14

B Western Actors Encyclopedia

B Western Actors Encyclopedia

Facts, Photos and Filmographies
for More than 250 Familiar Faces

by
Ted Holland

McFarland & Company, Inc., Publishers
Jefferson, North Carolina, and London

British Library Cataloguing-in-Publication data available

Library of Congress Cataloguing-in-Publication Data

Holland, Ted, 1945–
  B western actors encyclopedia.

  Bibliography: p. 479.
  Includes index.
  1. Western films – Dictionaries. 2. Motion picture
actors and actresses – United States – Biography –
Dictionaries. I. Title.
PN1995.9.W4H57   1989   791.43′09′093278   88-42566

ISBN 0-89950-306-3 (lib. bdg.; 50# acid-free natural paper)

Printed in the United States of America.

McFarland & Company, Inc., Publishers
  Box 611, Jefferson, North Carolina 28640

To Gerri
with love

Acknowledgments

Loads of thanks to: God for ideas, strength and patience; Gerri Russell and Pam Wilborn for turning tons of handwritten Sanskrit into neatly typed readable pages; the reference staff of the Charlotte Mecklenburg Public Library (Main Branch) for digging up a lot of weird books and answering a couple of million questions; Lojuana Blue of Copytype, Inc., for spending an entire Friday morning xeroxing the manuscript; Anne Russell for letting us turn her living room into something akin to Six Gun Playhouse; and the many who crawled around their attics looking for that long-lost autographed picture of Hoot Gibson.

Table of Contents

The Sidekicks   205

The Cowgirls   305

The Bad Guys   387

Preface

The *B Western Actors Encyclopedia* is all about dashing and daring heroes, dastardly conniving villains, sweet and lovely ladies in distress and comical sidekicks.

It is all about a genre of film that reflected an era when right was right, wrong was wrong and a man could only count on his horse, his six-gun, his guitar and the Sons of the Pioneers... An era when all good Americans believed in God, Mom, apple pie and Gabby Hayes.

It's about untarnished legends like Hopalong Cassidy, Roy Rogers, and Gene Autry; it's about hard fightin' cowboys like Reb Russell, Jack Perrin and Big John Kimbrough (who?) that never quite made it to legend status; about their pals, their gals and their wurstest enemies.

On these pages you can read all about the white-hatted hero who, in the span of 54 minutes, could sing a half dozen songs to a beautiful girl, kill 40 cattle rustlers, save the entire western United States from an Indian attack, and still have time to kiss his horse before he rode off into the sunset... At least until next week when he had to do it all over again.

The *B Western Actors Encyclopedia* is about a time long since passed when "headin' 'em off at the pass" was an honorable profession.

Introduction

Welcome to the world of the B Western; or more appropriately, welcome to the world of B Western people.

Originally I had planned to title this effort "The B Western Encyclopedia." However I was reminded by my editor that this was not a "film" book, but in reality a "people" book. A book about people and characters (or both) that breathed life into one of the world's most popular and unique film genres.

This book centers around the heroes, the sidekicks, the villains and the ladies of the B Westerns. I attempted to go past the all-familiar faces that everybody knows: Roy Rogers, Gene Autry, Dale Evans, . . . and so forth, and to reflect upon and pull into focus those lesser-known and — in film critic jargon — "obscure" performers.

The B Western Actors Encyclopedia was written simply because as a lover and student of B Westerns, I couldn't find one like it. There are plenty of books on the cowboy heroes, both individually and collectively. There is a great book by David Rothel on the sidekicks; the bad guys occupy bits and parts of several books. The most slighted category has been the B Western leading lady. With the exception of Dale Evans and Jennifer Holt, there is close to zip in printed existence.

The B Western Actors Encyclopedia is an effort to pull into full circle the personalities responsible for this popular filmdom genre, with career sketches and filmographies.

There also exists within a deep reflection of the directors and studios which shaped and produced the B Western.

One of the most important parts of this book is the filmographical listings. They are done in a way to reflect the performer's relationship to other individuals of the era. For example, the filmographies in the Heroes section lists not only the title and year of each hero's films but also the studio, leading lady, sidekick and director.

Filmographies contain the following code abbreviations:

H – Hero
SK – Sidekick
LL – Leading Lady
CB – Cowboy

The filmographies only reflect performers' appearances in series B Westerns. Hero filmographies list starring vehicles or, in the case of Russell Hayden and Jane Ellison, et al., important sidekick appearances. Sidekick filmographies list films in which the actor appeared as a sidekick to a cowboy hero. Leading ladies and bad guys speak for themselves.

A note about the leading ladies: inclusion in this section was based on the quantity and quality of films made. Also an attempt was made to balance the section between leading ladies of the early sparse B period and those of the more prolific later period.

Almost as important as those actors and Western notables covered in the book is the list of those not covered.

You won't find in any measurable space such legendary Western figures as Shane or the Magnificent Seven or Gary Cooper, Alan Ladd or the Lone Ranger. The reason is simple; these folks didn't appear in B Westerns.

John Wayne is here, not the classic Wayne of *Big Jake* or *The Sons of Katie Elder*, but a younger Wayne learning his cowboy craft on the backlots of small indie studios like Monogram.

The B Western Actors Encyclopedia also includes a section of capsule career sketches of some familiar B Western players that really didn't fit into any of the book's major categories.

THE
HEROES

The Legend of the Cowboy Hero

For my seventh birthday I got a Hopalong Cassidy wristwatch, a Red Ryder six-shooter and a rifle set, a Roy Rogers Ranch figure set — complete with Pat Brady's jeep Nelliebelle — and three comic books, a Johnny Mack Brown, a Wild Bill Elliott and a Rex Allen.

That morning I spent ridding the neighborhood of a villainous gang of cattle rustlers; the afternoon was reserved for my usual Saturday P.M. pursuit: watching "B" Western heroes in action on channel thirteen's Six Gun Playhouse. That day they ran a superduper double feature — Tom Tyler in *Cheyenne Rides Again* and Tim McCoy in *Bulldog Courage.*

*   *   *

When Gene Autry sang no woman was gonna break his heart "as long as I have my hoss" in one of his 1930s features, he somewhat summed up the philosophy of those hard-ridin', straight-shootin', headin'-'em-off-at-the-pass, white-hatted, white-horsed heroes of those 56-minute, low-budgeted-one-take, shot-in-three-days horse operas released between 1930 and 1954 most commonly known as B Westerns.

Heroes always had the fastest horse, the fanciest shirt, the hardest left hook, a hat that wouldn't fall off even in the darndest fight, and a shootin' iron that never needed reloading. Even on his worst day a hero could outride, outshoot, outsing, outfight, outrope, outromance and outthink any varmint that ever rode the wild and woolly celluloid West. And he always got the girl at the end of the picture.

1

In profile, the B Western hero was basically a drifting cowboy whose sense of chivalry and sometimes just plain bad luck caused him to wander into situations of dire distress.

Ofttimes he could remedy the problem by simply catching a bank robber or a gang of horse thieves. On other occasions he would solve a murder mystery and free a wrongly accused man; avenge the murder of a sidekick or relative; or save a ranch, stagecoach line, freight line, railroad or occasionally the entire West from the dastardly clutches of a blackhearted villain.

> "Where I come from men don't go round
> slappin' kids."
>   Hopalong Cassidy
>   *Renegade Trail*

The B Western cowboy hero was always the champion of the downtrodden and the helpless; be they a damsel in distress, a frightened youngster, a defenseless old-timer or a saddle pal in trouble.

He was a combination lawman, counselor, preacher, doctor, civil rights worker and general all-round jack of good deeds.

The men who wore these heroes' clothes were an unusual and widely varied breed of actor and man.

Some, like Tom Mix, Hoot Gibson, Tim McCoy and Buck Jones, led personal lives that were more adventurous and death-defying than anything they portrayed on the screen.

Those with an acute business sense — Gene Autry, William "Hopalong Cassidy" Boyd and Roy Rogers — parlayed their screen popularity into multimillion-dollar business empires.

For some, like a youthful John Wayne, B Westerns marked the beginning of a brilliant screen career. For others, some of whom were major film stars in the silent era, like Bob Custer, Jack Luden and Jack Perrin, B's marked the end.

They came to ride the B Western range by various roads. Some, like Buster Crabbe, Johnny Mack Brown and Bob Steele, became screen heroes because of well developed athletic ability. Others, like Autry, Jimmy Wakely, Eddie Dean and Tex Ritter, were successful recording artists before saddling up in Hollywood.

Mix, Gibson, Whip Wilson, Sunset Carson and others were actually working cowboys and rodeo performers.

Some of them, like Charles Starrett, Bob Steele and Gene Autry, made scores of features while the likes of Reb Russell, Smith Ballew and Eddie Dew made only a few.

Many had unforgettable trademarks that are forever etched in our

memories and dreams—Lash LaRue and his cracking bullwhip, Wild Bill
Elliott, his guns turned backward in his holsters, the solid black figure of
Hoppy Cassidy—while others have long since ridden off into some long-
forgotten Poverty Row sunset.

*   *   *

Bob Allen

Bob Allen made his splash across the B Western movie screen in a series of six films produced by Columbia Pictures in 1936 and 1937. The films, directed by Spencer G. Bennett, were collectively known as the Texas Rangers series.

Allen, whose real name was Irving Theodore Baehr, had begun his film career in 1926 while still a student at Dartmouth College. A top college athlete (boxing and polo), Allen was chosen to do stunt work in Richard Arlen's The Quarterback, which was being filmed on the Dartmouth campus.

After working as a model and airline pilot, Allen was signed as contract player by Warner Bros. in 1931. He subsequently did work in stage productions in Southern California and even made several appearances on Broadway. He returned to film work in 1934 when he signed a contract with Columbia. He appeared in several mysteries and costarred in three Westerns with Tim McCoy, who was Columbia's top cowboy star at the time.

Allen's work in the McCoy films impressed the Columbia brass so much that, when McCoy left the studio, Bob Allen was moved up to fill his slot, hence beginning the Rangers series. The series ended in 1937 when Allen left Columbia for more dramatic roles that were being offered him over at 20th Century–Fox.

In 1939 he returned to the Broadway stage and continued to do stage and film work into the 1970s.

Allen was born on March 28, 1906, in Mt. Vernon, New York.

Bob Allen Filmography

1936: *The Unknown Ranger* (Columbia; Spencer G. Bennett) *LL* Martha Tibbetts; *Rio Grande Ranger* (Columbia; Spencer G. Bennett) *LL* Iris Meredith. **1937:** *Ranger Courage* (Columbia; Spencer G. Bennett) *LL* Martha Tibbetts; *Law of the Ranger* (Columbia; Spencer G. Bennett) *LL* Elaine Shepard; *Reckless Ranger* (Columbia; Spencer G. Bennett) *LL* Louise Small; *The Rangers Step In* (Columbia; Spencer G. Bennett) *LL* Eleanor Stewart.

Bob Allen

Rex Allen
"The Arizona Cowboy"

Horse: Koko, the Miracle Horse of the Movies
Sidekicks: Slim Pickens, Fuzzy Knight, Buddy Ebsen

Rex Allen was born in Wilcox, Arizona, on December 31, 1922. In 1939 he won a statewide talent contest and quickly got a job singing on the radio.

Rex Allen and Koko.

In 1946 he joined the National Barn Dance, one of the top country and western radio shows in the country.

In 1949 he was signed to do a series of Western films by Republic Pictures. His first, released in 1950, was appropriately titled *The Arizona Cowboy*. The next year Allen placed in the top five cowboy stars.

He made 35 films for Republic between 1950 and the end of the B Western era in 1954.

Rex starred in the TV show *Frontier Doctor* in 1958. After that he continued to make records, personal appearances and TV commercials as well as serving as a narrator for a series of Walt Disney wildfire films.

His son Rex Allen, Jr., is one of today's top country and western performers.

Rex' faithful steed Koko, the Miracle Horse of the Movies, passd away in 1968 at the age of 28.

Rex Allen Filmography

1950: *The Arizona Cowboy* (Republic; R.G. Springsteen) *SK* Gordon Jones, *LL* Teala Loring; *Hills of Oklahoma* (Republic; R.G. Springsteen) *SK* Fuzzy Knight, *LL* Elizabeth Fraser; *Redwood Forest Trail* (Republic; Philip Ford) *LL* Jeff Donnell; *Under Mexicali Stars* (Republic; George Blair) *SK* Buddy Ebsen, *LL* Dorothy Patrick. **1951:** *Silver City Bonanza* (Republic; George Blair) *SK* Buddy Ebsen, *LL* Mary Ellen Kay; *Thunder in God's Country* (Republic; George Blair) *SK* Buddy Ebsen, *LL* Mary Ellen Kay; *Rodeo King & the Senorita* (Republic; Philip Ford) *SK* Buddy Ebsen, *LL* Mary Ellen Kay; *Utah Wagon Train* (Republic; Philip Ford) *SK* Buddy Ebsen, *LL* Penny Edwards. **1952:** *Colorado Sundown* (Republic; William Witney) *SK* Slim Pickens, *LL* Mary Ellen Kay; *The Last Musketeer* (Republic; William Witney) *SK* Slim Pickens, *LL* Mary Ellen Kay; *Border Saddlemates* (Republic; William Witney) *SK* Slim Pickens, *LL* Mary Ellen Kay; *Old Oklahoma Plains* (Republic; William Witney) *SK* Slim Pickens, *LL* Elaine Edwards; *South Pacific Trail* (Republic; William Witney) *SK* Slim Pickens, *LL* Estelita Rodriguez. **1953:** *Old Overland Trail* (Republic; William Witney) *SK* Slim Pickens, *LL* Virginia Hall; *Iron Mountain Trail* (Republic; William Witney) *SK* Slim Pickens, *LL* Nan Leslie; *Down Laredo Way* (Republic; William Witney) *SK* Slim Pickens, *LL* Dona Drake, Marjorie Lord; *Shadows of Tombstone* (Republic; William Witney)*SK* Slim Pickens, *LL* Jeanne Cooper; *Red River Shore* (Republic; Harry Keller) *SK* Slim Pickens, *LL* Lyn Thomas. **1954:** *Phantom Stallion* (Republic; Harry Keller) *SK* Slim Pickens, *LL* Carla Balenda.

Gene Austin

Gene Austin was a first-rate singer, musician and songwriter. His recording of "My Blue Heaven" holds the distinction of being the first documented million seller in recording history.

Austin was born in Gainesville, Texas, June 24, 1900.

He appeared in and provided music for such films as *Sadie McKee* with Joan Crawford and *Klondike Annie* with Mae West in 1936.

Gene starred in *Songs and Saddles* for Colony Pictures in 1939 and also made some musical shorts.

He enjoyed a long and distinguished career and made personal appearances and TV guest shots well into the 1960s.

Gene Austin passed away in Palm Springs, California on January 24, 1972.

Gene Austin Filmography

1938: *Songs and Saddles* (Colony; Harry Fraser) *LL* Lynne Berkeley.

Gene Autry

Horse: Champion, Champion Jr.
Sidekicks: Smiley Burnette, Sterling Halloway, Pat Buttram, Gabby Hayes

Gene Autry, the dean of the singing cowboys, may be the most successful star to ever ride the B Western trails of the silver screen, both in terms of popularity and revenue. Autry became *Motion Picture Herald*'s number one Western box office star in 1937 and remained in that position through 1942.

He was born Orvon Gene Autry in Tioga, Texas, on September 29, 1907, the son of a poor tenant farmer. When Gene was still a boy his family settled near Ravia, Oklahoma. As a youth he learned to ride horses, play the guitar and sing.

When he was a young man Autry got a job as a telegrapher in Chelsea where he used to while away the long hours, singing and writing songs. One day Will Rogers heard Autry's voice and suggested he become a professional singer.

Gene took Rogers' advice and went off to New York City to show and sell his talents. When nothing came of the trip, he returned to Oklahoma and got a job on radio station KVOO in Tulsa where he was billed as "Oklahoma's yodeling cowboy."

Autry scored his first recording hit with a ballad entitled "That Silver Haired Daddy of Mine."

In 1933 he joined the National Barn Dance, which was broadcast nationwide from WLS in Chicago, and recorded his first real cowboy song, 'The Yellow Rose of Texas."

Nat Levine, president of Mascot Pictures, gave Autry and his radio pal

Gene Autry and Champion.

Smiley Burnette bit parts in Ken Maynard's 1934 vehicle *I'm Old Santa Fe.*

Mascot then starred Autry in a chapter serial, *The Phantom Empire,* in 1935.

That same year Autry, with Burnette and his horse Champion, made the first of 58 B Western features for Republic Pictures: *Tumbling Tumbleweeds.*

After only a year on the screen Autry's popularity was so great he was the industry's third-ranked Western star.

Autry continued his domination of the Westerns until 1942 when he left the screen and entered the service, serving as a tech sergeant in the Air Transport Command until the end of World War II.

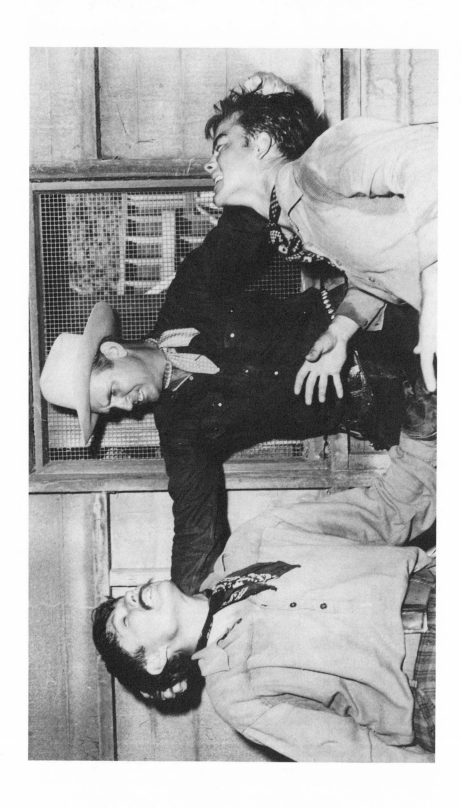

Upon his release in 1945, he made six films for Republic before forming his own production company, Flying A's Productions, which signed a distribution pact with Columbia Pictures. Flying A's and Columbia released Autry Films.

All the while he was making films, Autry continued his recording career scoring with such hits as "Tumbling Tumbleweeds" (1935), "There's a Goldmine in the Sky" (1938), "Have I Told You Lately That I Love You" (1948) and the unforgettable "Rudolph the Red Nosed Reindeer" in 1949. In 1950 Gene turned his production efforts toward the medium of television. He starred in 91 episodes of the *Gene Autry Show* for CBS-TV. The series ran until 1956.

Autry and Flying A's also produced shows such as *Range Rider, Annie Oakley, Buffalo Bill Jr.* and *The Adventures of Champion*.

In 1953 Gene made his final B Western, *The Last of the Pony Riders*.

Gene also made personal appearances nationwide in his Gene Autry World Championship Rodeo.

In 1960 Gene Autry retired from the screen to concentrate on his investments. Today he continues to rule his vast empire of holdings, the best known of which is the American Baseball League's California Angels.

Note: Gene's horse Champion (original name Lindy) was born in Oklahoma on May 20, 1927, and passed away in 1944. There were two Champion Jr.'s, the best-remembered debuting in the 1948 film *The Strawberry Roan*. This horse, which died in 1976, was seen on the Champion TV series.

Gene Autry Filmography

1935: *Tumbling Tumbleweeds* (Republic; Joseph Kane) *SK* Smiley Burnette, *LL* Lucille Brown; *Melody Trail* (Republic; Joseph Kane) *SK* Smiley Burnette, *LL* Ann Rutherford; *The Sagebrush Troubador* (Republic; Joseph Kane) *SK* Smiley Burnette, *LL* Barbara Pepper; *The Singing Vagabond* (Republic; Carl Pierson) *SK* Smiley Burnette, *LL* Ann Rutherford, Barbara Pepper. **1936:** *Red River Valley* (TV: *Man of the Frontier*) (Republic; B. Reeves Eason) *SK* Smiley Burnette, *LL* Frances Grant; *Comin' Round the Mountain* (Republic; Mack V. Wright) *SK* Smiley Burnette, *LL* Ann Rutherford; *The Singing Cowboy* (Republic; Mack V. Wright) *SK* Smiley Burnette, *LL* Lois Wilde; *Guns and Guitars* (Republic; Joseph Kane) *SK* Smiley Burnette, *LL* Dorothy Dix; *Oh, Susannah* (Republic; Joseph Kane)

Gene Autry in a scene from The Old West.

SK Smiley Burnette, *LL* Frances Grant; *Ride, Ranger Ride* (Republic; Joseph Kane) *SK* Smiley Burnette, *LL* Kay Hughes; *The Big Show* (Republic; Mack V. Wright) *SK* Smiley Burnette, *LL* Kay Hughes, Sally Payne; *The Old Corral* (Republic; Joseph Kane) *SK* Smiley Burnette, *LL* Hope Manning. **1937:** *Round Up Time in Texas* (Republic; Joseph Kane) *SK* Smiley Burnette, *LL* Maxine Doyle; *Git Along Little Dogies* (Republic; Joseph Kane) *SK* Smiley Burnette, *LL* Judith Allen; *Rootin' Tootin' Rhythm* (Republic; Mack V. Wright) *SK* Smiley Burnette, *LL* Armida; *Yodelin' Kid from Pine Ridge* (Republic; Joseph Kane) *SK* Smiley Burnette, *LL* Betty Bronson; *Public Cowboy #1* (Republic; Joseph Kane) *SK* Smiley Burnette, *LL* Ann Rutherford; *Boots and Saddles* (Republic; Joseph Kane) *SK* Smiley Burnette, *LL* Judith Allen; *Manhattan Merry Go Round* (Republic; Charles Riesner) *SK* Smiley Burnette, *LL* Ann Dvorak; *Springtime in the Rockies* (Republic; Joseph Kane) *SK* Smiley Burnette, *LL* Polly Rowles. **1938:** *The Old Barn Dance* (Republic; Joseph Kane) *SK* Smiley Burnette, *LL* Helen Valkis; *Gold Mine in the Sky* (Republic; Joseph Kane) *SK* Smiley Burnette, *LL* Carol Hughes; *Man from Music Mountain* (Republic; Joseph Kane) *SK* Smiley Burnette, *LL* Carol Hughes, Sally Payne; *Prairie Moon* (Republic; Ralph Staub) *SK* Smiley Burnette, *LL* Shirley Deane; *Rhythm of the Saddle* (Republic; George Sherman) *SK* Smiley Burnette, *LL* Peggy Moran; *Western Jamboree* (Republic; Ralph Staub) *SK* Smiley Burnette, *LL* Jean Rouverol. **1939:** *Home on the Prairie* (Republic; Jack Townley) *SK* Smiley Burnette, *LL* June Storey; *Mexicali Rose* (Republic; George Sherman) *SK* Smiley Burnette, *LL* Luana Walters; *Blue Montana Skies* (Republic; B. Reeves Eason) *SK* Smiley Burnette, *LL* June Storey; *Mountain Rhythm* (Republic; B. Reeves Eason) *SK* Smiley Burnette, *LL* June Storey; *Colorado Sunset* (Republic; George Sherman) *SK* Smiley Burnette, *LL* June Storey; *In Old Monterey* (Republic; Joseph Kane) *SK* Smiley Burnette, Gabby Hayes, *LL* June Storey; *Rovin' Tumbleweeds* (Republic; George Sherman) *SK* Smiley Burnette *LL* Mary Carlisle; *South of the Border* (Republic; George Sherman) *SK* Smiley Burnette, *LL* Lupita Tovar, June Storey, Mary Lee. **1940:** *Rancho Grande* (Republic; Frank McDonald) *SK* Smiley Burnette, *LL* June Storey, Mary Lee; *Shooting High* (20th Century–Fox; Alfred E. Green) *LL* Jane Withers, Marjorie Weaver; *Gaucho Serenade* (Republic; Frank McDonald) *SK* Smiley Burnette, *LL* June Storey, Mary Lee; *Carolina Moon* (Republic; Frank McDonald) *SK* Smiley Burnette, *LL* June Storey, Mary Lee; *Ride Tenderfoot Ride* (Republic; Frank McDonald) *SK* Smiley Burnette, *LL* June Storey, Mary Lee; *Melody Ranch* (Republic; Joseph Santley) *SK* Jimmy Durante, Gabby Hayes, *LL* Ann Miller. **1941:** *Ridin' on a Rainbow* (Republic; Lew Landers) *SK* Smiley Burnette, *LL* Mary Lee, Carol Adams; *Back in the Saddle* (Republic; Lew Landers) *SK* Smiley Burnette, *LL* Mary Lee, Jacqueline Wells; *The Singing Hill* (Republic; Lew Landers) *SK* Smiley Burnette, *LL* Mary Lee, Virginia Dale; *Sunset in*

Wyoming (Republic; William Morgan) *SK* Smiley Burnette, *LL* Maris Wrixon; *Under Fiesta Stars* (Republic; Frank McDonald) *SK* Smiley Burnette, *LL* Carol Hughes; *Down Mexico Way* (Republic; Joseph Santley) *SK* Smiley Burnette, *LL* Fay McKenzie; *Sierra Sue* (Republic; William Morgan) *SK* Smiley Burnette, *LL* Fay McKenzie. **1942:** *Cowboy Serenade* (Republic; William Morgan) *SK* Smiley Burnette, *LL* Fay McKenzie; *Heart of the Rio Grande* (Republic; William Morgan) *SK* Smiley Burnette, *LL* Fay McKenzie; *Home in Wyomin'* (Republic; William Morgan) *SK* Smiley Burnette, *LL* Fay McKenzie; *Stardust on the Sage* (Republic; William Morgan) *SK* Smiley Burnette, *LL* Louise Currie; *Call of the Canyon* (Republic; Joseph Santley) *SK* Smiley Burnette, *LL* Ruth Terry; *Bells of Capistrano* (Republic; William Morgan) *SK* Smiley Burnette, *LL* Virginia Grey. **1946:** *Sioux City Sue* (Republic; Frank McDonald) *SK* Sterling Holloway, *LL* Lynne Roberts. **1947:** *Trail to San Antone* (Republic; John English) *SK* Sterling Holloway, *LL* Peggy Stewart; *Twilight on the Rio Grande* (Republic; Frank McDonald) *SK* Sterling Holloway, *LL* Adele Mara; *Saddle Pals* (Republic; Lesley Selander) *SK* Sterling Holloway, *LL* Lynne Roberts; *Robin Hood of Texas* (Republic; Lesley Selander *SK* Sterling Holloway, *LL* Lynne Roberts; *The Last Roundup* (Columbia; John English) *LL* Jean Heather, Carol Thurston. **1948:** *The Strawberry Roan* (Columbia; John English) *SK* Pat Buttram, Rufe Davis, *LL* Gloria Henry. **1949:** *Loaded Pistols* (Columbia; John English) *SK* Chill Wills, *LL* Barbara Britton; *The Big Sombrero* (Columbia; Frank McDonald) *LL* Elena Verdugo; *Riders of the Whistling Pines* (Columbia; John English) *LL* Patricia White; *Rim of the Canyon* (Columbia; John English) *LL* Nan Leslie; *The Cowboy and the Indians* (Columbia; John English) *LL* Sheila Ryan; *Riders in the Sky* (Columbia; John English) *SK* Pat Buttram, *LL* Gloria Henry. **1950:** *Sons of New Mexico* (Columbia; John English) *LL* Gail Davis; *Mule Train* (Columbia; John English) *SK* Pat Buttram, *LL* Sheila Ryan; *Cowtown* (Columbia; John English) *LL* Gail Davis; *Beyond the Purple Hills* (Columbia; John English) *SK* Pat Buttram, *LL* Jo Dennison; *Indian Territory* (Columbia; John English) *SK* Pat Buttram, *LL* Gail Davis; *The Blazing Hills* (Columbia; John English) *SK* Pat Buttram, *LL* Lynne Roberts. **1951:** *Gene Autry and the Mounties* (Columbia; John English) *SK* Pat Buttram, *LL* Elena Verdugo; *Texans Never Cry* (Columbia; Frank McDonald) *SK* Pat Buttram, *LL* Gail Davis; *Whirlwind* (Columbia; John English) *SK* Smiley Burnette, *LL* Gail Davis; *Silver Canyon* (Columbia; John English) *SK* Pat Buttram, *LL* Gail Davis; *Hills of Utah* (Columbia; John English) *SK* Pat Buttram, *LL* Elaine Riley; *Valley of Fire* (Columbia; John English) *SK* Pat Buttram, *LL* Gail Davis. **1952:** *The Old West* (Columbia; George Archainbaud) *SK* Pat Buttram, *LL* Gail Davis; *Night Stage to Galveston* (Columbia; George Archainbaud) *SK* Pat Buttram, *LL* Virginia Houston; *Apache Country* (Columbia; George Archainbaud) *SK* Pat Buttram, *LL* Carolina Cotton; *Barbed Wire* (Columbia; George Archainbaud)

SK Pat Buttram, *LL* Anne James; *Wagon Team* (Columbia; George Archainbaud) *SK* Pat Buttram, *LL* Gail Davis; *Blue Canadian Skies* (Columbia; George Archainbaud) *SK* Pat Buttram, *LL* Gail Davis. **1953:** *Winning of the West* (Columbia; George Archainbaud) *SK* Smiley Burnette, *LL* Gail Davis; *On Top of Old Smokey* (Columbia; George Archainbaud) *SK* Smiley Burnette, *LL* Gail Davis, Sheila Ryan; *Goldtown Ghost Riders* (Columbia; George Archainbaux) *SK* Smiley Burnette, *LL* Gail Davis; *Pack Train* (Columbia; George Archainbaud) *SK* Smiley Burnette, *LL* Gail Davis, Sheila Ryan; *Saginaw Trail* (Columbia; George Archainbaud) *SK* Smiley Burnette, *LL* Connie Marshall; *Last of the Pony Riders* (Columbia; George Archainbaud) *SK* Smiley Burnette.

Bob Baker

Horse: Apache
Sidekick: Fuzzy Knight

Singing Cowboy Bob Baker starred in a dozen Western thrillers for Universal pictures between 1937 and 1939. His sidekick for several of the features was Fuzzy Knight and his main leading lady was Marjorie Reynolds, who is better known as Peg, the belabored wife of Chester A. Riley, on TV's *The Life of Riley.*

Baker was christened Leland Weed and entered the world in Forest City, Iowa, on November 8, 1914. As a teenager he got a job as a cowpoke on a cattle ranch in Colorado.

Before joining The National Barn Dance radio program, he served as a radio performer and radio singer.

In 1936 his old friend Max "Alabi" Terhune got him an audition with Universal, who at the time was looking for someone to cash in on the singing cowboy craze that was sweeping films. Baker got the job and made his first feature, *Courage of the West,* in 1937.

After a dozen films, Universal demoted Baker from star to featured player in the Frontier Marshall series with Knight and star Johnny Mack Brown. He made six of these features. In 1943 he began the Trail Blazers series at Monogram with Hoot Gibson and Ken Maynard but was later dropped.

In 1943 Bob Baker retired from the screen.

Baker served in the Korean War and worked in Arizona as a police officer.

In 1969 he suffered a series of heart attacks. Bob Baker passed away, August 30, 1975, at the Veterans Hospital in Prescott, Arizona.

Bob Baker (left) with George Cleveland in the 1939 movie The Phantom Stage.

Bob Baker Filmography

1937: *Courage of the West* (Universal; Joseph H. Lewis) *SK* Fuzzy Knight, *LL* Lois January; *The Singing Outlaw* (Universal; Joseph Lewis) *SK* Fuzzy Knight, *LL* Joan Barclay. **1938:** *The Black Bandit* (Universal; George Waggner) *LL* Marjorie Reynolds; *Border Wolves* (Universal; Joseph Lewis) *SK* Fuzzy Knight, *LL* Constance Moore; *Ghost Town Riders* (Universal; George Waggner) *LL* Fay Shannon; *Guilty Trails* (Universal; George Waggner) *LL* Marjorie Reynolds; *The Last Stand* (Universal; Joseph H. Lewis) *SK* Fuzzy Knight, *LL* Marjorie Reynolds; *The Outlaw Express* (Universal; George Waggner) *LL* Cecilia Callejo; *Prairie Justice* (Universal; George Waggner) *LL* Dorothy Fay; *Western Trails* (Universal; George Waggner) *LL* Marjorie Reynolds. **1939:** *Honor of the West* (Universal; George Waggner) *LL* Marjorie Bell; *The Phantom Stage* (Universal; George Waggner) *LL* Marjorie Reynolds.

Smith Ballew

Golden-voiced Smith Ballew was the 20th Century–Fox entry into the 1930s singing cowboy sweepstakes. He withdrew from the race after starring in five films in 1937 and 1938, the best known of which was *Rawhide,* which costarred baseball legend Lou Gehrig.

Ballew hailed from Palestine, Texas, where he ws born in 1912. While a student at the University of Texas he got a job as a radio singer. He soon formed his own band and began a career in vaudeville.

His first brush with the cinema came in the form of musical shorts in the early thirties. From 1933 to 1934 he dubbed the voice for John Wayne's Singing Sandy films at Monogram. Ballew made his acting debut in a film called *Palm Springs.*

Producer Sol Lesser tabbed him to star in the Fox series, and in 1938 he made the list of top ten cowboys. He then suddenly fell from screen sight but continued his singing career into the late 1950s.

Smith Ballew Filmography

1937: *Roll Along Cowboy* (20th Century–Fox; Gus Miens) *LL* Cecilia Parker; *Western Gold* (20th Century–Fox; Howard Bretherton) *LL* Heather Angel. **1938:** *Panamint's Bad Man* (20th Century–Fox; Ray Taylor) *LL* Evelyn Daw; *Hawaiian Buckaroo* (20th Century–Fox; Ray Taylor) *LL* Evelyn Knapp; *Rawhide* (20th Century–Fox; Ray Taylor) *SK* Lou Gehrig, *LL* Evelyn Knapp.

Jim Bannon

Missouri-born Jim Bannon portrayed Red Ryder in a series of four films released by Eagle Lion Pictures in 1949. His costars were Don Reynolds as Little Beaver and Marin Sais as the Duchess.

Bannon was born in Kansas City in 1918, and, following a great collegiate athletic career, he landed a job as a sportscaster in St. Louis, eventually working his way to the West Coast.

He began in films in the early forties as a combination stuntman and bit player, and developed into a competent actor.

In 1945, when Columbia Pictures decided to bring the popular *I Love a Mystery* radio series to the screen, Bannon was chosen to play the central

Smith Ballew

character, Detective Jack Packard. He repeated the role the following year in *The Devil's Mask.*

In 1948 he starred in the 12-chapter Republic serial *Dangers of the Canadian Mounted.*

Following the "Ryder" series, Bannon continued in films as a character actor and occasionally did stunt work.

He played Uncle Sandy on *The Adventures of Champion*, which starred Gene Autry's famous horse, on CBS-TV in 1955 and 1956.

Jim Bannon Filmography

1948: *Dangers of the Canadian Mounted* (serial) (Republic; Yakima Canutt, Fred Brannon) *LL* Virginia Belmont. **1949:** *Ride Ryder Ride* (Eagle Lion; Lewis Collins) *SK* Don Reynolds, Marin Sais, Emmett Lynn, *LL* Peggy Stewart; *Roll Thunder Roll* (Eagle Lion; Lewis Collins) *SK* Don Reynolds, Marin Sais, Emmett Lynn, *LL* Nancy Gates; *The Fighting Redhead* (Eagle Lion; Lewis Collins) *SK* Don Reynolds, Marin Sais, Emmett Lynn, *LL* Peggy Stewart; *Cowboy and the Prize Fighter* (Eagle Lion; Lewis Collins) *SK* Don Reynolds, Marin Sais, Emmett Lynn, *LL* Karen Randle.

Don "Red" Barry

Horse: Cyclone
Sidekicks: Wally Vernon, Emmett Lynn, Slim Andrews, Fuzzy St. John, Dub Taylor

Don "Red" Barry rates as one of Movie Land's all-time great character actors. His career spanned five decades.

A native Texan, Barry attended the Texas School of Movies and began acting in summer stock companies and made his film debut in C.B. De Mille's 1933 melodrama *This Day and Age.* He also appeared in the National Road Company production of *Tobacco Road.*

He returned to the screen in 1937 with parts in such films as *Dead End* and films in the Dr. Kildare series.

In 1939 he came to Republic Pictures and began his Western career with featured parts in Roy Rogers' *Day of Jesse James* and the Three Mesquiteers' *Wyoming Outlaw.* In 1940 Republic starred him in a serialized version of Fred Harmon's popular Red Ryder comic strip. The film also gave Don Barry the "Red" nickname tag that would endure his remaining film career.

On the heels of the popular chapter play, Barry debuted in the first of 29 Westerns for Republic. His leading lady for 15 of the films was Lynn Merrick. His wife, Helen Talbott, also served as his leading lady in two of the films. Barry at one time was married to a popular B Western heroine Peggy Stewart.

Barry's series for Republic lasted until 1945. He appeared in scores of films and TV series over the next decades and taught the dramatic arts to young performers.

Left to right: Little Beaver (Don Reynolds), Red Ryder (Jim Bannon), the Duchess (Marin Sais) and Buckskin (Emmett Lynn) in The Fighting Redhead *(1949).*

Don "Red" Barry

Red Barry was born Donald Barry DeAcosta in Houston, Texas, on January 11, 1212. On July 17, 1980, at the age of 69, Don Barry shot and killed himself in North Hollywood, California.

Don "Red" Barry Filmography

1940: *Adventures of Red Ryder* (serial) (Republic; William Witney, John English) *SK* Tommy Cook, Maude P. Allen, *LL* Vivian Coe; *One Man's Law* (Republic; George Sherman) *SK* Dub Taylor, *LL* Janet Waldo; *The Tulsa Kid* (Republic; George Sherman) *LL* Luana Walters; *Frontier Vengeance* (Republic; Nate Watt) *LL* Betty Moran; *Texas Terrors* (Republic; George Sherman) *SK* Al St. John, *LL* Julie Duncan, Ann Pennington; *Ghost Valley Raiders* (Republic; George Sherman) *LL* Lona Andre. **1941:** *Wyoming Wildcat* (Republic; George Sherman) *SK* Syd Saylor, *LL* Julie Duncan; *The Phantom Cowboy* (Republic; George Sherman) *LL* Virginia Carroll; *Two Gun Sheriff* (Republic; George Sherman) *LL* Lynn Merrick; *Desert Bandit* (Republic; George Sherman) *LL* Lynn Merrick; *Kansas Cyclone* (Republic; George Sherman) *LL* Lynn Merrick, Dorothy Sebastian; *The Apache Kid* (Republic; George Sherman) *SK* Al St. John, *LL* Lynn Merrick; *Death Valley Outlaws* (Republic; George Sherman) *LL* Lynn Merrick;

A Missouri Outlaw (Republic; George Sherman) *SK* Al St. John, *LL* Lynn Merrick. **1942:** *Arizona Terror* (Republic; George Sherman) *SK* Al St. John, *LL* Lynn Merrick; *Stagecoach Express* (Republic; George Sherman) *SK* Al St. John, *LL* Lynn Merrick; *Jesse James Jr.* (Republic; George Sherman) *SK* Al St. John, *LL* Lynn Merrick; *Cyclone Kid* (Republic; George Sherman) *SK* Slim Andrews, *LL* Lynn Merrick; *The Sombrero Kid* (Republic; George Sherman) *SK* Slim Andrews, *LL* Lynn Merrick; *Outlaws of Pineridge* (Republic; William Witney) *SK* Emmett Lynn, *LL* Lynn Merrick; *Sundown Kid* (Republic; Elmer Clifton) *SK* Emmett Lynn, *LL* Helen MacKellar, Linda Johnson. **1943:** *Dead Man's Gulch* (Republic; John English) *SK* Emmett Lynn, *LL* Lynn Merrick; *Carson City Cyclone* (Republic; Howard Bretherton) *SK* Emmett Lynn, *LL* Lynn Merrick; *Days of Old Cheyenne* (Republic; Elmer Clifton) *SK* Emmett Lynn, *LL* Lynn Merrick; *Fugitive from Sonora* (Republic; Howard Bretherton) *SK* Wally Vernon, *LL* Lynn Merrick; *Black Hills Express* (Republic; John English) *SK* Wally Vernon, *LL* Ariel Heath; *The Man from the Rio Grande* (Republic; Howard Bretherton) *SK* Wally Vernon, *LL* Nancy Gay; *Canyon City* (Republic; Spencer Bennet) *SK* Wally Vernon, *LL* Helen Talbot; *California Joe* (Republic; Spencer Bennet) *SK* Wally Vernon, *LL* Helen Talbot. **1944:** *Outlaws of Santa Fe* (Republic; Howard Bretherton) *SK* Wally Vernon, *LL* Helen Talbot.

Noah Beery, Jr.

Noah Beery, Jr., ranks as one of the film colony's all-time great character actors and as one of the screen's most recognizable faces. TV fans best know him as James Garner's dad "Rocky" on the hit series *The Rockford Files.*

You might say that Beery was Hollywood born and bred; his father, Noah Beery, Sr., ranks as one of the screen's all-time top villains, and his uncle was the noted screen star Wallace Beery.

Born in Hollywood in 1916, Noah Jr. made his movie debut at the age of four with his dad (and Douglas Fairbanks) in *The Mark of Zorro.*

While Beery was featured in such classic Western serials as *Heroes of the West* (1932), *Fighting with Kit Carson* (1933), *Riders of Death Valley* (1941) and *Overland Mail* (1942) and had costarring roles in "B"s like *The Carson City Kid* with Roy Rogers, he starred in only two B Western features early in his career for little-known Sunset Films.

Beery went on to make scores of films and TV shows and is currently active in film work.

Noah Beery, Jr.

Noah Beery, Jr. Filmography

1935: *Devils Canyon* (Sunset; Cliff Smith); *Five Bad Men* (Sunset; Cliff Smith) *SK* Buffalo Bill. Jr., Wally Wales, *LL* Sally Darling.

Rex Bell

Rex Bell is probably best known to movie aficionados as the man who married the "It" girl Clara Bow, the famous sexy siren of the silent film era in 1931.

Bell was a "Poverty Row" cowboy. That is, he made his Western films for small, almost obscure studios in the early to mid-thirties. Poverty Row features were earmarked by extremely low budgets and sometimes even lower production values.

Rex Bell

Bell was born George Francis Beldham in Chicago, Illinois, on October 16, 1905, and became a top-notch football player at the University of Iowa.

The handsome Bell got a bit part in John Ford's 1927 feature salute starring soon to be B Western star George O'Brien.

Bell met Bow in 1930 when he appeared in *True to the Navy*, which starred Clara and Frederic March. Their relationship culminated with a highly publicized elopement followed by Clara Bow's official retirement from the screen.

A part in the 1931 serial *Battling with Buffalo Bill* gained the attention of Monogram Pictures producer Trem Carr, who decided to star Bell in a series of films. His first was *From Broadway to Cheyenne* in 1932. He made nine films for Monogram in 1932 and 1933. In 1935 and 1936 Bell made films for Resolute and Colony Pictures. He made 19 B Westerns all together.

In 1942 Rex Bell retired from films to concentrate on his business and ranching interests and politics; in 1954 he was elected lieutenant governor of Nevada. He passed away on July 4, 1962, of a heart attack.

Rex Bell Filmography

1932: *Arm of the Law* (Monogram; Louis King) *LL* Lina Basquette, Dorothy Revier, Marceline Day; *From Broadway to Cheyenne* (Monogram; Harry Fraser) *LL* Marceline Day; *The Man from Arizona* (Monogram; Harry Fraser) *LL* Naomi Judge; *Lucky Larrigan* (Monogram; J.P. McCarthy) *LL* Helen Foster; *The Diamond Trail* (Monogram; Harry Fraser) *LL* Frances Rich. **1933:** *Crashing Broadway* (Monogram; John P. McCarthy) *LL* Doris Hill; *Rainbow Ranch* (Monogram; Harry Fraser) *LL* Cecilia Parker; *The Fighting Texans* (Monogram; Armand Schaefer) *LL* Luana Walters, Betty Mack; *The Fugitive* (Monogram; Harry Fraser) *LL* Cecilia Parker. **1935:** *Fighting Pioneers* (Resolute; Harry Fraser) *SK* Buzz Barton, *LL* Ruth Mix; *Gun Fire* (Resolute; Harry Fraser) *SK* Buzz Barton, *LL* Ruth Mix; *Saddle Aces* (Resolute; Harry Fraser) *SK* Buzz Barton, *LL* Ruth Mix; *The Tonto Kid* (Resolute; Harry Fraser) *SK* Buzz Barton, *LL* Ruth Mix. **1936:** *Too Much Beef* (Colony; Robert Hill) *SK* Horace Murphy, *LL* Connie Bergen; *West of Nevada* (Colony; Robert Hill) *SK* Fuzzy St. John, *LL* Joan Barclay; *The Idaho Kid* (Colony; Robert Hill) *LL* Marion Shilling; *Men of the Plains* (Colony; Robert Hill) *LL* Joan Barclay; *Law and Lead* (Colony; Robert Hill) *LL* Harley Wood; *Stormy Trails* (Colony; Sam Newfield) *LL* Lois Wilde.

Bill "Cowboy Rambler" Boyd

Sidekicks: Art Davis, Lee Powell

Bill "Cowboy Rambler" Boyd is better known for his prolific recording career than he is for the half dozen films he made for PRC in 1942.

Boyd was born in Fannin County, Texas, in 1910. While still a teenager the talented Boyd got his own radio show. He continued to be a daily radio performer until the 1970s.

In 1942 PRC, in need of a singing cowboy, paired Boyd with Art Davis and Lee Powell for the series of films, the high point of which was the music.

Boyd recorded hundreds of sides for RCA Records, his best known being "The New Steel Guitar Rag" and "The Spanish Two Step."

Bill died on December 7, 1977, at his ranch in Dallas, Texas.

A PRC poster advertising Texas Man Hunt *(1942) starring Bill Boyd, Art Davis and Lee Powell.*

Bill "Cowboy Rambler" Boyd Filmography

1942: *Texas Manhunt* (PRC; Peter Stewart [Sam Newfield]) *SK* Art Davis, Lee Powell, *LL* Julie Duncan; *Raiders of the West* (PRC; Peter Stewart [Sam Newfield]) *SK* Art Davis, Lee Powell, *LL* Virginia Carroll; *Rolling Down the Great Divide* (PRC; Peter Stewart [Sam Newfield]) *SK* Art Davis, Lee Powell, *LL* Wanda McKay; *Tumbleweed Trail* (PRC; Peter Stewart [Sam Newfield]) *SK* Art Davis, Lee Powell, *LL* Marjorie Manners; *Prairie Pals* (Peter Stewart [Sam Newfield]) *SK* Art Davis, Lee Powell, *LL* Esther Estrella; *Along the Sundown Trail* (PRC; Peter Stewart [Sam Newfield]) *SK* Art Davis, Lee Powell, *LL* Julie Duncan.

William "Hopalong Cassidy" Boyd

Horse: Topper
Sidekicks: Gabby Hayes, Jimmy Ellison, Russell Hayden, Andy Clyde, Harvey Clark, Frank Darien, Britt Wood, Jay Kirby, Brad King, George Reeves, Jimmy Rogers, Rand Brooks, Edgar Buchanan (TV)

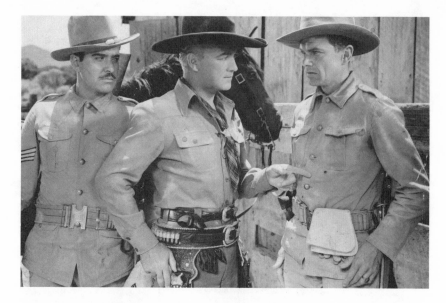

William Boyd (center) with Morris Ankrum (left) and unknown actor in a scene from Doomed Caravan *(1941).*

The Hopalong Cassidy pictures rank as the most successful Western film series produced and as one of the most successful overall series in motion picture history. Beginning with *Hopalong Cassidy* in 1935 and ending with *False Paradise* in 1948, the 66 Cassidy films also rate as some of the finest B Westerns ever produced.

The character of Hopalong Cassidy was created by Clarence E. Mulford in a series of very successful novels in the early 1900s. Cassidy, as created by Mulford, was a hard-drinking, loud-cussin', evil-tempered but straight-shootin' cowpoke on the Bar 20 Ranch. The nickname "Hopalong" was gleaned from the fact that Cassidy limped considerably due to an old gunshot wound.

To millions of fans, former silent film actor William Boyd *was* Hopalong Cassidy. Boyd was born William Lawrence Boyd on June 5, 1898, in Hendrysburg, Ohio. When his father died Boyd was forced to quit school and go to work as an oil field roustabout. On his way to adulthood he worked as a truck driver, miner, auto salesman and lumberjack.

He got involved in the fledgling movie industry as an extra and made his acting debut in a 1919 film called *Why Change Your Wife?* Boyd became a top leading man in such silent fetures as *The Volga Boatman, Jim the Conquerer, Yankee Clipper* and *The Leatherneck.* He also starred in the 1931 classic *The Painted Desert* which featured a youthful actor named Clark Gable.

William Boyd as Hopalong Cassidy.

The year of 1931 was a disastrous one for Boyd. A case of mistaken identity in a scandal almost ruined his career. A stage actor named William Boyd was arrested in conjunction with a notorious Hollywood beach party, but the papers carried Boyd's picture with the scandal story. Despite all his pleas of "You got the wrong man," the damage was done and he was out of work for two years.

After returning to filmmaking in 1933, Boyd was chosen by producer Harry Sherman to portray Cassidy.

The early Hoppy films were the best of the series. The first 41 were released by Paramount, the remainder by United Artists.

In the mid-forties Boyd realized what a national phenomenon the Cassidy films were proving to be, and he bought the rights to all the films and the Cassidy name. His first step was to release the films to the nation's newest darling... television. The TV popularity of the series was magnanimous. Boyd licensed all kinds of Hoppy paraphernalia: lunch boxes, coloring books, records, games, watches, cap pistols, etc., all with the famous Hoppy logo.

In 1950 he began a Hoppy radio series for the Mutual Radio Network, and he began producing the 106 half-hour episodes of the *Hopalong Cassidy* TV show.

In 1953 Boyd retired from the screen to lord over the Hoppy empire he controlled. In 1968 he contracted cancer, and ill health befell him the last few years of his life. William Boyd died of Parkinson's disease on September 12, 1972.

William "Hopalong Cassidy" Boyd Filmography

1935: *Hopalong Cassidy* (Paramount; Howard Bretherton) *SK* Jimmy Ellison, *LL* Paula Stone; *The Eagle's Brood* (Paramount; Howard Bretherton) *SK* Jimmy Ellison, Gabby Hayes, *LL* Joan Woodbury; *Bar 20 Rides Again* (Paramount; Howard Bretherton) *SK* Jimmy Ellison, Gabby Hayes, *LL* Jean Rouverol. **1936:** *Call of the Prairie* (Paramount; Howard Bretherton) *SK* Jimmy Ellison, Gabby Hayes, *LL* Muriel Evans; *Three on the Trail* (Paramount; Howard Bretherton) *SK* Jimmy Ellison, Gabby Hayes, *LL* Muriel Evans; *Heart of the West* (Paramount; Howard Bretherton) *SK* Jimmy Ellison, Gabby Hayes, *LL* Lynn Gilbert; *Hopalong Cassidy Returns* (Paramount; Nate Watt) *SK* Gabby Hayes, *LL* Gail Sheridan, Evelyn Brent; *Trail Dust* (Paramount; Nate Watt) *SK* Gabby Hayes, Jimmy Ellison, *LL* Gwynne Shipman. **1937:** *Borderland* (Paramount; Nate Watt) *SK* Gabby Hayes, Jimmy Ellison, *LL* Nora Lane, Charlene Wyatt; *Hills of Old Wyoming* (Paramount; Nate Watt) *SK* Gabby Hayes, *LL* Gail Sheridan; *North of the Rio Grande* (Paramount; Nate Watt) *SK* Gabby Hayes, Russell Hayden, *LL* Bernadine Hayes; *Rustler's Valley* (Paramount; Nate Watt) *SK* Gabby Hayes, Russell Hayden, *LL* Muriel Evans; *Hopalong Rides Again* (Paramount; Lesley Selander) *SK* Gabby Hayes, Russell Hayden, *LL* Nora Lane; *Texas Trail* (Paramount; David Selman) *SK* Gabby Hayes, Russell Hayden, *LL* Judith Allen. **1938:** *Partners of the Plains* (Paramount; Lesley Selander) *SK* Russell Hayden, Harvey Clark, *LL* Gwen Gaze; *Cassidy of the Bar 20* (Paramount; Lesley Selander) *SK* Harvey Clark, Russell Hayden, *LL* Nora Lane, Margaret Marquis; *Pride of the West*

William Boyd and Evelyn Venable in The Frontiersman *(1938).*

(Paramount; Lesley Selander) *SK* Russell Hayden, Gabby Hayes, *LL* Charlotte Field; *Heart of Arizona* (Paramount; Lesley Selander) *SK* Russell Hayden, Gabby Hayes, *LL* Natalie Morehead, Dorothy Short; *Bar 20 Justice* (Paramount; Lesley Selander) *SK* Russell Hayden; Gabby Hayes, *LL* Gwen Gaze; *In Old Mexico* (Paramount; Edward Venturini) *SK* Russell Hayden, Gabby Hayes, *LL* Betty Amann, Jan Clayton; *The Frontiersman* (Paramount; Lesley Selander) *SK* Russell Hayden, Gabby Hayes, *LL* Evelyn Venable. **1939:** *Sunset Trail* (Paramount; Lesley Selander) *SK* Russell Hayden, Gabby Hayes, *LL* Charlotte Wynters, Jan Clayton; *Silver on the Sage* (Paramount; Lesley Selander) *SK* Russell Hayden, Gabby Hayes, *LL* Ruth Rogers; *Renegade Trail* (Paramount; Lesley Selander) *SK* Russell Hayden, Gabby Hayes, *LL* Charlotte Wynters; *Range War* (Paramount; Lesley Selander) *SK* Russell Hayden, *LL* Betty Moran; *Law of the Pampas* (Paramount; Nate Watt) *SK* Russell Hayden, *LL* Steffi Duna. **1940:** *Sante Fe Marshall* (Paramount; Lesley Selander) *SK* Russell Hayden, Britt Wood, *LL* Marjorie Rambeau, Bernadine Hayes; *Hidden Gold* (Paramount; Lesley Selander) *SK* Russell Hayden, Britt Wood, *LL* Ruth Rogers; *Stagecoach War* (Paramount; Lesley Selander) *SK* Russell Hayden, *LL* Julie Carter; *Three Men from Texas* (Paramount; Lesley Selander) *SK* Russell Hayden, Andy Clyde, *LL* Esther Estrella. **1941:** *Doomed Caravan* (Paramount; Lesley Selander) *SK* Russell Hayden, Andy Clyde, *LL* Minna Gombell; *In Old Colorado* (Paramount; Howard Bretherton) *SK* Russell Hayden, Andy

Clyde, *LL* Margaret Hayes; *Border Vigilantes* (Paramount; Derwin Abrahams) *SK* Russell Hayden, Andy Clyde, *LL* Frances Gifford; *Pirates on Horseback* (Paramount; Lesley Selander) *SK* Russell Hayden, Andy Clyde, *LL* Eleanor Stewart; *Wide Open Town* (Paramount; Lesley Selander) *SK* Russell Hayden, Andy Clyde, *LL* Evelyn Brent; *Riders of the Timberline* (Paramount; Lesley Selander) *SK* Andy Clyde, Brad King, *LL* Eleanor Stewart; *Stick to Your Guns* (Paramount; Lesley Selander) *SK* Andy Clyde, Brad King, *LL* Jacqueline "Jennifer" Holt; *Outlaws of the Desert* (Paramount; Howard Bretherton) *SK* Andy Clyde, Brad King, *LL* Jean Phillips; *Secrets of the Wasteland* (Paramount; Derwin Abrahams) *SK* Andy Clyde, Brad King, *LL* Barbara Britton; *Twilight on the Trail* (Paramount; Howard Bretherton) *SK* Andy Clyde, Brad King, *LL* Wanda McKay. **1942:** *Undercover Man* (United Artists; Lesley Selander) *SK* Andy Clyde, Jay Kirby, *LL* Nora Lane, Esther Estrella. **1943:** *Hoppy Serves a Writ* (United Artists; George Archainbaud) *SK* Andy Clyde, Jay Kirby, *LL* Jan Christy; *Border Patrol* (United Artists; Lesley Selander) *SK* Andy Clyde, Jay Kirby, *LL* Claudia Drake; *The Leather Burners* (United Artists; Joseph E. Henabery) *SK* Andy Clyde, Jay Kirby, *LL* Shelley Spencer; *Colt Comrades* (United Artists; Lesley Selander) *SK* Andy Clyde, Jay Kirby, *LL* Gayle Lord; *Bar 20* (United Artists; Lesley Selander) *SK* Andy Clyde, George Reeves, *LL* Betty Blythe; *False Colors* (United Artists; George Archainbaud) *SK* Andy Clyde, Jimmy Rogers, *LL* Claudia Drake; *Lost Canyon* (United Artists; Lesley Selander) *SK* Andy Clyde, Jay Kirby, *LL* Lola Lane; *Riders of the Deadline* (United Artists; Lesley Selander) *SK* Andy Clyde, Jimmy Rogers, *LL* Frances Woodward. **1944:** *Texas Masquerade* (United Artists; George Archainbaud) *SK* Andy Clyde, Jimmy Rogers, *LL* Mady Correll; *Lumber Jack* (United Artists; Lesley Selander) *SK* Andy Clyde, Jimmy Rogers, *LL* Ellen Hall; *Mystery Man* (United Artists; George Archainbaud) *SK* Andy Clyde, Jimmy Rogers, *LL* Eleanor Stewart; *Forty Thieves* (United Artists; Lesley Selander) *SK* Andy Clyde, Jimmy Rogers, *LL* Louise Currie. **1946:** *The Devil's Playground* (United Artists; George Archainbaud) *SK* Andy Clyde, Rand Brooks, *LL* Elaine Riley; *Fool's Gold* (United Artists; George Archainbaud) *SK* Andy Clyde, Rand Brooks, *LL* Jane Randolph. **1947:** *Unexpected Guest* (United Artists; George Archainbaud) *SK* Andy Clyde, Rand Brooks, *LL* Una O'Connor, Patricia Tate; *Dangerous Venture* (United Artists; George Archainbaud) *SK* Andy Clyde, Rand Brooks, *LL* Elaine Riley; *The Marauders* (United Artists; George Archainbaud) *SK* Andy Clyde, Rand Brooks, *LL* Dorinda Clifton, Mary Newton; *Hoppy's Holiday* (United Artists; George Archainbaud) *SK* Andy Clyde, Rand Brooks, *LL* Mary Ware. **1948:** *Silent Conflict* (United Artists; George Archainbaud) *SK* Andy Clyde, Rand Brooks, *LL* Virginia Belmont; *The Dead Don't Dream* (United Artists; George Archainbaud) *SK* Andy Clyde, Rand Brooks, *LL* Mary Ware; Sinister Journey (United Artists;

George Archainbaud) *SK* Andy Clyde, Rand Brooks, *LL* Elaine Riley; *False Paradise* (United Artists; George Archainbaud) *SK* Andy Clyde, Rand Brooks, *LL* Elaine Riley; *Borrowed Trouble* (United Artists; George Archainbaud) *SK* Andy Clyde, Rand Brooks, *LL* Elaine Riley; *Strange Gamble* (United Artists; George Archainbaud) *SK* Andy Clyde, Rand Brooks, *LL* Elaine Riley.

Johnny Mack Brown

Horse: Rebel
Sidekicks: Raymond Hatton, Fuzzy Knight, Syd Saylor, Max Terhune, Bob Baker, Tex Ritter, Jimmy Ellison

Alabama-born Johnny Mack Brown made the transition from prolific gridiron great to an even more prolific B Western superstar. Between 1930 and his retirement in 1952 Johnny Mack Brown starred in over 130 sagebrush classics.

While some cowboys made their mark as jolly, happy-go-lucky singing cowpokes, Mack Brown's character image was always one of a rough, tough, no-nonsense hero, eager to bring about justice with an equally quick fist or trigger finger.

Brown hailed from Dothan, Alabama, where he was born on September 1, 1904. He entered the University of Alabama in 1924 and quickly gained a reputation as a top-notch football player. As a freshman playing halfback he had a 100-yard scoring run against Kentucky. In 1926 Brown led the team to the Rose Bowl and to top it off, caught a 65-yard pass for the game-winning TD over Georgia Tech.

The following year Brown and his Crimson Tide teammates returned to the Rose Bowl. Once again it was Brown's heroics that led to victory. This time he intercepted a pass and returned it for a score with the clock running out for a 20–19 win over Washington.

He was also voted to the 1927 All-American squad.

Upon graduation, Johnny accepted a position at his alma mater as an assistant football coach. Following the Rose Bowl, however, Johnny Mack Brown had taken a screen test and was soon called to Hollywood. He made his debut in the 1927 film *Bugle Call.* He appeared in such silent films as *The Fair Co Ed* with Marion Davies and *Our Dancing Daughter* with Joan Crawford.

He made his Western debut in 1930 in an MGM picture called *Montana Moon,* also co-starring Joan Crawford. That was soon followed by the film

Johnny Mack Brown and Rebel.

that was to make the name of Johnny Mack Brown a household name —
Billy the Kid.

After starring in two Western serials, *Fighting with Kit Carson*
(Mascot, 1933) and *Rustlers of Red Dog* (Universal, 1935), Brown got a
chance to star in his own series of films when he signed with Supreme Pictures in 1935. He made eight films for Supreme in 1935 and 1936, then
moved over to Republic for eight more.

In 1939 Johnny began a series of films for Universal. The films, which
paired Brown with sidekick Fuzzy Knight, were acclaimed to be his best
films and placed him among the top ten cowboy stars.

In 1943 Johnny was contracted to Monogram where he would remain
until his retirement in 1952, after which he relegated his performing to TV
guest shots.

In 1965 Johnny returned to the screen for parts in *The Bounty Hunter* and *Requiem for a Gunfighter*. He made his last film, *Apache Uprising*, in 1966.

Johnny Mack Brown passed away on November 14, 1974.

Johnny Mack Brown Filmography

1930: *Montana Moon* (MGM; Malcolm St. Clair) *SK* Cliff Edwards, *LL* Joan Crawford, Dorothy Sebastian; *Billy the Kid* (MGM; King Vidor) *LL* Kay Johnson. **1931:** *The Great Meadow* (MGM; Charles Brabin) *LL* Eleanor Boardman, Anita Louise; *Lasca of the Rio Grande* (Universal; Edward Laemmle) *LL* Dorothy Burgess. **1932:** *The Vanishing Frontier* (Paramount; Phil Rosen) *LL* Evelyn Knapp, Zazu Pitts. **1933:** *Fighting with Kit Carson* (serial) (Mascot; Armand Schaefer, Colbert Clark) *LL* Betsy King Ross. **1935:** *Rustlers of Red Dog* (serial) (Universal; Lew Landers) *SK* Raymond Hatton, *LL* Joyce Compton; *Between Men* (Supreme; R.N. Bradbury) *LL* Beth Marion; *The Courageous Avenger* (Supreme; R.N. Bradbury) *LL* Helen Erikson; *Branded a Coward* (Supreme; Sam Newfield) *SK* Syd Saylor, *LL* Billie Seward. **1936:** *Valley of the Lawless* (Supreme; R.N. Bradbury) *LL* Joyce Compton; *Desert Phantom* (Supreme; S. Roy Luby) *LL* Sheila Mannors; *Rogue of the Range* (Supreme; S. Roy Luby) *LL* Lois January; *Everyman's Law* (Supreme; Albert Ray) *LL* Beth Marion; *The Crooked Trail* (Supreme; S. Roy Luby) *LL* Lucile Brown; *Undercover Man* (Republic; Albert Ray) *LL* Suzanne Karen. **1937:** *The Gambling Terror* (Republic; Sam Newfield) *LL* Iris Meredith; *Trail of Vengeance* (Republic; Sam Newfield) *LL* Iris Meredith; *Lawless Land* (Republic; Albert Ray) *LL* Louise Stanley; *Bar Z Bad Men* (Republic; Sam Newfield) *LL* Lois January; *Guns in the Dark* (Republic; Sam Newfield) *LL* Claire Rochelle; *A Lawman Is Born* (Republic; Sam Newfield) *SK* Al St. John, *LL* Iris Meredith, Mary MacLaren; *Wild West Days* (serial) (Universal; Ford Beebe, Cliff Smith) *SK* Frank Yaconelli, *LL* Lynn Gilbert; *Boot Hill Brigade* (Republic; Sam Newfield) *LL* Claire Rochelle. **1938:** *Flaming Frontiers* (serial) (Universal; Ray Taylor, Alan James) *LL* Eleanor Hansen. **1939:** *The Oregon Trail* (Universal; Ford Beebe, Saul A. Goodkind) *SK* Fuzzy Knight, *LL* Louise Stanley; *Desperate Trails* (Universal; Albert Ray) *SK* Fuzzy Knight, Bob Baker, *LL* Frances Robinson; *Oklahoma Frontier* (Universal; Ford Beebe) *SK* Fuzzy Knight, Bob Baker, *LL* Anne Gwynne; *Chip of the Flying U* (Universal; Ralph Staub) *SK* Fuzzy Knight, Bob Baker), *LL* Doris Weston. **1940:** *Riders of Pasco Basin* (Universal; Ray Taylor) *SK* Fuzzy Knight, Bob Baker, *LL* Frances Robinson; *Badman from Red Butte* (Universal; Ray Taylor) *SK* Fuzzy Knight, Bob Baker, *LL* Anne Gwynne; *Son of Roaring Dawn* (Universal; Ford Beebe) *SK* Fuzzy Knight, *LL* Nell O'Day, Jeannie

Kelly; *Ragtime Cowboy Joe* (Universal; Ray Taylor) *SK* Fuzzy Knight, *LL* Nell O'Day, Lynn Merrick; *Law and Order* (Universal; Ray Taylor) *SK* Fuzzy Knight, *LL* Nell O'Day; *Pony Post* (Universal; Ray Taylor) *SK* Fuzzy Knight, *LL* Nell O'Day. **1941:** *Boss of Bullion City* (Universal; Ray Taylor) *SK* Fuzzy Knight, *LL* Nell O'Day, Maria Montez; *Bury Me Not on the Lone Prairie* (Universal; Ray Taylor) *SK* Fuzzy Knight, *LL* Nell O'Day, Kathryn Adams; *Law of the Range* (Universal; Ray Taylor) *SK* Fuzzy Knight, *LL* Nell O'Day; *Rawhide Rangers* (Universal; Ray Taylor) *SK* Fuzzy Knight, *LL* Nell O'Day, Kathryn Adams; *Man from Montana* (Universal; Ray Taylor) *SK* Fuzzy Knight, *LL* Nell O'Day, Jeanne Kelly; *The Masked Rider* (Universal; Ford Beebe) *SK* Fuzzy Knight, *LL* Nell O'Day, Virginia Carroll; *Arizona Cyclone* (Universal; Joseph H. Lewis) *SK* Fuzzy Knight, *LL* Nell O'Day, Kathryn Adams; *Fighting Bill Fargo* (Universal; Ray Taylor) *SK* Fuzzy Knight, *LL* Nell O'Day, Jeanne Kelly;. **1942:** *Stagecoach Buckaroo* (Universal; Ray Taylor) *SK* Fuzzy Knight, *LL* Nell O'Day, Anne Nagel; *The Silver Bullet* (Univeral; Joseph H. Lewis) *SK* Fuzzy Knight, *LL* Jennifer Holt; *Boss of Hangtown Mesa* (Universal; Joseph H. Lewis) *SK* Fuzzy Knight, *LL* Helen Deverell; *Deep in the Heart of Texas* (Universal; Elmer Clifton) *SK* Tex Ritter, Fuzzy Knight, *LL* Jennifer Holt; *Little Joe the Wrangler* (Universal; Lewis Collins) *SK* Tex Ritter, Fuzzy Knight, *LL* Jennifer Holt; *The Old Chisholm Trail* (Universal; Elmer Clifton) *SK* Tex Ritter, Fuzzy Knight, *LL* Jennifer Holt. **1943:** *Tenting Tonight on the Old Campground* (Universal; Lewis Collins) *SK* Tex Ritter, Fuzzy Knight, *LL* Jennifer Holt; *Cheyenne Roundup* (Universal; Ray Taylor) *SK* Tex Ritter, Fuzzy Knight, *LL* Jennifer Holt; *Raiders of San Joaquin* (Universal; Lewis Collins) *SK* Tex Ritter, Fuzzy Knight, *LL* Jennifer Holt; *The Stranger from Pecos* (Monogram; Lambert Hillyer) *SK* Raymond Hatton, *LL* Christine MacIntyre; *The Lone Star Trail* (Universal; Ray Taylor) *SK* Tex Ritter, Fuzzy Knight, *LL* Jennifer Holt; *Six Gun Gospel* (Monogram; Lambert Hillyer) *SK* Raymond Hatton, *LL* Inna Gest; *Outlaws of Stampede Pass* (Monogram; Wallace Fox) *SK* Raymond Hatton, *LL* Ellen Hall; *The Texas Kid* (Monogram; Lambert Hillyer) *SK* Raymond Hatton, *LL* Shirley Patterson. **1944:** *Raiders of the Border* (Monogram; John P. McCarthy) *SK* Raymond Hatton, *LL* Ellen Hall; *Partners of the Trail* (Monogram; Lambert Hillyer) *SK* Raymond Hatton, *LL* Christine McIntyre; *Lawmen* (Monogram; Lambert Hillyer) *SK* Raymond Hatton, *LL* Jan Wiley; *Range Land* (Monogram; Lambert Hillyer) *SK* Raymond Hatton, *LL* Sarah Padden, Ellen Hall; West of the Rio Grande (Monogram; Lambert Hillyer) *SK* Raymond Hatton, *LL* Christine McIntyre; *Land of the Outlaws* (Monogram; Lambert Hillyer) *SK* Raymond Hatton, *LL* Nan Holiday; *Land of the Valley* (Monogram; Howard Bretherton) *SK* Raymond Hatton, *LL* Lynne Carver; *Ghost Guns* (Monogram; Lambert Hillyer) *SK* Raymond Hatton, *LL* Evelyn Finley, Sarah Padden. **1945:** *The Navajo Trail* (Monogram; Howard

Bretherton) *SK* Raymond Hatton, *LL* Jennifer Holt; *Gunsmoke* (Monogram; Howard Bretherton) *SK* Raymond Hatton, *LL* Jennifer Holt; *Stranger from Santa Fe* (Monogram; Lambert Hillyer) *SK* Raymond Hatton, *LL* Beatrice Gray, Joann Curtis; *Flame of the West* (Monogram; Lambert Hillyer) *SK* Raymond Hatton, *LL* Joan Woodbury, Lynne Carver; *The Lost Trail* (Monogram; Lambert Hillyer) *SK* Raymond Hatton, *LL* Jennifer Holt; *Frontier Feud* (Monogram; Lambert Hillyer) *SK* Raymond Hatton, *LL* Christine McIntyre. **1946:** *Border Bandits* (Monogram; Lambert Hillyer) *SK* Raymond Hatton, *LL* Rosa Del Rosario; *Drifting Along* (Monogram; Derwin Abrahams) *SK* Raymond Hatton, *LL* Lynne Carver; *The Haunted Mine* (Monogram; Derwin Abrahams) *SK* Raymond Hatton, *LL* Linda Johnson; *Under Arizona Skies* (Monogram; Lambert Hillyer) *SK* Raymond Hatton, *LL* Reno Blair; *The Gentleman from Texas* (Monogram; Lambert Hillyer) *SK* Raymond Hatton, *LL* Reno Blair, Claudia Drake, Christine McIntyre; *Trigger Fingers* (Monogram; Lambert Hillyer) *SK* Raymond Hatton, *LL* Jennifer Holt; *Shadows on the Range* (Monogram; Lambert Hillyer) *SK* Raymond Hatton, *LL* Jan Bryant; *Silver Range* (Monogram; Lambert Hillyer) *SK* Raymond Hatton, *LL* Jan Bryant. **1947:** *Raiders of the South* (Monogram; Lambert Hillyer) *SK* Raymond Hatton, *LL* Evelyn Brent, Reno Blair; *Valley of Fear* (Monogram; Lambert Hillyer) *SK* Raymond Hatton, *LL* Christine McIntyre; *Trailing Danger* (Monogram; Lambert Hillyer) *SK* Raymond Hatton, *LL* Peggy Wynne; *Land of the Lawless* (Monogram; Lambert Hillyer) *SK* Raymond Hatton, *LL* Christine McIntyre, June Harrison; *The Law Comes to Gunsight* (Monogram; Lambert Hillyer) *SK* Raymond Hatton, *LL* Reno Blair; *Code of the Saddle* (Monogram; Thomas Carr) *SK* Raymond Hatton, *LL* Kay Morley; *Flashing Guns* (Monogram; Lambert Hillyer) *SK* Raymond Hatton, *LL* Jan Bryant; *Prairie Express* (Monogram; Lambert Hillyer) *SK* Raymond Hatton, *LL* Virginia Belmont; *Gun Talk* (Monogram; Lambert Hillyer) *SK* Raymond Hatton, *LL* Christine McIntyre, Geneva Gray. **1948:** *Overland Trails* (Monogram; Lambert Hillyer) *SK* Raymond Hatton, *LL* Virginia Belmont; *Crossed Trails* (Monogram; Lambert Hillyer) *SK* Raymond Hatton, *LL* Lynne Carver, Kathy Frye; *Frontier Agent* (Monogram; Lambert Hillyer) *SK* Raymond Hatton, *LL* Reno Blair; *Trigger Man* (Monogram; Howard Bretherton) *SK* Raymond Hatton, *LL* Virginia Carroll; *Back Trail* (Monogram; Christ Cabanne) *SK* Raymond Hatton, *LL* Mildred Coles; *Range Justice* (Monogram; Ray Taylor) *SK* Max Terhune, *LL* Felice Ingersol; *The Fighting Ranger* (Monogram; Lambert Hillyer) *SK* Raymond Hatton, *LL* Christine Larson; *The Sheriff of Medicine Bow* (Monogram; Lambert Hillyer) *SK* Raymond Hatton, Max Terhune, *LL* Evelyn Finley; *Gunning for Justice* (Monogram; Ray Taylor) *SK* Raymond Hatton, Max Terhune, *LL* Evelyn Finley; *Hidden Danger* (Monogram; Ray Taylor) *SK* Raymond Hatton, Max Terhune, *LL* Christine Larson. **1949:** *Law of the*

West (Monogram; Ray Taylor) *SK* Max Terhune, *LL* Gerry Patterson; *Trail's End* (Monogram; Lambert Hillyer) *SK* Max Terhune, *LL* Kay Morley; *West of El Dorado* (Monogram; Ray Taylor) *SK* Max Terhune, *LL* Reno Browne; *Western Renegades* (Monogram; Wallace Fox) *SK* Max Terhune, *LL* Jane Adams, Constance Worth; *Stampede* (Allied Artists; Lesley Selander) *LL* Gale Storm. **1950:** *West of Wyoming* (Monogram; Wallace Fox) *LL* Gail Davis; *Over the Border* (Monogram; Wallace Fox) *LL* Wendy Waldron; *Six Gun Mesa* (Monogram; Wallace Fox) *LL* Gail Davis; *Law of the Panhandle* (Monogram; Lewis Collins) *LL* Jane Adams; *Outlaw Gold* (Monogram; Wallace Fox) *LL* Jane Adams. **1951:** *Colorado Ambush* (Monogram; Lewis Collins) *LL* Lois Hall, Christine McIntyre; *Man from Sonora* (Monogram; Lewis Collins) *LL* Phyllis Coates; *Blazing Bullets* (Monogram; Wallace Fox) *LL* Lois Hall; *Montana Desperado* (Monogram; Wallace Fox) *LL* Virginia Herrick; *Oklahoma Justice* (Monogram; Lewis Collins) *SK* James Ellison, *LL* Phyllis Coates, Barbara Allen; *Whistling Hills* (Monogram; Derwin Abrahams) *SK* Jimmy Ellison, *LL* Noel Neill, Pamela Duncan; *Texas Lawmen* (Monogram; Lewis Collins) *SK* Jimmy Ellison. **1952:** *Texas City* (Monogram; Lewis Collins) *SK* Jimmy Ellison, *LL* Lois Hall, Lorna Thayer; *Man from the Black Hills* (Monogram; Thomas Carr) *SK* Jimmy Ellison; *Dead Man's Trail* (Monogram; Lewis Collins) *SK* Jimmy Ellison, *LL* Barbara Allen; *Canyon Ambush* (Monogram; Lewis Collins) *LL* Phyllis Coates.

Buffalo Bill, Jr.
(Jay Wilsey)

During his teen years Jay Wilsey (born in Cheyenne, Wyoming, 1902) developed into a first-class trick rider and rodeo performer while making a living as a working cowboy.

While performing in a wild West show in the early twenties, Wilsey began to make films for Artclass Pictures. When he was given starring roles, the studio changed his name to Buffalo Bill, Jr.

In 1924 he signed with the famous Pathé Studios and in 1926 moved to Universal. While at Universal he also became active in producing and directing films.

When the sound era came about, Bill found himself relegated to making Westerns for such independent Poverty Row studios as Big 4, West Coast, Cosmos, Syndicate, Imperial and American, his longest stint being a four-picture deal with Superior.

Buffalo Bill, Jr., made his last starring vehicle, *The Whirlwind Rider,*

Buffalo Bill, Jr.

in 1935. His last few years as an actor were spent as a featured player in films starring the likes of Tom Mix, Ken Maynard, Gene Autry and George Houston.

After finishing *The Lone Rider in Ghost Town* for PRC in 1941, Buffalo Bill, Jr. retired from the screen.

Buffalo Bill, Jr. Filmography

1930: *Bar L Ranch* (Big 4; Harry S. Webb) *LL* Betty Baker; *The Cheyenne Kid* (West Coast; Jacques Jacard) *LL* Joan Jacard. **1931:** *Westward Bound* (Syndicate; Harry Webb) *LL* Allene Ray; *Trails of the Golden West* (Cosmos; Leander Decordova) *LL* Wanda Hawley; *Pueblo Terror* (Cosmos; Alan James) *LL* Wanda Hawley. **1932:** *Riders of the Golden Gulch* (West Coast; Clifford Smith) *LL* Mary Dunn; *The Texan* (Principal; Clifford Smith) *LL* Lucille Brown. **1933:** *The Fighting Cowboy* (Superior Talking Pix; Denver Dixon) *LL* Genee Boutel, Marin Sais. **1934:** *Lightning Bill* (Superior Talking Pix; Denver Dixon) *LL* Alma Rayford; *Pals of the Prairie* (Imperial; Charles Hutchinson) *LL* Victoria Vinton; *Rawhide Romance* (Superior Talking Pix; Denver Dixon) *LL* Genee Boutel; *Riding Speed* (Superior Talking Pix; Buffalo Bill, Jr.) *LL* Joile Benet. **1935:** *Trails of Adventure* (American; Buffalo Bill, Jr.) *LL* Edna Aslin; *The Whirlwind Rider* (American; Robert Horner)*LL* Genee Boutel.

Rod Cameron

Horse: Knight
Sidekicks: Eddie Dew, Fuzzy Knight, Ray Whitley

Rod Cameron is best known for his early action-adventure television series, *City Detective, Coronado 9* and *State Trooper.*

Back in 1944 and 1945, Cameron made a series of six B Westerns for Univeral Studios with Fuzzy Knight, Ray Whitley and Eddie Dew as sidekicks.

Cameron was born Roderick Cox in Calgary, Canada, on December 7, 1912, and worked on construction and as a trucker and skin diver before becoming a bit player in films in 1939.

In 1945 he landed the lead in the film *Salome, Where She Danced* opposite Yvonne De Carlo. He starred in such A Westerns as *Calvary Scout, Ride the Man Down* and *Santa Fe Passage.*

Perhaps Cameron's best action role was in *The Secret Sercice in Darkest Africa,* a serial he made for Republic in 1943.

Rod Cameron Filmography

1944: *Boss of Boomtown* (Universal; Ray Taylor) *SK* Fuzzy Knight, Ray Whitley, *LL* Vivian Austin; *Trigger Trail* (Universal; Lewis Collins) *SK*

Rod Cameron

Fuzzy Knight, Ray Whitley, Eddie Dew, *LL* Vivian Austin; *Riders of the Santa Fe* (Universal; Wallace Fox) *SK* Fuzzy Knight, Ray Whitley, Eddie Dew, *LL* Jennifer Holt; *The Old Texas Trail* (Universal; Lewis Collins) *SK* Fuzzy Knight, Ray Whitley, Eddie Dew, *LL* Marjorie Clemments, Virginia Christine. **1945:** *Beyond the Pecos* (Universal; Lambert Hillyer) *SK* Fuzzy Knight, Ray Whitley, Eddie Dew, *LL* Jennifer Holt; *Renegades of the Rio Grande* (Universal; Howard Bretherton) *SK* Fuzzy Knight, Ray Whitley, Eddie Dew, *LL* Jennifer Holt.

Harry Carey

Henry DeWitt Carey, better known as Harry, rates as one of moviedom's all-time great action and aventure stars. He starred in one of

Harry Carey

the most famous adventure films ever made, *Trader Horn* (MGM, 1930). The film, a jungle epic, was unique in that it as actually shot on location in Africa, and according to reports the making of the film was as much an adventure as was its story line. In fact, a disease contracted while on location was responsible for costing Carey's co-star, Edwina Booth, her career.

Carey also starred in one of the most famous B Westerns ever made ... *Powder Smoke Range*, the 1935 epic which introduced the Three Mesquiteers to the screen.

Carey became involved in the entertainment business strictly by

An RKO poster advertising Powdersmoke Range *(1935) starring Harry Carey.*

accident. He was born in the Bronx, New York, on January 16, 1878, and while studying law at N.Y.U. he contracted pneumonia. While recuperating he wrote a play which he produced and starred in.

In 1909 he made a film called *Bill Sharkey's Revenge*, which led to his working with legendary pioneer director D.W. Griffith. He eventually signed with Universal Pictures. By the early twenties he was considered one of Hollywood's top stars. However, when the talkies arrived in the late twenties, Harry found himself without a contract and out of work. This condition did not last long for him. He made three action serials *(The Vanishing Legion, The Last of the Mohicans* and *The Devil Horse)* for Mascot in 1931 and 1932. He also made his first B's for Artclass.

Carey's sound Western work was not relegated to the B's. He also made Western features like the critically acclaimed 1932 film *Law and Order* with Walter Huston. This film is the precursor of the many Earps vs. Clantons O.K. Corral shoot-out pictures that came later.

In 1935 and 1936 he made more B's for Poverty Row's Ajax. The cast of *Powder Smoke Range* read like a who's who of twenties and thirties Western film stars; Hoot Gibson, Bob Steele, Tom Tyler, Big Boy Williams, Wally Wales, Buddy Roosevelt and Buffalo Bill, Jr. were featured. In 1936, Harry Carey made another super "B" with Gibson and Tyler... *The Last Outlaw.*

In 1938 he starred in *The Law West of Tombstone* with a youthful Tim Holt. After that Harry became a character actor, and was still active in film work when he passed away on September 21, 1947.

Following in his father's footsteps, Harry Carey, Jr. became noted for his work in Western films.

Harry Carey Filmography

1929: *The Trail of '98* (MGM; Clarence Brown) *LL* Delores Del Rio. **1931:** *The Vanishing Legion* (serial) (Mascot; Ford Beebe, B. Reeves Eason) *SK* Rex, King of the Wild Horses, *LL* Edwina Booth. **1932:** *Without Honors* (Art Class; William Nigh) *LL* Mae Busch; *Border Devils* (Art Class; William Nigh) *LL* Kathleen Collins; *The Last of the Mohicans* (serial) (Mascot; Ford Beebe, B. Reeves Eason) *LL* Edwina Booth, Lucille Brown; *The Night Rider* (Art Class; William Nigh) *LL* Eleanor Fair; *The Devil Horse* (serial) (Mascot; Otto Brower, Richard Talmadge) *SK* Apache, King of the Wild Horses, *LL* Greta Granstedt; *Law and Order* (Universal; Edward Cahn) *SK* Walter Huston. **1933:** *Man of the Forest* (Paramount; Henry Hathaway) *SK* Randolph Scott, *LL* Verna Hillie; *The Thundering Herd* (Paramount; Henry Hathaway) *SK* Randolph Scott, *LL* Judith Allen. **1935:** *Wagon Trail* (Ajax; Harry Fraser) *LL* Gertrude Messinger; *Rustler's Paradise* (Ajax;

Harry Fraser) *LL* Gertrude Messinger, Carmen Bailey; *Powdersmoke Range* (RKO; Wallace Fox) *SK* 3 Mesquiteers, *LL* Boots Mallory; *The Last of the Clintons* (Ajax; Harry Fraser) *LL* Betty Mack. **1936:** *Aces Wild* (Commodore; Harry Fraser) *LL* Gertrude Messinger; *Ghost Town* (Commodore; Harry Fraser) *LL* Ruth Findlay, Jane Novak; *The Last Outlaw* (RKO; Christy Cabanne) *SK* Hoot Gibson, Tom Tyler, *LL* Margaret Callahan; *Wild Mustang* (Ajax; Harry Fraser) *SK* Sonny (the Marvel Horse), *LL* Barbara Fritchie. **1938:** *The Law West of Tombstone* (RKO; Glenn Tyson) *SK* Tim Holt, *LL* Evelyn Brent, Jean Rouverol.

Johnny Carpenter

Little-known Johnny Carpenter is probably best known as John Forbes, the star of the 1956 cult Western classic *I Killed Wild Bill Hickok,* a film he wrote and produced. Carpenter had been a bit player in B Westerns in the late 1940s.

His first starring film was *Badman's Gold* for Eagle Lion in 1951. It was a one-shot that was moderately received by the public. In 1953 and 1954 he wrote, produced and starred in two B's for United Artists.

He changed his onscreen name to Forbes in 1955 for a film called *Outlaw Treasure.*

Following the release of the Hickock film, Forbes/Carpenter retired from the screen. (See photo, p. 44.)

Johnny Carpenter Filmography

1951: *Badman's Gold* (Eagle Lion; Robert Tansey) *LL* Alyn Lockwood. **1953:** *Son of the Renegade* (United Artists; Reg Brown) *LL* Lori Irving. **1954:** *The Lawless Rider* (United Artists; Yakima Canutt) *LL* Rose Bascom.

Sunset Carson

Horse: Cactus
Sidekick: Smiley Burnette

Sunset Carson's 1945 film, *The Cherokee Flash,* ranks as one of the best B Westerns ever made.

Johnny Carpenter

Carson is also recognized as one of the screen's most natural cowboy actors, mainly because he was a cowboy long before he was an actor.

Born Michael James Harrison in Plainview, Texas, on November 12, 1927, Carson began performing in rodeos at the age of eight. By the time he reached his teens he was a mater trick rider, roper, bulldogger and broncobuster.

He became interested in the theatre and enrolled in acting classes at the Pasadena Playhouse. Sunset landed a part in the 1942 film *Stagedoor Canteen*.

Sunset Carson

That year he auditioned for Republic Pictures but was turned down cold.

Sunset spent a year in the service and, upon returning to Hollywood, to his amazement Republic signed him to a seven-year contract. In his first features released in 1944, Sunset was actually billed second to Gene Autry's old sidekick Smiley Burnette.

When Burnette left to co-star with Charles Starrett in the Durango Kid series at Columbia, Sunset was upped to star status. Republic poured its top leading ladies Peggy Stewart and Linda Stirling and its nastiest villain Roy Barcroft into the Carson features, and while the films were overall of good quality, Republic was never satisfied with the fans' acceptance of Carson; so after 15 movies they negated the final five years of his contract.

Sunset moved over to Astor Pictures to release five more Western adventure films between 1948 and 1950. The Astor series never matched the quality of the films he had made at Republic.

Sunset had a short-lived radio series, *The Black Bandit*, in 1950. He also appeared as a trick rider and sharpshooter with the Clyde Beatty Circus.

The past several years have seen Sunset as host of the TV series *Six Gun Heroes* on the South Carolina Public Television Network. The series showcases B Westerns.

Late 1985 found Sunset hard at work before the cameras filming a science fiction epic in North Carolina.

Sunset Carson Filmography

1944: *Call of the Rockies* (Republic; Lesley Selander) *SK* Smiley Burnette, *LL* Ellen Hall; *Bordertown Trail* (Republic; Lesley Selander) *SK* Smiley Burnette, *LL* Ellen Lowe; *Firebrands of Arizona* (Republic; Lesley Selander) *SK* Smiley Burnette, *LL* Peggy Stewart; *Code of the Prairie* (Republic; Spencer Bennett) *SK* Smiley Burnette, *LL* Peggy Stewart. **1945:** *Sheriff of Cimarron* (Republic; Yakima Canutt) *SK* Olin Howlin, *LL* Linda Stirling; *Santa Fe Saddlemates* (Republic; Thomas Carr) *SK* Olin Howlin, *LL* Linda Stirling; *Oregon Trail* (Republic; Thomas Carr) *LL* Peggy Stewart; *Bandits of the Badlands* (Republic; Thomas Carr) *LL* Peggy Stewart; *Rough Riders of Cheyenne* (Republic; Thomas Carr) *LL* Peggy Stewart; *The Cherokee Flash* (Republic; Thomas Carr) *LL* Linda Stirling. **1946:** *Days of Buffalo Bill* (Republic; Thomas Carr) *LL* Peggy Stewart; *Red River Renegades* (Republic; Thomas Carr) *LL* Peggy Stewart; *Rio Grande Raiders* (Republic; Thomas Carr) *LL* Linda Stirling; *Alias Billy the Kid* (Republic; Thomas Carr) *LL* Peggy Stewart; *The El Paso Kid* (Republic; Thomas Carr) *LL* Marie Harmon. **1948:** *Fighting Mustang* (Astor; Oliver Drake) *LL* Patricia Starling; *Deadline* (Astor; Oliver Drake) *LL* Patricia Starling; *Sunset Carson Rides Again* (Astor; Oliver Drake) *LL* Patricia Starling. **1949:** *Rio Grande* (Astor; Norman Sheldon) *LL* Evohn Keyes. **1950** (filmed in 1947): *Battling Marshall* (Astor; Oliver Drake) *LL* Patricia Starling.

Lane Chandler

Horse: Raven

When an auto mechanic by the name of Robert L. Oakes talked a movie director into letting him act in films, he changed his name to Lane Chandler.

That was in 1923. Chandler's career as a motion picture star and character actor lasted well into the late 1960s. He played good guys and bad guys, sheriffs and rustlers alike.

Oakes was born in South Dakota on June 4, 1899, and quit college to be a tourist bus driver in Yellowstone Park before drifting to Los Angeles.

For the first couple of years of his acting career, Chandler was basically little more than an extra, but soon his parts got bigger until in the mid-twenties Paramount decided that Chandler was one of its hottest leading man properties. The other was a guy named Cooper . . . Gary Cooper. Paramount hipsters even concocted a "competition" between the two.

Chandler was cast in top roles in big-budget, big-star productions, but with the advent of sound the studio was forced to choose between the two actors. Paramount cast its die with Cooper. Like that of Harry Carey and others, the talkies put a dent in the career of Chandler.

Chandler soon returned to the screen in serials like *The Lightning Express* for Universal and a series of B Westerns for Willis Kent. The eight films he made for Kent in 1931 and 1932 were long on action but short on most everything else. He finished his "B" career with two films for Empire Films. In 1938 he was one of the featured players in the serial version of *The Lone Ranger.*

As a character actor he appeared in such films as *Sampson and Delilah, Northwest Mounted Police, Saratoga Trunk, Duel in the Sun* and *The Plainsman* (with Cooper) and scores of B Westerns and TV shows.

Lane Chandler passed away on September 14, 1972, in Hollywood, California.

Lane Chandler Filmography

1930: *Firebrand Jordan* (Big 4; Alan James) *LL* Aline Goodwin. **1931:** *Hurricane Horseman* (Kent; Armand Schaeffer) *LL* Marie Quillan; *Riders of Rio* (Roundup Pictures; Robert Tansey) *LL* Karla Cowan. **1932:** *The Cheyenne Cyclone* (Kent/First Division; Armand Schaeffer) *LL* Connie Lamont; *Battling Buckaroo* (Kent; Armand Schaeffer) *LL* Doris Hill; *Guns for*

Lane Chandler

Hire (Kent; Lew Collins) *LL* Sally Darling; *Lawless Valley* (Kent; J.P. McGowan) *LL* Gertrude Messinger; *The Reckless Rider* (Kent; Armand Schaeffer) *LL* Phyllis Barrington; *Texas Tornado* (Kent; Oliver Drake) *LL* Doris Hill; *Wyoming Whirlwind* (Kent; Armand Schaeffer) *LL* Adele Tracy. **1934:** *The Lone Bandit* (Empire; J.P. McGowan) *LL* Doris Brook; *The Outlaw Tamer* (Empire; J.P. McGowan) *LL* Blanche Mehaffey (Janet Morgan).

Michael Chapin see **The Rough Ridin' Kids**

Edmond Cobb

Every B Western fan knows Edmond Cobb as a villain in dozens of films in the thirties and forties. But Cobb, who was a star of silent Westerns,

Edmond Cobb

got his one shot at B Western heroics in a film made in 1934 as *Racketeer Roundup* and re-released in 1935 by Beaumont Films as *Gunners and Guns*. The film paired Cobb with a horse called Black King — the horse with the human brain.

Cobb was born in Albuquerque, New Mexico, in 1892 and began making films around 1910. He starred in Westerns and serials during the twenties but fell to supporting roles at the beginning of the talkie era.

He appeared in over 50 Westerns as a bad guy and was a featured player in more than a dozen serials including *Gordon of Ghost City* with Buck Jones, *Rustlers of Red Dog* with Johnny Mack Brown, *The Miracle Rider* with Tom Mix and *Zorro Rides Again*.

Cobb continued to make films into the mid-1960s and died of a heart attack on August 15, 1974, in Woodland Hills, California.

Edmond Cobb Filmography

1935: *Gunners and Guns (Racketeer Roundup)* (Beaumont; Robert Hoyt) *SK* Black King, *LL* Edna Aslin.

Bill Cody

Horse: Chico
Sidekicks: Andy Shuford, Bill Cody, Jr.

Canadian-born William Joseph (Bill) Cody was among that group of cowboy stars that made the transition from the silent screen to the talkies.

Cody, after attending college at St. John's University (Minnesota), joined the Metropolitan Stock Company and did stage plays. In 1924 he became a bit player in Westerns at Pathé Studios.

The year 1925 saw Bill Cody starring in a series of Westerns such as *Dangerous Odds, Riders of Mystery,* and *The Fighting Sheriff* for Independent Pictures. He made a total of eight pictures for Independent before moving to Associated Exhibitors in 1926, back to Pathé in 1927 and 1928, and finally to Universal in 1929.

When the sound films came about, Bill had little trouble finding work. He was signed by Monogram and made eight features for them in 1931 and 1932.

Bill then drifted into a series of films for some of Poverty Row's most obscure studios such as Spectrum, Aywon and Crescent before retiring in 1936.

One unique aspect of Cody's sound films was that his sidekick was always a youngster. First, Andy Shuford at Monogram and later, his own son Bill Cody, Jr.

Born January 5, 1891 in Winnipeg, Canada, Bill Cody died January 1, 1948, in Santa Monica, California.

Bill Cody Filmography

1931: *Dugan of the Badlands* (Monogram; R.N. Bradbury) *SK* Andy Shuford, *LL* Blanche Mehaffey; *The Montana Kid* (Monogram; Harry Fraser) *SK* Andy Shuford, *LL* Doris Hill; *Oklahoma Jim* (Monogram; Harry Fraser) *SK* Andy Shuford, *LL* Marion Burns. **1932:** *Ghost City* (Monogram; Harry Fraser) *SK* Andy Shuford, *LL* Helen Forrest; *Mason of the Mounted* (Monogram; Harry Fraser) *SK* Andy Shuford, *LL* Nancy Drexel; *Law of the North* (Monogram; Harry Fraser) *SK* Andy Shuford, *LL* Nadine Dore; *Texas Pioneers* (Monogram; Harry Fraser) *SK* Andy Shuford, *LL* Sheila Mannors; *Law of Wanted Men* (Monogram; Harry Fraser) *SK* Andy Shuford, *LL* Sheila Mannors. **1934:** *Frontier Days* (Spectrum; Bob Hill) *SK* Bill Cody, Jr., *LL* Ada Ince; *Border Guns* (Aywon; Jack Nelson)

A Bill Cody studio still.

SK Bill Cody, Jr., *LL* Blanche Mehaffey; *The Border Menace* (Aywon; Jack Nelson) *LL* Miriam Rice. **1935:** *Six Gun Justice* (Spectrum; Robert Hill) *LL* Ethel Jackson; *The Cyclone Ranger* (Spectrum; Robert Hill) *LL* Nena Quartero; *The Texas Rambler* (Spectrum; Robert Hill) *LL* Catherine Cotter; *The Vanishing Riders* (Spectrum; Bob Hill) *SK* Bill Cody, Jr., *LL* Ethel Jackson; *Lawless Borders* (Spectrum; John P. McCarthy) *LL* Molly O'Day; *The Reckless Buckaroo* (Crescent; Harry Fraser) *SK* Bill Cody, Jr., *LL* Betty Mack; *Western Racketeers* (Aywon; Robert J. Horner) *LL* Edna Aslin. **1936:** *Blazing Justice* (Spectrum; Al Herman) *LL* Gertrude Messinger; *Outlaws of the Range* (Spectrum; Al Herman) *SK* Bill Cody, Jr., *LL* Catherine Cotter.

Spade Cooley

The story of Donnell Clyde Cooley, better known as Spade because of his affinity for card playing, is one of the most tragic in the annals of show biz.

Cooley, "The King of Western Swing," was born in Pack Saddle, Oklahoma, in 1910. Fiddle playing was a tradition in his family, and Spade became an expert on the instrument at a very early age. He moved to southern California in 1934 and earned a living as a musician.

He became a stand-in for Roy Rogers at Republic.

He formed his own band in the early forties and they soon became the nation's top Western swing aggregation.

Cooley began making short musical films in the mid-1940s and also provided the musical relief for B Westerns like Charles Starrett's *Texas Panhandle* in 1945.

In the late forties he made two Westerns for an outfit called Friedgen Productions, but the films weren't released until 1950 and were distributed by Astor Pictures. Later in 1950 he made one film for Eagle Lion.

Shortly after that Spade Cooley suffered a heart attack. Upon recovery he continued his musical career.

In 1961 he killed his wife during a violent argument and was sentenced to prison where he suffered a second heart attack.

While playing a law enforcement benefit in 1969, Spade Cooley suffered a final heart attack and died backstage.

Spade Cooley Filmography

1950: *The Kid from Gower Gulch* (Astor; Oliver Drake) *LL* Wanda Cantlon; *The Silver Bandit* (Astor; Elmer Clifton) *LL* Virginia Jackson; *Border Outlaws* (Eagle Lion; Richard Talmadge) *LL* Maria Hart.

Ray "Crash" Corrigan

Milwaukee-born Ray Bernard adopted his Crash Corrigan monicker from the character he played in his first starring vehicle, the 1936 Republic serial *The Undersea Kingdom*. The character, like Corrigan himself, was a rugged athlete and bodybuilder.

Corrigan got involved in the film industry first in the early thirties as a physical fitness instructor to some of Tinseltown's top stars.

In 1934 he began doing stunt work in adventure films and eventually landed a contract with Republic Pictures.

On the heels of the popularity of *Undersea Kingdom*, Corrigan landed the part of Tucson Smith in the studio's new Mesquiteers series with Bob Livingston and Max Terhune. The Mesquiteers films went over big and Corrigan remained in the series for the first 24 films.

In 1940 he, along with Max Terhune, left Republic to start a new series of trio films at Monogram. . . *The Range Busters*. The third member of the group was Dusty King.

Corrigan made a total of 20 Range Busters before deciding to retire from the screen in 1944 to concentrate on his real estate holdings including Corriganville — an authentic Western town often used as a set for cowboy flicks.

Crash Corrigan died in 1977.

Ray "Crash" Corrigan Filmography

1936: *The Three Mesquiteers* (Republic; Ray Taylor) *SK* Bob Livingston, Syd Saylor, *LL* Kay Hughes; *Ghost Town Gold* (Republic; Joseph Kane) *SK* Bob Livingston, Max Terhune, *LL* Kay Hughes; *Roarin' Lead* (Republic; Mack Wright, Sam Newfield) *SK* Bob Livingston, Max Terhune, *LL* Christine Maple; **1937:** *Riders of the Whistling Skull* (Republic; Mack Wright) *SK* Bob Livingston, Max Terhune, *LL* Mary Russell; *Hit the Saddle* (Republic; Mack Wright) *SK* Bob Livingston, Max Terhune, *LL* Rita Cansino; *Gunsmoke Ranch* (Republic; Joseph Kane) *SK* Bob Livingston, Max Terhune, *LL* Julia Thayer; *Come on Cowboys* (Republic; Joseph Kane) *SK*

Ray "Crash" Corrigan

Bob Livingston, Max Terhune, *LL* Maxine Doyle; *Range Defenders* (Republic; Mack Wright) *SK* Bob Livingston, Max Terhune, *LL* Eleanor Stewart; *Heart of the Rockies* (Republic; Joseph Kane) *SK* Bob Livingston, Max Terhune, *LL* Lynn Roberts; *The Trigger Trio* (Republic; William Witney) *SK* Ralph Byrd, Max Terhune, *LL* Sondra Corday; *Wild Horse Rodeo* (Republic; George Sherman) *SK* Bob Livingston, Max Terhune, *LL* June Martel; *The Painted Stallion* (serial) (Republic; William Witney, Alan James, Ray Taylor) *SK* Hoot Gibson, *LL* Julia Thayer; **1938:** *The Purple Vigilantes* (Republic; George Sherman) *SK* Bob Livingston, Max Terhune, *LL* Joan Barclay; *Call the Mesquiteers* (Republic; John English) *SK* Bob Livingston, Max Terhune, *LL* Lynn Roberts; *Outlaws of the Sonora* (Republic; George Sherman) *SK* Bob Livingston, Max Terhune, *LL* Jean Joyce; *Riders of the Black Hills* (Republic; George Sherman) *SK* Bob Livingston, Max Terhune, *LL* Ann Evers; *Heroes of the Hills* (Republic; George Sherman) *SK* Bob Livingston, Max Terhune, *LL* Priscilla Lawson; *Pals of the Saddle* (Republic; George Sherman) *SK* John Wayne, Max Terhune, *LL* Doreen McKay; *Overland Stage Raiders* (Republic; George Sherman) *SK* John Wayne, Max Terhune, *LL* Louise Brooks; *Santa Fe Stampede* (Republic; George Sherman) *SK* John Wayne, Max Terhune, *LL* June Martel; *Red River Range* (Republic; George Sherman) *SK* John Wayne, Max Terhune, *LL* Polly Moran; **1939:** *The Night Riders* (Republic; George Sherman) *SK* John Wayne, Max Terhune, *LL* Doreen McKay, Ruth Rogers; *Three Texas Steers* (Republic; George Sherman) *SK* John Wayne, Max Terhune, *LL* Carole Landis, Colette Lyons; *Wyoming Outlaw* (Republic; George Sherman) *SK* John Wayne, Max Terhune, *LL* Adele Pearce, Katharine Kentworthy; *New Frontier* (Republic; George Sherman) *SK* John Wayne, Max Terhune, *LL* Phyllis Isley. **1940:** *The Range Busters* (Monogram; S. Roy Luby) *SK* Dusty King, Max Terhune, *LL* Luana Walters; *Trailing Double Trouble* (Monogram; S. Roy Luby) *SK* Dusty King, Max Terhune, *LL* Lita Conway; *West of Pinto Basin* (Monogram; S. Roy Luby) *SK* Dusty King, Max Terhune, *LL* Gwen Gaze. **1941:** *Trail of the Silver Spur* (Monogram; S. Roy Luby) *SK* Dusty King, Max Terhune, *LL* Dorothy Short; *The Kid's Last Ride* (Monogram; S. Roy Luby) *SK* Dusty King, Max Terhune, *LL* Luana Walters; *Tumbledown Ranch in Arizona* (Monogram; S. Roy Luby) *SK* Dusty King, Max Terhune, *LL* Sheila Darcy, Marian Kirby; *Wrangler's Roost* (Monogram; S. Roy Luby) *SK* Dusty King, Max Terhune, *LL* Gwen Gaze; *Fugitive Valley* (Monogram; S. Roy Luby) *SK* Dusty King, Max Terhune, *LL* Julie Duncan; *Saddle Mountain Roundup* (Monogram; S. Roy Luby) *SK* Dusty King, Max Terhune, *LL* Lita Conway; *Tonto Basin Outlaws* (Monogram; S. Roy Luby) *SK* Dusty King, Max Terhune, *LL* Jan Wiley; *Underground Rustlers* (Monogram; S. Roy Luby) *SK* Dusty King, Max Terhune, *LL* Gwen Gaze. **1942:** *Thunder River Feud* (Monogram; S. Roy Luby) *SK* Dusty King, Max Terhune, *LL* Jan Wiley; *Rocky River Renegades* (Monogram; S. Roy Luby) *SK* Dusty King, Max Terhune, *LL* Christine McIntyre; *Boot Hill Bandits* (Monogram; S. Roy Luby) *SK* Dusty King, Max Terhune, *LL* Jean Brooks; *Texas Trouble Shooters* (Monogram; S. Roy Luby) *SK* Dusty King, Max Terhune, *LL* Julie Duncan; *Arizona Stagecoach* (Monogram; S. Roy Luby) *SK* Dusty King, Max Terhune, *LL* Nell O'Day. **1943:** *Land of Hunted Men* (Monogram; S. Roy Luby) *SK* Dennis Moore, Max Terhune, *LL* Phyllis Adair; *Cowboy Commandoes* (Monogram; S. Roy Luby) *SK* Dennis Moore; Max Terhune, *LL* Evelyn Finley; *Black Market Rustlers* (Monogram; S. Roy Luby) *SK* Dennis Moore, Max Terhune, *LL* Evelyn Finley; *Bullets and Saddles* (Monogram; Anthony Marshall) *SK* Dennis Moore, Max Terhune, *LL* Julie Duncan.

Buster Crabbe

Horse: Falcon
Sidekick: Al "Fuzzy" St. John

Buster Crabbe is best known among action film fans as the King of the Serials, stemming from the fact that he made nine chapter plays in his career including the enormously popular trio of Flash Gordon adventures.

Buster was born Clarence Linden Crabbe on February 7, 1908, in Oakland, California. His family moved to Hawaii when Buster was two, and during his developing years he evolved into a fantastic swimmer.

In 1928 as a member of the U.S. Olympic team, he won a bronze medal in both the 400 and 1500 meter events in Amsterdam. The next year he enrolled at the University of Southern California and worked his way through school as a movie extra. In the 1932 Olympics Buster led the American team, winning a gold medal in the 400 meters. Before his career was over he would hold 16 swimming records. His performance at the Los Angeles Olympics gained him a successful screen test with Paramount Pictures.

Crabbe's first film was *King of the Jungle,* in which he played a Tarzan-like jungle man. In 1933 he made a big step upward, landing the lead in the 12-chapter serial *Tarzan the Fearless.* Buster also had featured parts in several of Paramount's Zane Grey Western films.

In 1936 he made the first of the Flash Gordon serials. Other serials quickly followed: *Red Barry* (1937, *Flash Gordon's Trip to Mars* (1938), *Buck Rogers* (1939) and *Flash Gordon Conquers the Universe* (1940).

In 1940 Producers Releasing Corporation signed Crabbe to take over the lead in its Billy the Kid series from the departing Bob Steele. In early 1941 PRC released *Billy the Kid Wanted,* the first of 36 B Westerns Buster and his sidekick Fuzzy Q. Jones would make for the company between 1941 and 1946.

Along the way, PRC yielded to pressure groups who objected to the series' glorification of the name of a known killer, and changed the name of Crabbe's character to Billy Carson.

In 1946 Crabbe left PRC to work in feature films and more serials.

Buster also ventured into television; first with an exercise program in early 1950, and then as the star of *Capt. Gallant of the Foreign Legion* in 1955. The series co-starred Crabbe's son Cuffy and Fuzzy Knight.

Noted for his youthful physique, Buster continued making personal appearances, films, commercials, and TV shows into the late 1970s.

Buster Crabbe passed away April 23, 1983, in Scottsdale, Arizona.

Buster Crabbe in one of his many Western roles.

Buster Crabbe Filmography

1935: *Nevada* (Paramount; Charles Barton) SK Raymond Hatton, LL Kathleen Burke. **1936:** *Drift Fence* (Paramount; Otto Lovering) SK Tom Keene, LL Katherine Demille; *Desert Gold* (Paramount; James Hogan) SK Tom Keene, LL Marsha Hunt; *The Arizona Raiders* (Paramount; James Hogan) SK Raymond Hatton, LL Marsha Hunt, Jane Rhodes. **1941:** *Billy the Kid Wanted* (PRC; Sherman Scott [Sam Newfield]) SK Al St. John; *Billy the Kid's Roundup* (PRC; Sherman Scott [Sam Newfield]) SK Al St. John, LL Joan Barclay. **1942:***Billy the Kidd Trapped* (PRC; Sherman Scott [Sam Newfield]) SK Al St. John, LL Anne Jeffries; *Billy the Kid's Smoking Guns* (PRC; Sherman Scott [Sam Newfield]) SK Al St. John, LL Joan Barclay; *Law and Order* (PRC; Sherman Scott [Sam Newfield]) SK Al St. John, LL Wanda McKay, Sarah Padden; *Sheriff of Sage Valley* (PRC;

Buster Crabbe as Flash Gordon (also pictured, Jean Rogers).

Sherman Scott [Sam Newfield]) *SK* Al St. John, *LL* Maxine Leslie; *The Mysterious Rider* (PRC; Sam Newfield) *SK* Al St. John, *LL* Caroline Burke.
1943: *The Kid Rides Again* (PRC; Sherman Scott) *SK* Al St. John, *LL* Iris Meredith; *Fugitive of the Plains* (PRC; Sam Newfield) *SK* Al St. John, *LL* Maxine Leslie; *Western Cyclone* (PRC; Sam Newfield) *SK* Al St. John, *LL* Marjorie Manners; *Cattle Stampede* (PRC; Sam Newfield) *SK* Al St. John, *LL* Frances Gladwin; *The Renegade* (PRC; Sam Newfield) *SK* Al St. John, *LL* Lois Ransom; *Blazing Frontier* (PRC; Sam Newfield) *SK* Al St. John, *LL* Marjorie Manners; *Devil Riders* (Billy Carson series) (PRC; Sam Newfield)

SK Al St. John, *LL* Patty McCarthy. **1944:** *Frontier Outlaws* (PRC; Sam Newfield) *SK* Al St. John, *LL* Frances Gladwin, Marin Sais; *Thundering Gunslingers* (PRC; Sam Newfield) *SK* Al St. John, *LL* Frances Gladwin; *Valley of Vengeance* (PRC; Sam Newfield) *SK* Al St. John, *LL* Evelyn Finley; *Fuzzy Settles Down* (PRC; Sam Newfield) *SK* Al St. John, *LL* Patty McCarthy; *Rustlers Hideout* (PRC; Sam Newfield) *SK* Al St. John, *LL* Patty McCarthy; *Wild Horse Phantom* (PRC; Sam Newfield) *SK* Al St. John, *LL* Elaine Morey; *Oath of Vengeance* (PRC; Sam Newfield) *SK* Al St. John, *LL* Mady Lawrence; *The Drifter* (PRC; Sam Newfield) *SK* Al St. John, *LL* Carol Parker. **1945:** *His Brother's Ghost* (PRC; Sam Newfield) *SK* Al St. John; *Shadows of Death* (PRC; Sam Newfield) *SK* Al St. John, *LL* Donna Dax; *Gangsters Den* (PRC; Sam Newfield) *SK* Al St. John; *Stagecoach Outlaws* (PRC; Sam Newfield) *SK* Al St. John, *LL* Frances Gladwin; *Border Badmen* (PRC; Sam Newfield) *SK* Al St. John, *LL* Lorraine Miller, Marin Sais; *Fighting Bill Carson* (PRC; Sam Newfield) *SK* Al St. John, *LL* Kay Hughes; *Prairie Rustlers* (PRC; Sam Newfield) *SK* Al St. John, *LL* Evelyn Finley. **1946:** *Lightning Raiders* (PRC; Sam Newfield) *SK* Al St. John, *LL* Mady Lawrence; *Gentlemen with Guns* (PRC; Sam Newfield) *SK* Al St. John, *LL* Patricia Knox; *Terrors on Horseback* (PRC; Sam Newfield) *SK* Al St. John, *LL* Patti McCarty; *Ghost of Hidden Valley* (PRC; Sam Newfield) *SK* Al St. John, *LL* Jean Carlin; *Prairie Badmen* (PRC; Sam Newfield) *SK* Al St. John, *LL* Patricia Knox; *Overland Riders* (PRC; Sam Newfield) *SK* Al St. John, *LL* Patti McCarty; *Outlaws of the Plains* (PRC; Sam Newfield) *SK* Al St. John, *LL* Patti McCarty.

Ken Curtis

Sidekicks: Big Boy Williams, Andy Clyde, Guy Kibbee

Ken Curtis is best known as Marshal Matthew Dillon's crotchety scutter of a sidekick and part-time deputy Festus Hagen on *Gunsmoke*, a role he played for 11 seasons on the popular TV series.

Curtis graced the B Western screen when he made a series of musical Western features for Columbia Pictures between 1945 and 1947. He made eight in all beginning with *Rhythm Roundup*. These films were more like Western jamborees than hard-hitting adventures. Songs always outnumbered the bad guys, and the cast included comics like Andy Clyde and Guy Kibbee and musical groups such as Bob Wills and his Texas Playboys and the Hoosier Hotshots.

Curtis was born in Lamar, Colorado, on July 2, 1916, and was blessed with a truly outstanding singing voice.

In 1949 he joined the famed Sons of the Pioneers, replacing original member Tim Spencer, and remained with them until 1953.

He made one serial, *Don Daredevil Rides Again*, for Republic Pictures in 1951 in which he played a masked Zorroesque hero.

Ken Curtis joined the *Gunsmoke* cast in 1964, replacing the departed Dennis (Chester) Weaver, and remained there until the show was cancelled in 1975.

In 1983 he co-starred in the short-lived NBC series *The Yellow Rose*.

Ken Curtis Filmography

1945: *Rhythm Roundup* (Columbia; Vernon Keays) *SK* Big Boy Williams, Raymond Hatton, *LL* Cheryl Walker; *Song of the Prairie* (Columbia; Ray Nazarro) *SK* Big Boy Williams; Andy Clyde, *LL* June Storey, Jeff Donnell. **1946:** *Throw a Saddle on a Star* (Columbia; Ray Nazarro) *SK* Big Boy Williams, Andy Clyde, *LL* Jeff Donnell, Adelle Roberts; *That Texas Jamboree* (Columbia; Ray Nazarro) *SK* Big Boy Williams, Andy Clyde, *LL* Jeff Donnell, Carolina Cotton, Claire Carleton; *Cowboy Blues* (Columbia; Ray Nazarro) *SK* Big Boy Williams, Guy Kibbee, *LL* Jeff Donnell, Carolina Cotton; *Singing on the Trail* (Columbia; Ray Nazarro) *SK* Big Boy Williams, Guy Kibbee, *LL* Jeff Donnell; *Lone Star Moonlight* (Columbia; Ray Nazarro) *SK* Guy Kibbee, *LL* Joan Barton. **1947:** *Over the Santa Fe Trail* (Columbia; Ray Nazarro) *SK* Guy Kibbee, Big Boy Williams, *LL* Jennifer Holt. **1949:** *Riders of the Pony Express* (Screen Craft; Michael Salle) *SK* Shug Fisher, *LL* Cathy Douglas; *Stallion Canyon* (Astor; Harry Fraser) *SK* Shug Fisher, *LL* Carolina Cotton. **1951:** *Don Daredevil Rides Again* (serial) (Republic; Fred Brannon) *LL* Aline Towne.

Bob Custer

Back in the silent film era of the 1920s Bob Custer was a top Western action film star. For FBO Studios Custer made films like *A Man of Nerve* and *Trigger Fingers*, and saved leading ladies such as Jean Arthur from dastardly evil villains. However when the silent era gave way to talking pictures, Custer was one of the many silent screen performers who found himself out of work.

Ken Curtis (with June Storey, left, and Jeff Donnell) in one of his singing cowboy roles.

Bob Custer

He signed with the independent Syndicate Studios in 1929 and did six films for them. In 1931 and 1932 he made Westerns for Big 4 and ended his film career with several pictures for Reliable in 1936 and 1937.

Custer's best sound film work came in the 1934 Mascot serial *Law of the Wild* in which he teamed with Rin Tin Tin, Jr.; Rex, king of the wild horses; and cross-eyed comedian Ben Turpin.

Custer was born Raymond Anthony Glenn in Frankfurt, Kentucky, on October 18, 1898. He attended the University of Kentucky and later became a trick rider and rodeo performer. In 1920 he went to California and found work as a movie extra. In 1924 he signed with FBO for $100 a week.

Custer retired from the screen in 1938 to work in the shipbuilding industry and later went to work for the City of Los Angeles.

Bob Custer passed away December 7, 1974, of a heart attack.

Bob Custer Filmography

1929: *Riders of the Rio Grande* (Syndicate; J.P. McGowan) *LL* Edna Aslin. **1930:** *Parting of the Trails* (Syndicate; J.P. McGowan) *LL* Vivian Ray; *Under Texas Skies* (Syndicate; J.P. McGowan) *LL* Natalie Kingston; *Covered Wagon Trails* (Syndicate; J.P. McGowan) *LL* Phyliss Bainbridge. **1931:** *Riders of the North* (Syndicate; J.P. McGowan) *LL* Blanche Mehaffey; *Son of the Plains* (Syndicate; R.N. Bradbury) *SK* Al "Fuzzy" St. John, *LL* Doris Phillips; *Law of the Rio Grande* (Syndicate; Bennett Cohen, Forrest Sheldon) *LL* Betty Mack; *Headin' for Trouble* (Big 4; J.P. McGowan) *LL* Betty Mack; *Quick Trigger Lee* (Big 4; J.P. McGowan) *LL* Caryl Lincoln. **1932:** *Mark of the Spur* (Big 4; J.P. McGowan) *LL* Lillian Rich; *Scarlet Brand* (Big 4; Fred Allen) *LL* Betty Mack. **1934:** *Law of the Wild* (serial) (Mascot; B. Reeves Eason, Armand Schaeffer) *SK* Ben Turpin, *LL* Lucile Brown. **1936:** *Ambush Valley* (Reliable; Raymond Samuels, [Bernard Ray]) *LL* Victoria Vinton; *Vengeance of Rannah* (Reliable; Franklyn Shamray, [Bernard Ray]) *SK* Rin Tin Tin, Jr., *LL* Victoria Vinton. **1937:** *Santa Fe Rides* (Reliable; Raymond Samuels, [Bernard Ray]) *LL* Eleanor Stewart.

Eddie Dean

Horses: Flash, Copper, White Cloud
Sidekicks: Roscoe Ates, Lash LaRue, Emmett Lynn

Eddie Dean, composer of the country and western classic "One Has My Name the Other Has My Heart," was one of several B Western stars who prior to a film career was a star of the radio airwaves.

Dean, born Eddie Dean Glossup in Posey, Texas, in 1910, began in vaudeville as a singer. In 1930 he got his first radio show in Tulsa, Oklahoma, and soon joined the famous National Barn Dance and later was the crooner on the very popular *Judy Canova Show*.

Around 1936 Dean, in between radio performances, began getting jobs as a bit player in films, especially Westerns such as Tex Ritter's *Golden Trail*.

Dean got his break in the 1944 Mattox production of *The Harmony Trail*. While Ken Maynard was listed as the film's major star, co-star Dean handled most of the action and music. Even though the film was only a limited release, Dean's performance and audience reaction got him a contract with PRC. Eddie Dean made 18 films for the studio between 1945 and

1948. Most critics agree the best part of the Dean films was his voice. In fact, many argue that voicewise Dean was the best of the singing cowboy lot.

An interesting note on Dean's films is that his co-star early on in the series was Lash LaRue. LaRue's work in the films gave him his shot to star in a series of his own.

When his series ended, Dean returned to performing his music on radio and in rodeos around the country. He continued to get bit parts in films and on TV. He can be remembered as the yodeling cop on *The Beverly Hillbillies*.

Today Eddie Dean continues to live in California and often performs at the Palomino nightclub in North Hollywood.

Eddie Dean Filmography

1945: *Song of Old Wyoming* (PRC; Robert Emmett Tansey) *SK* Lash LaRue, Emmett Lynn, *LL* Jennifer Holt, Sarah Padden. **1946:** Romance of the West (PRC; Robert Emmett Tansey) *SK* Emmett Lynn, *LL* Joan Barton; *The Caravan Trail* (PRC; Robert Emmett Tansey) *SK* Emmett Lynn, Lash LaRue, *LL* Jean Carlin; *Colorado Serenade* (PRC; Robert Emmett Tansey) *SK* Roscoe Ates, *LL* Mary Kenyon; *Driftin' River* (PRC; Robert Emmett Tansey) *SK* Roscoe Ates, *LL* Shirley Patterson; *Tumbleweed Trail* (PRC; Robert Emmett Tansey) *SK* Roscoe Ates, *LL* Shirley Patterson; *Stars Over Texas* (PRC; Robert Emmett Tansey) *SK* Roscoe Ates, *LL* Shirley Patterson; *Wild West* (PRC; Robert Emmett Tansey) *SK* Lash LaRue, *LL* Louise Currie, Jean Carlin, Sarah Padden. **1947:** *Wild Country* (PRC; Ray Taylor) *SK* Roscoe Ates, *LL* Peggy Wynn; *Range Beyond the Blue* (PRC; Ray Taylor) *SK* Roscoe Ates, *LL* Helen Mowery; *West to Glory* (PRC; Ray Taylor) *SK* Roscoe Ates, *LL* Delores Castle; *Black Hills* (PRC; Ray Taylor) *SK* Roscoe Ates, *LL* Shirley Patterson; *Shadow Valley* (PRC; Ray Taylor) *SK* Roscoe Ates, *LL* Jennifer Holt. **1948:** *Check Your Guns* (PRC; Ray Taylor) *SK* Roscoe Ates, *LL* Nancy Gates; *Tornado Range* (PRC; Ray Taylor) *SK* Roscoe Ates, *LL* Jennifer Holt; *The Westward Trail* (PRC; Ray Taylor) *SK* Roscoe Ates, *LL* Phyllis Planchard, Eileen Hardin; *The Hawk of Powder River* (PRC; Ray Taylor) *SK* Roscoe Ates, *LL* Jennifer Holt, June Carson; *The Tioga Kid* (PRC; Ray Taylor) *SK* Roscoe Ates, *LL* Jennifer Holt.

Eddie Dean

Eddie Dew

Eddie Dew had one of the shortest B Western careers on record. He starred in only three films in 1943 and 1944 and then slipped into moviola oblivion.

Dew had been a bit player at Republic when suddenly the studio decided to make him a star. They created a series especially for him. Dew was to play John Paul Revere, a new hero, and they even gave him Smiley Burnette as a sidekick.

The first two films of the series, *Beyond the Last Frontier* and *Raiders of Sunset Pass,* were dismal flops. Dew was given a pink slip, and Bob Livingston was called upon to take over, but the project was scrapped after one more film.

Dew went over to Universal and sidekicked (with Fuzzy Knight and Ray Whitley) Rod Cameron for five films in 1944 and 1945.

Eddie Dew

Universal gave Dew one last chance to make it as a matinee cowboy when they starred him in *Trail to Gunsight*, but it too was ill received by the fans, and Eddie Dew drifted off into the sunset.

Eddie Dew Filmography

1943: *Beyond the Last Frontier* (Republic; Howard Bretherton) *SK* Smiley Burnette, *LL* Lorraine Miller; *Raiders of Sunset Pass* (Republic; John English) *SK* Smiley Burnette, *LL* Jennifer Holt. **1944:** *Trail to Gunsight* (Universal; Vernon Keyes) *SK* Fuzzy Knight, *LL* Maris Wrixon; *Lucky Cowboy* (short) (Paramount; Josef Berne) *LL* Julie Gibson.

Wild Bill Elliott

Horses: Thunder, Sonny
Sidekicks: Gabby Hayes, Bobby Blake

The self-proclaimed "peaceable" man with his guns settin' buttfirst in his holsters, Gordon "Wild Bill" Elliott ranks with Rogers, Autry and Cassidy as the most famous of the action Western stars. He gleaned the monicker "Wild Bill" from his portrayal of Wild Bill Hickock in the popular 1938 Columbia serial *The Great Adventures of Wild Bill Hickok*, which was his first starring role.

With the exception of singing, Elliott was all that a cowboy hero should be. He was handsome, rugged and athletic in appearance, a good horseman and able to handle trouble with either fists or shootin' irons. Elliott, especially in the Red Ryder role, was a hero who never went looking for trouble; in fact he tried his darndest to avoid it.

Elliott was born Gordon Nance in Pattonsburgh, Missouri, on October 16, 1903. He began riding at the age of five and was an expert roper, bulldogger and rodeo performer by his teens. As a boy, his hero was the legendary silent film star William S. Hart.

After attending Rockhurst College, he headed for Hollywood and gained stage experience at the Pasadena Playhouse. During that time he changed his name to Gordon Elliott.

His first film *The Plastic Age*, starring Clara Bow, was released in 1925. Elliott appeared in over 60 films before he made his first Western, Dick Foran's *Trailin' West*, in 1936. In 1936 he got a bigger dose of celluloid traildust, appearing with Gene Autry in *Boots and Saddles* and with Smith Ballew in *Roll Along Cowboy*.

Columbia Pictures was well pleased with the box office reception that Elliott received in the Hickok serial and wasted no time in launching a series of Elliott films, beginning with *In Early Arizona* in 1938.

The following year he made another popular serial, *Overland with Kit Carson*, and picked up Dub Taylor as sidekick in his series.

In 1941 Columbia paired Elliott with Tex Ritter for eight films. Elliott made 25 films for Columbia before departing for Republic in 1943.

His first film for his new studio was *Calling Wild Bill Elliott*, which teamed him with Gabby Hayes and leading lady Anne Jeffreys. This combination made a half dozen films before Elliott took on the role of Red Ryder in the film *Tucson Raiders* in 1944.

Hayes was in the initial outing but yielded sidekicking duties to young Bobby Blake, who portrayed Little Beaver in Elliott's 16 Ryder films.

In 1946 Elliott gave up the Red Ryder role to Rocky Lane and moved

Wild Bill Elliott

up to bigger budget Westerns, his first being *In Old Sacramento.* He also changed his billing to William Elliott.

In 1951 Wild Bill Elliott left Republic for Monogram. He made his last starring Western, *The 49'ers,* in 1954.

Still under contract to Monogram, now called Allied Artists, Elliott starred in several mystery dramas before retiring to his Nevada ranch in 1957.

Wild Bill Elliott died on November 6, 1965.

Wild Bill Elliott Filmography

1938: *The Great Adventures of Wild Bill Hickok* (serial) (Columbia; Mack V. Wright, Sam Nelson) *LL* Carole Wayne; *In Early Arizona* (Columbia; Joseph Levering) *LL* Dorothy Gulliver. **1939:** *Frontiers of '49* (Columbia; Joseph Levering) *LL* Luana Dealcaniz; *Lone Star Pioneers* (Columbia; Joseph Levering) *LL* Dorothy Gulliver; *The Law Comes to Texas* (Columbia; Joseph Levering) *LL* Veda Ann Borg; *Overland with Kit Carson* (serial) (Columbia; Sam Nelson, Norman Deming) *SK* Richard Fiske, *LL* Iris Meredith; *Taming of the West* (Columbia; Norman Deming) *SK* Dub Taylor, *LL* Iris Meredith. **1940:** *Pioneers of the Frontier* (Columbia; Sam Nelson) *SK* Dub Taylor, *LL* Linda Winters; *The Man from Tumbleweeds* (Columbia; Joseph H. Lewis) *SK* Dub Taylor, *LL* Iris Meredith; *The Return of Wild Bill* (Columbia; Joseph H. Lewis) *SK* Dub Taylor, *LL* Iris Meredith, Luana Walters; *Prairie Schooners* (Columbia; Sam Nelson) *SK* Dub Taylor, *LL* Evelyn Young; *Beyond the Sacramento* (Columbia; Lambert Hillyer) *SK* Dub Taylor, *LL* Evelyn Keyes; *Wildcat of Tucson* (Columbia; Lambert Hillyer) *SK* Dub Taylor, *LL* Evelyn Young. **1941:** *Across the Sierras* (Columbia; D. Ross Lederman) *SK* Dub Taylor, Richard Fiske, *LL* Luana Walters; *North from the Lone Star* (Columbia; Lambert Hillyer) *SK* Dub Taylor, Richard Fiske, *LL* Dorothy Fay; *The Return of Daniel Boone* (Columbia; Lambert Hillyer) *SK* Dub Taylor, *LL* Betty Miles; *Hands Across the Rockies* (Columbia; Lambert Hillyer) *SK* Dub Taylor, *LL* Mary Daily; *The Son of Davy Crockett* (Columbia; Lambert Hillyer) *SK* Dub Taylor, *LL* Iris Meredith; *King of Dodge City* (Columbia; Lambert Hillyer) *SK* Tex Ritter, Dub Taylor, *LL* Judith Linden; *Roaring Frontiers* (Columbia; Lambert Hillyer) *SK* Tex Ritter, *LL* Ruth Ford. **1942:** *Lone Star Vigilantes* (Columbia; Wallace Fox) *SK* Tex Ritter, *LL* Virginia Carpenter, Luana Walters; *Bullets for Bandits* (Columbia; Robert Lee Johnson) *SK* Tex Ritter, *LL* Dorothy Short; *North of the Rockies* (Columbia; Lambert Hillyer) *SK* Tex Ritter, *LL* Shirley Patterson; *The Devil's Trail* (Columbia; Lambert Hillyer) *SK* Tex Ritter, *LL* Eileen O'Hearn; *Prairie Gunsmoke* (Columbia; Lambert Hillyer) *SK* Tex Ritter, *LL* Virginia Carroll; *Vengeance of the West* (Columbia; Lambert Hillyer) *SK* Tex Ritter, *LL* Adele Mara; *The Valley of Vanishing Men* (Columbia; Spencer Bennett) *SK* Slim Summerville, *LL* Carmen Morales. **1943:** *Calling Wild Bill Elliott* (Republic; Spencer Bennett) *SK* Gabby Hayes, *LL* Anne Jeffreys; *The Man from Thunder River* (Republic; John English) *SK* Gabby Hayes, *LL* Anne Jeffreys; *Death Valley Manhunt* (Republic; John English) *SK* Gabby Hayes, *LL* Anne Jeffreys; *Wagon Tracks West* (Republic; Howard Bretherton) *SK* Gabby Hayes, *LL* Anne Jeffreys; *Overland Mail Robbery* (Republic; John English) *SK* Gabby Hayes, *LL* Anne Jeffreys, Nancy Gay; **1944:** *Hidden Valley Outlaws* (Republic; Howard Bretherton) *SK* Gabby Hayes, *LL* Anne

Jeffreys; *Tucson Raiders* (Red Ryder series, hereafter cited as R.R.) (Republic; Spencer Bennett) *SK* Gabby Hayes, Bobby Blake, Alice Fleming, *LL* Peggy Stewart, Ruth Lee; *Marshal of Reno* (R.R.) (Republic; Wallace Grissell) *SK* Gabby Hayes, Bobby Blake, Alice Fleming; *The San Antonio Kid* (R.R.) (Republic; Howard Bretherton) *SK* Bobby Blake, Alice Fleming, *LL* Linda Stirling; *Cheyenne Wildcat* (R.R.) (Republic; Lesley Selander) *SK* Bobby Blake, Alice Fleming, *LL* Peggy Stewart; *Vigilantes of Dodge City* (R.R.) (Republic; Wallace Grissell) *SK* Bobby Blake, Alice Fleming, *LL* Linda Stirling; *Sheriff of Las Vegas* (R.R.) (Republic; Lesley Selander) *SK* Bobby Blake, Alice Fleming, *LL* Peggy Stewart. **1945:** *The Great Stagecoach Robbery* (R.R.) (Republic; Lesley Selander) *SK* Bobby Blake, Alice Fleming, *LL* Sylvia Arslan; *Lone Texas Ranger* (R.R.) (Republic; Spencer Bennett) *SK* Bobby Blake, Alice Fleming, *LL* Helen Talbot; *Phantom of the Plains* (R.R.) (Republic; Lesley Selander) *SK* Bobby Blake, Alice Fleming, *LL* Virginia Christine; *Marshal of Laredo* (R.R.) (Republic; R.G. Springsteen) *SK* Bobby Blake, Alice Fleming, *LL* Peggy Stewart; *Colorado Pioneers* (R.R.) (Republic; R.G. Springsteen) *SK* Bobby Blake, Alice Fleming; *Wagon Wheels Westward* (R.R.) *SK* Bobby Blake, Alice Fleming, *LL* Linda Stirling. **1946:** *California Gold Rush* (R.R.) (Republic; R.G. Springsteen) *SK* Bobby Blake, Alice Fleming, *LL* Peggy Stewart; *Sun Valley Cyclone* (R.R.) (Republic; R.G. Springsteen) *SK* Bobby Blake, Alice Fleming; *In Old Sacramento* (Republic; Joseph Kane) *LL* Constance Moore; *Conquest of Cheyenne* (R.R.) (Republic; R.G. Springsteen) *SK* Bobby Blake, Alice Fleming, *LL* Peggy Stewart; *Sheriff of Redwood Valley* (R.R.) (Republic; R.G. Springsteen) *SK* Bobby Blake, Alice Fleming, *LL* Peggy Stewart. **1947:** *Wyoming* (Republic; Joseph Kane) *SK* Gabby Hayes, *LL* Vera Ralston, Virginia Grey; *The Fabulous Texan* (Republic; Edward Ludwig) *LL* Catherine McLeod, Ruth Donnelly. **1948:** *In Old Los Angeles* (Republic; Joseph Kane) *LL* Catherine McLeod, Estelita Rodriguez; *The Gallant Legion* (Republic; Joseph Kane) *LL* Adrian Booth. **1949:** *The Last Bandit* (Republic; Joseph Kane) *SK* Andy Devine, *LL* Adrian Both, Minna Gombell; *Hellfire* (Republic; R.G. Springsteen) *LL* Marie Windsor. **1950:** *The Savage Horde* (Republic; Joseph Kane) *LL* Adrian Booth, Barbara Fuller; *The Showdown* (Republic; Dorrell & Stuart McGowan) *LL* Marie Windsor. **1951:** *The Longhorn* (Monogram; Lewis Collins) *LL* Phyllis Coates; *Waco* (Monogram; Lewis Collins) *LL* Pamela Blake. **1952:** *Kansas Territory* (Monogram; Lewis Collins) *SK* Fuzzy Knight, *LL* Peggy Stewart; *Fargo* (Monogram; Lewis Collins) *SK* Fuzzy Knight, *LL* Phyllis Coates; *The Maverick* (Allied Artists; Thomas Carr) *LL* Phyllis Coates. **1953:** *The Homesteaders* (Allied Artists; Lewis Collins); *Rebel City* (Allied Artists; Thomas Carr) *LL* Marjorie Lord; *Topeka* (Allied Artists; Thomas Carr) *SK* Fuzzy Knight, *LL* Phyllis Coates; *Vigilante Terror* (Allied Artists; Lewis Collins) *SK* Fuzzy Knight, *LL* Mary Ellen Kay. **1954:** *Bitter Creek* (Allied

Artists; Thomas Carr) *LL* Beverly Garland, Veda Ann Borg; *The 49'ers* (Allied Artists; Thomas Carr) *LL* Virginia Grey.

Jimmy "Shamrock" Ellison

Handsome Jimmy Ellison began his Western career as Hopalong Cassidy's youthful sidekick Johnny Nelson. In fact, in the eight "Hoppys" he did between 1935 and 1937, he got the girl more times than Cassidy did.

Ellison, born James Smith in Guthrie Center, Iowa, in 1910, was raised on a cattle ranch in Montana and decided to become an actor when his family moved to southern California. He joined a stock company and performed around the country before debuting in *Party Girl* (Warner Bros., 1934). In 1935 he became Nelson in the popular Cassidy series. In 1937 he was given a major part in *The Plainsman*, the C.B. De Mille Western epic starring Gary Cooper.

For the next dozen years Ellison would appear on screen in a wide variety of roles in comedies, dramas and musicals. Some of his films include *Charley's Aunt* (1941, with Jack Benny), *Undying Monster* (1942), *The Gang's All Here* (1943, with Alice Faye and Carmen Miranda) and *Johnny Doesn't Live Here Anymore* (1944).

In 1950 he returned to the B Westerns with a series for Lippert Pictures, co-starring (and coproduced by) another former Cassidy sidekick, Russ Hayden. In the series of six films all directed by Thomas Carr, Ellison played "Shamrock" and Hayden, "Lucky." Fuzzy Knight and Raymond Hatton played their sidekicks and Betty Adams served as leading lady. The fact that the films had almost identical casts perpetrated rumors that they had all been filmed in one shooting.

The year 1950 also saw Ellison star in one of the all-time Western cult classics, *I Killed Geronimo*, released by Eagle Lion.

Ellison went to Monogram to serve as Johnny Mack Brown's partner in a half dozen oaters in 1951 and 1952, after which he retired from film work.

Jimmy "Shamrock" Ellison Filmography

1935: *Hopalong Cassidy* (Paramount; Howard Bretherton) *SK* H. Cassidy, *LL* Paula Stone; *The Eagle's Brood* (Paramount; Howard Bretherton) *SK* H. Cassidy, *LL* Joan Woodbury; *Bar 20 Rides Again* (Paramount; Howard

Jimmy Ellison

Bretherton) *SK* H. Cassidy, *LL* Jean Rouverol. **1936:** *Call of the Prairie* (Paramount; Howard Bretherton) *SK* H. Cassidy, *LL* Lynn Gilbert; *Three on the Trail* (Paramount; Howard Bretherton) *SK* H. Cassidy; *LL* Muriel Evans; *Heart of the West* (Paramount; Howard Bretherton) *SK* H. Cassidy; *LL* Lynn Gilbert; *Trail Dust* (Paramount; Nate Watt) *SK* H. Cassidy, *LL* Gwynne Shipman. **1937:** *Border Land* (Paramount; Nate Watt) *SK* H. Cassidy, *LL* Nora Lane. **1950:** *Hostile Country* (Lippert; Thomas Carr) *SK* Russell Hayden, Fuzzy Knight, Raymond Hatton, *LL* Betty Adams; *Marshall of Heldorado* (Lippert; Thomas Carr) *SK* Russell Hayden, Fuzzy Knight, Raymond Hatten, *LL* Betty Adams; *Colorado Ranger* (Lippert;

Thomas Carr) *SK* Russell Hayden, Fuzzy Knight, Raymond Hatton, *LL* Betty Adams; *West of the Brazos* (Lippert; Thomas Carr) *SK* Russell Hayden, Raymond Hatton, Fuzzy Knight, *LL* Betty Adams; *Crooked River* (Lippert; Thomas Carr) *SK* Russell Hayden, Raymond Hatton, Fuzzy Knight, *LL* Betty Adams; *Fast on the Draw* (Lippert; Thomas Carr) *SK* Russell Hayden, Raymond Hatton, Fuzzy Knight, *LL* Betty Adams; *I Killed Geronimo* (Eagle Lion; John Hoffman) *LL* Virginia Herrick; **1951:** *Oklahoma Justice* (Monogram; Lewis Collins) *SK* Johnny Mack Brown, *LL* Phyllis Coates; *Whistling Hills* (Monogram; Derwin Abrahams) *SK* Johnny Mack Brown, *LL* Noel Neill, Pamela Duncan; *Texas Lawmen* (Monogram; Lewis Collins) *SK* Johnny Mack Brown. **1952:** *Texas City* (Monogram; Lewis Collins) *SK* Johnny Mack Brown, *LL* Lois Hall, Lorna Thayer; *Man from the Black Hills* (Monogram; Thomas Carr) *SK* Johnny Mack Brown. *Dead Man's Trail* (Monogram; Lewis Collins) *SK* Johnny Mack Brown, *LL* Barbara Allen.

Tex Fletcher
"The Lonely Cowboy"

Tex Fletcher was the biggest B Western star that never was... The reason: Fletcher made only one film. That was the 1939 Grand National musical action epic *Six Gun Rhythm*.

The film, however, has gained such a cult following among Western film fans that when the subject of the most popular cowboys is discussed, quite often along with the names of Autry, Rogers, Jones, and Mix, there appears the name of Tex Fletcher.

Fletcher hailed from the small New York town of Harrison, where he was born under the name of Jerry Bisceglia. He was introduced to cowboys and Westerns as a boy when he got a job at a local theater.

In 1926 he left home and became a performer with the Buffalo Bill Wild West Show. His singing and guitar playing landed him his own radio show in Yankton, South Dakota. There he acquired the Lonely Cowboy tag because of the "broken-hearted" love songs he crooned. In 1932 Fletcher returned to New York and performed over WOR.

In 1938 he made several musical shorts, and E.W. Hammonds, the head of floundering Grand National Pictures, signed Tex to do a series of musical Westerns. *Six Gun Rhythm* was well received, but, before another Fletcher film could be made, Grand National declared bankruptcy and was out of business.

Tex Fletcher

Before Fletcher could land another deal, World War II broke out and he landed in the army. After his service stint, he returned to his New York radio show.

He cut several records for Decca, and in the 1950s and 1960s was a TV host in the New York area.

Tex Fletcher Filmography

1939: *Six Gun Rhythm* (Grand National; Sam Newfield) *LL* Joan Barclay.

Dick Foran

Horse: Smoke

John Nicholas (Dick) Foran made over 200 films in his career; only 12 of them were considered B Westerns.

Beginning in 1935, Foran and his Palomino Smoke were the Warner Bros. entry into the singing cowboy derby, and by 1937 Foran was rated number four on the top ten cowboy list. Though Foran was a more-than-competent actor and a believable action master, undoubtedly his biggest asset in his Westerns was his golden voice. Warner's Foran series as a whole was not up to Republic standards but was several cuts above other Western series.

Foran, whose father was a U.S. senator, was born in Flemington, New Jersey, on June 18, 1911, and was educated at Princeton University. A yen for adventure led him to take jobs as a seaman and an investigator with the Pennsylvania Railroad. Finally using the name Nick Foran, he became an actor in summer stock productions.

In 1934 Foran made his film debut in *Gentlemen Are Born.* He made his musical screen debut later that year in *Stand Up and Cheer,* which starred Warner Baxter and Shirley Temple. In 1935 he co-starred with Humphrey Bogart in *The Black Legion.*

Some fast talking to his bosses at Warners got him his first singing Western, *Moonlight on the Prairie.* In 1938 Foran moved to Universal Studios.

At Universal, Foran's contribution to Westerns came in the form of two action serials, *Winners of the West* in 1940, and *Riders of Death Valley,* Universal's 1941 million-dollar serial. The latter also starred, in addition to Foran, the likes of Buck Jones, Leo Carrillo, Big Boy Williams, Monte Blue and Charles Bickford as the villainous Wolf Reade.

Foran starred or was featured in every kind of film imaginable. He had parts in horror films such as *Horror Island, The Mummy's Hand* and *the Mummy's Tomb;* comedies like *My Little Chickadee* (with Mae West and W.C. Fields) and *Ride 'em Cowboy* (with Abbott and Costello and Johnny Mack Brown); dramas like *The Fighting 69th* and *The House of Seven*

The versatile Dick Foran.

Gables; Westerns such as *Fort Apache* (with John Wayne) and *The Doolins of Oklahoma,* and his one lone "B" for Universal, *Road Agent,* in 1941.

During the early days of television Foran could be spotted on such dramatic series as *Playhouse 90* and Kraft Mystery Theatre.

Dick Foran passed away on August 10, 1979, in Panorama City, California.

Dick Foran Filmography

1935: *Moonlight on the Prairie* (Warner Bros.; D. Ross Lederman) *LL* Sheila Mannors. **1936:** *Treachery Rides the Range* (Warner Bros.; Frank McDonald) *LL* Paula Stone; *Trailin' West* (Warner Bros.; Noel Smith) *LL* Paula Stone; *The California Mail* (Warner Bros.; Noel Smith) *LL* Linda Perry; *Song of the Saddle* (Warner Bros.; Louis King) *LL* Alma Lloyd. **1937:** *Guns of the Pecos* (Warner Bros.; Noel Smith) *LL* Anne Nagel; *Land Beyond the Law* (Warner Bros.; B. Reeves Eason) *LL* Linda Perry; *Cherokee Strip* (Warner Bros.; Noel Smith) *LL* Jane Bryan; *Blazing Sixes* (Warner Bros.; Noel Smith) *LL* Helen Valkis, Myra McKinney; *Empty Holsters* (Warner Bros.; B. Reeves Eason); *Devil's Saddle Legion* (Warner Bros.; Bobby Connolly) *LL* Anne Nagel; *Prairie Thunder* (Warner Bros.; B. Reeves Eason) *LL* Ellen Clancy. **1940:** *Winners of the West* (serial) (Universal; Forbe Beebe, Ray Taylor) *LL* Anne Nagel. **1941:** *Riders of Death Valley* (serial) (Universal; Forbe Beebe, Ray Taylor) *LL* Jeannie Kelly; *Road Agent* (Universal; Charles Lamont) *SK* Leo Carrillo, *LL* Anne Gwynne.

John Forbes *see* Johnny Carpenter

Hoot Gibson

Horse: Goldie
Sidekick: Skeeter Bill Robbins

One of the most famous of the screen's cowboys, Hoot Gibson was unique among Western heroes. He didn't sing like Autry or Rogers, wasn't a fast gunner like Tim McCoy or Johnny Mack Brown, and wasn't noted for fisticuffs like Bill Elliott or Rocky Lane. Quite often Hoot Gibson used smarts rather than violence to subdue a bad guy or rectify a hostile situation.

As opposed to many macho heroes, Gibson often appeared befuddled, stumbling and almost comical.

He was a superstar long before the advent of B Westerns. As one of the silent screen's top attractions, he made over 120 Westerns between 1912 and 1929, and by the mid-1920s was earning an unheard-of $14,500 a week.

Gibson was an all-around daredevil who worked as a cowboy, a rodeo performer, and had a penchant for racing anything, especially airplanes. He claimed to be the first movie stuntman, when a director paid him $2.50 to fall off a galloping horse in the early 1900s.

Hoot Gibson

"Hoot" was born Edmund Richard Gibson on August 6, 1892, in Tekamah, Nebraska. He reportedly got his nickname because he spent a good deal of his time hunting for owls. At 13 he ran away from home and joined a circus. In 1906 he found employment as a cowboy at the Miller 101 ranch in Ft. Bliss, Oklahoma. The next year he joined the Stanley-Atkinson Wild West Show.

He made his first films in 1911 and 1912. His career was interrupted in 1917 when he was called to duty in World War I. Gibson attained the rank of sergeant while in the U.S. Army Tank Corps.

In 1919, upon his discharge, he returned to films and began making his Westerns with a young director named John Ford at Universal. In 1921, Ford gave Gibson his first starring role in *Action*. Gibson became enormously popular during the twenties and was one of Universal's hottest properties.

When the sound era was ushered in, however, the studio felt that Gibson would not fare well in talking pictures, and overnight they cancelled his contract. Also that same year (1930), Gibson declared bankruptcy as a result of some bad investments.

The next year he signed with Allied and did 11 films for them between 1931 and 1933. Most of the Gibson films seen on TV are from that series. He then moved in quick succession to First Division and Diversion studios. He made *Powdersmoke Range* and *The Last Outlaw* for RKO, and a serial, *The Painted Stallion*, for Republic before retiring in 1939.

In 1943 he returned to the screen to star with Ken Maynard in the Trail Blazers series at Monogram. He did seven Trail Blazers films, followed by three with Bob Steele before retiring a second time.

Gibson returned to the screen once again in 1953 in a film called *The Marshal's Daughter* and in 1959 appeared in the John Wayne film *The Horse Soldiers*, which his old pal John Ford directed.

Gibson's private life was as adventurous as his films. He was married four times (including once to his leading lady, Sally Eilers). He was named Best All-Round Cowboy at the Pendleton (Oregon) rodeo in 1912. In 1931 he captured the National Air Races, and in 1933 he and Ken Maynard competed in an airplane match race which nearly ended in disaster when his plane crashed.

Hoot Gibson died of cancer on August 23, 1962.

Hoot Gibson Filmography

1929: *The Long, Long Trail* (Universal; Arthur Rosson) *LL* Sally Eilers; *Courtin' Wildcats* (Universal; Jerome Storm) *LL* Eugenia Gilbert. **1930:** *The Mounted Stranger* (Universal; Arthur Rosson) *LL* Louise Lorraine; *Trailin' Trouble* (Universal; Arthur Rosson) *LL* Margaret Quimby; *Roaring Ranch* (Universal; B. Reeves Eason) *LL* Sally Eilers; *Trigger Tricks* (Universal; B. Reeves Eason) *LL* Sally Eilers; *Spurs* (Universal; B. Reeves Eason) *LL* Helen Wright; *The Concentratin' Kid* (Universal; Arthur Rosson) *LL* Kathryn Crawford. **1931:** *Clearing the Range* (Allied; Otto Brower) *LL* Sally Eilers; *Wild Horse* (Allied; Richard Thorpe, Sidney Algier) *SK* Stepin Fetchit, Skeeter Bill Robbins, *LL* Alberta Vaughn; *Hard Hombre* (Allied; Otto Brower) *SK* Skeeter Bill Robbins, *LL* Lina Basquette. **1932:** *The Local Bad Man* (Allied; Otto Brower) *SK* Skeeter Bill Robbins, *LL* Sally Blaine; *The Gay Buckaroo* (Allied; Phil Rosen) *LL* Merna Kennedy; *Spirit of the West* (Allied; Otto Brower) *LL* Doris Hill; *A Man's Land* (Allied; Phil Rosen) *SK* Skeeter Bill Robbins, *LL* Marion Shilling; *The Cowboy Counsellor* (Allied; George Melford) *SK* Skeeter Bill Robbins, *LL* Sheila Mannors; *The Boiling Point* (Allied; George Melford) *SK* Skeeter Bill Robbins, *LL* Helen Foster.

1933: *The Dude Bandit* (Allied; George Melford) *SK* Skeeter Bill Robbins, *LL* Gloria Shea; *The Fighting Parson* (Allied; Harry Fraser) *SK* Skeeter Bill Robbins, *LL* Marceline Day. **1935:** *Sunset Range* (First Division; Ray McCarey) *LL* Mary Doran; *Swifty* (Diversion; Alan James) *LL* June Gale; *Rainbow's End* (First Division; Norman Spencer) *LL* June Gale; *Powder-smoke Range* (RKO; Wallace Fox) *SK* 3 Mesquiteers, *LL* Boots Mallory. **1936:** *Lucky Terror* (Diversion; Alan James) *LL* Lona Andre; *Feud of the West* (Diversion; Harry Fraser) *LL* Joan Barclay; *The Riding Avenger* (Diversion; Harry Fraser) *LL* Ruth Mix; *The Last Outlaw* (RKO; Christy Cabanne) *LL* Margaret Callahan; *Frontier Justice* (Diversion; Robert McGowan) *LL* Jane Barnes; *Cavalcade of the West* (Diversion; Harry Fraser) *LL* Marion Shilling. **1937:** *The Painted Stallion* (serial) (Republic; W. Witney, Alan James, Ray Taylor) *LL* Julia Thayer. **1943:** *Wild Horse Stampede* (Monogram; Alan James) *SK* Trail Blazers, *LL* Betty Miles; *The Law Rides Again* (Monogram; Alan James) *SK* Trail Blazers, *LL* Betty Miles; *Death Valley Rangers* (Monogram; Robert Tansey) *SK* Trail Blazers, *LL* Linda Brent. **1944:** *Westward Bound* (Monogram; Robert Tansey) *SK* Trail Blazers, *LL* Betty Miles; *Arizona Whirlwind* (Monogram; Robert Tansey) *SK* Trail Blazers, *LL* Myrna Dell; *Outlaw Trail* (Monogram; Robert Tansey) *SK* Trail Blazers, *LL* Jennifer Holt; *Sonora Stagecoach* (Monogram; Robert Tansey) *SK* Trail Blazers, *LL* Betty Miles; *The Utah Kid* (Monogram; Vernon Keyes) *SK* Bob Steele, *LL* Evelyn Eaton; *Marked Trails* (Monogram; J.P. McCarthy) *SK* Bob Steele, *LL* Veda Ann Borg; *Trigger Law* (Monogram; Vernon Keyes) *SK* Bob Steele, *LL* Beatrice Gray. **1953:** *The Marshal's Daughter* (United Artists; William Berke) *LL* Laurie Anders.

Kirby Grant

Sidekicks: Fuzzy Knight, Chinook the Wonder Dog

Actor, singer, musician and bandleader Kirby Grant is best known for his portrayal of Sky King, 'America's Flying Cowboy," in the Western adventure series that ran on NBC and ABC-TV from 1951 to 1954 and which has been a rerun favorite over the years.

Grant, born Kirby Grant Hoon in Butte, Montana, on November 24, 1911, was a violin prodigy as a child and gave a recital with the Seattle Symphony at the age of 12. He later studied at the University of Washington and at the American Conservatory of Music.

As a young man, Grant gave up classical music and opted for the more lucrative field of popular music, and formed his own dance band.

Kirby Grant

A job as a radio singer led to a contract with RKO Pictures.

In 1937 he made his film debut using the name Robert Stanton. Included in some of his early films were several George O'Brien Westerns like *Bullet Code*.

During World War II Grant entertained U.S. troops in Europe and North Africa, and in 1944 he signed with Universal. He made musicals and comedies like Olsen and Johnson's *Ghost Catchers* (1944) and in 1945 began a series of seven Westerns with Fuzzy Knight as his sidekick. When the series ended, he returned to musicals and comedies.

In 1949 Grant began a series for Monogram. In these films Grant portrayed a mountie with a four-legged companion, Chinook the Wonder Dog. The series ran 10 films and concluded in 1954.

When the Sky King series ended, Grant retired from acting to become involved in film and TV production and direction.

Grant often appeared at Western film fairs and was active until his death in 1987.

Kirby Grant Filmography

1945: *Bad Men of the Border* (Universal; Wallace Fox) *SK* Fuzzy Knight, *LL* Armida, Barbara Sears, Soledad Jiminez; *Code of the Lawless* (Universal; Wallace Fox) *SK* Fuzzy Knight, *LL* Poni Adams (Jane), Barbara Sears; *Trail to Vengeance* (Universal; Wallace Fox) *SK* Fuzzy Knight, *LL* Poni Adams. **1946:** *Gun Town* (Universal; Wallace Fox) *SK* Fuzzy Knight, *LL* Claire Carleton, Louise Currie; *Rustlers Roundup* (Universal; Wallace Fox) *SK* Fuzzy Knight, *LL* Jane Adams; *Lawless Breed* (Universal; Wallace Fox) *SK* Fuzzy Knight, *LL* Jane Adams; *Gunman's Code* (Universal; Wallace Fox) *SK* Fuzzy Knight, *LL* Jane Adams. **1949:** *Trail of the Yukon* (Monogram; William X. Crowley) *SK* Chinook, the Wonder Dog, *LL* Suzanne Dalbert, Iris Adrian; *The Wolf Hunters* (Monogram; Budd Boetticher) *SK* Chinook, the Wonder Dog, *LL* Jan Clayton, Helen Parrish. **1950:** *Snow Dog* (Monogram; Frank McDonald) *SK* Chinook, the Wonder Dog, *LL* Elena Verdugo; *Call of the Klondike* (Monogram; Frank McDonald) *SK* Chinook, the Wonder Dog, *LL* Anne Gwynne, Lynne Roberts. **1951:** *Yukon Manhunt* (Monogram; Frank McDonald) *SK* Chinook the Wonder Dog, *LL* Gail Davis; *Northwest Territory* (Monogram; Frank McDonald) *SK* Chinook the Wonder Dog, *LL* Gloria Saunders. **1952:** *Yukon Gold* (Monogram; Frank McDonald) *SK* Chinook the Wonder Dog, *LL* Martha Hyer. **1953:** *Fangs of the Arctic* (Monogram; Rex Bailey) *SK* Chinook the Wonder Dog, *LL* Lorna Hansen; *Northern Patrol* (Monogram; Rex Bailey) *SK* Chinook the Wonder Dog, *LL* Marion Carr, Claudia Drake, Gloria Talbot. **1954:** *Yukon Vengeance* (Allied Artists, William Beaudine) *SK* Monte Hale, *LL* Mary Ellen Kay, Carol Thurston.

Monte Hale

Horse: Pardner
Sidekicks: Paul Hurst, Emmett Lynn, Max Terhune

Republic Picture's cowboy Monte Hale was born in Ada, Oklahoma, on June 8, 1921, and grew up on a ranch near San Angelo, Texas, where he

Monte Hale

got his singing cowboy basic training (ridin', ropin', and singin') as a youngster. After high school he played in several local country and western groups and eventually landed a spot singing on the radio.

During World War II he joined a USO troupe and entertained the troops. While on tour he gained the attention of Phil Isley, a movie talent scout and father of actress Jennifer Jones.

He debuted in a film called *Steppin' in Society* in 1944 and the next year Republic hailed Hale as their next singing cowboy star. Beginning with *Home on the Range* in 1946, Hale made 19 films for the studio.

Lovely Adrian Booth was his leading lady in the first seven films, and Paul Hurst served sidekick duty in 13 of them starting with *Under Colorado Skies* in 1947.

Hale made his last film for Republic in 1950 and then resumed his singing career in a group headed by Tim Holt's old screen sidekick, Ray Whitley.

He also made personal appearances at rodeos and circuses.

Monte Hale Filmography

1946: *Home on the Range* (Republic; R.G. Springsteen) *LL* Adrian Booth; *Man from Rainbow Valley* (Republic; R.G. Springsteen) *SK* Emmett Lynn, *LL* Adrian Booth, Jo Ann Marlowe; *Out California Way* (Republic; Lesley Selander) *LL* Adrian Booth. **1947:** *Last Frontier Uprising* (Republic; Lesley Selander) *LL* Adrian Booth; *Along the Oregon Trail* (Republic; R.G. Springsteen) *SK* Max Terhune, *LL* Adrian Booth; *Under Colorado Skies* (Republic; R.G. Springsteen) *SK* Paul Hurst, *LL* Adrian Booth. **1948:** *California Firebrand* (Republic; Phillip Ford) *SK* Paul Hurst, *LL* Adrian Booth, Alice Tyrell; *The Timber Trail* (Republic; Phillip Ford) *LL* Lynne Roberts; *Son of God's Country* (Republic; R.G. Springsteen) *SK* Paul Hurst, *LL* Pamela Blake. **1949:** *Prince of the Plains* (Republic; Phillip Ford) *SK* Paul Hurst, *LL* Shirley Davis; *Law of the Golden West* (Republic; Phillip Ford) *SK* Paul Hurst, *LL* Gail Davis; *Outcasts of the Trail* (Republic; Phillip Ford) *SK* Paul Hurst, *LL* Jeff Donnell; *South of Rio* (Republic; Phillip Ford) *SK* Paul Hurst, *LL* Kay Christopher; *San Antone Ambush* (Republic; Phillip Ford) *SK* Paul Hurst, *LL* Bette Daniels; *Ranger of the Cherokee Strip* (Republic; Phillip Ford) *SK* Paul Hurst, *LL* Alice Talton; *Pioneer Marshall* (Republic; Phillip Ford) *SK* Paul Hurst, *LL* Nan Leslie. **1950:** *The Vanishing Westerner* (Republic; Phillip Ford) *SK* Paul Hurst, *LL* Aline Towne; *The Old Frontier* (Republic; Phillip Ford) *SK* Paul Hurst, *LL* Claudia Barrett; *The Missourians* (Republic; George Blair) *SK* Paul Hurst, *LL* Lyn Thomas.

Russell Hayden

Lucky Jenkins was young, hot headed, and though he meant well, he caused his saddle pal Hopalong Cassidy all sorts of problems. In fact, Hoppy spent as much time keeping Lucky out of trouble as he did chasing rustlers off the Bar 20 range.

Russ Hayden assumed the role of Lucky in 1937 after the departure of Hoppy's other young sidekick Johnny Nelson (Jimmy Ellison) and rode with the black-clad hero through two dozen film adventures before exiting in 1941.

Russell Hayden

From there, Hayden went to Columbia to co-star with Charles Starrett in eight films.

In 1942 Columbia gave Hayden his own series starting with *The Lone Prairie*. He even got to have a sidekick in the person of Dub Taylor. There were eight films in this series before it ended in 1944.

Two years down the trail Russ starred in four James Oliver Curwood Yukon adventures for Screen Guild.

In 1950, Hayden teamed with Jimmy Ellison to release six "Shamrock" (Ellison) and "Lucky" (Hayden) Western films. Hayden was also coproducer of the series.

Russ had bit parts in several Gene Autry films in the early fifties before turning his efforts to television. He starred with Jackie Coogan in a Western series called *Cowboy G Men*. He also produced two series, *Twenty Six Men* and *Judge Roy Bean*.

Russell "Lucky" Hayden contracted viral pneumonia and passed away on June 9, 1981, in Palm Springs, California.

Russell Hayden Filmography

1937: *Rustler's Valley* (Paramount; Nate Watt) *SK* Hopalong Cassidy, *LL* Muriel Evans; *North of the Rio Grande* (Paramount; Nate Watt) *SK* Hopalong Cassidy, *LL* Bernadine Hayes; *Hills of Old Wyoming* (Paramount; Nate Watt) *SK* Hopalong Cassidy, *LL* Gail Sheridan. **1938:** *Partners of the Plains* (Paramount; Lesley Selander) *SK* Hopalong Cassidy, *LL* Gwen Gaze; *Cassidy of the Bar 20* (Paramount; Lesley Selander) *SK* Hopalong Cassidy, *LL* Nora Lane, Margaret Marquis; *Heart of Arizona* (Paramount; Lesley Selander) *SK* Hopalong Cassidy, *LL* Natalie Morehead, Dorothy Short; *Bar 20 Justice* (Paramount; Lesley Selander) *SK* Hopalong Cassidy, *LL* Gwen Gaze; *Pride of the West* (Paramount; Lesley Selander) *SK* Hopalong Cassidy, *LL* Charlotte Field, *In Old Mexico* (Paramount; Edward Venturini) *SK* Hopalong Cassidy, *LL* Betty Amann, Jan Clayton; *Sunset Trail* (Paramount; Lesley Selander) *SK* Hopalong Cassidy, *LL* Charlotte Wynters; *The Frontiersman* (Paramount; Lesley Selander) *SK* Hopalong Cassidy, *LL* Evelyn Venable. **1939:** *Silver on the Sage* (Paramount; Lesley Selander) *SK* Hopalong Cassidy, *LL* Ruth Rogers; *Renegade Trail* (Paramount; Lesley Selander) *SK* Hopalong Cassidy, *LL* Charlotte Wynters; *Range War* (Paramount; Lesley Selander) *SK* Hopalong Cassidy, *LL* Betty Moran; *Law of the Pampas* (Paramount; Nate Watt) *SK* Hopalong Cassidy, *LL* Steffi Duna. **1940:** *Santa Fe Marshall* (Paramount; Lesley Selander) *SK* Hopalong Cassidy, *LL* Bernadine Hayes; *The Showdown* (Paramount; Howard Bretherton) *SK* Hopalong Cassidy, *LL* Jan Clayton; *Hidden Gold* (Paramount; Howard Bretherton) *SK* Hopalong Cassidy, *LL* Ruth Rogers; *Stagecoach War* (Paramount; Howard Bretherton) *SK* Hopalong Cassidy, *LL* Julie Carter; *3 Men from Texas* (Paramount; Howard Bretherton) *SK* Hopalong Cassidy, *LL* Esther Estrella; *Knights of the Range* (Paramount; Lesley Selander) *LL* Jean Parker; *Light of Western Stars* (Paramount; Lesley Selander) *LL* Jo Ann Sayers. **1941:** *Doomed Caravan* (Paramount; Howard Bretherton) *SK* Hopalong Cassidy, *LL* Minna Gombell; *In Old Colorado* (Paramount; Howard Bretherton) *SK* Hopalong Cassidy, *LL* Margaret Hayes; *Border Vigilantes* (Paramount; Derwin Abrahams) *SK* Hopalong Cassidy, *LL* Frances Gifford; *Pirates on Horseback* (Paramount; Lesley Selander) *SK* Hopalong Cassidy, *LL* Eleanor Stewart; *Wide Open*

Town (Paramount; Lesley Selander) *SK* Hopalong Cassidy, *LL* Evelyn Brent; *The Royal Mounted Patrol* (Columbia; Lambert Hillyer) *SK* Charles Starrett, *LL* Wanda McKay; *Riders of the Badlands* (Columbia; Howard Bretheron) *SK* Charles Starrett, *LL* Kay Hughes, Ilene Brewer. **1942:** *West of Tombstone* (Columbia; Howard Bretheron) *SK* Charles Starrett, *LL* Marcella Martin; *Lawless Plainsmen* (Columbia; William Berke) *SK* Charles Starrett, *LL* Luana Walters; *Down Rio Grande Way* (Columbia; William Berke) *SK* Charles Starrett, *LL* Rose Anne Stevens; *Riders of the North Land* (Columbia; William Berke) *SK* Charles Starrett, *LL* Shirley Patterson; *Bad Men of the Hills* (Columbia; William Berke) *SK* Charles Starrett, *LL* Luana Walters; *Overland to Deadwood* (Columbia; William Berke) *SK* Charles Starrett, *LL* Leslie Brooks; *The Lone Prairie* (Columbia; William Berke) *SK* Dub Taylor, *LL* Lucille Lambert; *A Tornado in the Saddle* (Columbia; William Berke) *SK* Dub Taylor, *LL* Alma Carroll. **1943:** *Riders of the Northwest Mounted* (Columbia; William Berke) *SK* Dub Taylor, *LL* Adele Mara; *Saddles and Sagebrush* (Columbia; William Berke) *SK* Dub Taylor, *LL* Ann Savage; *Silver City Raiders* (Columbia; William Berke) *SK* Dub Taylor, *LL* Alma Carroll; *Frontier Law* (Universal; Elmer Clifton) *SK* Fuzzy Knight, *LL* Jennifer Holt. **1944:** *Marshall of Gunsmoke* (Universal; Vernon Keyes) *SK* Tex Ritter, *LL* Jennifer Holt; *The Vigilantes Ride* (Columbia; William Berke) *SK* Dub Taylor, *LL* Shirley Patterson; *Wyoming Hurricane* (Columbia; William Berke) *SK* Dub Taylor, *LL* Alma Carroll; *The Last Horseman* (Columbia; William Berke) *SK* Dub Taylor, *LL* Ann Savage. **1946:** '*Neath Canadian Skies* (Screen Guild; B. Reeves Eason) *LL* Inez Cooper; *North of the Border* (Screen Guild; B. Reeves Eason) *LL* Inez Cooper. **1947:** *Where the North Begins* (Screen Guild; Howard Bretherton) *LL* Jennifer Holt; *Trail of the Mounties* (Screen Guild; Howard Bretherton) *LL* Jennifer Holt. **1950:** *Hostile Country* (Lippert; Thomas Carr) *SK* Jimmy Ellison, Fuzzy Knight, Raymond Hatton, *LL* Betty Adams; *Marshall of Heldorado* (Lippert; Thomas Carr) *SK* Jimmy Ellison, Fuzzy Knight, Raymond Hatton, *LL* Betty Adams; *Colorado Ranger* (Lippert; Thomas Carr) *SK* Jimmy Ellison, Fuzzy Knight, Raymond Hatton, *LL* Betty Adams; *West of the Brazos* (Lippert; Thomas Carr) *SK* Jimmy Ellison, Fuzzy Knight, Raymond Hatton, *LL* Betty Adams; *Crooked River* (Lippert; Thomas Carr) *SK* Jimmy Ellison, Fuzzy Knight, Raymond Hatton, *LL* Betty Adams; *Fast on the Draw* (Lippert; Thomas Carr) *SK* Jimmy Ellison, Fuzzy Knight, Raymond Hatton, *LL* Betty Adams.

Tim Holt

Horse: Lightning
Sidekicks: Ray Whitley, Emmett Lynn, Lee "Lasses" White, Cliff Edwards, Richard Martin

In the years between 1940 and 1952 Tim Holt made 47 B Western features for RKO Pictures.

Holt was Hollywood born and bred; his father Jack Holt had an illustrious film career that lasted from the silent era until 1950. His sister Jennifer rates with Dale Evans as one of the top leading ladies of the B Western era.

Tim, whose given name was John Charles Holt, Jr., was born in Beverly Hills, California, on February 5, 1918, and made his screen debut with his dad in 1928 in *The Red River Valley*. He grew up on a ranch and became an all-round athlete.

Holt attended the University of Southern California and began a career as a stage actor. In 1937 he got a featured part in the Barbara Stanwyck film *Stella Dallas*.

In his first meaty role at RKO he co-starred with Harry Carey in *The Law West of Tombstone;* that same year (1938) he backed up RKO's top cowboy star, George O'Brien, in *Renegade Ranger*. His performances caused RKO to purchase his contract from producer Walter Wanger.

In 1939 he got a role in John Ford's epic Western drama *Stagecoach*. In 1940 he was in *Swiss Family Robinson*.

Tim made his first "B" for the studio in 1940 and the following year he had made the top ten cowboy list. After 18 films, he enlisted in the Air Force in 1943. His service to his country earned him the Distinguished Flying Cross.

When the war was over, Tim returned to filmmaking. He resumed his Western series with RKO in 1947. He also appeared in such film classics as *My Darling Clementine* (1946) and *The Treasure of Sierra Madre* (1948).

Tim and trail partner Richard "Chito" Martin churned out Westerns until 1952 when RKO decided to get out of the "B" business.

After his Western career, Tim continued in films, starring in the 1957 science fiction thriller *The Monster That Challenged the World*.

In 1959 he retired from the screen to go into private business in Denver, Colorado. In the early seventies he moved to Oklahoma, purchased a ranch and hosted a local TV Western film show.

Tim Holt died of a brain tumor on February 15, 1973.

Tim Holt

Tim Holt Filmography

1940: *Wagon Train* (RKO; Edward Killy) *SK* Ray Whitley, Emmett Lynn, *LL* Martha O'Driscoll; *The Fargo Kid* (RKO; Edward Killy) *SK* Ray Whitley, Emmett Lynn, *LL* Jane Drummond. **1941:** *Along the Rio Grande* (RKO; Stuart Anthony) *SK* Ray Whitley, Emmett Lynn, *LL* Betty Jane Rhodes; *Robbers of the Range* (RKO; Edward Killy) *SK* Ray Whitley, Emmett Lynn, *LL* Virginia Vale; *Cyclone on Horseback* (RKO; Edward Killy) *SK* Ray Whitley, Lee "Lasses" White, *LL* Marjorie Reynolds; *Six Gun Gold* (RKO; David Howard) *SK* Ray Whitley, Lee "Lasses" White, *LL* Jan Clayton; *The Bandit Trail* (RKO; Edward Killy) *SK* Ray Whitley, Lee "Lasses" White, *LL* Janet Waldo; *Dude Cowboy* (RKO; David Howard) *SK* Ray Whitley, Lee "Lasses" White, *LL* Marjorie Reynolds, Louise Currie. **1942:** *Riding the Wind* (RKO; Edward Killy) *SK* Ray Whitley, Lee "Lasses" White, *LL* Mary Douglas; *Land of the Open Range* (RKO; Edward Killy) *SK* Ray Whitley, Lee "Lasses" White, *LL* Janet Waldo; *Come on Danger*

(RKO; Edward Killy) *SK* Ray Whitley, Lee "Lasses" White, *LL* Frances
Neal; *Thundering Hoofs* (RKO; Lesley Selander) *SK* Ray Whitley, Lee
"Lasses" White, *LL* Luana Walters; *Bandit Ranger* (RKO; Lesley Selander)
SK Cliff Edwards, *LL* Joan Barclay; *Pirates of the Prairie* (RKO; Howard
Bretherton) *SK* Cliff Edwards, *LL* Nell O'Day. **1943:** *Fighting Frontier*
(RKO; Lambert Hillyer) *SK* Cliff Edwards, Eddie Dew, *LL* Ann Summers;
Sagebrush Law (RKO; Sam Nelson) *SK* Cliff Edwards, *LL* Joan Barclay;
The Avenging Rider (RKO; Sam Nelson) *SK* Cliff Edwards, *LL* Ann Sum-
mers; *Red River Robin Hood* (RKO; Lesley Selander) *SK* Cliff Edwards, Ed-
die Dew, *LL* Barbara Moffett. **1947:** *Thunder Mountain* (RKO: Lew Land-
ers) *SK* Richard Martin, *LL* Martha Hyer; *Under the Tonto Rim* (RKO: Lew
Landers) *SK* Richard Martin, *LL* Nan Leslie; *Wild Horse Mesa* (RKO: Wal-
lace Grissell) *SK* Richard Martin, *LL* Nan Leslie. **1948:** *Western Heritage*
(RKO: Wallace Grissell) *SK* Richard Martin, *LL* Nan Leslie; *Guns of Hate*
(RKO; Lesley Selander) *SK* Richard Martin, *LL* Nan Leslie; *The Arizona
Ranger* (RKO; John Rawlins) *SK* Richard Martin, *LL* Nan Leslie; *Indian
Agent* (RKO; Lesley Selander) *SK* Richard Martin, Lee "Lasses" White, *LL*
Nan Leslie; *Gun Smugglers* (RKO; Frank McDonald) *SK* Richard Martin,
LL Martha Hyer. **1949:** *Brothers of the Saddle* (RKO; Lesley Selander) *SK*
Richard Martin, *LL* Virginia Cox, Carol Forman; *Rustlers* (RKO; Lesley
Selander) *SK* Richard Martin, *LL* Martha Hyer, Lois Andrews; *Stagecoach
Kid* (RKO; Lew Landers) *SK* Richard Martin, *LL* Jeff Donnell, Carol
Hughes; *Masked Raiders* (RKO; Lesley Selander) *SK* Richard Martin, *LL*
Marjorie Lord; *The Mysterious Desperado* (RKO; Lesley Selander) *SK*
Richard Martin, *LL* Movita. **1950:** *Riders of the Range* (RKO; Lesley
Selander) *SK* Richard Martin, *LL* Jacqueline White; *Dynamite Pass* (RKO;
Lew Landers) *SK* Richard Martin, *LL* Lynne Roberts; *Storm Over Wyo-
ming* (RKO; Lesley Selander) *SK* Richard Martin, *LL* Noreen Nash; *Rider
from Tucson* (RKO; Lesley Selander) *SK* Richard Martin) *LL* Elaine Riley,
Veda Ann Borg; *Border Treasure* (RKO; George Archainbaud) *SK* Richard
Martin, *LL* Jane Nigh; *Rio Grande Patrol* (RKO; Lesley Selander) *SK*
Richard Martin, *LL* Jane Nigh. **1951:** *Law of the Badlands* (RKO; Lesley
Selander) *SK* Richard Martin, *LL* Joan Dixon; *Saddle Legion* (RKO; Lesley
Selander) *SK* Richard Martin, *LL* Dorothy Malone; *Gun Play* (RKO; Lesley
Selander) *SK* Richard Martin, *LL* Joan Dixon; *Pistol Harvest* (RKO; Lesley
Selander) *SK* Richard Martin, *LL* Joan Dixon; *Hot Lead* (RKO; Stuart
Gilmore) *SK* Richard Martin, *LL* Joan Dixon; *Overland Telegraph* (RKO;
Lesley Selander) *SK* Richard Martin, *LL* Gail Davis. **1952:** *Trail Guide*
(RKO; Lesley Selander) *SK* Richard Martin, *LL* Linda Douglas; *Road Agent*
(RKO; Lesley Selander) *SK* Richard Martin, *LL* Noreen Nash, Dorothy
Patrick; *Target* (RKO; Stuart Gilmore) *SK* Richard Martin, *LL* Linda
Douglas; *Desert Passage* (RKO; Lesley Selander) *SK* Richard Martin, *LL*
Joan Dixon, Dorothy Patrick.

George Houston

Sidekick: Fuzzy St. John

George Houston portrayed the Lone Rider in a series of 11 films released by PRC in 1941 and 1942. The films co-starred PRC perennial sidekick Al "Fuzzy" St. John. PRC dropped Houston and continued the Lone Rider series with Bob Livingston in the lead role.

George Houston was born in Hampton, New Jersey, in 1898. His father was a minister. George attended Rutgers University, studied voice at the Juilliard School of Music and served in the U.S. Army during World War I.

After his discharge he opened a voice school in New York. Later he joined the American Opera Company.

In 1934 Houston made his film debut in *The Melody Lingers On.* Prior to the Lone Rider series, Houston had starred in only one Western, *Frontier Scout,* made in 1938 for Grand National. Because of Grand National's financial straits, no subsequent Houston films were made.

His contract with PRC was a result of his performance in his lone Grand National vehicle.

George Houston suffered a heart attack and died on November 12, 1944.

George Houston Filmography

1938: *Frontier Scout* (Grand National; Sam Newfield) *SK* Fuzzy St. John, *LL* Beth Marion. **1941:** *The Lone Rider Rides On* (PRC; Sam Newfield) *SK* Fuzzy St. John, *LL* Hillary Brooke; *The Lone Rider Crosses the Rio* (PRC; Sam Newfield) *SK* Fuzzy St. John, *LL* Roquell Verrin; *The Lone Rider in Ghost Town* (PRC; Sam Newfield) *SK* Fuzzy St. John, *LL* Alaine Brandes; *The Lone Rider in Frontier Fury* (PRC; Sam Newfield) *SK* Fuzzy St. John, *LL* Hillary Brooke; *The Lone Rider Ambushed* (PRC; Sam Newfield) *SK* Fuzzy St. John, *LL* Maxine Leslie; *The Lone Rider Fights Back* (PRC; Sam Newfield) *SK* Fuzzy St. John, *LL* Dorothy Short. **1942:** *The Lone Rider and the Bandit* (PRC; Sam Newfield) *SK* Fuzzy St. John, *LL* Vicki Lester; *The Lone Rider in Cheyenne* (PRC; Sam Newfield) *SK* Fuzzy St. John, *LL* Ella Neal; *Texas Justice* (PRC; Sam Newfield) *SK* Fuzzy St. John, *LL* Wanda McKay, Claire Rochelle; *Border Roundup* (PRC; Sam Newfield) *SK* Fuzzy St. John, *LL* Patricia Knox; *Outlaws of Boulder Pass* (PRC; Sam Newfield) *SK* Fuzzy St. John, *LL* Marjorie Manners.

Jack Hoxie and an unknown actress in one of the B Westerns he made for Majestic.

Jack Hoxie

Horse: Scout

Jack Hoxie's mark on the B Western came in six films he made for Majestic in 1932 and 1933. The features were all of the high action variety.

During the 1920s Hoxie had been a top silent cowboy star at Universal but was dismissed when the talkies arrived.

Hoxie, who also used the names Art Hoxie and Hartford Hoxie in films, was born in Oklahoma on January 20, 1890. When his family moved to Iowa, he worked as a farmhand when not competing in rodeos. In 1914 he won the National Riding Championship and got a job in a wild West show.

In 1917 he started in films as a stuntman and got his first lead in 1919 in the serial *Lightning Bryce.* In 1921 Universal signed him and gave him the "Jack" tag. He made his last film in 1935.

In 1937, Hoxie and a partner formed the Jack Hoxie Circus which starred Jack.

Jack Hoxie was an excellent horseman.

Jack passed away in Oklahoma in 1965. His brother, Al Hoxie, was also a silent Western star in the twenties.

A note about the Hoxie sound films: Hoxie was an excellent horseman and stuntman, but as an actor he was a bust, and his inability to deliver even the simplest line convincingly drew chuckles from the public and the ire of the critics.

Jack Hoxie Filmography

1932: *Outlaw Justice* (Majestic; Armand Schaeffer) *LL* Dorothy Gulliver; *Gold* (Majestic; Otto Brower) *LL* Alice Day; *The Law and the Lawless* (Majestic; Armand Schaeffer) *LL* Hilda Moore. **1933:** *Via Pony Express* (Majestic; Lew Collins) *LL* Marceline Day; *Gun Law* (Majestic; Lew Collins) *LL* Betty Boyd; *Trouble Busters* (Majestic; Lew Collins) *LL* Kaye Edwards.

Eileen Jansen *see* The Rough Ridin' Kids

Art Jarrett

Art Jarrett found himself in pretty much the same predicament, as did Tex Fletcher, as far as B Westerns were concerned: that is he was signed by Grand National Pictures, but following the release of his first film, *Trigger Pals* (1939), the company went bankrupt.

Jarrett was a big-band and radio singer who had appeared in films like *Dancing Lady* with Joan Crawford.

Jarrett continued his musical career and in 1950 hosted his own Western musical show, *Rhythm Rodeo*, on the Dumont Television Network.

Art Jarrett Filmography

1939: *Trigger Pals* (Grand National; Sam Newfield.) *SK* Lee Powell, Fuzzy St. John, *LL* Dorothy Fay.

Herb Jeffreys

During the thirties and forties there flourished a thriving black film industry. Films were written, directed and produced by blacks, with all-black casts, and they were shown in black theaters across the nation.

Herb Jeffreys was the black film industry's contribution to the B Western.

Jeffreys was a jazz singer with Earl "Fatha" Hines' band when *The Bronze Buckaroo* and *Harlem Rides the Range* were released in 1939. In the larger cities on the East Coast the films were also shown in major white theaters. The screenplay for *Harlem* was written by Spencer Williams, Jr. (better known to TV fans as Andrew H. Brown, the Kingfish's prize sucker on *The Amos and Andy Show* in the early fifties).

Jeffreys enjoyed a long and flourishing career as a vocalist and is perhaps best known as the vocalist on Duke Ellington's 1941 hit "Flamingo."

Herb Jeffreys Filmography

1939: *The Bronze Buckaroo* (Sack Amusement; Richard Kahn); *Harlem Rides the Range* (Hollywood Pictures; Richard Kahn).

Buck Jones

Horse: Silver

Even if he had never made a motion picture, Buck Jones would be a hero. He led a life as adventuresome as any screenwriter could concoct.

Jones was born December 12, 1891, in Vincennes, Indiana, and his given name was Charles Fredrick Gebhart. He got the nickname "Buck" as a boy.

He grew up on a ranch in Red Rock, Oklahoma, and by the time he reached his teens had become an expert horseman. At the age of 16 he left home and became a mechanic for an auto racing team in Indianapolis.

While still 16, he joined the army and saw action against Pancho Villa on the Mexican border. He reenlisted and was sent to the Philippines to help quell the Moro insurrection. While there, he was wounded by a sniper and transferred back stateside. He attained the rank of sergeant before his discharge in 1913.

Buck got a job at the Miller 101 Ranch and became a featured attraction in the Miller 101 Wild West Show. He also worked as a test driver for the Stutz Bearcat Auto Company and at one time was a performer with Ringling Brothers' Circus.

Buck began in movies as a $5-a-day extra and stuntman at Universal and Fox Studios and gradually worked his way up to bigger roles. Buck made his first feture, *The Last Straw*, in 1919.

Fox decided to star Jones in Westerns because they needed a way to keep their main cowboy star—Tom Mix—in line, and they felt suitable competition from the likes of Jones was the way to do it.

Buck Jones circa 1932.

The public's response to Jones surprised Fox, and over the next nine years Jones made over 50 films for the studio and was rated with William S. Hart and Mix as one of the silent screen's top cowboys.

In 1928 Buck Jones decided to leave the studio to produce his own films, but his timing was bad. He lost a great deal of money in the 1929 stock market crash, production of motion pictures changed with the arrival of sound, and Jones's first feature, *The Big Hop*, was a dismal failure.

After touring with a circus, Jones signed with Columbia Pictures in 1931 and made 27 films before going to Universal in 1934.

Although his Universal features were good, his best work came in the

Buck Jones and Silver.

five serial chapter plays he made there: *Gordon of Ghost City, The Red Rider, Roaring West, The Phantom Rider* and *Riders of Death Valley.* He also made one for Columbia, *White Eagle,* in 1941. Jones was also active in the production and direction of his films at Universal.

In 1937 he returned to Columbia for a series of six films. Buck later teamed with Tim McCoy and Raymond Hatton in 1941 to star in the eight films of the well-received *Rough Riders* series.

Buck had completed work on his last film, *Dawn of the Great Divide,*

Buck Jones and Mary Doran in a scene from Ridin' for Justice *(Columbia, 1932).*

in late 1942 and became part of a national war bond tour. On Thanksgiving night he was in Boston, Massachusetts, as a guest of the city and had participated in the annual turkey day parade. While he was enjoying himself at the Coconut Grove nightclub a terrible fire broke out. The club was poorly constructed and without enough exits; the holocaust took over 500 lives, including that of Buck Jones, who was badly burned trying to help others get out of the blaze. The date was November 28, 1942.

Buck Jones was one of the most popular of the screen cowboys, and at one point his fan club, the Buck Jones Rangers, numbered over four million members.

Buck Jones Filmography

1928: *The Big Hop* (Buck Jones Prod.; James W. Horne) *LL* Jobyna Ralston.
1930: *Shadow Ranch* (Columbia; Louis King) *LL* Margeurite de la Motte,
Kate Price; *The Lone Rider* (Columbia; Louis King) *LL* Vera Reynolds; *Men
Without Law* (Columbia; Louis King) *LL* Carmelita Geraghty, Lydia
Knott; *The Dawn Trail* (Columbia; Christy Cabanne) *LL* Miriam Seegar.
1931: *Desert Vengeance* (Columbia; Louis King) *LL* Barbara Bedford; *The
Avenger* (Columbia; Roy Wm. Neill) *LL* Dorothy Revier; *The Texas
Ranger* (Columbia; D. Ross Lederman) *LL* Carmelita Geraghty; *The
Fighting Sheriff* (Columbia; Louis King) *LL* Loretta Sayers; *Branded* (Co-
lumbia; D. Ross Lederman) *LL* Ethel Kenyon; *Border Law* (Columbia;
Louis King) *LL* Lupita Tovar; *Range Feud* (Columbia; D. Ross Lederman)
LL Susan Fleming; *The Deadline* (Columbia; Lambert Hillyer) *LL* Loretta
Sayers. **1932:** *Ridin' for Justice* (Columbia; D. Ross Lederman) *LL* Mary
Doran; *One Man Law* (Columbia; Lambert Hillyer) *LL* Shirley Grey; *South
of the Rio Grande* (Columbia; Lambert Hillyer) *LL* Mona Maris; *Hello
Trouble* (Columbia; Lambert Hillyer) *LL* Lina Basquette; *White Eagle* (Co-
lumbia; Lambert Hillyer) *LL* Barbara Weeks; *McKenna of the Mounted*
(Columbia; D. Ross Lederman) *LL* Greta Granstedt. **1933:** *Forbidden Trail*
(Columbia; Lambert Hillyer) *LL* Barbara Weeks; *Treason* (Columbia;
George B. Seitz) *LL* Shirley Grey; *Sundown Rider* (Columbia; Lambert
Hillyer) *LL* Barbara Weeks; *California Trail* (Columbia; Lambert Hillyer)
LL Helen Mack; *Unknown Valley* (Columbia; Lambert Hillyer) *LL* Cecilia
Parker; *Thrill Hunter* (Columbia; George B. Seitz) *LL* Dorothy Revier;
Gordon of Ghost City (serial) (Universal; Ray Taylor) *LL* Madge Bellamy.
1934: *The Fighting Code* (Columbia; Lambert Hillyer) *LL* Diane Sinclair;
The Fighting Rangers (Columbia; George B. Seitz) *LL* Dorothy Revier; *Man
Trailer* (Columbia; Lambert Hillyer) *LL* Cecilia Parker; *Rocky Rhodes*
(Universal; Al Roboch) *LL* Sheila Terry, Lydia Knott; *When a Man Sees
Red* (Universal; Alan James) *LL* Peggy Campbell, Dorothy Revier; *The Red
Rider* (serial) (Universal; Lew Landers) *LL* Marion Shilling. **1935:** *The
Crimson Trail* (Universal; Al Roboch) *LL* Polly Ann Young; *Stone of Silver
Creek* (Universal; Nick Grinde) *LL* Peggy Campbell, Noel Francis, Marion
Shilling; *Outlawed Guns* (Universal; Ray Taylor) *LL* Ruth Channing, Joan
Gale; *Border Brigands* (Universal; Nick Grinde) *LL* Lona Andre; *The
Throwback* (Universal; Ray Taylor) *LL* Muriel Evans; *The Ivory Handled
Gun* (Universal; Ray Taylor) *LL* Charlotte Wynters; *Roaring West* (serial)
(Universal; Ray Taylor) *SK* Frank McGlynn, *LL* Muriel Evans. **1936:** *Sun-
set of Power* (Universal; Ray Taylor) *LL* Dorothy Dix; *Silver Spurs* (Uni-
versal; Ray Taylor) *LL* Muriel Evans; *For the Service* (Universal; Buck
Jones) *LL* Beth Marion; *The Cowboy and the Kid* (Universal; Ray Taylor)
LL Dorothy Revier; *Ride 'Em Cowboy* (Universal; Lesley Selander) *LL* Luana

Walters; *Boss Rider of Gun Creek* (Universal; Lesley Selander) *LL* Muriel Evans; *Empty Saddles* (Universal; Lesley Selander) *LL* Louise Brooks, Claire Rochelle; *The Phantom Rider* (serial) (Universal; Ray Taylor) *LL* Marla Skelton, Diana Gibson. **1937:** *Sand Flow* (Universal; Lesley Selander) *LL* Lita Chevret; *Left Handed Law* (Universal; Lesley Selander) *LL* Nena Quartero; *Smoke Tree Range* (Universal; Lesley Selander) *LL* Muriel Evans; *Black Aces* (Universal; Buck Jones) *LL* Kay Linaker; *Law for Tombstone* (Universal; Buck Jones) *LL* Muriel Evans; *Boss of Lonely Valley* (Universal; Ray Taylor) *LL* Muriel Evans; *Sudden Bill Dorn* (Universal; Ray Taylor) *LL* Noel Francis, Evelyn Brent; *Headin' East* (Columbia; Ewing Scott) *LL* Ruth Coleman; *Hollywood Roundup* (Columbia; Ewing Scott) *LL* Helen Twelvetrees. **1938:** *California Frontier* (Columbia; Elmer Clifton) *LL* Carmen Bailey; *The Overland Express* (Columbia; Drew Eberson) *LL* Marjorie Reynolds; *Law of the Texan* (Columbia; Elmer Clifton) *LL* Dorothy Fay; *Stranger from Arizona* (Columbia; Elmer Clifton) *LL* Dorothy Fay. **1940:** *Wagons Westward* (Republic; Lew Landers) *LL* Anita Louise. **1941:** *Arizona Bound* (Monogram; Spencer G. Bennet) *SK* Rough Riders, *LL* Luana Walters, Kathryn Sheldon; *The Gunman from Bodie* (Monogram; Spencer G. Bennet) *SK* Rough Riders, *LL* Christine McIntyre; *Forbidden Trails* (Monogram; R.N. Bradbury) *SK* Rough Riders, *LL* Christine McIntyre; *White Eagle* (serial) (Columbia; James W. Horne) *SK* Raymond Hatton, *LL* Dorothy Fay; *Riders of Death Valley* (serial) (Universal; Ray Taylor, Ford Beebe) *SK* Dick Foran, Leo Carrillo, Big Boy Williams, *LL* Jeannie Kelly. **1942:** *Below the Border* (Monogram; Howard Bretherton) *SK* Rough Riders, *LL* Linda Brent; *Ghost Town Law* (Monogram; Howard Bretherton) *SK* Rough Riders, *LL* Virginia Carpenter; *Down Texas Way* (Monogram; Howard Bretherton) *SK* Rough Riders, *LL* Luana Walters; *Riders of the West* (Monogram; Howard Bretherton) *SK* Rough Riders, *LL* Christine McIntyre, Sarah Padden; *West of the Law* (Monogram; Howard Bretherton) *SK* Rough Riders, *LL* Evelyn Cook; *Dawn on the Great Divide* (Monogram; Howard Bretherton) *SK* Raymond Hatton, *LL* Mona Barrie, Christine McIntyre, Betty Blythe.

Tom Keene

Horse: Rusty, the Wonder Horse
Sidekicks: Roscoe Ates, Edgar Kennedy, Slim Andrews, Frank Yaconelli

Ask connoisseurs of the B Western film genre just who the best actor of the bunch was, and nine times out of ten you'll get the answer "Tom Keene."

Tom Keene

Keene, who also made films under the names George Duryea and Richard Powers, was a highly literate, superbly educated individual who was a star of the legitimate stage long before he butted a saddle and rode the celluloid range.

Keene/Duryea/Powers was born in Smokey Hollow, New York, on December 30, 1904. He was orphaned at the age of six and raised by his aunt. He attained a bachelor of arts degree from Columbia University and began his stage career with a small New England–based stock company.

Soon he found himself with the lead in several New York City productions.

For two years he headed the cast of the international touring company of the hit play *Abie's Irish Rose.*

He made his screen debut in Cecil B. De Mille's 1929 film *The Godless Girl*, and in 1930 when he signed a contract with RKO, he was given the name Tom Keene. Keene's first horse opera for the studio was *Pardon My Gun.* Over the next three years he made 13 more Westerns for the company.

An interesting thing about Keene's career was that, along with his B's, he also made quality films and A Westerns. He starred in *Our Daily Bread,* King Vidor's 1934 film of the Depression, and Paramount's *Sunset Pass* with Randolph Scott.

In 1936 Keene signed with Crescent Films to make a series of historical Western dramas. The outstanding point about these films was Keene's leading ladies. Rita Cansino Hayworth co-starred in *Rebellion* and *Old Louisiana*, and Lorraine Hayes Day was featured in *The Law Commands.*

The year 1937 found Keene at Monogram where he made Westerns until 1942. After that he changed his name to Powers and became a character actor in such varied productions as *Dig That Uranium* (1956) with the Bowery Boys, *Indian Agent* with Tim Holt and *Berlin Express* (both 1948) with Robert Ryan.

Cancer took the life of Tom Keene on August 6, 1963.

Tom Keene Filmography

1930: *The Dude Wrangler* (World Wide; Richard Thorpe) *LL* Lina Basquette; *Pardon My Gun* (RKO; Robert Delacey) *LL* Sally Starr. **1931:** *Sundown Trail* (RKO; Robert Hill) *LL* Marion Shilling; *Freighters of Destiny* (RKO; Fred Allen) *SK* Frank Rice, *LL* Barbara Kent. **1932:** *Partners* (RKO; Fred Allen) *SK* Ben Corbett, *LL* Nancy Drexel; *Saddle Buster* (RKO; Fred Allen) *SK* Ben Corbett, *LL* Helen Forest; *Ghost Valley* (RKO; Fred Allen) *LL* Merna Kennedy, Kate Campbell; *Beyond the Rockies* (RKO; Fred Allen) *LL* Rochelle Hudson; *Come on Danger* (RKO; Robert Hill) *SK* Roscoe Ates, *LL* Julie Haydon; *Renegades of the West* (RKO; Casey Robinson) *SK* Roscoe Ates, *LL* Betty Furness. **1933:** *Scarlet River* (RKO; Otto Brower) *SK* Roscoe Ates, *LL* Betty Furness, Dorothy Wilson; *Son of the Border* (RKO; Lloyd Nosler) *SK* Edgar Kennedy, *LL* Julie Haydon; *Sunset Pass* (Paramount; Henry Hathaway) *SK* Randolph Scott, *LL* Kathleen Burke; *The Cheyenne Kid* (RKO; Robert Hill) *SK* Roscoe Ates, *LL* Mary Mason; *Crossfire* (RKO; Otto Brower) *SK* Edgar Kennedy, *LL* Betty

Furness. **1936:** *Desert Gold* (Paramount; James Hogan) *SK* Buster Crabbe (star), *LL* Marsha Hunt; *Drift Fence* (Paramount; Otto Lovering) *SK* Buster Crabbe (star), *LL* Katherine De Mille; *Rebellion* (Crescent; Lynn Shores) *LL* Rita Cansino. **1937:** *Battle of Greed* (Crescent; Harold Higgin) *LL* Gwynne Shipman; *Old Louisiana* (Crescent; I.V. Wallat) *LL* Rita Cansino; *Under Strange Flags* (Crescent; I.V. Wallat) *LL* Luana Walters; *The Law Commands* (Crescent; William Nigh) *LL* Lorraine Hayes (Day); *Drums of Destiny* (Crescent; Ray Taylor) *LL* Edna Lawrence; *Raw Timber* (Crescent; Ray Taylor) *LL* Peggy Keyes; *God's Country and the Man* (Monogram; R.N. Bradbury) *LL* Betty Compson, Charlotte Henry; *Where Trails Divide* (Monogram; R.N. Bradbury) *LL* Eleanor Stewart, Lorraine Randall; *Romance of the Rockies* (Monogram; R.N. Bradbury) *LL* Beryl Wallace. **1938:** *The Painted Trail* (Monogram; Robert Hill) *LL* Eleanor Stewart. **1941:** *Wanderers of the West* (Monogram; Robert Hill) *SK* Slim Andrews, *LL* Betty Miles, Sugar Dawn; *Dynamite Canyon* (Monogram; Robert E. Tansey) *SK* Slim Andrews, *LL* Evelyn Finley, Sugar Dawn; *The Driftin' Kid* (Monogram; Robert E. Tansey) *SK* Slim Andrews, Frank Yaconelli, *LL* Betty Miles; *Riding the Sunset Trail* (Monogram; Robert E. Tansey) *SK* Slim Andrews, Frank Yaconelli, *LL* Betty Miles, Sugar Dawn; *Lone Star Law Men* (Monogram; Robert E. Tansey) *SK* Frank Yaconelli, *LL* Betty Miles, Sugar Dawn. **1942:** *Western Mail* (Monogram; Robert E. Tansey) *SK* Frank Yaconelli, *LL* Jean Trent; *Arizona Roundup* (Monogram; Robert E. Tansey) *SK* Frank Yaconelli, *LL* Hope Blackwood, Sugar Dawn; *Where Trails End* (Monogram; Robert E. Tansey) *SK* Frank Yaconelli, *LL* Joan Curtis. **1950:** *Desperadoes of the West* (serial) (Republic; Fred C. Brannon) *LL* Judy Clark.

Paul Kelly

Handsome Paul Kelly was one of the top leading men of the whole B picture era that flourished in the thirties and forties. He starred in dozens of dramas, horror films and comedies during the period. He was the pilot who flew Johnny Weissmuller and Maureen O'Sullivan to the Big Apple in *Tarzan's New York Adventure* (MGM, 1942).

Born in 1899, Kelly made his first screen appearance in 1920 in the silent film *Uncle Sam of Freedom Ridge.*

His contribution to B Westerns came in 1936 and 1937, when Fox Studios starred him in a pair of features.

He also appeared in several A Westerns like Errol Flynn's *San Antonio* (Warner Bros., 1945).

Paul Kelly

Paul Kelly made over 100 films before his death in 1956.
He made his last screen appearance posthumously in the 1957 film
Bailout at 43,000 Ft.

Paul Kelly Filmography

1936: *The Country Beyond* (Fox; Eugene Ford) *LL* Rochelle Hudson; *It Happened Out West* (Fox; Howard Bretherton) *LL* Judith Allen.

John Kimbrough

After Republic Pictures successfully starred Washington Redskins quarterback slingin' Sammy Baugh in its 1941 serial *King of the Texas Rangers,* 20th Century–Fox decided to promote the talents of former Texas A&M gridiron-great John Kimbrough, then a running back for the New York Americans of the American Football League.

They released a pair of B Westerns starring Kimbrough in March of 1942; but the critics pooh-poohed the productions, the fans didn't exactly storm the box office to see big John, and World War II prevented Kimbrough from any further movie adventures. When he was released from the service, he returned to the pro football wars. From 1946 to 1948 he starred with the Los Angeles Dons of the All-American Football Conference, and his 17 TDs rank him as the twelfth all-time leading rusher in the history of the long-defunct league.

John Kimbrough Filmography

1942: *Lone Star Ranger* (20th Century–Fox; James Tinling) *LL* Sheila Ryan; *Sundown Jim* (20th Century–Fox; James Tinling) *LL* Virginia Gilmore, Arlean Whelan.

John "Dusty" King

John "Dusty" King was the musical member of the Range Busters in a series of 20 trio Westerns released by Monogram Pictures between 1940 and 1943. The other original members were Crash Corrigan and Max Terhune and later on, David Sharpe and Dennis Moore.

King was born Miller McLeod Everson in Cincinnati, Ohio, on July 11, 1909. He was educated at the University of Cincinnati and in 1932 got a job with a local radio station as an announcer and singer. He was a vocalist with the Ben Bernie Orchestra when he got a chance to do musical shorts for the movies.

King made his acting debut in the 1934 serial *The Adentures of Frank Merriwell* and was in the *Ace Drummond* serial in 1936. He also appeared in such delightful musical comedies as *Three Smart Girls Grow Up* with Deanna Durbin.

In 1940 he signed with Monogram to do the Range Busters series. After the series ended, King made only a few screen appearances before retiring in 1946.

John "Dusty" King Filmography

1940: *The Range Busters* (Mongram; S. Roy Luby) *SK* Ray Corrigan, Max Terhune, *LL* Luana Walters; *Trailing Double Trouble* (Monogram; S. Roy Luby) *SK* Ray Corrigan, Max Terhune, *LL* Lita Conway; *West of Pinto Basin* (Monogram; S. Roy Luby) *SK* Ray Corrigan, Max Terhune, *LL* Gwen Gaze. **1941:** *Trail of the Silver Spur* (Monogram; S. Roy Luby) *SK* Ray Corrigan, Max Terhune, *LL* Dorothy Short; *The Kid's Last Ride* (Monogram; S. Roy Luby) *SK* Ray Corrigan, Max Terhune, *LL* Luana Walters; *Tumbledown Ranch in Arizona* (Monogram; S. Roy Luby) *SK* Ray Corrigan, Max Terhune, *LL* Sheila Darcy; *Wranglers Roost* (Monogram; S. Roy Luby) *SK* Ray Corrigan, Max Terhune, *LL* Gwen Gaze; *Fugitive Valley* (Monogram; S. Roy Luby) *SK* Ray Corrigan, Max Terhune, *LL* Julie Duncan; *Saddle Mountain Roundup* (Monogram; S. Roy Luby) *SK* Ray Corrigan, Max Terhune, *LL* Lita Conway, *Tonto Basin Outlaws* (Monogram; S. Roy Luby) *SK* Ray Corrigan, Max Terhune, *LL* Jan Wiley; *Underground Rustlers* (Monogram; S. Roy Luby) *SK* Ray Corrigan, Max Terhune, *LL* Gwen Gaze. **1942:** *Thunder River Feud* (Monogram; S. Roy Luby) *SK* Ray Corrigan, Max Terhune, *LL* Jan Wiley; *Rocky River Renegades* (Monogram; S. Roy Luby) *SK* Ray Corrigan, Max Terhune, *LL* Christine McIntyre; *Boot Hill Bandits* (Monogram; S. Roy Luby) *SK* Ray Corrigan, Max Terhune, *LL* Jean Brooks; *Texas Trouble Shooters* (Monogram; S. Roy Luby) *SK* Ray Corrigan, Max Terhune, *LL* Julie Duncan; *Arizona Stage Coach* (Monogram; S. Roy Luby) *SK* Ray Corrigan, Max Terhune, *LL* Nell O'Day; *Texas to Bataan* (Monogram; Robert Tansey) *SK* Max Terhune, David Sharpe, *LL* Marjorie Manners; *Trail Riders* (Monogram; Robert Tansey) *SK* Max Terhune, David Sharpe, *LL* Evelyn Finley. **1943:** *Two Fisted Justice* (Monogram; Robert Tansey) *SK* Max Terhune, David Sharpe, *LL* Gwen Gaze; *Haunted Ranch* (Monogram; Robert Tansey) *SK* Max Terhune, David Sharpe, *LL* Julie Duncan.

Fred Kohler, Jr.

Fred Kohler, Jr., the son of one of B-Westerndom's greatest bad guys, Fred Kohler, Sr., starred as the hero of two films for Commodore Pictures in 1935 before following in his dad's villainous footsteps.

John "Dusty" King

Fred Kohler, Jr.

1935: *The Pecos Kid* (Commodore; William Berke) *LL* Ruth Findlay; *Toll of the Desert* (Commodore; William Berke) *LL* Betty Mack.

Allan "Rocky" Lane
"America's Fightin'est Cowboy"

Horse: Black Jack
Sidekicks: Eddy Waller, Chubby Johnson, Bobby Blake

If I ever have to face a gang of muggers in a dark alley, I don't want Hulk Hogan or Smokin' Joe Frazier by my side; I want Rocky Lane. Lane was the hardest hitting of the two-fisted cowboys, and he made better use of the excellent Republic stunt team than did anyone else. Every Lane adventure had at least one well-staged jaw rattling brawl in a saloon, jail, cafe or stage depot; sometimes all of the above.

Lane came by his athletic ability honestly. He lettered in football, basketball and baseball while attending Notre Dame University.

Lane became interested in acting and joined an Ohio-based stock company; he later got the lead in the road company production of *Hit the Deck.* He quit for a while to become a photographer.

He was offered a film contract in 1929 and debuted in *Not Quite Decent* for Fox Films.

In 1932 he signed with Warner Bros. He appeared with Shirley Temple in *Stowaway* in 1936 and signed with RKO in 1938.

Rocky Lane made his Western film debut in *The Law West of Tombstone* with Harry Carey and Tim Holt. In 1940 his career took off when he signed with Republic Pictures. He made four action serials, three of them Westerns for the studio, and in 1944 began his own Western series.

In 1946 he took over the role of Red Ryder from Wild Bill Elliott and made seven Ryder films.

In 1947 he began his most famous series for Republic — the one with his stallion, Black Jack, and Eddy Waller as his sidekick, Nugget Clark. There were 32 of these films and they made Rocky Lane a top-ten cowboy and a household name.

Lane made his last "B" in 1953. In the mid fifties he toured with circuses and rodeos and got bit parts in films. His final screen appearance was *Posse from Hell* in 1961.

From 1961 to 1966 Lane served as the voice of TV's famous talking equine, "Mr. Ed."

Allan "Rocky" Lane

Born Harry Albershart on September 22, 1904 in Mishawaka, Indiana, Allan "Rocky" Lane died October 27, 1973, of cancer.

Allan "Rocky" Lane Filmography

1940: *King of the Royal Mounted* (serial) (Republic; William Witney, John English) *LL* Lita Conway. **1942:** *King of the Mounties* (serial) (Republic; William Witney) *LL* Peggy Drake; *Dare Devils of the West* (serial) (Republic; John English) *LL* Kay Aldridge. **1944:** *Silver City Kid* (Republic; John English) *SK* Wally Vernon, *LL* Peggy Stewart; *Stagecoach to Monterey* (Republic; Lesley Selander) *SK* Wally Vernon, *LL* Peggy Stewart; *Sheriff of Sundown* (Republic; Lesley Selander) *SK* Max Terhune, *LL* Linda Stirling. **1945:** *The Topeka Terror* (Republic; Howard Bretherton) *LL* Linda Stirling; *Corpus Christi Bandits* (Republic; Wallace Grissel) *LL* Helen Talbot; *Trail of Kit Carson* (Republic; Lesley Selander) *LL* Helen Talbot. **1946:** *Santa Fe Uprising* (Red Ryder series, hereafter cited as R.R.) (Republic; R.G. Springsteen) *SK* Bobby Blake, Martha Wentworth; *Stagecoach to Denver* (R.R.) (Republic; R.G. Springsteen) *SK* Bobby Blake, Martha Wentworth, *LL* Peggy Stewart. **1947:** *Vigilantes of Boomtown* (R.R.) (Republic; R.G. Springsteen) *SK* Bobby Blake, Martha Wentworth, *LL* Peggy Stewart; *Homesteaders of Paradise Valley* (R.R.) (Republic; R.G. Springsteen) *SK* Bobby Blake, Martha Wentworth, *LL* Ann Todd; *Oregon Trail Scouts* (R.R.) (Republic; R.G. Springsteen) *SK* Bobby Blake, Martha Wentworth. *Rustlers of Devil's Canyon* (R.R.) (Republic; R.G. Springsteen) *SK* Bobby Blake, Martha Wentworth, *LL* Peggy Stewart; *Marshal of Cripple Creek* (R.R.) (Republic; R.G. Springsteen) *SK* Bobby Blake, Martha Wentworth; *The Wild Frontier* (Republic; Phillip Ford) *SK* Eddy Waller; *Bandits of Dark Canyon* (Republic; Phillip Ford) *SK* Eddy Waller, *LL* Linda Johnson. **1948:** *Oklahoma Badlands* (Republic; Yakima Canutt) *SK* Eddy Waller, *LL* Mildred Coles; *The Bold Frontiersman* (Republic; Phillip Ford) *SK* Eddy Waller; *Carson City Raiders* (Republic; Yakima Canutt) *SK* Eddy Waller, *LL* Beverly Jons; *Marshal of Amarillo* (Republic; Phillip Ford) *SK* Eddy Waller, *LL* Mildred Coles; *Desperadoes of Dodge City* (Republic; Phillip Ford) *SK* Eddy Waller, *LL* Mildred Coles; *The Denver Kid* (Republic; Phillip Ford) *SK* Eddy Waller; *Sundown in Santa Fe* (Republic; R.G. Springsteen) *SK* Eddy Waller, *LL* Jean Dean; *Renegades of Sonora* (Republic; R.G. Springsteen) *SK* Eddy Waller. **1949:** *Sheriff of Wichita* (Republic; R.G. Springsteen) *SK* Eddy Waller, *LL* Lyn Wilde; *Death Valley Gunfighter* (Republic; R.G. Springsteen) *SK* Eddy Waller, *LL* Gail Davis; *Frontier Marshal* (Republic; Fred C. Brannon) *SK* Eddy Waller, *LL* Gail Davis; *The Wyoming Bandit* (Republic; Phillip Ford) *SK* Eddy Waller; *Bandit King of Texas* (Republic; Fred C. Brannon) *SK* Eddy Waller,

LL Helen Stanley; *Navajo Trail Raiders* (Republic; R.G. Springsteen) *SK* Eddy Waller, *LL* Barbara Bestar; *Powder River Rustlers* (Republic; Phillip Ford) *SK* Eddy Waller, *LL* Gerry Ganzer. **1950:** *Gunmen of Abilene* (Republic; Fred C. Brannon) *SK* Eddy Waller, *LL* Donna Hamilton; *Code of the Silver Sage* (Republic; Fred C. Brannon) *SK* Eddy Waller, *LL* Kay Christopher; *Salt Lake Raiders* (Republic; Fred C. Brannon) *SK* Eddy Waller, *LL* Martha Hyer; *Covered Wagon Raid* (Republic; R.G. Springsteen) *SK* Eddy Waller, *LL* Lyn Thomas; *Vigilante Hideout* (Republic; Fred C. Brannon) *SK* Eddy Waller, *LL* Virginia Herrick; *Frisco Tornado* (Republic; R.G. Springsteen) *SK* Eddy Waller, *LL* Martha Hyer; *Rustlers on Horseback* (Republic; Fred C. Brannon) *SK* Eddy Waller, *LL* Claudia Barrett. **1951:** *Rough Riders of Durango* (Republic; Fred C. Brannon) *LL* Aline Towne; *Night Riders of Montana* (Republic; Fred C. Brannon) *SK* Chubby Johnson, *LL* Claudia Barrett; *Wells Fargo Gunmaster* (Republic; Phillip Ford) *SK* Chubby Johnson, *LL* Mary Ellen Kay; *Fort Dodge Stampede* (Republic; Harry Keller) *SK* Chubby Johnson, *LL* Mary Ellen Kay; *Desert of Lost Men* (Republic; Harry Keller) *LL* Mary Ellen Kay. **1952:** *Captive of Billy the Kid* (Republic; Fred C. Brannon) *LL* Penny Edwards; *Leadville Gunslinger* (Republic; Harry Kellar) *SK* Eddy Waller, *LL* Elaine Riley; *Black Hills Ambush* (Republic; Harry Kellar) *SK* Eddy Waller, *LL* Leslye Banning; *Thundering Caravans* (Republic; Harry Kellar) *SK* Eddy Waller, *LL* Mona Knox; *Desperadoes Outpost* (Republic; Phillip Ford) *SK* Eddy Waller, *LL* Claudia Barrett. **1953:** *Marshal of Cedar Rock* (Republic; Harry Kellar) *SK* Eddy Waller, *LL* Phyllis Coates; *Savage Frontier* (Republic; Harry Kellar) *SK* Eddy Waller, *LL* Dorothy Patrick; *Bandits of the West* (Republic; Harry Kellar) *SK* Eddy Waller, *LL* Cathy Downs; *El Paso Stampede* (Republic; Harry Kellar) *SK* Eddy Waller, *LL* Phyllis Coates.

Lash LaRue

Horse: Rush
Sidekick: Fuzzy St. John

Lash LaRue, "the King of the Bullwhip," has famous B Western screen director Robert Tansey to thank for his movie success. It was Tansey who suggested that LaRue, a previously unsuccessful actor, take up the bullwhip and develop it as a screen gimmick.

Born Alfred LaRue on June 14, 1917, in Gretna, Louisiana, Lash studied drama in college to correct a speech problem he had had since childhood. After some stage work he did a screen test for Warner Bros., however, they turned him down because he looked and acted like another Warner contractee — Humphrey Bogart.

In 1945 he signed a one-year contract with Universal and appeared in the serial *The Master Key*. It was during this time he developed his bullwhip ability.

PRC selected LaRue to play an outlaw, the Cheyenne Kid, in Eddie Dean's *The Song of Old Wyoming*, and LaRue made appearances in several other Dean features.

Beginning with *The Law of the Lash* in 1947, LaRue starred in eight films for PRC using his character "Cheyenne."

In 1948 the series continued at Screen Guild. From 1950–1952 LaRue's films were produced by Western Adventure Films.

After his film career faded, Lash appeared in carnies and rodeos, and today he is still active making personal appearances at Western film fairs and in low-budget indy films.

Lash LaRue's personal life has been plagued by several unsuccessful marriages and bundles of trouble with the IRS.

Lash LaRue Filmography

1947: *Law of the Lash* (PRC; Ray Taylor) *SK* Fuzzy St. John, *LL* Mary Scott; *Border Feud* (PRC; Ray Taylor) *SK* Fuzzy St. John, *LL* Gloria Marlen; *Pioneer Justice* (PRC; Ray Taylor) *SK* Fuzzy St. John, *LL* Jennifer Holt; *Ghost Town Renegades* (PRC; Ray Taylor) *SK* Fuzzy St. John, *LL* Jennifer Holt; *Stage to Mesa City* (PRC; Ray Taylor) *SK* Fuzzy St. John, *LL* Jennifer Holt; *Return of the Lash* (PRC; Ray Taylor) *SK* Fuzzy St. John, *LL* Mary Maynard; *The Fighting Vigilantes* (PRC; Ray Taylor) *SK* Fuzzy St. John, *LL* Jennifer Holt; *Cheyenne Takes Over* (PRC; Ray Taylor) *SK* Fuzzy St. John, *LL* Nancy Gates. **1948:** *Dead Man's Gold* (Screen Guild; Ray Taylor) *SK* Fuzzy St. John, *LL* Peggy Stewart; *Mark of the Lash* (Screen Guild; Ray Taylor) *SK* Fuzzy St. John, *LL* Suzi Crandall; *Frontier Revenge* (Screen Guild; Ray Taylor) *SK* Fuzzy St. John, *LL* Peggy Stewart. **1949:** *Outlaw Country* (Screen Guild; Ray Taylor) *SK* Fuzzy St. John, *LL* Nancy Saunders; *Son of Billy the Kid* (Screen Guild; Ray Taylor) *SK* Fuzzy St. John, *LL* Marion Colby, June Carr; *Son of a Badman* (Screen Guild; Ray Taylor) *SK* Fuzzy St. John, *LL* Noel Neill. **1950:** *The Daltons' Women* (Howco; Thomas Carr) *SK* Fuzzy St. John, *LL* Pamela Blake, Jacqueline Fontaine. **1951:** *King of the Bullwhip* (Western Adventure; Ron Ormond) *SK* Fuzzy St. John, *LL* Anne Gwynne; *The Thundering Trail* (Western Adventure; Ron Ormond) *SK* Fuzzy St. John, *LL* Sally Anglim; *The Vanishing Outpost* (Western Adventure; Ron Ormond) *SK* Fuzzy St. John, *LL* Sue Hussey. **1952:** *The Black Lash* (Western Adventure; Ron Ormond)

Lash LaRue

SK Fuzzy St. John, *LL* Peggy Stewart; *The Frontier Phantom* (Western Adventure; Ron Ormond) *SK* Fuzzy St. John, *LL* Virginia Herrick.

Rex Lease

Rex Lease made scores of silent and sound Westerns. He was at times a hero, other times a villain, and often, late in his career, just a bit player.

Rex Lease

Lease starred in eight B Westerns between 1930 and 1935 for such long-extinct studios as Tiffany, World Wide, and Superior. He also starred in two Western chapter plays, *The Sign of the Wolf* in 1931 and *Custer's Last Stand* in 1935.

Lease was born in Central City, Virginia, on February 11, 1903. He began his professional acting career with an Ohio-based stock company after studying theology at Ohio Wesleyan College.

He began in films in 1922 and got his first leading part in 1925 in the film *Clancey's Kosher Wedding*. The next year he starred in the serial *The Mystery Pilot* and signed with F.B.O. Studios, where he remained until the end of the silents.

Rex Lease died January 6, 1966, in Hollywood, California.

Rex Lease Filmography

1930: *The Utah Kid* (Tiffany; Richard Thorpe) *LL* Dorothy Sebastian. **1931:** *In Old Cheyenne* (World Wide; Stuart Paton) *LL* Dorothy Gulliver; *The Sign of the Wolf* (serial) (Metropolitan; Forrest Sheldon, Harry S. Webb) *LL* Virginia Brown Faire. **1935:** *The Cowboy and the Bandit* (Superior; Al Herman) *LL* Janet Morgan (Blanche Mehaffey); *Cyclone of the Saddle* (Superior; Elmer Clifton) *LL* Janet Chandler; *Pals of the Range* (Superior; Elmer Clifton); *Fighting Caballero* (Superior; Elmer Clifton) *LL* Dorothy Gulliver; *The Ghost Rider* (Superior; Jack Levine) *LL* Ann Carol; *Rough Riding Ranger* (Superior; Elmer Clifton) *LL* Janet Chandler. **1936:** *Custer's Last Stand* (Stage & Screen; Elmer Clifton) *LL* Ruth Mix, Lona Andre.

Bob Livingston

Horse: Starlight

Hard-riding Bob Livingston is best remembered as Stoney Brooke, leader of the Three Mesquiteers. He portrayed Brooke in 29 films for Republic Pictures between 1936 and 1941.

Born Robert Randall in Quincey, Illinois, on December 9, 1890, his brother Jack Randall was also a top B Western star of the thirties.

The Randall family moved to Glensdale, California, when Bob was 12. Before becoming an actor Bob worked as a cowboy, a sailor and as a reporter for a Los Angeles newspaper.

In 1929 he entered films as a bit player and in 1933 was signed by MGM.

In 1936 Republic starred him in their serial *The Vigilantes Are Coming* and the feature *The Bold Caballero*.

On break from the Mesquiteers series he starred in *The Lone Ranger Rides Again*, one of Republic's better serials.

In 1941 he left Republic to take over the lead in *The Lone Rider* series from George Houston at PRC.

He made six Lone Riders before returning to Republic in 1944 and

Bob Livingston and Starlight.

assuming the role of John Paul Revere in Eddie Dew's ill-fated film series. After two films the series was dropped.

Livingston continued to play in films until 1950 when he retired from acting to concentrate on script writing.

Bob Livingston Filmography

1936: *The Bold Cabellero* (Republic; Wells Root) *LL* Heather Angel; *The Three Mesquiteers* (Republic; Ray Taylor) *SK* Ray Corrigan, Syd Saylor, *LL* Kay Hughes; *Ghost Town Gold* (Republic; Joseph Kane) *SK* Ray Corrigan, Max Terhune, *LL* Kay Hughes; *The Vigilantes Are Coming* (serial) (Republic; Ray Taylor, Mack V. Wright) *SK* Big Boy Williams, Raymond Hatton, *LL* Kay Hughes; *Roarin' Lead* (Republic; Mack V. Wright, Sam Newfield) *SK* Ray Corrigan, Max Terhune, *LL* Christine Maple. **1937:**

Riders of the Whistling Skull (Republic; Mack V. Wright) *SK* Ray Corrigan, Max Terhune, *LL* Mary Russell; *Hit the Saddle* (Republic; Mack V. Wright) *SK* Ray Corrigan, Max Terhune, *LL* Rita Cansino; *Gunsmoke Ranch* (Republic; Joseph Kane) *SK* Ray Corrigan, Max Terhune, *LL* Julia Thayer; *Come on Cowboys* (Republic; Joseph Kane) *SK* Ray Corrigan, Max Terhune, *LL* Maxine Doyle; *Range Defenders* (Republic; Mac V. Wright) *SK* Ray Corrigan, Max Terhune, *LL* Eleanor Stewart; *Heart of the Rockies* (Republic; Joseph Kane) *SK* Ray Corrigan, Max Terhune, *LL* Lynn Roberts; *Wild Horse Rodeo* (Republic; George Sherman) *SK* Ray Corrigan, Max Terhune, *LL* June Martel. **1938:** *The Purple Vigilantes* (Republic; George Sherman) *SK* Ray Corrigan, Max Terhune, *LL* Joan Barclay; *Call the Mesquiteers* (Republic; John English) *SK* Ray Corrigan, Max Terhune, *LL* Lynn Roberts; *Outlaws of Sonora* (Republic; George Sherman) *SK* Ray Corrigan, Max Terhune, *LL* Jean Joyce; *Riders of the Black Hills* (Republic; George Sherman) *SK* Ray Corrigan, Max Terhune, *LL* Ann Evers; *Heroes of the Hills* (Republic; George Sherman) *SK* Ray Corrigan, Max Terhune, *LL* Priscilla Lawson. **1939:** *The Lone Ranger Rides Again* (serial) (Republic; William Witney, John English) *SK* Chief Thundercloud, *LL* Jinx Falkenberg; *The Kansas Terrors* (Republic; George Sherman) *SK* (3 Mesq.) Raymond Hatton, Duncan Renaldo, *LL* Jacqueline Wells; *Cowboys from Texas* (Republic; George Sherman) *SK* Raymond Hatton, Duncan Renaldo, *LL* Carole Landis, Betty Compson. **1940:** *Heroes of the Saddle* (Republic; William Witney) *SK* Raymond Hatton, Duncan Renaldo, *LL* Patsy Lee Parsons, Loretta Weaver; *Pioneers of the West* (Republic; Les Orlebeck) *SK* Raymond Hatton, Duncan Renaldo, *LL* Beatrice Roberts; *Covered Wagon Days* (Republic; George Sherman) *SK* Raymond Hatton, Duncan Renaldo, *LL* Kay Griffith, Ruth Robinson; *Rocky Mountain Rangers* (Republic; George Sherman) *SK* Raymond Hatton, Duncan Renaldo, *LL* Rosella Towne; *Oklahoma Renegades* (Republic; Nate Watt) *SK* Raymond Hatton, Duncan Renaldo, *LL* Florine McKinney; *Under Texas Skies* (Republic; George Sherman) *SK* Bob Steele, Rufe Davis, *LL* Lois Ranson; *The Trail Blazers* (Republic; George Sherman) *SK* Bob Steele, Rufe Davis, *LL* Pauline Moore; *Lone Star Raiders* (Republic; George Sherman) *SK* Bob Steele, Rufe Davis, *LL* June Johnson. **1941:** *Prairie Pioneers* (Republic; Les Orlebeck) *SK* Bob Steele, Rufe Davis, *LL* Esther Estrella; *Pals of the Pecos* (Republic; Les Orlebeck) *SK* Bob Steele, Rufe Davis, *LL* June Johnson; *Saddlemates* (Republic; Les Orlebeck) *SK* Bob Steele, Rufe Davis, *LL* Gale Storm; *Gangs of Sonora* (Republic; John English) *SK* Bob Steele, Rufe Davis, *LL* June Johnson. **1942:** *Overland Stagecoach* (Lone Rider Series) (PRC; Sam Newfield) *SK* Fuzzy St. John, *LL* Julie Duncan. **1943:** *Wild Horse Rustlers* (PRC; Sam Newfield) *SK* Fuzzy St. John, *LL* Linda Johnson; *Death Rides the Plains* (PRC; Sam Newfield) *SK* Fuzzy St. John, *LL* Nica Doret; *Wolves of the Range* (PRC; Sam Newfield) *SK* Fuzzy St.

John, LL Frances Gladwin; *Law of the Saddle* (PRC; Melville De Lay) *SK* Fuzzy St. John, *LL* Betty Miles; *Raiders of Red Gap* (PRC; Sam Newfield) *SK* Fuzzy St. John, *LL* Myrna Dell. **1944:** *Pride of the Plains* (John Paul Revere Series) (Republic; Wallace Fox) *SK* Smiley Burnette, *LL* Nancy Gay; *Beneath Western Skies* (Republic; Spencer Bennett) *SK* Smiley Burnette, Joe Stauch, Jr., *LL* Effie Laird; *The Laramie Trail* (Republic; John English) *SK* Smiley Burnette, *LL* Linda Brent; *The Big Bonanza* (Republic; George Archainbaud) *SK* Richard Arlen, Gabby Hayes, *LL* Jane Frazee, Lynne Roberts.

Jack Luden

Sidekick: Tuffy

Cowboy star Jack Luden was born John Luden in Reading, Pennsylvania, on February 6, 1902. He was the son of Jacob C. Luden of Luden's cough drops fame. He studied medicine at Johns Hopkins University but was bitten by the acting bug before completing his studies.

In 1925 he enrolled in Paramount Studios Junior School of Acting in New York and the following year made his screen debut in *Fascinating Youth.* That year he got his first leading role in a film called *That Old Army Game* and made his first Western, *Shootin' Irons,* for F.B.O. that led to a series of Western films.

When the sound era arrived, Luden found himself out of work as an actor. A decade later he returned to the screen to star in four low-budget Westerns for Columbia.

He made a few subsequent appearances as a character actor in such films as *Guadalcanal Diary* and the serial *King of the Royal Mounted* before disappearing once again.

Jack Luden Filmography

1938: *Rolling Caravans* (Columbia; Joseph Levering) *SK* Tuffy (dog), *LL* Eleanor Stewart; *Stagecoach Days* (Columbia; Joseph Levering) *SK* Tuffy, *LL* Eleanor Stewart; *Pioneer Trail* (Columbia; Joseph Levering) *SK* Tuffy, *LL* Joan Barclay, Marin Sais; *Phantom Gold* (Columbia; Joseph Levering) *SK* Tuffy, *LL* Beth Marion.

Jack Luden

Tim McCoy

Horses: Starlight, Midnight

Tim McCoy's entrance into the world of motion pictures was unique. While most cowboys began as bit players, stuntmen or singers, McCoy's film career began when he was appointed technical adviser for the 1923 film classic *The Covered Wagon.* He was working as an Indian agent in Wyoming and was considered one of the country's top experts on American Indian lore.

He was born Timothy John Fitzgerald McCoy in Saginaw, Michigan, on April 10, 1891, and attended St. Ignatius College in Chicago, Illinois.

Tim inherited a ranch in Wyoming where he studied Indian customs and language. He also worked for the U.S. Bureau of Indian Affairs.

Tim McCoy

During World War I he served with the adjutant general's office and achieved the rank of lieutenant colonel before his discharge in 1919.

In 1925 he got a supporting role in Paramount's *The Thundering Herd* and later signed a contracted with MGM.

A series of silent Westerns led to an appearance on the top ten cowboy list. McCoy demanded authenticity in regards to Western lifestyle aspects of his films.

The era of sound was little obstacle to McCoy. He made a serial, *The Indians Are Coming*, for Universal in 1930.

Tim McCoy

In 1931 he began a series of two dozen films for Columbia, serving with the company until 1935.

Most of the McCoy films seen on TV are from a series he made in 1935 and 1936 for independent Puritan Pictures.

Tim left films for a short time to appear with the Ringling Brothers–Barnum and Bailey Circus and in 1938 organized his own wild West show, but the show folded and left McCoy in dire financial debt.

He quickly returned to the screen for four films with Monogram, seven with Victory and seven with PRC between 1938 and 1940.

In 1941 he, along with Buck Jones and Raymond Hatton, launched the Rough Riders series at Monogram.

In 1942 he ran for the U.S. Senate but lost, and reenlisted in the service.

Seeing action in Europe, he earned the rank of full colonel and was awarded the Bronze Star for bravery in combat.

He appeared in circuses and wild West shows until the early 1960s, and had a cameo role in *Around the World in 80 Days*.

His last film appearance was in 1965 in *Requiem for a Gunfighter*.

Tim passed away in 1984 at the age of 93. McCoy is often considered the quickest on the draw of the B Western cowboys.

Tim McCoy Filmography

1930: *The Indians Are Coming* (serial) (Universal; Henry McRae) LL Allene Ray. **1931:** *The One Way Trail* (Columbia; Ray Taylor) LL Polly Ann Young, Doris Hill; *Shotgun Pass* (Columbia; J.P. McGowan) LL Virginia Lee Corbin; *The Fighting Marshall* (Columbia; D. Ross Lederman) LL Dorothy Gulliver. **1932:** *The Fighting Fool* (Columbia; Lambert Hillyer) LL Marceline Day, Ethel Wales; *Texas Cyclone* (Columbia; D. Ross Lederman) LL Shirley Grey; *The Riding Tornado* (Columbia; D. Ross Lederman) LL Shirley Grey; *Two Fisted Law* (Columbia; D. Ross Lederman) LL Alice Day; *Daring Danger* (Columbia; D. Ross Lederman) LL Alberta Vaughn; *Cornered* (Columbia; B. Reeves Eason) LL Shirley Grey; *The Western Code* (Columbia; J.P. McCarthy) LL Nora Lane; *Fighting for Justice* (Columbia; Otto Brower) LL Joyce Compton; *End of the Trail* (Columbia; D. Ross Lederman) LL Luana Walters. **1933:** *Man of Action* (Columbia; George Melford) LL Caryl Lincoln; *Silent Men* (Columbia; D. Ross Lederman) LL Florence Britton; *The Whirlwind* (Columbia; D. Ross Lederman) LL Alice Dahl; *Rusty Rides Alone* (Columbia; D. Ross Lederman) LL Barbara Weeks. **1934:** *Beyond the Law* (Columbia; D. Ross Lederman) LL Shirley Grey; *The Prescott Kid* (Columbia; David Selman) LL Sheila Mannors; *The Westerner* (Columbia; David Selman) LL Marion Shilling. **1935:** *Square Shooter* (Columbia; David Selman) LL Jacqueline Wells; *Law Beyond the Range* (Columbia; Ford Beebe) LL Billie Seward; *The Revenge Rider* (Columbia; David Selman) SK Bob Allen, LL Billie Seward; *Fighting Shadows* (Columbia; David Selman) SK Bob Allen, LL Geneva Mitchell; *Justice of the Range* (Columbia; David Selman) LL Billie Seward; *The Outlaw Deputy* (Puritan; Otto Brower) LL Nora Lane; *Riding Wild* (Columbia; David Selman) LL Billie Seward; *The Man from Guntown* (Puritan; Ford Beebe) LL Billie Seward; *Bulldog Courage* (Puritan; Sam Newfield) LL Joan Woodbury. **1936:** *Roarin' Guns* (Puritan; Sam Newfield) LL Rosalinda Rice;

Border Caballero (Puritan; Sam Newfield) *LL* Lois January; *Lightnin' Bill Carson* (Puritan; Sam Newfield) *LL* Lois January; *Aces and Eights* (Puritan; Sam Newfield) *LL* Luana Walters; *The Lion's Den* (Puritan; Sam Newfield) *LL* Joan Woodbury; *Ghost Patrol* (Puritan; Sam Newfield) *LL* Claudia Dell; *The Traitor* (Puritan; Sam Newfield) *LL* Frances Grant. **1938:** *West of Rainbow's End* (Monogram; Alan James) *LL* Kathleen Eliott; *Code of the Rangers* (Monogram; Sam Newfield) *LL* Judith Ford; *Two Gun Justice* (Monogram; Alan James) *LL* Betty Compson, Joan Barclay; *Phantom Ranger* (Monogram; Sam Newfield) *LL* Suzanne Kaaren; *Lightning Carson Rides Again* (Victory; Sam Newfield) *LL* Joan Barclay; *Six Gun Trail* (Victory; Sam Newfield) *LL* Nora Lane. **1939:** *Code of the Cactus* (Victory; Sam Newfield.) *SK* Ben Corbett, *LL* Dorothy Short; *Texas Wildcats* (Victory; Sam Newfield) *SK* Ben Corbett, *LL* Joan Barclay; *Outlaw's Paradise* (Victory; Sam Newfield) *SK* Ben Corbett, *LL* Joan Barclay; *The Fighting Renegade* (Victory; Sam Newfield) *SK* Ben Corbett, *LL* Joyce Bryant; *Straight Shooter* (Victory; Sam Newfield) *SK* Ben Corbett, *LL* Julie Sheldon. **1940:** *Texas Renegades* (PRC; Peter Stewart [Sam Newfield]) *LL* Nora Lane; *Frontier Crusader* (PRC; Peter Stewart [Sam Newfield]) *LL* Dorothy Short; *Gun Code* (PRC; Peter Stewart [Sam Newfield]) *LL* Ina Guest; *Arizona Gangbusters* (PRC; Peter Stewart [Sam Newfield]) *LL* Pauline Haddon; *Riders of Black Mountain* (PRC; Peter Stewart [Sam Newfield]) *LL* Pauline Haddon. **1941:** *Outlaws of the Rio Grande* (PRC; Peter Stewart [Sam Newfield]) *LL* Virginia Carpenter; *The Texas Marshall* (PRC; Peter Stewart [Sam Newfield]) *LL* Kay Leslie; *Arizona Bound* (Monogram; Spencer G. Bennett) *SK* Rough Riders, *LL* Luana Walters, Kathryn Sheldon; *The Gunman from Bodie* (Monogram; Spencer G. Bennett) *SK* Rough Riders, *LL* Christine McIntyre; *Forbidden Trails* (Monogram; R.N. Bradbury) *SK* Rough Riders, *LL* Christine McIntyre. **1942:** *Below the Border* (Monogram; Howard Bretherton) *SK* Rough Riders, *LL* Linda Brent; *Ghost Town Law* (Monogram; Howard Bretherton) *SK* Rough Riders, *LL* Virginia Carpenter; *Down Texas Way* (Monogram; Howard Bretherton) *SK* Rough Riders, *LL* Luana Walters; *Riders of the West* (Monogram; Howard Bretherton) *SK* Rough Riders, *LL* Christine McIntyre, Sarah Padden; *West of the Law* (Monogram; Howard Bretherton) *SK* Rough Riders, *LL* Evelyn Cook.

Ken Maynard

Horse: Tarzan
Sidekicks: Frank Rice, Frank Yaconelli

Ken Maynard

Ken Maynard and Tarzan rank as one of Western filmdom's greatest cowboy and wonder-horse teams. Maynard was an excellent horseman but gained a reputation as a very temperamental and often hard-to-work-with actor.

Maynard was born July 21, 1895, in Mission, Texas, and at 14 he ran away from home to join a traveling medicine show. After his short adventure he returned home and was quickly enrolled in military school by his angry parents.

He served as an army engineer during World War I and upon his release began performing in rodeos. In 1920 he won the national trick riding
title and in 1923, while performing with the Ringling Brothers Circus, he
was approached by a movie talent scout; that led to his screen role in *Janice
Meredith* in 1924.

His first Western feature was *$50,000 Reward* made for Davis Studios.
After several more pictures he signed with the much larger First National
Film Corporation. Maynard's films for First National are regarded as some
of the best silent Westerns ever made.

At the dawn of the sound era in 1929 Maynard signed with Universal
and very easily made the silent-to-talky transition.

By the end of 1930 Maynard was making films for Tiffany Studios.
After 11 films he left for World Wide and seven features before returning
to Universal in 1933.

In 1934 Ken Maynard made two films for Mascot. These films, the
serial *Mystery Mountain* and *In Old Santa Fe*, are note-worthy because
they introduced to the world Gene Autry and Smiley Burnette and set the
framework for the scores of musical Westerns that would follow.

In 1935 Maynard was at Columbia; 1937–1938, Grand National; and
1939–1940, Colony, before retiring temporarily from the screen.

Maynard came out of retirement in 1943 to co-star in the Trail Blazers
series at Monogram, but after six films Maynard left the series.

He made his last feature in 1944, *Harmony Trail.* The film, which was
not released nationally until 1947, featured Eddie Dean, who by that time
was a major Western star.

In the late forties he toured with the Cole Brothers Circus and made
rodeo appearances around the country and in England.

Ken Maynard passed away in 1973.

Ken Maynard Filmography

1929: *The Royal Rider* (First National; Harry Joe Brown) *LL* Olive Has-
brouck; *The Wagon Master* (Universal; Harry Joe Brown) *LL* Edith
Roberts; *Senor Americano* (Universal; Harry Joe Brown) *SK* Frank Yaco-
nelli, *LL* Kathryn Crawford. **1930:** *Parade of the West* (Universal; Harry
Joe Brown) *SK* Frank Yaconelli, *LL* Gladys McConnell; *Lucky Larkin* (Uni-
versal; Harry Joe Brown) *LL* Nora Lane; *The Fighting Legion* (Universal;
Harry Joe Brown) *SK* Frank Rice, *LL* Dorothy Dwan; *Mountain Justice*
(Universal; Harry Joe Brown) *LL* Kathryn Crawford; *Song of the Caballero*
(Universal; Harry Joe Brown) *SK* Frank Rice, *LL* Doris Hill; *Sons of the
Saddle* (Universal; Harry Joe Brown) *SK* Frank Rice, *LL* Doris Hill; *Fighting
Thru* (Tiffany; William Nigh) *LL* Carmelita Geraghty. **1931:** *The Two Gun*

Man (Tiffany; Phil Rosen) *LL* Nita Martin, Lucille Powers; *Alias the Bad-man* (Tiffany; Phil Rosen) *LL* Virginia Brown Faire; *The Arizona Terror* (Tiffany; Phil Rosen) *LL* Lina Basquette, Nena Quartero; *Range Law* (Tiffany; Phil Rosen) *LL* Frances Dade; *Branded Men* (Tiffany; Phil Rosen) *LL* June Clyde; *The Pocatello Kid* (Tiffany; Phil Rosen) *LL* Marceline Day. **1932:** *The Sunset Trail* (Tiffany; B. Reeves Eason) *SK* Frank Rice, *LL* Ruth Hiatt; *Texas Gun Fighter* (Tiffany; Phil Rosen) *LL* Sheila Mannors; *Hell Fire Austin* (Tiffany; Forrest Sheldon) *LL* Ivy Merton; *Whistlin' Dan* (Tiffany; Phil Rosen) *LL* Joyzelle Joyner; *Dynamite Ranch* (World Wide; Forrest Sheldon) *LL* Ruth Hall; *Come on Tarzan* (World Wide; Alan James) *LL* Kate Campbell; *Between Fighting Men* (World Wide; Forrest Sheldon) *LL* Ruth Hall; *Tombstone Canyon* (World Wide; Forrest Sheldon) *LL* Cecilia Parker. **1933:** *Drum Taps* (World Wide; J.P. McGowan) *LL* Dorothy Dix; *The Phantom Thunderbolt* (World Wide; Alan James) *SK* Frank Rice, *LL* Frances Dade; *The Lone Avenger* (World Wide; Alan James) *LL* Muriel Gordon; *King of the Arena* (Universal; Alan James) *LL* Lucille Brown; *The Fiddlin' Buckaroo* (Universal; Ken Maynard) *SK* Frank Rice, *LL* Gloria Shea; *The Trail Drive* (Universal; Alan James) *SK* Frank Rice, *LL* Cecilia Parker; *Strawberry Roan* (Universal; Alan James) *SK* Frank Yaconelli, *LL* Ruth Hall; *Fargo Express* (World Wide; Alan James) *LL* Helen Mack; *Gun Justice* (Universal; Alan James) *LL* Cecilia Parker. **1934:** *Wheels of Destiny* (Universal; Alan James) *LL* Dorothy Dix; *Honor of the Range* (Universal; Alan James) *LL* Cecilia Parker; *Smoking Guns* (Universal; Alan James) *LL* Gloria Shea; *In Old Santa Fe* (Mascot; David Howard) *SK* Gene Autry, Smiley Burnette, *LL* Evelyn Knapp; *Mystery Mountain* (serial) (Mascot; B. Reeves Eason) *SK* Gene Autry, Smiley Burnette, *LL* Verna Hillie. **1935:** *Western Frontier* (Columbia; Al Herman) *LL* Lucille Brown, Nora Lane; *Western Courage* (Columbia; Spencer G. Bennett) *LL* Geneva Mitchell, Betty Blythe; *Lawless Riders* (Columbia; Spencer G. Bennett) *SK* Frank Yaconelli, *LL* Geneva Mitchell; *Heir to Trouble* (Columbia; Spencer G. Bennett) *LL* Joan Perry. **1936:** *The Cattle Thief* (Columbia; Spencer G. Bennett) *LL* Geneva Mitchell; *Avenging Waters* (Columbia; Spencer G. Bennett) *LL* Beth Marion; *Heroes of the Range* (Columbia; Spencer G. Bennett) *LL* June Gale; *The Fugitive Sheriff* (Columbia; Spencer G. Bennett) *LL* Beth Marion. **1937:** *Boots of Destiny* (Grand National; Arthur Rosson) *LL* Claudia Dell; *Trailing Trouble* (Grand National; Arthur Rosson) *LL* Lona Andre. **1938:** *Whirlwind Horseman* (Grand National; Bob Hill) *LL* Joan Barclay; *Six Shootin' Sheriff* (Grand National; Harry Fraser) *LL* Marjorie Reynolds. **1939:** *Flaming Lead* (Colony; Sam Newfield) *LL* Eleanor Stewart. **1940:** *Death Rides the Range* (Colony; Sam Newfield) *LL* Fay McKenzie; *Phantom Rancher* (Colony; Harry Fraser) *LL* Dorothy Short; *Lightning Strikes West* (Colony; Harry Fraser) *LL* Claire Rochelle. **1943:** *Wild Horse Stampede* (Monogram; Alan James) *SK* Trail Blazers, *LL* Betty Miles; *The*

Law Rides Again (Monogram; Alan James) *SK* Trail Blazers, *LL* Betty Miles; *Blazing Guns* (Monogram; Robert Tansey) *SK* Trail Blazers, *LL* Kay Forrester; *Death Valley Rangers* (Monogram; Robert Tansey) *SK* Trail Blazers, *LL* Linda Brent. **1944:** *Westward Bound* (Monogram; Robert Tansey) *SK* Trail Blazers, *LL* Betty Miles; *Arizona Whirlwind* (Monogram; Robert Tansey) *SK* Trail Blazers, *LL* Myrna Dell; **1947:** (made in 1944) *Harmony Trail* aka *White Stallion* (Astor; Robert Tansey) *SK* Eddie Dean, Max Terhune, *LL* Ruth Roman.

Kermit Maynard

Horse: Rocky

Kermit Maynard was the younger brother of Ken Maynard. He was born on September 20, 1897, in Indiana and attended Indiana University, where he studied law for a while. He developed into an excellent horseman and athlete. He played halfback for Indiana and joined a semipro basketball team.

Kermit was working for Hormel Meat Packing Company when his brother called him to Hollywood and got him a job as a stuntman at First National Studios. He also got bit parts in films. He began using the name "Tex" Maynard and in 1927 signed to do a series of Westerns with Rayart.

When the sound era came in, Kermit found himself once again doubling for the likes of Tom Tyler, Rex Bell, George O'Brien and his brother Ken. After several featured parts in Westerns, Kermit signed to do a series of films with Maurice Conn's Ambassador Pictures. The films were to be Northwest Mounted Police adventures based on the writings of James Oliver Curwood. They began with *The Fighting Trooper* in 1934 and ended 17 films later in 1937. Halfway through the series the Mountie aspects was dropped, and the remainder of the series were straight Westerns.

When the series ended, Kermit Maynard became a top stuntman and featured player (usually a villain) in scores of B Westerns. He retired from stunt work in 1958 to work with the Screen Extras Guild.

Kermit Maynard passed away on January 16, 1971.

Kermit Maynard Filmography

1934: *The Fighting Trooper* (Ambassador; Ray Taylor) *LL* Barbara Worth. **1935:** *Northern Frontier* (Ambassador; Sam Newfield) *LL* Eleanor Hunt;

Kermit Maynard and Rocky.

Wilderness Mail (Ambassador; Forrest Sheldon) *SK* Syd Saylor, *LL* Doris Brook; *Code of the Mounted* (Ambassador; Sam Newfield) *LL* Lillian Miles; *The Red Blood of Courage* (Ambassador; Jack English) *LL* Ann Sheridan; *Trails of the Wild* (Ambassador; Sam Newfield) *SK* Fuzzy Knight, *LL* Billie Seward; *His Fighting Blood* (Ambassador; John English) *LL* Polly Ann Young; *Timber War* (Ambassador; Sam Newfield) *LL* Lucille Lund. **1936:** *Song of the Trail* (Ambassador; Russell Hopton) *SK* Fuzzy Knight, *LL* Evelyn Brent, Antoinette Lees; *Wildcat Trooper* (Ambassador; Elmer Clifton) *SK* Fuzzy Knight, *LL* Lois Wilde; *Phantom Patrol* (Ambassador; Charles Hutchinson) *LL* Joan Barclay. **1937:** *Valley of Terror* (Ambassador; Al Herman) *LL* Harley Wood; *Whistling Bullets* (Ambassador; John English) *LL* Harley Wood; *The Fighting Texan* (Ambassador; Charles Abbott) *LL* Elaine Shepard; *Galloping Dynamite* (Ambassador; Harry Fraser) *LL* Ariane Allen; *Rough Ridin' Rhythm* (Ambassador; J.P.

Ray Middleton

McGowan) *LL* Beryl Wallace, Betty Mack; *Roaring Six Guns* (Ambassador; J.P. McGowan) *LL* Mary Hayes.

Ray Middleton

If the *Guinness Book of World Records* had a category for shortest career of a movie cowboy, Ray Middleton would be the record holder.

Middleton was Republic's contract player who had appeared in such films as *Gangs of Chicago* when the studio's movers and shakers decided to build him into a cowboy hero.

In 1941 on the heels of co-starring roles in two John Wayne vehicles, *Lady from Louisiana* and *Lady for a Night*, Republic starred Middleton in his first, last and only B Western—*Hurricane Smith.* As they say in the business: they ran Ray Middleton up the cowboy flagpole and nobody saluted.

Middleton remained under contract to Republic until the 1950s. He starred in *I Dream of Jeannie* (1952), Republic's production of the Stephen Foster story.

Ray Middleton Filmography

1941: *Hurricane Smith* (Republic; Bernard Vorhaus) *LL* Jane Wyatt.

Tom Mix

Horses: Tony, Tony Jr.

Tom Mix is a movie legend; his name is uttered in the same breath with those of Rudolph Valentino, Greta Garbo, Marilyn Monroe and Humphrey Bogart. He is the granddaddy of every Western hero that was or is. Mix wasn't the first cinema cowboy, but he was the first to make it to superstardom, capturing the fancy of the world in the process and, in short, laying the groundwork pattern for all who followed.

At the height of his career in the mid-twenties, Mix lived in a mansion, owned a fleet of Rolls Royces and commanded $20,000 a week from Fox Studios.

Thomas Edwin Mix was born January 6, 1881, in Mix Run, Pennsylvania. His family had a military background, and Tom studied at the Virginia Military Institute. He enlisted to fight in the Spanish-American War and was wounded in battle while in Cuba. He also served in the Philippines and in China during the Boxer Rebellion. After his discharge, he trained horses for the British during the Anglo-Boer War in South Africa.

In 1902 he was made sheriff of Sequatchie County, Tennessee, subsequently becoming a federal marshal and at one point joining the Texas Rangers.

In 1909 Mix became the livestock foreman at the famous Miller 101 Ranch in Oklahoma and began competing in rodeos.

That same year he won the National Riding Championship in Prescott, Arizona. He repeated this honor in 1911.

His first movie appearance was in William Selig's *Ranch Life in the*

Tom Mix and Tony, Jr.

Great Southwest in 1910. He made one- and two-reel films for Selig for the next seven years, making about $150 a week. Fox Studios offered Mix more money, and in 1918 he signed a long-term contract.

Mix, who did his own stunt work, is credited with developing the action Western of the time, a format that would be the prototype for the B Western.

The fan reaction to his films was so great that by 1921 he had replaced William S. Hart as the top movie cowboy and had a fan club that numbered two million.

Tom Mix (left) in a scene from My Pal the King, *1932.*

Mix spent a decade at Fox before leaving for F.B.O. There he made a series of films that, while nontalking, did feature sound effects.

In 1929 Tom Mix and Tony retired from the screen to star in the gigantic Sells and Floto Circus and Wild West Show.

In 1932 Universal Pictures offered Tom the sum of $10,000 a week to make a Western series. He made nine fetures for Universal beginning with *Destry Rides Again.*

Mix retired from the screen again in 1934. This time he bought a circus and renamed it the Tom Mix Circus.

In 1935 Tom made his last screen appearance in the Mascot serial *The Miracle Rider.*

In 1938 Tom merged his circus with his former employers', Sells and Floto.

On October 12, 1940, after completing a performance in Tucson, Arizona, Tom Mix was killed in a car crash on U.S. Highway 80. He was buried in Hollywood's Forrest Lawn Cemetery.

Mix was married five times, and his daugher Ruth was a leading lady in several B Westerns of the early thirties.

Tom actually had three movie horses . . . Old Blue in the early 1900s, Tony during his glory days, and Tony Jr. in his years at Universal.

Tom Mix Filmography

1932: *Destry Rides Again* (Universal; Alan James, Ben Stoloff) *SK* Tony, *LL* Claudia Dell; *Riders of Death Valley* (Universal; Albert Rogell) *SK* Tony, *LL* Lois Wilson; *My Pal, the King* (Universal; Kurt Neumann) *SK* Tony, *LL* Noel Francis; *The Texas Badman* (Universal; Edward Laemmle) *SK* Tony Jr., *LL* Lucille Powers. **1933:** *The Fourth Horseman* (Universal; Hamilton McFadden) *SK* Tony Jr., *LL* Margaret Lindsay; *Terror Trail* (Universal; Armand Schaeffer) *SK* Tony Jr., *LL* Naomi Judge; *Hidden Gold* (Universal; Arthur Rosson) *SK* Tony Jr., *LL* Judith Barry; *Flaming Guns* (Universal; Arthur Rosson) *SK* Tony Jr., *LL* Ruth Hall; *The Rustlers Roundup* (Universal; Henry McRae) *SK* Tony Jr., *LL* Diane Sinclair. **1935:** *The Miracle Rider* (serial) (Mascot; B. Reeves Eason, Armand Schaeffer) *SK* Tony Jr., *LL* Joan Gale.

Dennis Moore

Dennis Moore was born Dennis Meadows in Fort Worth, Texas, on January 26, 1908. He worked as a commercial airline pilot before turning to films in the early 1930s.

One of his early screen appearances was in the 1935 John Wayne B Western *The Dawn Rider*. Over the next few years his parts consisted of mostly assorted villains and gangsters.

In late 1941 and 1942 he appeared in several of George Houston's Lone Rider films at PRC, his role evolving into that of a semi-sidekick to Houston and Fuzzy St. John. He also had a part in Buck Jones's final film, *Dawn on the Great Divide*.

In 1943 Monogram drafted Moore to fill the void created when Dusty King departed the Range Busters series. Moore appeared in the final four films of the series.

Moore made his greatest screen contribution in the genre of the action chapter play. He was featured in such serials as *The Purple Monster Strikes* (1945), *The Master Key* (1945) and *Blazing the Overland Trail* (1956).

Dennis Moore

He is also remembered as the villain in Lash LaRue's classic "B," *King of the Bull Whip.*

Dennis Moore passed away on March 1, 1964.

Dennis Moore Filmography

1943: *Land of Hunted Men* (Monogram; S. Roy Luby) *SK* Range Busters, *LL* Phyllis Adair; *Cowboy Commandos* (Monogram; S. Roy Luby) *SK*

Range Busters, *LL* Evelyn Finley; *Black Market Rustlers* (Monogram; S. Roy Luby) *SK* Range Busters, *LL* Evelyn Finley; *Bullets and Saddles* (Monogram; Anthony Marshall) *SK* Range Busters, *LL* Julie Duncan.

Wayne Morris

Most film historians consider the release of Wayne Morris's 1954 film *Two Guns and a Badge* as the official end of the B Western era. At that time all of the major B series films had ceased production and the major stars were either dead, retired or, in the case of Roy Rogers and Gene Autry, working in the medium of television.

Morris had begun his film series for Monogram/Allied Artists in 1951 with *Sierra Passage*. The series consisted of eight films.

Morris was born Bertram DeWayne Morris on February 17, 1914, in Los Angeles and made his film debut in the 1936 film *China Clipper*.

His first major film part was as the title character in *Kid Galahad* (Warner Bros., 1937), a boxing epic which starred Edward G. Robinson and Humphrey Bogart. As a Warner Bros. contract player he appeared in A Westerns like *Badmen of Missouri* and *Valley of the Giants*, and he starred in the highly-acclaimed *Brother Rat*.

When World War II came along, Morris departed Hollywood to serve in the navy as a pilot and flew nearly 60 combat missions.

He returned to the screen in 1947 but was relegated to parts in B pictures.

Morris continued to work in films until his death due to a heart attack on September 14, 1959.

Wayne Morris Filmography

1951: *Sierra Passage* (Monogram; Frank McDonald) *LL* Lola Albright. **1952:** *Desert Pursuit* (Monogram; George Blair) *LL* Virginia Grey. **1953:** *Star of Texas* (Allied Artists; Thomas Carr); *The Marksman* (Allied Artists; Lewis Collins) *LL* Elena Verdugo; *The Fighting Lawman* (Allied Artists; Thomas Carr) *LL* Virginia Grey; *Texas Badman* (Allied Artists; Lewis Collins) *LL* Elaine Riley. **1954:** *The Desperado* (Allied Artists; Thomas Carr) *LL* Beverly Garland; *Two Guns and a Badge* (Allied Artists; Lewis Collins) *LL* Beverly Garland.

Wayne Morris (left), Beverly Garland and Roy Barcroft in a scene from Two Guns and a Badge *(Allied Artists, 1954).*

James Newill

Sidekicks: Dave O'Brien, Guy Wilkerson

James Newill starred in the *Renfrew of the Royal Mounted* series released by Grand National and Monogram between 1937 and 1940. Only two of the eight films were released by Grand National who initiated the series; the remainder by Monogram when Grand National went bankrupt.

Newill was born in Pittsburgh, Pennslvania, on August 12, 1911. He majored in music at the University of Southern California and entered vaudeville as a singer.

In 1936 he was discovered by a movie talent scout and the following year made his screen debut in James Cagney's *Something to Sing About.*

He was working as a radio singer when he signed with Grand National to do the films based on the popular Renfrew radio series. The first film, *Renfrew of the Royal Mounted,* was released in December 1937.

James Newill in Murder on the Yukon *(Monogram, 1940), one of the films in the* Renfrew of the Royal Mounted *series.*

When the Renfrews ended, Newill went to PRC to make the Texas Rangers series, which starred his old Mountie sidekick Dave O'Brien.

Along with Guy Wilkerson, Newill and O'Brien made 14 Ranger films until PRC replaced Newill with Tex Ritter for the duration of the series.

In 1945 he retired from films and returned to his musical career.

In the early 1950s Newill made 13 half-hour Renfrew adventures for TV.

James Newill Filmography

1937: *Renfrew of the Royal Mounted* (Grand National; Al Herman) *LL* Carol Hughes. **1938:** *On the Great White Trail* (Grand National; Al Herman) *LL* Terry Walker. **1939:** *Crashing Thru* (Monogram; Elmer Clifton)

LL Jean Carmen; *Fighting Mad* (Monogram; Sam Newfield) *SK* Dave O'Brien, *LL* Sally Blane; *Yukon Flight* (Monogram; Ralph Staub) *SK* Dave O'Brien, *LL* Louise Stanley. **1940:** *Danger Ahead* (Monogram; Ralph Staub) *SK* Dave O'Brien, *LL* Dorothea Kent; *Murder on the Yukon* (Monogram; Louis Gasnier) *SK* Dave O'Brien, *LL* Polly Ann Young; *Sky Bandits* (Monogram; Ralph Staub) *SK* Dave O'Brien, *LL* Louise Stanley. **1942:** *The Rangers Take Over* (Texas Rangers) (PRC; Al Herman) *SK* Dave O'Brien, Guy Wilkerson, *LL* Iris Meredith. **1943:** *Bad Men of Thunder Gap* (PRC; Al Herman) *SK* Dave O'Brien, Guy Wilkerson, *LL* Janet Shaw; *West of Texas (Shootin' Irons)* (PRC; Oliver Drake) *SK* Dave O'Brien, Guy Wilkerson, *LL* Frances Gladwin; *Border Buckaroos* (PRC; Oliver Drake) *SK* Dave O'Brien, Guy Wilkerson, *LL* Christine McIntyre; *Fighting Valley* (PRC; Oliver Drake) *SK* Dave O'Brien, Guy Wilkerson, *LL* Patti McCarty; *Trail of Terror* (PRC; Oliver Drake) *SK* Dave O'Brien, Guy Wilkerson, *LL* Patricia Knox; *Return of the Rangers* (PRC; Elmer Clifton) *SK* Dave O'Brien, Guy Wilkerson, *LL* Nell O'Day; *Boss of Rawhide* (PRC; Elmer Clifton) *SK* Dave O'Brien, Guy Wilkerson, *LL* Nell O'Day. **1944:** *Gunsmoke Mesa* (PRC; Harry Fraser) *SK* Dave O'Brien, Guy Wilkerson, *LL* Patti McCarty; *Outlaw Roundup* (PRC; Harry Fraser) *SK* Dave O'Brien, Guy Wilkerson, *LL* Helen Chapman; *Guns of the Law* (PRC; Elmer Clifton) *SK* Dave O'Brien, Guy Wilkerson; *The Pinto Bandit* (PRC; Elmer Clifton) *SK* Dave O'Brien, Guy Wilkerson, *LL* Mady Lawrence; *Spook Town* (PRC; Elmer Clifton) *SK* Dave O'Brien, Guy Wilkerson, *LL* Mady Lawrence; *Brand of the Devil* (PRC; Harry Fraser) *SK* Dave O'Brien, Guy Wilkerson, *LL* Ellen Hall.

Dave "Tex" O'Brien

Dave O'Brien was James Newill's sidekick in the Renfrew adventure series and then graduated to star of the Texas Ranger Westerns with Newill, Tex Ritter, and Guy Wilkerson.

O'Brien was born in Big Spring, Texas, on May 13, 1912.

He debuted in 1933's *Jennie Gerhart* (Paramount) which starred Sylvia Sidney. He evolved as a bit player and a stunt double before securing a lead part in the 1936 serial *Black Coin.*

He did the Renfrew series from 1937 to 1940, and the first Ranger film was released in 1942. He did 22 of the series for PRC before they ceased in 1945.

Near the end of the Texas Ranger films, Dave signed with MGM to star in the Pete Smith Specialties short-film series. In the more than 70 Smith films he made, O'Brien was often a writer and director as well as star.

Dave "Tex" O'Brien

Dave later became a writer for the Red Skelton TV and radio shows.

He passed away on November 18, 1969.

Dave "Tex" O'Brien Filmography

1937: *Renfrew of the Royal Mounted* (series: 8 films) (Grand National; Albert Herman) *SK* James Newill, *LL* Carol Hughes. **1938:** *On the Great White Trail* (Grand National; Albert Herman) *SK* James Newill. **1939:** *Crashing Thru* (Grand National; Elmer Clifton) *SK* James Newill, *LL* Jean Carmen; *Water Rustlers* (Singing Cowgirl Series) (Grand National; Samuel Diege) *SK* Dorothy Page; *Ride 'em Cowgirl* (Grand National; Samuel Diege) *SK* Dorothy Page; *The Singing Cowgirl* (Grand National; Samuel Diege) *SK* Dorothy Page; *Fighting Mad* (Renfrew series cont.) (Monogram; Sam Newfield) *SK* James Newill, *LL* Sally Blane; *Yukon Flight* (Monogram; Ralph Staub) *SK* James Newill, *LL* Louise Stanley. **1940:** *Danger Ahead* (Monogram; Ralph Staub) *SK* James Newill, *LL* Dorothea Kent, Maude Allen; *Murder on the Yukon* (Monogram; Louis Gasnier) *SK* James Newill, *LL* Polly Ann Young; *Sky Bandits* (Monogram; Ralph Staub) *SK* James Newill, *LL* Louise Stanley. **1942:** *The Rangers Take Over* (series: 22 films) (PRC; Albert Herman) *SK* Texas Rangers, *LL* Iris Meredith. **1943:** *Bad Men of Thunder Gap* (PRC; Albert Herman) *SK* Texas Rangers, *LL* Janet Shaw, Lucille Vance; *West of Texas* (aka *Shootin' Irons*) (PRC; Oliver Drake) *SK* Texas Rangers, *LL* Frances Gladwin, Marilyn Hare; *Border Buckaroos* (PRC; Oliver Drake) *SK* Texas Rangers, *LL* Christine McIntyre, Eleanor Counts; *Fighting Valley* (PRC; Oliver Drake) *SK* Texas Rangers, *LL* Patti McCarty, Mary MacLaren; *Trail of Terror* (PRC; Oliver Drake) *SK* Texas Rangers, *LL* Patricia Knox, Rose Plummer; *Return of the Rangers* (PRC; Elmer Clifton) *SK* Texas Rangers, *LL* Nell O'Day; *Boss of Rawhide* (PRC; Elmer Clifton) *SK* Texas Rangers, *LL* Nell O'Day, Lucille Vance. **1944:** *Gunsmoke Mesa* (PRC; Harry Fraser) *SK* Texas Rangers, *LL* Patti McCarty; *Outlaw Roundup* (PRC; Harry Fraser) *SK* Texas Rangers, *LL* Helen Chapman; *Guns of the Law* (PRC; Elmer Clifton) *SK* Texas Rangers; *The Pinto Bandit* (PRC; Elmer Clifton) *SK* Texas Rangers, *LL* Mady Lawrence; *Spook Town* (PRC; Elmer Clifton) *SK* Texas Rangers, *LL* Mady Lawrence; *Brand of the Devil* (PRC; Elmer Clifton) *SK* Texas Rangers, *LL* Ellen Hall; *Gangsters of the Frontier* (PRC; Elmer Clifton) *SK* Texas Rangers, *LL* Patti McCarty; *Dead or Alive* (PRC; Harry Fraser) *SK* Texas Rangers, *LL* Marjorie Clements; *The Whispering Skull* (PRC; Harry Fraser) *SK* Texas Rangers. **1945:** *Marked for Murder* (PRC; Elmer Clifton) *SK* Texas Rangers, *LL* Marilyn McConnell; *Enemy of the Law* (PRC; Harry Fraser) *SK* Texas Rangers, *LL* Kay Hughes; *Three in the Saddle* (PRC;

Elmer Clifton) *SK* Texas Rangers, *LL* Lorraine Miller; *Frontier Fugitives* (PRC; Elmer Clifton) *SK* Texas Rangers, *LL* Lorraine Miller; *Flaming Bullets* (PRC; Harry Fraser) *SK* Texas Rangers, *LL* Patricia Knox.

George O'Brien

Horse: Mike
Sidekicks: Chill Wills, Syd Saylor, Ray Whitley

George O'Brien was one of the few Western stars that did all of his own riding and stunt work; horsefalls, horse to stagecoach transfers and the age-old bulldoggin' the bad guy outa the saddle and over a cliff were all right up George's alley. In the decade between 1930 and 1940, O'Brien starred in 40 B Westerns for Fox and RKO studios.

O'Brien was born in San Francisco on April 19, 1900. He developed into a superior athlete in high school and excelled in boxing and baseball. While in the navy during World War I, O'Brien won the U.S. Naval Light Heavyweight Boxing Championship.

Upon his discharge, he entered the Premed program at Santa Clara State College where he took up dramatics as an extracurricular activity.

In 1922 he met Tom Mix when his father, a policeman, was assigned to escort Mix around the Bay City. Mix got the young man a job at Fox as an assistant cameraman, and after a few bit parts O'Brien was one of over 60 actors who auditioned for the lead role in John Ford's 1924 production of *The Iron Horse*. Ford selected the unknown O'Brien and gave him a contract for $125 a week.

During the silent era he also starred in such first-rate films as *Sunrise* (1927) and *Noah's Ark* (1929).

When the talkies arrived, O'Brien became a Western star. His first "B" was *The Lone Star Ranger* made in 1930. He remained with Fox until 1935 before signing with RKO.

His initial film for RKO was one of his best, the lively action saga *Daniel Boone.*

From 1938 to 1939 he made films with Ray Whitley and Chill Wills as his sidekicks. During that period he ranked number four on the top ten cowboys list.

When World War II broke out George reenlisted in the navy and saw action in the Pacific. He returned to Hollywood in 1946 but was relegated to character parts for the next few years. He appeared with John Wayne in

George O'Brien

Fort Apache and *She Wore a Yellow Ribbon* and starred with the Three Stooges in *Gold Raiders* in 1951.

He retired from the screen in the early fifties to produce films for the U.S. military.

In 1964 he returned to the screen for a part in *Cheyenne Autumn*.

George O'Brien Filmography

1930: *The Lone Star Ranger* (Fox; A.F. Erickson) *LL* Sue Carol, Elizabeth Patterson; *Rough Romance* (Fox; A.F. Erickson) *LL* Helen Chandler; *Last of the Duanes* (Fox; Alfred L. Werker) *LL* Lucille Brown, Myrna Loy. **1931:** *Fair Warning* (Fox; Alfred L. Werker) *LL* Louise Huntington; *A Holy Terror* (Fox; Irving Cummings) *LL* Sally Eilers, Rita LaFoy; *Riders of the Purple Sage* (Fox; Hamilton McFadden) *LL* Marguerite Churchill, Yvonne Pelletier. **1932:** *Rainbow Trail* (Fox; David Howard) *SK* Roscoe Ates, *LL* Cecilia Parker; *The Gay Caballero* (Fox; Alfred Werker) *LL* Cecilia Parker; *Mystery Ranch* (Fox; David Howard) *LL* Cecilia Parker; *The Golden West* (Fox; David Howard) *LL* Janet Chandler, Marion Burns. **1933:** *Robbers Roost* (Fox; David Howard) *LL* Maureen O'Sullivan; *Smoke Lightning* (Fox; David Howard) *LL* Virginia Sale, Nell O'Day, Betsy King Ross; *Life in the Raw* (Fox; Louis King) *LL* Claire Trevor; *The Last Trail* (Fox; James Tinling) *SK* El Brendel, *LL* Claire Trevor, Lucille Laverne. **1934:** *Frontier Marshall* (Fox; Lewis Seiler) *LL* Irene Bentley; *The Dude Ranger* (Fox; Edward Cline) *SK* Syd Saylor, *LL* Irene Hervey. **1935:** *When a Man's a Man* (Fox; Edward Cline) *LL* Dorothy Wilson; *The Cowboy Millionaire* (Fox; Edward Cline) *SK* Edgar Kennedy, *LL* Evelyn Bostock; *Thunder Mountain* (Fox; David Howard) *LL* Barbara Fritchie, Frances Grant. **1936:** *O'Malley of the Mounted* (20th Century–Fox; David Howard) *LL* Irene Ware; *The Border Patrolman* (Fox; David Howard) *LL* Polly Ann Young, Mary Doran; *Daniel Boone* (RKO; David Howard) *LL* Heather Angel. **1937:** *Park Avenue Logger* (RKO; David Howard) *LL* Beatrice Roberts; *Hollywood Cowboy* (RKO; Ewing Scott) *LL* Cecilia Parker. **1938:** *Gun Law* (RKO; David Howard) *SK* Ray Whitley, *LL* Rita Oehmen; *Border G-Man* (RKO; David Howard) *SK* Ray Whitley, *LL* Lorraine Johnson (Day); *The Painted Desert* (RKO; David Howard) *SK* Ray Whitley, *LL* Lorraine Johnson (Day); *The Renegade Ranger* (RKO; David Howard) *SK* Tim Holt, Ray Whitley, *LL* Rita Hayworth; *Lawless Valley* (RKO; David Howard) *SK* Chill Wills, *LL* Kay Sutton. **1939:** *Arizona Legion* (RKO; David Howard) *SK* Chill Wills, *LL* Lorraine Johnson (Day); *Trouble in Sundown* (RKO; David Howard) *SK* Chill Wills, Ray Whitley, *LL* Rosiland Keith; *Racketeers of the Range* (RKO; D. Ross Lederman) *SK* Chill Wills, *LL* Marjorie Reynolds; *Timber Stampede* (RKO; David Howard) *SK* Chill

Wills, *LL* Marjorie Reynolds; *Marshal of Mesa City* (RKO; David Howard) *LL* Virginia Vale; *The Fighting Gringo* (RKO; David Howard) *LL* Lupita Tovar. **1940:** *Legion of the Lawless* (RKO; David Howard) *LL* Virginia Vale; *Bullet Code* (RKO; David Howard) *LL* Virginia Vale; *Prairie Law* (RKO; David Howard) *LL* Virginia Vale; *Stage to Chino* (RKO; Edward Kelly) *LL* Virginia Vale; *Triple Justice* (RKO; David Howard) *LL* Virginia Vale. **1951:** *Gold Raiders* (United Artists; Edward Bernds) *SK* Three Stooges, *LL* Sheila Ryan.

Dorothy Page
"The Singing Cowgirl"

Radio performer Dorothy Page holds the distinction of being the only cowgirl to ever star in her own B Western series.

The "singing cowgirl" series consisted of a trio of films released in 1939 by about-to-go-bankrupt Grand National Pictures. She was given a comic sidekick in Vince Barnett and a romantic interest/sidekick in B Western regular Dave O'Brien, who handled all the action sequences in the pictures. Because of their horrid financial straits, Grand National never survived 1939, and the series died with the studio.

Dorothy Page first came into prominence in the early thirties as a country singer on an NBC radio show called *The Paducah Plantation*. By 1935 she had her own weekly show on the network and had broken into the movies by appearing in such B musicals as *King Solomon on Broadway*.

When the cowgirl series ended, Ms. Page found little film work and returned to the radio.

Dorothy Page Filmography

1939: *Water Rustlers* (Grand National; Samuel Diege) *SK* Dave O'Brien, Vince Barnett; *Ride 'em Cowgirl* (Grand National; Samuel Diege) *SK* Dave O'Brien, Vince Barnett; *The Singing Cowgirl* (Grand National; Samuel Diege) *SK* Vince Barnett, Dave O'Brien, *LL* Dorothy Short.

Dorothy Page in a scene from Ride 'Em Cowgirl, *one of three films in her singing cowgirl series for Grand National Pictures.*

Jack Perrin

Horse: Starlight the Wonder Horse
Sidekicks: Ben Corbett, Brave Heart (a dog)

Jack Perrin began his film career with small parts in the famous Mack Sennett comedies of the early 1900s.

He evolved into one of the silent screen's top serial stars during the 1920s. Among his best chapter plays were *The Lion Man* in 1919, *The Vanishing West* in 1928 and *The Jade Box*, the first serial to be released in both silent and sound versions. In between serials he made dozens of Westerns and adventure films.

His most outstanding contribution to B Westerns was a series of features and shorts he made with Ben Corbett in the early thirties called the Bud 'n' Ben Westerns. The Bud 'n' Ben films were released by Reliable Pictures.

Jack Perrin

He also made pictures for a number of Poverty Row outfits including Rayton, Big 4, Syndicate, Cosmos and Atlantic. His longest series were four films for Cosmos in 1931 and a like number for Atlantic in 1936.

Perrin was born on July 26, 1896, in Three Rivers, Michigan, and while still a child, moved to southern California with his family.

He got his first featured part in the 1917 film *Toton the Apache.*

At the completion of the Atlantic film series, he made appearances in several B Westerns in supporting roles before retiring in the early forties.

Jack Perrin Filmography

1929: *Overland Bound* (Rayton; Leo Maloney) *SK* Wally Wales, *LL* Allene Ray. **1930:** *Beyond the Rio Grande* (Big 4; Harry Webb) *SK* Buffalo Bill, Jr., *LL* Charlene Burt; *Ridin' Law* (Big 4; Harry Webb) *LL* Rene Borden; *Phantom of the Desert* (Syndicate; Harry Webb) *LL* Eva Novak; *The Apache Kid's Escape* (Robert J. Horner Prod.; Robert J. Horner) *LL* Josephine Hill. **1931:** *Wild West Whoopee* (Cosmos; Robert J. Horner) *SK* Buzz Barton, *LL* Josephine Hill; *The Kid from Arizona* (Cosmos; Robert J. Horner) *LL* Josephine Hill; *The Sheriff's Secret* (Cosmos; James Hogan) *LL* Dorothy Bauer; *Lariats and Sixshooters* (Cosmos; Alvin J. Neitz [Alan James]) *LL* Ann Lee, Virginia Bell. **1932:** *Forty-five Calibre Echo* (Horner Prod.; Bruce Mitchell) *SK* Ben Corbett, *LL* Eleanor Fair. **1933:** *Girl Trouble* (series) (Reliable; Bernard B. Ray) *SK* Ben Corbett, *LL* Lola Tate, Mary Draper. **1934:** *Arizona Nights* (Reliable; Bernard B. Ray) *SK* Ben Corbett; *Rawhide Mail* (Reliable; Bernard B. Ray) *LL* Lillian Gilmore; *Rainbow Riders* (Reliable; Bennett Cohen) *SK* Bud 'n' Ben, *LL* Virginia Browne Faire; *Ridin' Gents* (Reliable/Astor; Bennett Cohen) *SK* Ben Corbett, *LL* Doris Hill; *The Cactus Kid* (Reliable; Harry Webb) *LL* Jayne Regan; *Loser's End* (Reliable; Bernard B. Ray) *LL* Tina Menard. **1935:** *North of Arizona* (Reliable; Harry S. Webb) *LL* Blanche Mehaffey; *Texas Jack* (Reliable; Bernard B. Ray) *LL* Jayne Regan; *Wolf Riders* (Reliable; Harry Webb) *LL* Lillian Gilmore, Nancy Deshon. **1936:** *Gun Grit* (Atlantic; Lester Williams [William Berke]) *SK* Brave Heart, *LL* Ethel Beck; *Hair Trigger Casey* (Atlantic; Harry Fraser) *LL* Betty Mack; *Desert Justice* (Atlantic; Lester Williams) *SK* Brave Heart, *LL* Mary Ann Downing; *Wildcat Saunders* (Atlantic; Harry Fraser) *LL* Blanche Mehaffey.

Lee Powell

Lee Powell was the first actor to portray the Lone Ranger on the silver screen. He did this in the highly successful Republic serial, *The Lone Ranger,* in 1938.

As far as B Westerns are concerned, Powell was never a headliner; he was always sort of a "Lucky Jenkins"–type sidekick, somewhere between the main hero and the comedy relief.

In 1939 he starred with crooner Art Jarrett and Fuzzy St. John in *Trigger Pals* for Grand National. This originally was to be the first of a series of films but Grand National's faulty financial condition turned it into a one-shot.

In 1942 he made a half dozen films at PRC with Bill "Cowboy Rambler" Boyd as the main lead.

In mid-1942 Powell joined the U.S. Marines and saw action in the Pacific. On July 20, 1944, Lee Powell was killed in action. He was 35 years old.

Lee Powell Filmography

1938: *The Lone Ranger* (serial) (Republic; William Witney, John English) *SK* Chief Thundercloud, *LL* Lynn Roberts. **1939:** *Trigger Pals* (Grand National; Sam Newfield) *SK* Art Jarrett, *LL* Dorothy Fay. **1942:** *Texas Manhunt* (PRC; Peter Stewart) *SK* Bill "Cowboy Rambler" Boyd, *LL* Julie Duncan; *Raiders of the West* (PRC; Peter Stewart) *SK* Bill "Cowboy Rambler" Boyd, *LL* Virginia Carroll; *Rolling Down the Great Divide* (PRC; Peter Stewart) *SK* Bill "Cowboy Rambler" Boyd, *LL* Wanda McKay; *Tumbleweed Trail* (PRC; Peter Stewart) *SK* Bill "Cowboy Rambler" Boyd, *LL* Marjorie Manners; *Prairie Pals* (PRC; Peter Stewart) *SK* Bill "Cowboy Rambler" Boyd, *LL* Esther Estrella; *Along the Sundown Trail* (PRC; Peter Stewart) *SK* Bill "Cowboy Rambler" Boyd, *LL* Julie Duncan.

John Preston

In 1935 veteran B Western writer/director Robert Emmett Tansey created, wrote, produced and directed a two-film series of "North" Westerns which featured a character called Morton of the Mounties and his four-legged compadres Dynamite, the Wonder Horse and Captain (King of the Dogs).

He chose a little-known actor, John Preston, to play the title role. Following the films, Preston once again ventured into anonymity.

Lee Powell in the title role of Republic's popular serial The Lone Ranger *(1938). Chief Thundercloud played the sidekick role.*

John Preston Filmography

1935: *Courage of the North* (Stage & Screen; Robert Emmett Tansey) *SK* Dynamite, the Wonder Horse, Captain (King of the Dogs), *LL* June Love; *Timber Terrors* (Stage & Screen; Robert Emmett Tansey) *SK* Dynamite, the Wonder Horse, Captain (King of the Dogs), *LL* Marla Bratton.

Jack Randall

Sidekicks: Frank Yaconelli, Fuzzy St. John

Cowboy heroes and their guns have always been a subject of interest to movie fans. There is of course the age-old joke of endlessly firing 20 and 30 shooters that never had to be reloaded, but over the years movie Western weapons ran the full gamut of gimmickry. Some heroes carried one gun, some two; Bill Elliott carried his backwards in his holster, the Lone Ranger used silver bullets. On TV there was the Rifleman's rapid-fire Winchester, Josh Randall's mare's leg on *Wanted Dead or Alive* and Johnny Ringo's .45 that fired a shotgun blast. But in his 1939 Monogram release *Trigger Smith*, Jack Randall carried two of moviedom's most unique .45s. They were triggerless and could be fired only by fanning the hammer.

Randall was the brother of fellow cowboy star Bob Livingston and made 22 features for Monogram between 1937 and 1940.

Randall was a capable vocalist and actor, but he was also an outstanding stuntman, and his films reflected his daredevil ability.

He was born Addison Randall in San Fernando, California, on May 12, 1906, and began in show business as a vocalist in vaudeville. He made his screen debut in 1934 but had only small parts until Monogram signed him in 1937.

His first feature film, *Riders of the Dawn* (1937), was directed by R.N. Bradberry, the father of Western star Bob Steele.

In 1942 he enlisted in the Army Air Corps and attained the rank of captain before his discharge in 1945.

Returning to film work and while filming a serial, *the Royal Mounted Rides Again*, Jack Randall suffered a fatal fall from a horse. He died July 16, 1945.

Jack Randall

Jack Randall Filmography

1937: *Riders of the Dawn* (Monogram; R.N. Bradbury) LL Peggy Keyes; *Stars Over Arizona* (Monogram; R.N. Bradbury) SK Horace Murphy, LL Kathleen Elliott; *Danger Valley* (Monogram; R.N. Bradbury) LL Lois Wilde. **1938:** *Where the West Begins* (Monogram; J.P. McGowan) SK Fuzzy Knight, LL Luana Walters; *Land of Fighting Men* (Monogram; Alan

James) *LL* Louise Stanley; *Gunsmoke Trail* (Monogram; Sam Newfield) *SK* Fuzzy St. John, *LL* Louise Stanley; *Man's Country* (Monogram; Robert Hill) *LL* Marjorie Reynolds; *Mexicali Kid* (Monogram; Wallace Fox) *LL* Eleanor Stewart; *Gun Packer* (Monogram; Wallace Fox) *LL* Louise Stanley; *Wild Horse Canyon* (Monogram; Robert Hill) *SK* Frank Yaconelli, *LL* Dorothy Short. **1939:** *Drifting Westward* (Monogram; Robert Hill) *SK* Frank Yaconelli, *LL* Edna Duran, Carmen Bailey; *Trigger Smith* (Monogram; Alan James) *SK* Frank Yaconelli, *LL* Joyce Bryant; *Across the Plains* (Monogram; Spencer Bennett) *SK* Frank Yaconelli, *LL* Joyce Bryant; *Oklahoma Terror* (Monogram; Spencer Bennett) *SK* Fuzzy St. John, *LL* Virginia Carroll; *Overland Mail* (Monogram; Robert Hill) *LL* Jean Joyce. **1940:** *Pioneer Days* (Monogram; Harry S. Webb) *SK* Frank Yaconelli, *LL* June Wilkins; *The Cheyenne Kid* (Monogram; Raymond K. Johnson) *SK* Frank Yaconelli, *LL* Louise Stanley; *Covered Wagon Trails* (Monogram; Raymond K. Johnson) *LL* Sally Cairns; Land of the Six Guns (Monogram; Raymond K. Johnson) *LL* Louise Stanley; *The Kid from Santa Fe* (Monogram; Raymond K. Johnson) *LL* Claire Rochelle, Clarene Curtis; *Riders from Nowhere* (Monogram; Raymond K. Johnson) *LL* Margaret Roach; *Wild Horse Range* (Monogram; Raymond K. Johnson) *SK* Frank Yaconelli, *LL* Phyllis Ruth.

Duncan Renaldo

Horse: Diablo
Sidekicks: Leo Carrillo, Martin Garralaga

Duncan Renaldo is best known as TV's "Robin Hood of the Old West—The Cisco Kid." Renaldo first portrayed the colorful character created by O. Henry in the 1945 Monogram release *The Cisco Kid Returns.*

The Cisco Kid film series had begun back in 1929 with Warner Baxter playing the lead. Baxter did three films, *In Old Arizona, The Cisco Kid* (1931), and *The Return of the Cisco Kid* (1939). These films were all released by Fox Studios. Later in 1939, Cesar Romero assumed the role for six films before Fox, now Twentieth Century–Fox, abandoned the series in 1941.

When Monogram began production on the Cisco series, they chose Renaldo for the lead.

Renaldo was born either in Spain, or Camden, New Jersey, in April 1904. He studied music in Europe and South America and appeared throughout Europe as a working musician and an artist.

Duncan Renaldo

In 1921 he was hired to design stage productions for the New York-based Metropolitan Opera Company. Soon, however, he turned to acting on the stage and became active in film production around New York City.

He was discovered by a movie talent scout in 1927 while appearing in a production of *Her Cardboard Lover,* and made his screen debut in the 1928 film *The Devil's Skipper.*

In 1930 he got a featured part in Harry Carey's adventure classic *Trader Horn.*

In the mid-1930s, in the midst of a flourishing film career, Renaldo had problems with the U.S. Immigration Service, who claimed he was in the country illegally.

When he cleared his citizenship problems up, he signed with Republic Pictures and became part of The Three Mesquiteers series, portraying Rico in seven films beginning with *The Kansas Terrors* in 1939.

Going to Monogram in 1945, he made three Cisco features before relinquishing the role to Gilbert Roland in 1946.

Three years later United Artists revived the Cisco series and once again Renaldo was Cisco with Leo Carrillo as Pancho. They made five films in 1949 and 1950.

In the early fifties production began on the popular Cisco Kid TV series with Renaldo and Carrillo, the last episodes being filmed in 1955. With the series in reruns, Renaldo made many personal appearances around the country as Cisco.

He died of a heart attack on September 30, 1980, in Golita, California.

Duncan Renaldo Filmography

1939: *The Kansas Terrors* (Republic; George Sherman) *SK* 3 Mesquiteers, *LL* Jacqueline Wells; *Cowboys from Texas* (Republic; George Sherman) *SK* 3 Mesquiteers, *LL* Carole Landis. **1940:** *Heroes of the Saddle* (Republic; William Witney) *SK* 3 Mesquiteers, *LL* Patsy Lee Parsons, Loretta Weaver; *Pioneers of the West* (Republic; Marcel Perez) *SK* 3 Mesquiteers, *LL* Dorothy Earle; *Covered Wagon Days* (Republic; George Sherman) *SK* 3 Mesquiteers, *LL* Kay Griffith; *Rocky Mountain Rangers* (Republic; George Sherman) *SK* 3 Mesquiteers, *LL* Rosella Towne; *Oklahoma Renegades* (Republic; Nate Watt) *SK* 3 Mesquiteers, *LL* Florine McKinney. **1945:** *The Cisco Kid Returns* (Monogram; John P. McCarthy) *SK* Martin Garralaga, *LL* Cecilia Callejo; *The Cisco Kid in Old Mexico* (Monogram; Phil Rosen) *SK* Martin Garralaga, *LL* Gwen Kenyon; *South of the Rio Grande* (Monogram; Lambert Hillyer) *SK* Martin Garralaga, *LL* Armida. **1949:** *The Valiant Hombre* (United Artists; Wallace Fox) *SK* Leo Carrillo, *LL* Barbara Billingsley; *The Gay Amigo* (United Artists; Wallace Fox) *SK* Leo Carrillo, *LL* Armida; *The Daring Caballero* (United Artists; Wallace Fox) *SK* Leo Carrillo, *LL* Kippee Valez; *Satan's Cradle* (United Artists; Ford Beebe) *SK* Leo Carrillo, *LL* Anne Savage. **1950:** *Girl from San Lorenzo* (United Artists; Derwin Abrahams) *SK* Leo Carrillo, *LL* Jane Adams.

Tex Ritter

Horse: White Flash
Sidekicks: Arkansas Slim Andrews, Horace Murphy, Hank Worden, Snub
  Pollard, Syd Saylor, Fuzzy Knight

Few, if any, Western film fans can ever forget Tex Ritter's voice echo-
ing "Do not forsake me oh my darling" in the background as Marshal Will
Kane (Gary Cooper) strode down that dusty street to face Frank Miller and
his gang of killers alone in the 1952 classic *High Noon.* The song and Ritter's
delivery of it were good enough to take an Oscar that year.

Often billed as "America's Favorite Cowboy," Tex Ritter made scores
of hit records, and he made 58 B Westerns between 1936 and 1945.

He was born Woodward Maurice Ritter on January 12, 1907, in Mur-
vaul, Texas, and learned to play guitar and sing folksongs from black farm-
hands as a youngster.

He attended the University of Texas for a while, before dropping out
to take a job as a singer over radio station KRPC in Houston.

Tex moved to New York where he began appearing in stage plays and
was a good enough actor to land a part in a Broadway show. New York
is where he picked up the nickname Tex. While in New York, Tex's radio
career began to flourish. He hosted *The New York City Barn Dance,* was
the storyteller on *Lone Star Rangers* and got parts in radio dramas. In 1932
he took the part of Tex Mason on the popular *Bobby Benson's B Bar B
Riders* show. He also began recording that year.

In 1936 producer Edward Finney signed Tex to make musical Westerns
for Grand National Pictures. His first was *Song of the Gringo.* Tex made
a dozen films for the company. In 1938 when Finney quit Grand National
to go to work at Monogram, Tex followed suit.

Ritter and Finney churned out 20 films for Monogram before Tex
signed with Columbia Pictures in 1941. At Columbia he was paired with
Wild Bill Elliott for a series of films.

The following year he went to Universal and was teamed with Johnny
Mack Brown for seven films, with Russell Hayden for one and starred in
a couple of his own.

In 1944 Tex became a member of the Texas Rangers trio at PRC, making eight films in that series. At the conclusion of the Rangers series Tex
abandoned films and began to concentrate on his recording career.

He had some monstrous country hits including "Deck of Cards,"
"Hillbilly Heaven," "Rhye Whiskey" and of course "High Noon." For his
efforts, he is enshrined in the Country Music Hall of Fame.

Tex married Dorothy Fay, who was his leading lady in four films. His

Tex Ritter

son John Ritter is a popular actor and starred in the TV series *Three's Company.*

Tex passed away on July 2, 1974.

Tex Ritter Filmography

1936: *Song of the Gringo* (Grand National; John P. McCarthy) *SK* Fuzzy Knight, *LL* Joan Woodbury; *Headin' for the Rio Grande* (Grand National; R.N. Bradbury) *SK* Syd Saylor, Snub Pollard, *LL* Eleanor Stewart. **1937:** *Arizona Days* (Grand National; John English) *SK* Syd Saylor, *LL* Eleanor Stewart; *Trouble in Texas* (Grand National; R.N. Bradbury) *LL* Rita Cansino; *Hittin' the Trail* (Grand National; R.N. Bradbury) *SK* Snub Pollard, Heber Snow (Hank Worden); *Sing, Cowboy, Sing* (Grand National; R.N. Bradbury) *SK* Fuzzy St. John, Hank Worden, *LL* Louise Stanley; *Riders of the Rockies* (Grand National; R.N. Bradbury) *SK* Snub Pollard, Hank Worden, *LL* Louise Stanley; *The Mystery of the Hooded Horseman* (Grand National; Ray Taylor) *SK* Hank Worden, *LL* Iris Meredith. **1938:** *Tex Rides with the Boy Scouts* (Grand National; Ray Taylor) *SK* Snub Pollard, Hank Worden, *LL* Marjorie Reynolds; *Frontier Town* (Grand National; Ray Taylor) *SK* Snub Pollard, Hank Worden, *LL* Anne Evers; *Rollin' Plains* (Grand National; Al Herman) *SK* Snub Pollard, Hank Worden, *LL* Hariett Bennett; *Utah Trail* (Grand National; Al Herman) *SK* Horace Murphy, Snub Pollard, *LL* Adele Pearce; *Starlight Over Texas* (Monogram; Al Herman) *SK* Horace Murphy, Snub Pollard, *LL* Carmen Laroux; *Where the Buffalo Roam* (Monogram; Al Herman) *SK* Horace Murphy, Snub Pollard, *LL* Dorothy Short. **1939:** *Song of the Buckaroo* (Monogram; Al Herman) *SK* Snub Pollard, Horace Murphy, *LL* Jinx Falkenberg, Mary Ruth, Dorothy Fay; *Sundown on the Prairie* (Monogram; Al Herman) *SK* Horace Murphy, Hank Worden, *LL* Dorothy Fay; *Rollin' Westward* (Monogram; Al Herman) *SK* Horace Murphy, Hank Worden, *LL* Dorothy Fay; *Man from Texas* (Monogram; Al Herman) *LL* Ruth Rogers; *Down the Wyoming Trail* (Monogram) *SK* Horace Murphy, *LL* Mary Brodel; *Riders of the Frontier* (Monogram; Spencer Bennett) *LL* Jean Joyce, Marin Sais; *Westbound Stage* (Monogram; Spencer Bennett) *LL* Muriel Evans. **1940:** *Rhythm of the Rio Grande* (Monogram; Al Herman) *SK* Arkansas Slim Andrews, *LL* Suzan Dale; *Pals of the Silver Sage* (Monogram; Al Herman) *SK* Arkansas Slim Andrews, *LL* Clarissa Curtis; *The Cowboy from Sundown* (Monogram; Spencer Bennett) *SK* Roscoe Ates, *LL* Pauline Haddon; *The Golden Trail* (Monogram; Al Herman) *SK* Slim Andrews, *LL* Patsy Moran, Ina Guest; *Rainbow Over the Range* (Monogram; Al Herman) *SK* Slim Andrews, *LL* Dorothy Fay; *Roll, Wagons, Roll* (Monogram; Al Herman) *LL* Muriel Evans; *Arizona Frontier* (Monogram; Al Herman) *SK* Slim Andrews, *LL* Evelyn Finley; *Take Me Back to Oklahoma* (Monogram; Al Herman) *SK* Slim Andrews; *Rollin' Home to Texas* (Monogram; Al Herman) *SK* Slim Andrews, *LL* Virginia Carpenter. **1941:** *Ridin' the Cherokee Trail* (Monogram; Spencer G. Bennett) *SK* Slim Andrews, *LL* Betty Miles; *The Pioneers* (Monogram; Al Herman) *SK* Slim Andrews, Red Foley, *LL*

Wanda McKay; *King of Dodge City* (Columbia; Lambert Hillyer) *SK* Bill Elliott, Dub Taylor, *LL* Judith Linden; *Roaring Frontiers* (Columbia; Lambert Hillyer) *SK* Bill Elliott, *LL* Ruth Ford. **1942:** *Lone Star Vigilantes* (Columbia; Wallace Fox) *SK* Bill Elliott, *LL* Virginia Carpenter, Luana Walters; *Bullets for Bandits* (Columbia; Wallace Fox) *SK* Bill Elliott, *LL* Dorothy Short; *North of the Rockies* (Columbia; Lambert Hillyer) *SK* Bill Elliott, *LL* Shirley Patterson; *The Devil's Trail* (Columbia; Lambert Hillyer) *SK* Bill Elliott, *LL* Eileen O'Hearn; *Prairie Gunsmoke* (Columbia; Lambert Hillyer) *SK* Bill Elliott, *LL* Virginia Carroll; *Vengeance of the West* (Columbia; Lambert Hillyer) *SK* Bill Elliott, *LL* Adele Mara; *Deep in the Heart of Texas* (Universal; Elmer Clifton) *SK* Johnny Mack Brown, Fuzzy Knight, *LL* Jennifer Holt; *Little Joe the Wrangler* (Universal; Lewis Collins) *SK* Johnny Mack Brown, Fuzzy Knight, *LL* Jennifer Holt; *The Old Chisholm Trail* (Universal; Elmer Clifton) *SK* Johnny Mack Brown, Fuzzy Knight, *LL* Jennifer Holt. **1943:** *Tenting Tonight on the Old Camp Ground* (Universal; Lewis Collins) *SK* Johnny Mack Brown, Fuzzy Knight, *LL* Jennifer Holt; *Cheyenne Roundup* (Universal; Ray Taylor) *SK* Johnny Mack Brown, Fuzzy Knight, *LL* Jennifer Holt; *Raiders of San Joaquin* (Universal; Lewis Collins) *SK* Johnny Mack Brown, Fuzzy Knight, *LL* Jennifer Holt; *The Lone Star Trail* (Universal; Ray Taylor) *SK* Johnny Mack Brown, Fuzzy Knight, *LL* Jennifer Holt; *Arizona Trail* (Universal; Vernon Keays) *SK* Fuzzy Knight, *LL* Janet Shaw. **1944:** *Marshal of Gunsmoke* (Universal; Vernon Keays) *SK* Fuzzy Knight, Russell Hayden, *LL* Jennifer Holt; *Oklahoma Raiders* (Universal; Lewis Collins) *SK* Fuzzy Knight, *LL* Jennifer Holt; *Gangsters of the Frontier* (series) (PRC; Elmer Clifton) *SK* Texas Rangers, *LL* Patti McCarty; *Dead or Alive* (PRC; Elmer Clifton) *SK* Texas Rangers, *LL* Marjorie Clements; *The Whispering Skull* (PRC; Elmer Clifton) *SK* Texas Rangers. **1945:** *Marked for Murder* (PRC; Elmer Clifton) *SK* Texas Rangers, *LL* Marilyn McConnell; *Enemy of the Law* (PRC; Harry Fraser) *SK* Texas Rangers, *LL* Kay Hughes; *Three in the Saddle* (PRC; Harry Fraser) *SK* Texas Rangers, *LL* Lorraine Miller; *Frontier Fugitives* (PRC; Harry Fraser) *SK* Texas Rangers, *LL* Lorraine Miller; *Flaming Bullets* (PRC; Harry Fraser) *SK* Texas Rangers, *LL* Patricia Knox.

Roy Rogers
"The King of the Cowboys"

Horse: Trigger, the Smartest Horse in the Movies
Sidekicks: Gabby Hayes, Smiley Burnette, Raymond Hatton, Pat Brady, Andy Devine, Gordon Jones, Big Boy Williams, Pinky Lee

Roy Rogers circa 1950.

Roy Rogers was born Leonard Slye on November 12, 1912, in Cincinnati, Ohio. In 1930 he moved to California and worked as a fruit picker and a truck driver. As a youngster, Slye had learned to sing and play guitar. In 1934 he changed his name to Dick Weston, and along with Bob Nolan, Hugh Farr and Tim Spencer formed a country and western singing group called the Sons of the Pioneers. After getting their own radio show on station KFWB in Los Angeles, they added Pat Brady to the group and signed a contract with Decca Records.

In 1935 the Sons of the Pioneers broke into the movies with an appearance in the film *The Old Homestead*. Over the next two years movie fans saw the Pioneers in several Gene Autry and Charles Starrett B Westerns.

Dick Weston left the group in 1937 and went out on his own, getting bit parts in films starring Autry and the Three Mesquiteers. He also auditioned for Universal Pictures, which was in the market for a youthful singing cowboy. Weston lost the spot to Bob Baker.

In early 1938 Weston signed with Republic Pictures and changed his name to Roy Rogers. His first starring vehicle, *Under Western Stars*, was released on April 20, 1938. The film paired Roy with Gene Autry's longtime sidekick Smiley Burnette. Roy went on to star in 79 films for Republic before retiring from B Westerns to devote his energies to television in 1951. His last Western was *Pals of the Golden West*.

When Gene Autry left films in 1942 to enter the U.S. Air Corps, Roy Rogers became the movie industry's top-grossing cowboy star; a position that he maintained until the end of the era in 1953. Roy's fortieth film, *The Cowboy and the Senorita*, introduced as his leading lady a young actress named Dale Evans. Republic decided the chemistry was right to make the Rogers-Evans combination a top box-office draw. Together they made 20 films between 1944 and 1947.

In 1946 Roy's wife Arlene passed away, and the following year Roy and Dale were married.

Roy was always supported by the best of Western sidekicks. He made 40 films with the legendary Gabby Hayes. Others who rode with him included Smiley Burnette, Andy Devine, Raymond Hatton, Pinky Lee, Big Boy Williams, Gordon Jones and Pat Brady.

His golden Palomino, Trigger, was dubbed "the smartest horse in the movies" and reportedly had a repertoire of over 70 tricks.

His adventure series *The Roy Rogers Show*, starring Roy, Dale, Trigger and Pat Brady, ran on NBC from 1951 to 1957.

Roy made big-screen appearances with Bob Hope in *The Son of Paleface* in 1952 and *Alias Jesse James* in 1959. He returned to the movies in 1975 to star in *MacKintosh & T.J.*

Today Roy and Dale live in Chatsworth, California, home of the Roy Rogers Museum.

Roy Rogers Filmography

1938: *Under Western Stars* (Republic; Joseph Kane) *SK* Smiley Burnette, *LL* Carol Hughes; *Billy the Kid Returns* (Republic; Joseph Kane) *SK* Smiley Burnette, *LL* Lynne Roberts; *Come on Rangers* (Republic; Joseph Kane)

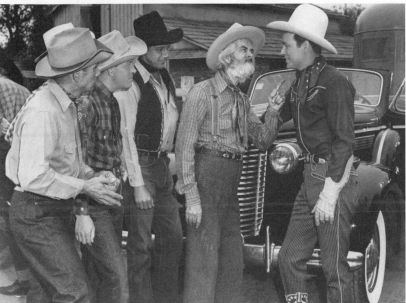

Top: *Roy Rogers and Trigger in* Man from Music Mountain *(Republic, 1943).* Bottom: *Roy and his comic sidekick Gabby Hayes in* Lights of Old Santa Fe *(Republic, 1944).*

Roy Rogers in his second Western, Billy the Kid Returns *(Republic, 1938). The other actor with the gun is Wade Boteler.*

SK Raymond Hatton, *LL* Mary Hart; *Shine on Harvest Moon* (Republic; Joseph Kane) *LL* Mary Hart. **1939:** *Rough Riders Roundup* (Republic; Joseph Kane) *SK* Raymond Hatton, *LL* Mary Hart; *Frontier Pony Express* (Republic; Joseph Kane) *SK* Raymond Hatton, *LL* Mary Hart; *Southward Ho* (Republic; Joseph Kane) *SK* Gabby Hayes, *LL* Mary Hart; *In Old Caliente* (Republic; Joseph Kane) *SK* Gabby Hayes, *LL* Katherine De Mille; *Wall Street Cowboy* (Republic; Joseph Kane) *SK* Gabby Hayes, Raymond Hatton, *LL* Ann Baldwin; *The Arizona Kid* (Republic; Joseph Kane) *SK* Gabby Hayes, *LL* Sally March; *Saga of Death Valley* (Republic; Joseph Kane) *SK* Gabby Hayes, *LL* Doris Day; *Days of Jesse James* (Republic; Joseph Kane) *SK* Gabby Hayes, *LL* Pauline Moore. **1940:** *Young Buffalo Bill* (Republic; Joseph Kane) *SK* Gabby Hayes, *LL* Pauline Moore; *The Carson City Kid* (Republic; Joseph Kane) *SK* Gabby Hayes, *LL* Pauline Moore; *Ranger and the Lady* (Republic; Joseph Kane) *SK* Gabby Hayes, *LL* Jacqueline Wells; *Colorado* (Republic; Joseph Kane) *SK* Gabby Hayes, *LL* Pauline Moore; *Young Bill Hickock* (Republic; Joseph Kane) *SK* Gabby Hayes, *LL* Jacqueline Wells; *The Border Legion* (Republic; Joseph Kane) *SK* Gabby Hayes, *LL* Carol Hughes. **1941:** *Robin Hood of the Pecos* (Republic; Joseph Kane) *SK* Gabby Hayes, *LL* Marjorie Reynolds; *In Old Cheyenne* (Republic; Joseph Kane) *SK* Gabby Hayes, *LL* Joan Woodbury; *Sheriff of Tombstone* (Republic; Joseph Kane) *SK* Gabby Hayes, *LL* Sally Payne;

Nevada City (Republic; Joseph Kane) *SK* Gabby Hayes, *LL* Sally Payne; *Bad Man of Deadwood* (Republic; Joseph Kane) *SK* Gabby Hayes, *LL* Carol Adams; *Jesse James at Bay* (Republic; Joseph Kane) *SK* Gabby Hayes, *LL* Sally Payne, Gale Storm; *Red River Valley* (Republic; Joseph Kane) *SK* Gabby Hayes, *LL* Sally Payne, Gale Storm. **1942:** *The Man from Cheyenne* (Republic; Joseph Kane) *SK* Gabby Hayes, *LL* Sally Payne, Gale Storm, Lynne Carver; *South of Santa Fe* (Republic; Joseph Kane) *SK* Gabby Hayes, *LL* Linda Hayes; *Sunset on the Desert* (Republic; Joseph Kane) *SK* Gabby Hayes, *LL* Lynne Carver; *Romance on the Range* (Republic; Joseph Kane) *SK* Gabby Hayes, *LL* Sally Payne, Linda Hayes; *Sons of the Pioneers* (Republic; Joseph Kane) *SK* Gabby Hayes, *LL* Maris Wrixon; *Sunset Serenade* (Republic; Joseph Kane) *SK* Gabby Hayes, *LL* Joan Woodbury, Helen Parrish; *Heart of the Golden West* (Republic; Joseph Kane) *SK* Gabby Hayes, *LL* Ruth Terry; *Ridin Down the Canyon* (Republic; Joseph Kane) *SK* Gabby Hayes, *LL* Lorna Gray, Linda Hayes. **1943:** *Idaho* (Republic; Joseph Kane) *SK* Smiley Burnette, *LL* Virginia Grey; *King of the Cowboys* (Republic; Joseph Kane) *SK* Smiley Burnette, *LL* Peggy Moran; *Song of Texas* (Republic; Joseph Kane) *SK* Pat Brady, *LL* Sheila Ryan; *Silver Spurs* (Republic; Joseph Kane) *SK* Smiley Burnette, *LL* Phyllis Brooks; *Man from Music Mountain* (Republic; Joseph Kane) *SK* Pat Brady, *LL* Ruth Terry. **1944:** *Hands Across the Border* (Republic; Joseph Kane) *SK* Big Boy Williams, *LL* Ruth Terry; *Cowboy and the Senorita* (Republic; Joseph Kane) *SK* Big Boy Williams, Fuzzy Knight, *LL* Dale Evans, Mary Lee; *Yellow Rose of Texas* (Republic; Joseph Kane) *LL* Dale Evans; *Song of Nevada* (Republic; Joseph Kane) *LL* Dale Evans; *San Fernando Valley* (Republic; John English) *LL* Dale Evans; *Lights of Old Santa Fe* (Republic; Frank McDonald) *SK* Gabby Hayes, *LL* Dale Evans. **1945:** *Utah* (Republic; John English) *SK* Gabby Hayes, *LL* Dale Evans, Peggy Stewart; *Bells of Rosarita* (Republic; Frank McDonald) *SK* Gabby Hayes, *LL* Dale Evans; *Man from Oklahoma* (Republic; Frank McDonald) *SK* Gabby Hayes, *LL* Dale Evans; *Sunset in El Dorado* (Republic; Frank McDonald) *SK* Gabby Hayes, *LL* Dale Evans; *Don't Fence Me In* (Republic; John English) *SK* Gabby Hayes, *LL* Dale Evans. **1946:** *Along the Navajo Trail* (Republic; Frank McDonald) *SK* Gabby Hayes, *LL* Dale Evans, Estilita Rodriguez; *Song of Arizona* (Republic; Frank McDonald) *SK* Gabby Hayes, *LL* Dale Evans; *Rainbow Over Texas* (Republic; Frank McDonald) *SK* Gabby Hayes, *LL* Dale Evans; *My Pal Trigger* (Republic; Frank McDonald) *SK* Gabby Hayes, *LL* Dale Evans; *Under Nevada Skies* (Republic; Frank McDonald) *SK* Gabby Hayes, *LL* Dale Evans; *Roll on Texas Moon* (Republic; William Witney) *SK* Gabby Hayes, *LL* Dale Evans; *Home in Oklahoma* (Republic; William Witney) *SK* Gabby Hayes, *LL* Dale Evans, Carol Hughes; *Heldorado* (Republic; William Witney) *SK* Gabby Hayes, *LL* Dale Evans. **1947:** *Apache Rose* (Republic; William Witney) *SK*

Olin Howlin, *LL* Dale Evans; *Bells of San Angelo* (Republic; William
Witney) *SK* Andy Devine, *LL* Dale Evans; *Springtime in the Sierras*
(Republic; William Witney) *SK* Andy Devine, *LL* Jane Frazee; *The Old
Spanish Trail* (Republic; William Witney) *SK* Andy Devine, *LL* Jane
Frazee, Estelita Rodriguez. **1948:** *The Gay Ranchero* (Republic; William
Witney) *SK* Andy Devine, *LL* Jane Frazee, Estelita Rodriguez; *Under
California Stars* (Republic; William Witney) *SK* Andy Devine, *LL* Jane
Frazee; *Eyes of Texas* (Republic; William Witney) *SK* Andy Devine, *LL*
Lynne Roberts; *Nighttime in Nevada* (Republic; William Witney) *SK* Andy
Devine, *LL* Adele Mara; *Grand Canyon Trail* (Republic; William Witney)
SK Andy Devine, *LL* Jane Frazee. **1949:** *The Far Frontier* (Republic; William
Witney) *SK* Andy Devine, *LL* Gail Davis; *Susanna Pass* (Republic; William
Witney) *LL* Dale Evans, Estelita Rodriguez; *Down Dakota Way* (Republic;
William Witney) *SK* Pat Brady, *LL* Dale Evans; *The Golden Stallion*
(Republic; William Witney) *SK* Pat Brady, *LL* Dale Evans, Estelita Rod-
riguez. **1950:** *Bells of Coronado* (Republic; William Witney) *SK* Pat Brady,
LL Dale Evans; *Twilight in the Sierras* (Republic; William Witney) *SK* Pat
Brady, *LL* Dale Evans, Estelita Rodriguez; *Trigger Jr.* (Republic; William
Witney) *SK* Pat Brady, *LL* Dale Evans; *Sunset in the West* (Republic;
William Witney) *SK* Gordon Jones, *LL* Estelita Rodriguez, Penny Edwards;
North of the Great Divide (Republic; William Witney) *SK* Gordon Jones,
LL Penny Edwards; *Trail of Robin Hood* (Republic; William Witney) *SK*
Gordon Jones, *LL* Penny Edwards. **1951:** *Spoilers of the Plains* (Republic;
William Witney) *SK* Gordon Jones, *LL* Penny Edwards; *Heart of the
Rockies* (Republic; William Witney) *SK* Gordon Jones, *LL* Penny Edwards;
In Old Amarillo (Republic; William Witney) *SK* Pinky Lee, *LL* Penny Ed-
wards, Estelita Rodriguez; *South of Caliente* (Republic; William Witney)
SK Pinky Lee, *LL* Dale Evans; *Pals of the Golden West* (Republic; William
Witney) *SK* Pinky Lee, *LL* Dale Evans, Estelita Rodriguez.

Gilbert Roland

Gilbert Roland is the only Mexican to portray Latin adventurer the
Cisco Kid on the silver screen.

Roland played Cisco in a half dozen films for Monogram Pictures in
1946 and 1947 and some aficionados have declared his portrayal of the hero
as the best of the lot.

Roland was born in Chihuahua, Mexico, on December 11, 1905, the
son of a famous matador. His given name was Luis Antonio Damasco
Alonso.

He made his screen debut in 1925 in *This Plastic Age*, eventually becoming a leading man in silent romantic films. When the talkies came around, Roland was mostly relegated to gangster parts.

During World War II he served in the U.S. Army Air Corps and assumed the role of Cisco shortly after his discharge.

Upon completion of his Cisco stint, Roland continued to pursue a very busy screen career, appearing in such notable films as *Ten Tall Men* (1951), *The Wild and the Innocent* (1959), *Cheyenne Autumn* (1964), as well as many films produced in Mexico and Europe.

He is considered one of the screen's all-time most handsome leading men.

Gilbert Roland Filmography

1946: *The Gay Cavalier* (Monogram; William Nigh) *SK* Martin Garralaga, *LL* Ramsey Ames; *South of Monterey* (Monogram; William Nigh) *SK* Martin Garralaga, *LL* Marjorie Riordan; *Beauty and the Bandit* (Monogram; William Nigh) *SK* Martin Garralaga, *LL* Ramsey Ames. **1947:** *Riding the California Trail* (Monogram; William Nigh) *SK* Martin Garralaga, *LL* Teala Loring; *Robin Hood of Monterey* (Monogram; Christy Cabanne) *SK* Chris-Pin Martin, *LL* Evelyn Brent; *King of the Bandits* (Monogram; Christy Cabanne) *SK* Chris-Pin Martin, *LL* Angela Greene.

Cesar Romero

Devilishly handsome Cesar Romero played the part of the Cisco Kid from 1939 through 1941 in six films for Twentieth Century–Fox.

Romero was born in New York City on February 15, 1907, and began his career in entertainment as a dancer in vaudeville and eventually worked his way onto the Broadway stage.

He made his film debut in *The Thin Man* in 1934.

In 1939 he had a supporting role in *The Return of the Cisco Kid*, which starred the screen's original Cisco (Warner Baxter). He assumed the lead role in the next Cisco outing, *The Cisco Kid and the Lady*. He served in the coast guard during World War II. He returned to films upon discharge and is still active.

Romero is best known to TV fans as the villainous Joker on the campy *Batman* series.

Cesar Romero Filmography

1939: *The Cisco Kid and the Lady* (Twentieth Century–Fox; Herbert I. Leeds) *SK* Chris Pin Martin, *LL* Marjorie Weaver. **1940:** *Viva Cisco Kid* (Twentieth Century–Fox; Norman Foster) *SK* Chris Pin Martin, *LL* Jean Rogers; *Lucky Cisco Kid* (Twentieth Century–Fox; H. Bruce Humberstone) *SK* Chris Pin Martin, *LL* Mary Beth Hughes; *The Gay Caballero* (Twentieth Century–Fox; Otto Brower) *SK* Chris Pin Martin, *LL* Sheila Ryan. **1941:** *Romance on the Rio Grande* (Twentieth Century–Fox; Herbert Leeds) *SK* Chris Pin Martin, *LL* Lynne Roberts, Patricia Morrison; *Ride on Vaquero* (Twentieth Century–Fox; Herbert Leeds) *SK* Chris Pin Martin, *LL* Lynne Roberts, Joan Woodbury.

Buddy Roosevelt

Buddy Roosevelt was a major silent film cowboy star in the 1920s. He made films for Pathe, Universal and Paramount studios.

What set Roosevelt apart from his peers (Tom Mix, Hoot Gibson, Buck Jones, etc.) was his natural comedic talents.

While his pictures were exciting and action-filled, Roosevelt always managed to inject a sense of humor into his characters and into his films overall.

Roosevelt was born in Colorado on June 25, 1898, and was a bona fide cowboy when he entered the movies as a bit player in 1922. By 1924 he was starring in films for Artclass Studios. He eventually moved to larger studios.

When the sound era arrived, Roosevelt's stardom came to a screeching halt.

In 1931 he starred in one film, *Lightnin' Smith Returns*, for Syndicate Films.

In 1934 he signed to do four films with Superior Pictures. These features would be Roosevelt's last starring vehicles. He continued in films for several years as a character actor before retiring.

Buddy Roosevelt Filmography

1931: *Lightnin' Smith Returns* (Syndicate; Jack Irwin) *LL* Barbara Worth. **1934:** *Boss Cowboy* (Superior; Victor Adamson) *LL* Frances Morris, Fay McKenzie; *Circle Canyon* (Superior; Victor Adamson) *LL* June Matthews;

Buddy Roosevelt, left, with Lafe McKee (center) and Robert Homans in a scene from one of his movies.

Lightning Range (Superior; Victor Adamson) *LL* Patsy Bellamy; *Range Riders* (Superior; Victor Adamson) *LL* Barbara Starr.

The Rough Ridin' Kids
(Michael Chapin and Eileen Jansen)

In the early fifties Republic Pictures tried to capture the fancy and large box-office potential of the large juvenile B Western audience by creating a series of films about the adventures of two youngsters in the wild and woolly West. They called them the Rough Ridin' Kids.

For the leads they chose two youngsters with a fair amount of Hollywood experience, Michael Chapin and Eileen Jansen.

Eileen Jansen, despite her young age, was already a veteran screen performer having appeared in such films as *The Green Years* in 1946, and *A Miracle Can Happen* in 1948. Among Michael Chapin's credits was the 1949 melodrama *Strange Bargain*.

The series lasted four films; three released in 1951 and the final entry the following year.

The Rough Ridin' Kids Filmography

1951: *Buckaroo Sheriff of Texas* (Republic; Phillip Ford); *The Dakota Kid* (Republic; Phillip Ford); *Arizona Manhunt* (Republic; Fred C. Brannon). **1952:** *Wild Horse Ambush* (Republic; Fred C. Brannon).

Reb Russell

Horse: Rebel

Reb Russell is one of the B Western's most overlooked stars; in fact he falls into the category that most film historians deem obscure.

Russell and his white stallion Rebel flashed across the screen for a series of nine films produced by the Willis Kent Company in 1934 and 1935. his initial film was one of his best — *The Man from Hell*.

Russell's films were all action from start to finish.

He was born Fay H. Russell on May 31, 1905, in Paola, Kansas. An outstanding athlete in high school, he attended the University of Nebraska where he was named All Big 6 (now Big 8) quarterback. In 1929 he transferred to Northwestern, and there he lettered in football, wrestling and baseball. In 1930 he made the All-American list as a fullback.

In 1932 the six foot–220-pound Russell was among a group of athletes who were recruited by Universal Pictures for bit parts in their film *The All American.*

During 1932 and 1933 Russell played pro football. He starred with the New York Giants in 1932, and in 1933 with the Philadelphia Eagles.

He returned to Hollywood to co-star in *Fighting to Live* in 1934, before signing with Kent.

When the series with Kent ended, Russell decided to forgo any further screen Westerns and instead tour with a circus and wild West show.

Reb Russell and Rebel.

He retired to his ranch near Kansas City, Kansas, in 1940.
In the 1960s he became involved in politics and once ran unsuccessfully for the state senate in Kansas.
Reb Russell passed away March 16, 1978.

Reb Russell Filmography

1934: *Fighting to Live* (Principal; Edward F. Cline) *LL* Marion Shilling; *The Man from Hell* (Kent; Lew Collins) *LL* Ann D'Arcy; *Fighting Thru*

(Kent; Harry Fraser) *LL* Lucille Lund. **1935:** *Outlaw Rule* (Kent; S. Roy Luby) *LL* Betty Mack; *Range Warfare* (Kent; S. Roy Luby) *LL* Lucille Lund; *Arizona Badman* (Kent; S. Roy Luby) *LL* Lois January; *Blazing Guns* (Kent; Ray Heinz) *LL* Marion Shilling; *Border Vengeance* (Kent; Ray Heinz) *LL* Mary Jane Carey; *Cheyenne Tornado* (Kent; William O'Connor) *LL* Victoria Vinton; *Lightning Triggers* (Kent; S. Roy Luby) *LL* Yvonne Pelletier.

Fred Scott
"The Silvery Voiced Buckaroo"

Horse: White Knight
Sidekicks: Fuzzy St. John, Harry Harvey

Singing cowboy Fred Lee Scott was born in Fresno, California, on February 14, 1902. As a youngster he studied voice, and learned riding skills while living on a ranch.

He made his professional acting debut at the age of 16 as a member of the Fresno Community Players. In 1919 Scott entered vaudeville as a singer.

In the early twenties he began to get parts in silent films such as *Bride of the Storm.*

His big break came when, in 1929, former silent screen star Bebe Daniels heard Scott sing and got him a part in her musical *Rio Rita.*

Scott appeared in such films as *The Grand Parade, Swing High* and *Beyond Victory.*

In 1932 he left films and joined the San Francisco Opera Company.

In 1936 producer Jed Buell signed Scott to star in a series of musical Westerns for Spectrum Pictures. His first was *Romance Rides the Range.* In his third film Scott acquired Al "Fuzzy" St. John as his sidekick, and together they made seven films.

Fred Scott made a total of 13 pictures for Spectrum. The Company went bankrupt before they could release his final film for them — *Ridin' the Trail.* The film was subsequently released in 1942 by the Zeihm Company.

Fred Scott made his last Western, *Rodeo Rhythm,* for PRC that same year. Fred then returned to his stage career.

Fred Scott

Fred Scott Filmography

1936: *Romance Rides the Range* (Spectrum; Harry Fraser) *LL* Marion Shilling. **1937:** *The Singing Buckaroo* (Spectrum; Tom Gibson) *LL* Victoria Vinton; *Melody of the Plains* (Spectrum; Sam Newfield) *SK* Fuzzy St. John, *LL* Louise Small; *The Fighting Deputy* (Spectrum; Sam Newfield) *SK* Fuzzy St. John, *LL* Marjorie Beebe; *Moonlight on the Range* (Spectrum; Sam Newfield) *SK* Fuzzy St. John, *LL* Lois January; *The Roaming Cowboy* (Spectrum; Robert Hill) *SK* Fuzzy St. John, *LL* Lois January. **1938:** *The Rangers'*

Roundup (Spectrum; Sam Newfield) *SK* Fuzzy St. John, *LL* Christine McIntyre; *Knight of the Plains* (Spectrum; Sam Newfield) *SK* Fuzzy St. John, *LL* Marion Weldon; *Songs and Bullets* (Spectrum; Sam Newfield) *SK* Fuzzy St. John, *LL* Alice Ardell. **1939:** *Code of the Fearless* (Spectrum; Raymond K. Johnson) *SK* Harry Harvey, *LL* Claire Rochelle; *In Old Montana* (Spectrum; Raymond K. Johnson) *SK* Harry Harvey, *LL* Jean Carmen; *Two Gun Troubador* (Spectrum; Raymond K. Johnson) *SK* Harry Harvey, *LL* Claire Rochelle. **1940:** *Ridin' the Trail* (Zeihm, Inc.; Raymond K. Johnson) *SK* Harry Harvey, *LL* Iris Lancaster. **1942:** *Rodeo Rhythm* (PRC; Fred Neymyer) *LL* Patricia Red Path, Gloria Morse.

David Sharpe

If Yakima Canutt is considered the King of Stuntmen, then Missouri-born David Sharpe must be considered the Crown Prince. In fact it was the famous Canutt who taught Sharpe the ups 'n' downs of the dangerous profession.

Sharpe was born in St. Louis in 1911, but his family moved to Los Angeles when he was a youngster. He made his film debut in the 1924 production of *The Thief of Bagdad* which starred Douglas Fairbanks, Sr.

Sharpe concentrated on acrobatics and gymnastics while in school and won the National Tumbling Championship.

He returned to films in 1928 as a bit player and worked his way up the ladder until, by 1930, he was one of the stars of the Boy Friends series of comedy shorts which were produced by Hal Roach for MGM.

All the while working in the stunt/double trade, he got parts in a variety of films including such B's as *Gun Grit* with Jack Perrin and the Three Mesquiteers' *Wyoming Outlaw.*

In 1939 David Sharpe was one of the stars of the highly-rated Republic serial *Daredevils of the Red Circle,* and he also joined the topflight Republic stunt team.

In 1941 Monogram Pictures teamed Dave with Chief Thundercloud and the usually villainous Leroy Mason to make a one-shot trio Western, *The Silver Stallion.*

The following year he replaced Crash Corrigan in the Range Busters series. He did four films in the series before joining the Army Air Corps to serve in World War II.

He attained the rank of captain and after the war returned to films, basically concentrating on stunt work. He did make an occasional B Western appearance. He played the villain in Roy Rogers' *Bells of San Angelo.*

David Sharpe

He did stunt work on such early TV series as *The Cisco Kid, Zorro* and *Wild Bill Hickok,* and retired following work on the 1978 film *Heaven Can Wait.*

David Sharpe died of Parkinson's disease in Altadena, California, on March 30, 1980.

David Sharpe Filmography

1941: *Silver Stallion* (Monogram; Edward Finney) *SK* Chief Thundercloud, Leroy Mason, *LL* Janet Waldo. **1942:** *Texas to Bataan* (Monogram; Robert Tansey) *SK* Range Busters, *LL* Marjorie Manners; *Trail Riders* (Monogram; Robert Tansey) *SK* Range Busters, *LL* Evelyn Finley. **1943:** *Two-Fisted Justice* (Monogram; Robert Tansey) *SK* Range Busters, *LL* Gwen

Gaze; *Haunted Ranch* (Monogram; Robert Tansey) *SK* Range Busters, *LL* Julie Duncan.

Cal Shrum

Cal Shrum was a member of his brother Walt's musical group the Colorado Hillbillies when they made their screen debut in the 1938 Gene Autry film *The Old Barn Dance.*

Shrum landed bit parts in several Republic B Westerns before forming his own group, the Rhythm Rangers. The aggregation appeared in films like *Rolling Home to Texas* with Tex Ritter and *Thunder Over the Prairie* with Charles Starrett.

In 1944 Shrum made two films for an outfit called Three Crown Productions. The first one, called *Swing, Cowboy, Swing,* co-starred former Three Mesquiteer Max Terhune, and Shrum's leading lady in both films was his wife Alta Lee. His sidekick in the second film was Brad King, late of the Hopalong Cassidy series.

Both films stayed in the can until 1949 when they were released by Astor Pictures.

Shrum was born in Arkansas on July 10, 1910. He is probably best known as the writer of the country classic "When My Blue Moon Turns to Gold."

Cal Shrum Filmography

1949 (made in 1944): *Swing Cowboy Swing* (aka *Bad Man from Big Bend*) (Astor; Elmer Clifton) *SK* Max Terhune, *LL* Alta Lee; (made in 1944) *Trouble at Melody Mesa* (Astor; W.M. Connell) *SK* Brad King, *LL* Alta Lee.

Charles Starrett

Horse: Raider
Sidekicks: Smiley Burnette, Cliff Edwards, Russell Hayden, Arthur Hunnicutt, Dub Taylor, Tex Harding

Charles Starrett starred in more B Westerns than any other of the genre's cowboy heroes. He made 131 Western adventures between 1935 and

Charles Starrett and leading lady Iris Meredith in 1938.

1952, all for Columbia Pictures. He was rated as a top ten cowboy from 1937 till 1952.

Starrett is best known for his portrayal of black-clad masked avenger the Durango Kid, a role he performed in over 60 films.

Starrett was born in Athol, Massachusetts, on March 28, 1904. At the age of 13 he ran away from home and joined a vaudeville show. When his angry father caught up with him, he was quickly enrolled in a military school as a disciplinary measure.

He graduated from Dartmouth College, where he was an excellent football player. While at Dartmouth, he and soon-to-be-fellow-cowboy-star Bob Allen were among a group of athletes who were given bit parts in the 1926 film *The Quarterback*.

Starrett studied at the American Academy of Dramatic Arts and joined an Ohio-based theatrical company. By 1929 he had appeared in four Broadway plays. He was appearing on Broadway in *The Star of Bengal* when he was offered a movie contract by a talent scout. His debut film was *Fast and Loose*, a 1930 release starring Carole Lombard. Over the next four years he appeared in such films as *Touchdown* with Richard Arlen and *The Mask of Fu Manchu* with Boris Karloff.

In 1935 when Tim McCoy quit as Columbia Pictures' top cowboy, the studio signed Starrett to take his place. Starrett's long string of Columbia releases began later that year when the studio issued *The Gallant Defender*.

In his early years Starrett did not have a sidekick, but he had an excellent ensemble of supporting players including Iris Meredith, who was his leading lady in 18 films, and Dick Curtis, Columbia's chief resident bad guy.

Later he was paired with "Ukelele Ike" Cliff Edwards, "Stringbean" Arthur Hunnicutt, Hopalong Cassidy's former pal Russ Hayden, Jimmy Wakely's future saddle pal Cannonball Taylor, newcomer Tex Harding, and in 56 films with Smiley Burnette.

Starrett first played the Durango Kid in the 1940 film of the same name. The series, however, did not take off for another five years with the release of *The Return of the Durango Kid* in 1945.

Starrett released his last B in 1952 and retired from the screen.

Charles Starrett was one of the original founders of the Screen Actors Guild, which he and 17 other film actors laid the groundwork for in a 1933 meeting in Boris Karloff's garage.

Charles Starrett passed away on March 22, 1986, in Borrego Springs, California.

Charles Starrett Filmography

1935: *Gallant Defender* (Columbia; David Selman) *LL* Joan Perry; *Undercover Men* (Booth Dominions; Sam Newfield) *LL* Adrienne Dore. **1936:** *The Mysterious Avenger* (Columbia; Harry S. Webb) *LL* Joan Perry; *Secret Patrol* (Columbia; David Selman) *LL* Finis Barton; *Code of the Range* (Columbia; C.C. Coleman, Jr.) *LL* Mary Blake; *The Cowboy Star* (Columbia; David Selman) *LL* Iris Meredith; *Stampede* (Columbia; Ford Beebe) *LL* Finis Barton; *Dodge City Trail* (Columbia; C.C. Coleman, Jr.) *LL* Marion Weldon. **1937:** *Trapped* (Columbia; Leon Barsha) *LL* Peggy Stratford; *Two Gun Law* (Columbia; Leon Barsha) *LL* Peggy Stratford; *Two Fisted Sheriff* (Columbia; Leon Barsha) *LL* Barbara Weeks; *One Man Justice* (Columbia; Leon Barsha) *LL* Barbara Weeks; *The Old Wyoming Trail* (Columbia; Folmer Blangstead) *LL* Barbara Weeks; *Outlaws of the Prairie* (Columbia; Sam Nelson) *LL* Iris Meredith; *West Bound Mail* (Columbia; Folmer Blangstead) *LL* Rosiland Keith. **1938:** *Cattle Raiders* (Columbia; Sam Nelson) *LL* Iris Meredith; *Call of the Rockies* (Columbia; Alan James) *LL* Iris Meredith; *Law of the Plains* (Columbia; Sam Nelson) *LL* Iris Meredith;

Charles Starrett as the Durango Kid, a role he played in over 60 films for Columbia.

West of Cheyenne (Columbia; Sam Nelson) *LL* Iris Meredith; *South of Arizona* (Columbia; Sam Nelson) *LL* Iris Meredith; *The Colorado Trail* (Columbia; Sam Nelson) *LL* Iris Meredith; *West of Santa Fe* (Columbia; Sam Nelson) *LL* Iris Meredith; *Rio Grande* (Columbia; Sam Nelson) *LL* Ann Doran. **1939:** *The Thundering West* (Columbia; Sam Nelson) *LL* Iris Meredith; *Texas Stampede* (Columbia; Sam Nelson) *LL* Iris Meredith; *North of the Yukon* (Columbia; Sam Nelson) *LL* Linda Winters; *Spoilers of the Range* (Columbia; C.C. Coleman, Jr.) *LL* Iris Meredith; *Western Caravans* (Columbia; Sam Nelson) *LL* Iris Meredith; *The Man from Sundown* (Columbia; Sam Nelson) *LL* Iris Meredith; *Riders of Black River* (Columbia; Norman Deming) *LL* Iris Meredith; *Outpost of the Mounties* (Columbia; C.C. Coleman, Jr.) *LL* Iris Meredith; *The Stranger from Texas* (Columbia; Sam Nelson) *LL* Lorna Gray. **1940:** *Two Fisted Rangers* (Columbia; Joseph Lewis) *LL* Iris Meredith; *Bullets for Rustlers* (Columbia; Sam Nelson) *LL* Lorna Gray; *Blazing Six Shooters* (Columbia; Joseph Lewis) *LL* Iris Meredith; *Texas Stagecoach* (Columbia; Joseph Lewis) *LL* Iris Meredith; *The Durango Kid* (Columbia; Lambert Hillyer) *LL* Luana Walters; *West of Abilene* (Columbia; Ralph Cedar) *LL* Marjorie Cooley; *Thundering Frontier* (Columbia; D. Ross Lederman) *LL* Iris Meredith. **1941:** *The Pinto Kid* (Columbia; Lambert Hillyer) *LL* Louise Currie; *Outlaws of the Panhandle* (Columbia; Sam Nelson) *LL* Frances Robinson; *The Medico of Painted Springs* (Columbia; Lambert Hillyer) *LL* Terry Walker; *Thunder Over the Prairie* (Columbia; Lambert Hillyer) *SK* Cliff Edwards, *LL* Eileen O'Hearn; *Prairie Stranger* (Columbia; Lambert Hillyer) *SK* Cliff Edwards,

LL Patti McCarty; *The Royal Mounted Patrol* (Columbia; Lambert Hillyer) *SK* Russell Hayden, *LL* Wanda McKay; *Riders of the Badlands* (Columbia; Howard Bretherton) *SK* Cliff Edwards, Russell Hayden, *LL* Ilene Brewer, Kay Hughes. **1942:** *West of Tombstone* (Columbia; Howard Bretherton) *SK* Cliff Edwards, Russell Hayden, *LL* Marcella Martin; *Lawless Plainsmen* (Columbia; William Berke) *SK* Cliff Edwards, Russell Hayden, *LL* Luana Walters, Gwen Kenyon; *Down Rio Grande Way* (Columbia; William Berke) *SK* Russell Hayden, Britt Wood, *LL* Roseanne Stevens; *Riders of the Northland* (Columbia; William Berke) *SK* Russell Hayden, Cliff Edwards, *LL* Shirley Patterson; *Bad Men of the Hills* (Columbia; William Berke) *SK* Russell Hayden, Cliff Edwards, *LL* Luana Walters; *Overland to Deadwood* (Columbia; William Berke) *SK* Russell Hayden, Cliff Edwards, *LL* Leslie Brooks; *Riding Through Nevada* (Columbia; William Berke) *SK* Arthur Hunnicutt, *LL* Shirley Patterson; *Pardon My Gun* (Columbia; William Berke) *SK* Arthur Hunnicutt, *LL* Alma Carroll. **1943:** *The Fighting Buckaroo* (Columbia; William Berke) *SK* Arthur Hunnicutt, *LL* Kay Harris; *Law of the Northwest* (Columbia; William Berke) *SK* Arthur Hunnicutt, *LL* Shirley Patterson; *Frontier Fury* (Columbia; William Berke) *SK* Arthur Hunnicutt, *LL* Roma Aldrich; *Robin Hood of the Range* (Columbia; William Berke) *SK* Arthur Hunnicutt, *LL* Kay Harris; *Hail to the Rangers* (Columbia; William Berke) *SK* Arthur Hunnicutt, *LL* Leota Atcher; *Cowboy in the Clouds* (Columbia; Benjamin Kline) *SK* Dub Taylor, *LL* Julie Duncan. **1944:** *Cowboy Canteen* (Columbia; Lew Landers) *SK* Dub Taylor, *LL* Jane Frazee, Vera Vague; *Sundown Valley* (Columbia; Ben Kline) *SK* Dub Taylor, *LL* Jeanne Bates; *Riding West* (filmed in 1943) (Columbia; William Berke) *SK* Arthur Hunnicutt, *LL* Shirley Patterson; *Cowboy from Lonesome River* (Columbia; Ben Kline) *SK* Dub Taylor, *LL* Vi Athens; *Cyclone Prairie Rangers* (Columbia; Ben Kline) *SK* Dub Taylor, *LL* Constance Worth; *Saddle Leather Law* (Columbia; Ben Kline) *SK* Dub Taylor, *LL* Vi Athens. **1945:** *Rough Ridin' Justice* (Columbia; Derwin Abrahams) *SK* Dub Taylor, *LL* Betty Jane Graham; *Return of the Durango Kid* (Columbia; Derwin Abrahams) *SK* Tex Harding, *LL* Betty Roadman; *Rustlers of the Badlands* (Columbia; Derwin Abrahams) *SK* Dub Taylor, *LL* Sally Bliss; *Blazing the Western Trail* (Columbia; Vernon Keays) *SK* Dub Taylor, Tex Harding, *LL* Carole Matthews; *Outlaws of the Rockies* (Columbia; Ray Nazarro) *SK* Dub Taylor, Tex Harding, *LL* Carole Matthews; *Lawless Empire* (Columbia; Vernon Keays) *SK* Dub Taylor, Tex Harding, *LL* Mildred Law; *Texas Panhandle* (Columbia; Ray Nazarro) *SK* Dub Taylor, Tex Harding, *LL* Nanette Parks, Carolina Cotton; *Both Barrels Blazing* (Columbia; Derwin Abrahams) *SK* Dub Taylor, Tex Harding, *LL* Pat Parrish. **1946:** *Frontier Gun Law* (Columbia; Derwin Abrahams) *SK* Dub Taylor, Tex Harding, *LL* Jean Stevens; *Roaring Rangers* (Columbia; Ray Nazarro) *SK* Smiley Burnette, *LL* Adelle Roberts; *Gunning for Vengeance* (Columbia;

Ray Nazarro) *SK* Smiley Burnette, *LL* Marjean Neville; *Galloping Thunder* (Columbia; Ray Nazarro) *SK* Smiley Burnette, *LL* Adelle Roberts; *Two Fisted Stranger* (Columbia; Ray Nazarro) *SK* Smiley Burnette, *LL* Doris Houck; *The Desert Horseman* (Columbia; Ray Nazarro) *SK* Smiley Burnette, *LL* Adelle Roberts; *Heading West* (Columbia; Ray Nazarro) *SK* Smiley Burnette, *LL* Doris Houck; *Land Rush* (Columbia; Vernon Keays) *SK* Smiley Burnette, *LL* Doris Houck; *Terror Trail* (Columbia; Ray Nazarro) *SK* Smiley Burnette, *LL* Barbara Pepper; *The Fighting Frontiersman* (Columbia; Derwin Abrahams) *SK* Smiley Burnette, *LL* Helen Mowery. **1947:** *South of the Chisholm Trail* (Columbia; Derwin Abrahams) *SK* Smiley Burnette, *LL* Nancy Saunders; *The Lone Hand Texan* (Columbia; Ray Nazarro) *SK* Smiley Burnette, *LL* Mary Newton; *West of Dodge City* (Columbia; Ray Nazarro) *SK* Smiley Burnette, *LL* Nancy Saunders; *Law of the Canyon* (Columbia; Ray Nazarro) *SK* Smiley Burnette, *LL* Nancy Saunders; *Prairie Raiders* (Columbia; Derwin Abrahams) *SK* Smiley Burnette, *LL* Nancy Saunders; *The Stranger from Ponca City* (Columbia; Derwin Abrahams) *SK* Smiley Burnette, *LL* Virginia Hunter; *Riders of the Lone Star* (Columbia; Derwin Abrahams) *SK* Smiley Burnette, *LL* Virginia Hunter; *Buckaroo from Powder River* (Columbia; Ray Nazarro) *SK* Smiley Burnette, *LL* Eve Miller; *Last Days of Boot Hill* (Columbia; Ray Nazarro) *SK* Smiley Burnette, *LL* Virginia Hunter. **1948:** *Six Gun Land* (Columbia; Ray Nazarro) *SK* Smiley Burnette, *LL* Nancy Saunders; *Phantom Valley* (Columbia; Ray Nazarro) *SK* Smiley Burnette, *LL* Virginia Hunter; *West of Sonora* (Columbia; Ray Nazarro) *SK* Smiley Burnette, *LL* Anita Castle; *Whirlwind Raiders* (Columbia; Vernon Keays) *SK* Smiley Burnette, *LL* Nancy Saunders; *Blazing Across the Pecos* (Columbia; Ray Nazarro) *SK* Smiley Burnette, *LL* Patricia White; *Trail to Laredo* (Columbia; Ray Nazarro) *SK* Smiley Burnette, *LL* Virginia Maxey; *El Dorado Pass* (Columbia; Ray Nazarro) *SK* Smiley Burnette, *LL* Elena Verdugo; *Quick on the Trigger* (Columbia; Ray Nazarro) *SK* Smiley Burnette, *LL* Helen Parrish. **1949:** *Challenge of the Range* (Columbia; Ray Nazarro) *SK* Smiley Burnette, *LL* Paula Raymond; *Laramie* (Columbia; Ray Nazarro) *SK* Smiley Burnette, *LL* Marjorie Stapp; *South of Death Valley* (Columbia; Ray Nazarro) *SK* Smiley Burnette, *LL* Gail Davis; *Bandits of El Dorado* (Columbia; Ray Nazarro) *SK* Smiley Burnette; *Renegades of the Sage* (Columbia; Ray Nazarro) *SK* Smiley Burnette, *LL* Leslie Banning; *The Blazing Trail* (Columbia; Ray Nazarro) *SK* Smiley Burnette, *LL* Marjorie Stapp; *Desert Vigilante* (Columbia; Fred Sears) *SK* Smiley Burnette, *LL* Peggy Stewart; *Horsemen of the Sierras* (Columbia; Fred Sears) *SK* Smiley Burnette, *LL* Lois Hall. **1950:** *Trail of the Rustlers* (Columbia; Ray Nazarro) *SK* Smiley Burnette, *LL* Gail Davis; *Outcasts of Black Mesa* (Columbia; Ray Nazarro) *SK* Smiley Burnette, *LL* Martha Hyer; *Texas Dynamo* (Columbia; Ray Nazarro) *SK* Smiley Burnette, *LL* Lois Hall;

Streets of Ghost Town (Columbia; Ray Nazarro) *SK* Smiley Burnette, *LL* Mary Ellen Kay; *Across the Badlands* (Columbia; Fred F. Sears) *SK* Smiley Burnette, *LL* Helen Mowery; *Raiders of Tomahawk Creek* (Columbia; Fred F. Sears) *SK* Smiley Burnette, *LL* Kay Buckley; *Lightning Guns* (Columbia; Fred F. Sears) *SK* Smiley Burnette, *LL* Gloria Henry; *Frontier Outpost* (Columbia; Ray Nazarro) *SK* Smiley Burnette, *LL* Lois Hall. **1951:** *Prairie Roundup* (Columbia; Fred Sears) *SK* Smiley Burnette, *LL* Mary Castle; *Ridin' the Outlaw Trail* (Columbia; Fred Sears) *SK* Smiley Burnette, *LL* Sunny Vickers; *Fort Savage Raiders* (Columbia; Ray Nazarro) *SK* Smiley Burnette; *Snake River Desperadoes* (Columbia; Fred Sears) *SK* Smiley Burnette; *Bonanza Town* (Columbia; Fred Sears) *SK* Smiley Burnette; *Cyclone Fury* (Columbia; Ray Nazarro) *SK* Smiley Burnette; *The Kid from Amarillo* (Columbia; Ray Nazarro) *SK* Smiley Burnette; *Pecos River* (Columbia; Fred Sears) *SK* Smiley Burnette, *LL* Delores Sidener. **1952:** *Smoky Canyon* (Columbia; Fred Sears) *SK* Smiley Burnette, *LL* Dani Sue Nolan; *The Hawk of Wild River* (Columbia; Fred Sears) *SK* Smiley Burnette; *Laramie Mountains* (Columbia; Ray Nazarro) *SK* Smiley Burnette; *The Rough Tough West* (Columbia; Ray Nazarro) *SK* Smiley Burnette, *LL* Carolina Cotton; *Junction City* (Columbia; Ray Nazarro) *SK* Smiley Burnette, *LL* Kathleen Case; *The Kid from Broken Gun* (Columbia; Fred Sears) *SK* Smiley Burnette, *LL* Angela Stevens.

Bob Steele

Horse: Brownie
Sidekicks: Syd Saylor, Fuzzy St. John

Battlin' Bob Steele blazed his way through nearly 100 starring roles in B Westerns between the years 1930 and 1946. He also had featured roles in many others.

Steele was born Robert North Bradbury, Jr., on January 26, 1906, in Pendleton, Oregon, one of twin sons of film director R.N. Bradbury.

He made his screen debut at an early age when his dad starred Bob and his brother Bill in a series of two-reelers called *The Adventures of Bill and Bob.* The twins also appeared in vaudeville.

Steele was raised in Glendale, California, and attended Glendale High School, where one of his classmates was John Wayne. Steele also became a professional boxer for a while, which accounted for the excellent physical aspect of his onscreen performances and his ability to handle his own stunt work.

Bob Steele

In 1926 he began making films for his dad at Sunset Films.

In 1927 he changed his name from Bradbury to Steele and signed a contract with FBO. His first FBO release ws *The Mojave Kid*.

When FBO became RKO in 1929, Steele moved to Syndicate and, with the emergence of the sound era, several of his films released in 1929 and 1930 featured sound effects and music.

Bob's first all-talking feature was *Near the Rainbow's End*, released by Tiffany in 1930. He made eight films for Tiffany in 1930 and 1931, and six for World Wide before signing with Monogram in 1932. Five of the eight films he made for Monogram were directed by his father.

In 1934 Bob was signed by producer A.W. Hackel and made what are considered by B Western buffs to be some of the better and most overlooked films of the genre. Unlike most B Westerns, these films featured strong and oft-complicated storylines along with well-staged action sequences. The first fifteen films were released under the banner of Supreme Pictures; the final 16 by Republic.

From 1939 to 1940 Steele was with Metropolitan Pictures, and in late 1940 he initiated the Billy the Kid series at PRC. After three films, however, he yielded the role to Buster Crabbe and returned to Republic to join the Three Mesquiteers in the role of Tucson Smith. Steele made 19 Mesquiteer adventures between 1940 and 1943.

He then moved to Monogram to begin work on the Trail Blazers series with Ken Maynard and Hoot Gibson.

Steele closed his B career with a series of films at PRC in 1945 and 1946.

Bob Steele was equally adept at playing heroes and villains. His major film roles outside of Westerns were as bad buys. He was the teasing, taunting Curley in *Of Mice and Men* and was the vicious killer Canino in Humphrey Bogart's *The Big Sleep*.

In the fifties and sixties Steele appeared in countless films and TV shows including a stint as a regular on *F Troop*.

Bob Steele Filmography

1930: *The Cowboy and the Outlaw* (Sundicate; J.P. McGowan) *LL* Edna Aslin; *Near the Rainbow's End* (Tiffany; J.P. McGowan) *LL* Louise Lorraine; *Oklahoma Cyclone* (Tiffany; John P. McCarthy) *SK* Al St. John, *LL* Nita Ray; *Land of Missing Men* (Tiffany; John P. McCarthy) *SK* Al St. John, *LL* Caryl Lincoln; *Headin' North* (Tiffany; John P. McCarthy) *LL* Barbara Luddy. **1931:** *Sunrise Trail* (Tiffany; John P. McCarthy) *LL* Blanche Mehaffey; *The Ridin' Fool* (Tiffany; John P. McCarthy) *LL* Frances Morris, Josephine Velez; *The Nevada Buckaroo* (Tiffany; John P. McCarthy) *LL* Dorothy Dix; *Near the Trail's End* (Tiffany; Wallace Fox) *LL* Marion Shockley. **1932:** *South of Santa Fe* (World Wide; Bert Glennon) *LL* Janis Elliott; *Law of the West* (World Wide; R.N. Bradbury) *LL* Nancy Drexel; *Riders of the Desert* (World Wide; R.N. Bradbury) *LL* Gertrude Messenger; *Man from Hell's Edges* (World Wide; R.N. Bradbury) *LL* Nancy Drexel; *Son of Oklahoma* (World Wide; R.N. Bradbury) *LL* Carmen Laroux; *Hidden Valley* (Monogram; R.N. Bradbury) *LL* Gertrude Messinger; *Texas Buddies* (Tiffany/World Wide; R.N. Bradbury) *LL* Nancy Drexel; *Young Blood* (Monogram; Phil Rosen) *LL* Helen Foster, Naomi Judge; *The Fighting Champ* (Monogram; J.P. McCarthy) *LL* Arletta Duncan. **1933:** *Breed of the Border* (Monogram; R.N. Bradbury) *LL* Marion Byron; *The Gallant Fool* (Monogram; R.N. Bradbury) *LL* Arletta Duncan; *Galloping Romeo* (Monogram; R.N. Bradbury) *LL* Doris Hill; *The Rangers*

Code (Monogram; R.N. Bradbury) *LL* Doris Hill; *Trailing North* (Monogram; J.P. McCarthy) *LL* Doris Hill. **1934:** *A Demon for Trouble* (Supreme; Robert Hill) *LL* Gloria Shea, Carmen Laroux; *Brand of Hate* (Supreme; Lew Collins) *LL* Lucille Browne. **1935:** *Alias John Law* (Supreme; R.N. Bradbury) *LL* Roberta Gale; *Big Calibre* (Supreme; R.N. Bradbury) *LL* Peggy Campbell, Georgia O'Dell; *Kid Courageous* (Supreme; R.N. Bradbury) *LL* Renee Borden; *No Man's Range* (Supreme; R.N. Bradbury) *LL* Roberta Gale; *The Rider of the Law* (Supreme; R.N. Bradbury) *LL* Gertrude Messinger; *Smokey Smith* (Supreme; R.N. Bradbury) *LL* Mary Kornman; *Tombstone Terror* (Supreme; R.N. Bradbury) *LL* Kay McCoy, Hortense Petro, Ann Howard; *Western Justice* (Supreme; R.N. Bradbury) *LL* Renee Borden. **1936:** *the Kid Ranger* (Supreme; R.N. Bradbury) *LL* Joan Barclay; *Last of the Warrens* (Supreme; R.N. Bradbury) *LL* Margaret Marquis; *The Law Rides* (Supreme; R.N. Bradbury) *LL* Harley Wood, Margaret Mann; *Brand of the Outlaws* (Supreme; R.N. Bradbury) *LL* Margaret Marquis, Virginia True Boardman; *Cavalry* (Republic; R.N. Bradbury) *LL* Frances Grant; *Sundown Saunders* (Supreme; R.N. Bradbury) *LL* Catherine Cotter. **1937:** *The Gun Ranger* (Republic; R.N. Bradbury) *LL* Eleanor Stewart; *Lightnin' Crandall* (Republic; Sam Newfield) *LL* Lois January; *The Trusted Outlaw* (Republic; R.N. Bradbury) *LL* Lois January, Joan Barclay; *Gun Lords of Stirrup Basin* (Republic; Sam Newfield) *LL* Louise Stanley; *Border Phantom* (Republic; S. Roy Luby) *LL* Harley Wood; *Doomed at Sundown* (Republic; Sam Newfield) *LL* Lorraine Hayes (Day); *The Red Rope* (Republic; S. Roy Luby) *LL* Lois January; *Arizona Gunfighter* (Republic; Sam Newfield) *LL* Jean Carmen; *Ridin' the Lone Trail* (Republic; Sam Newfield) *LL* Claire Rochelle; *Colorado Kid* (Republic; Sam Newfield) *LL* Marion Weldon. **1938:** *Paroled to Die* (Republic; Sam Newfield) *LL* Kathleen Elliott; *Thunder in the Desert* (Republic; Sam Newfield) *LL* Louise Stanley; *The Feud Maker* (Republic; Sam Newfield) *LL* Marion Weldon; *Desert Patrol* (Republic; Sam Newfield) *LL* Marion Weldon; *Durango Valley Raiders* (Republic; Sam Newfield) *LL* Louise Stanley. **1939:** *Feud of the Range* (Metropolitan; Harry S. Webb) *LL* Gertrude Messinger; *Smokey Trails* (Metropolitan; Bernard B. Ray) *LL* Jean Carmen; *Mesquite Buckaroo* (Metropolitan; Harry S. Webb) *LL* Carolyn Curtis, Juanita Fletcher; *Riders of the Sage* (Metropolitan; Harry S. Webb) *LL* Claire Rochelle; *The Pal from Texas* (Metropolitan; Harry S. Webb) *LL* Claire Rochelle, Betty Mack; *El Diablo Rides* (Metropolitan; Ira Webb) *LL* Claire Rochelle. **1940:** *Wild Horse Valley* (Metropolitan; Ira Webb) *LL* Phyllis Adair; *Pinto Canyon* (Metropolitan; Raymond Johnson) *LL* Louise Stanley; *Billy the Kid Outlawed* (PRC; Peter Stewart [Sam Newfield]) *SK* Al St. John, *LL* Louise Currie; *Billy the Kid in Texas* (PRC; Peter Stewart [Sam Newfield]) *SK* Al St. John, *LL* Terry Walker; *The Trail Blazers* (Republic; George Sherman) *SK* 3 Mesquiteers, *LL* Pauline Moore; *Lone Star Raiders* (Republic; George

Sherman) *SK* 3 Mesquiteers, *LL* June Johnson; *Billy the Kid's Gun Justice* (PRC; Peter Stewart) *SK* Al St. John, *LL* Louise Currie. **1941:** *Billy the Kid's Range War* (PRC; Peter Stewart) *SK* Al St. John, *LL* Joan Barclay; *Prairie Pioneers* (Republic; Les Orlebeck) *SK* 3 Mesquiteers, *LL* Esther Estrella; *Pals of the Pecos* (Republic; Les Orlebeck) *SK* 3 Mesquiteers, *LL* June Johnson; *Billy the Kid's Fighting Pals* (PRC; Sherman Scott [Sam Newfield]) *SK* Al St. John, *LL* Phyllis Adair; *Saddlemates* (Republic; Les Orlebeck) *SK* 3 Mesquiteers, *LL* Gale Storm; *Gangs of Sonora* (Republic; John English) *SK* 3 Mesquiteers, *LL* June Johnson; *Outlaws of the Cherokee Trail* (Republic; Les Orlebeck) *SK* 3 Mesquiteers, *LL* Lois Collier; *Gauchos of El Dorado* (Republic; Les Orlebeck) *SK* 3 Mesquiteers, *LL* Lois Collier; *West of Cimarron* (Republic; Les Orlebeck) *SK* 3 Mesquiteers, *LL* Lois Collier. **1942:** *Code of the Outlaw* (Republic; John English) *SK* 3 Mesquiteers, *LL* Melinda Leighton; *Raiders of the Range* (Republic; John English) *SK* 3 Mesquiteers, *LL* Lois Collier; *Westward Ho* (Republic; John English) *SK* 3 Mesquiteers, *LL* Evelyn Brent; *The Phantom Plainsmen* (Republic; John English) *SK* 3 Mesquiteers, *LL* Lois Collier; *Shadows on the Sage* (Republic; Les Orlebeck) *SK* 3 Mesquiteers, *LL* Cheryl Walker; *Valley of Hunted Men* (Republic; John English) *SK* 3 Mesquiteers, *LL* Anna Marie Stewart. **1943:** *Thundering Trails* (Republic; Al Herman) *SK* 3 Mesquiteers, *LL* Nell O'Day; *The Blocked Trail* (Republic; Elmer Clifton) *SK* 3 Mesquiteers, *LL* Helen Deverall; *Santa Fe Scouts* (Republic; Howard Bretherton) *SK* 3 Mesquiteers, *LL* Lois Collier; *Riders of the Rio Grande* (Republic; Howard Bretherton) *SK* 3 Mesquiteers, *LL* Lorraine Miller; *Death Valley Rangers* (Monogram; Robert Tansey) *SK* Trail Blazers, *LL* Linda Brent. **1944:** *Westward Bound* (Monogram; Robert Tansey) *SK* Trail Blazers, *LL* Betty Miles; *Arizona Whirlwind* (Monogram; Robert Tansey) *SK* Trail Blazers, *LL* Myrna Dell; *Outlaw Trail* (Monogram; Robert Tansey) *SK* Trail Blazers, *LL* Jennifer Holt; *Sonora Stagecoach* (Monogram; Robert Tansey) *SK* Trail Blazers, *LL* Betty Miles; *The Utah Kid* (Monogram; Vernon Keays) *SK* Trail Blazers, *LL* Beatrice Gray, Evelyn Eaton; *Marked Trails* (Monogram; J.P. McCarthy) *SK* Hoot Gibson, *LL* Veda Ann Borg; *Trigger Law* (Monogram; Vernon Keays) *SK* Hoot Gibson, *LL* Beatrice Gray. **1945:** *Wildfire* (Screen Guild; Robert Tansey) *SK* Sterling Holloway, *LL* Virginia Maples; *The Navajo Kid* (PRC; Harry Fraser) *SK* Syd Saylor, *LL* Caren Marsh; *Northwest Trail* (Lippert; Derwin Abrahams) *LL* Joan Woodbury. **1946:** *Six Gun Man* (PRC; Harry Fraser) *SK* Syd Saylor, *LL* Jean Carlin; *Ambush Trail* (PRC; Harry Fraser) *SK* Syd Saylor, *LL* Lorraine Miller; *Thunder Town* (PRC; Harry Fraser) *SK* Syd Saylor, *LL* Ellen Hall.

Conway Tearle

Conway Tearle

Near the end of his long film career, former silent screen leading man Conway Tearle starred in four B Westerns for Beaumont Pictures in 1935 and 1936.

Tearle, the half brother of the distinguished British stage and screen actor Godfrey Tearle, was born Frederick Levy in England in 1878.

Beginning with *Virtuous Wives* in 1918, Tearle became one of the silent era's top leading men, specializing in soap opera–like melodramas. When

the silents gave way to sound, he became a character actor appearing in such diverse films as *Gold Diggers of 1929*, George Cukor's grandiose *Romeo & Juliet* in 1936, and *Klondike Annie* with Mae West.
	Tearle passed away in 1938.

Conway Tearle Filmography

1935: *The Judgment Book* (Beaumont; Charles Hutchinson) *LL* Bernadine Hayes; *Trail's End* (Beaumont; Al Herman) *LL* Claudia Dell. **1936:** *Desert Guns* (Beaumont; Charles Hutchinson) *LL* Margaret Morris; *Senor Jim* (Beaumont; Jacques Jaccard) *LL* Barbara Bedford, Betty Mack.

Tom Tyler

Horses: Ace, Baron

	Tom Tyler was born Vincent Markowski in Port Henry, New York, on August 9, 1903, and grew up in Detroit, Michigan. Markowski was a weight lifter and bodybuilder who worked as a coal miner, a merchant seaman and lumberjack as well as being a pro boxer and football player.
	He entered the film industry as sort of a jack-of-all-trades in 1924. He worked as a prop man, stuntman, bit player and extra.
	While playing a small part in the 1925 epic *Ben Hur*, Tyler was offered a contract to make Westerns for Joe Kennedy's FBO Studios. FBO was involved in a contract dispute with their top cowboy Fred Thompson and, rather than yield to his salary demands, they signed the unknown Tyler and gave the star his walking papers.
	Tyler's first starring vehicle was *Galloping Gallagher* released in 1925. He made more than 25 films before leaving the studio at the beginning of the sound era in 1929.
	In 1930 he signed to make features for Syndicate and made the serial *The Phantom of the West* for Mascot.
	The following year Tyler went to Monogram Pictures for a series of B Westerns and began to establish himself as a top serial star. He made *Battling with Buffalo Bill, The Jungle Mystery, Clancy of the Mounted* and *The Phantom of the Air* all for Universal in 1932 and 1933.
	After eight features he left Monogram for Freuler Films and a four-picture deal.

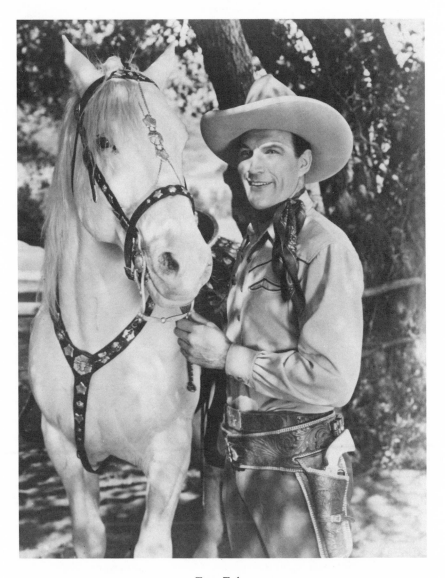

Tom Tyler

In 1934 Tyler was hired by Reliable Pictures and made 18 films for them over the next two years.

The year 1935 saw Tyler appearing in the classic B *Powdersmoke Range,* and in 1936 he was in *The Last Outlaw* with Hoot Gibson and Harry Carey.

In late 1936 and 1937 he made films for Victory Pictures.

Nineteen thirty-nine was a good year for Tom Tyler; he had featured parts in three of the all-time classic motion pictures: *Stagecoach, Gone with the Wind* and *Drums Along the Mohawk.* The following year a gauze-wrapped Tyler had the title role in *The Mummy's Hand.*

In 1941 Tom Tyler inked a pact with Republic Pictures and began his stint there by taking the lead role in one of the great all-time adventure serials, *The Adventures of Captain Marvel.* That year he also assumed the role of Stoney Brooke in the popular Three Mesquiteers series. He remained in that role for the final 13 films of the series which ended in 1943, the same year he made *The Phantom* serial for Columbia.

At the conclusion of the Mesquiteers series Tyler contracted an arthritic condition which put him out of work for two years. When he returned to work in 1945, he found good roles hard to come by. He got a few bit parts in major films like *San Antonio* with Errol Flynn and in the late forties made six B's with Jimmy Ellison and Russ Hayden.

Tom Tyler subsequently retired from the screen and went to live with his sister in Detroit.

He died of a heart attack on May 1, 1954.

Tom Tyler Filmography

1929: *Idaho Red* (FBO; Robert DeLacey) SK Frankie Darro, LL Patricia Caron. **1930:** *Call of the Desert* (Syndicate; J.P. McGowan) LL Sheila Legay; *The Canyon of Missing Men* (Syndicate; J.P. McGowan) LL Sheila Legay; *'Neath Western Skies* (Syndicate; J.P. McGowan) LL Lotus Thompson. **1931:** *The Phantom of the West* (serial) (Mascot; Ross Lederman) LL Dorothy Gulliver; *West of Cheyenne* (Syndicate; Harry S. Webb) LL Josephine Hill; *God's Country and the Man* (Syndicate; J.P. McCarthy) LL Betty Mack; *Rider of the Plains* (Syndicate; J.P. McCarthy) SK Andy Shuford, LL Lillian Bond; *Partners of the Trail* (Monogram; Wallace Fox) LL Betty Mack; *The Man from Death Valley* (Monogram; Lloyd Nosler) LL Betty Mack; *Two-Fisted Justice* (Monogram; G. Arthur Durlam) LL Barbara Weeks. **1932:** *Single-handed Sanders* (Monogram; Lloyd Nosler) LL Margaret Morris; *The Man from New Mexico* (Monogram; J.P. McCarthy) LL Caryl Lincoln; *Vanishing Men* (Monogram; Harry Fraser) LL Adele Lacy; *Honor of the Mounted* (Monogram; Harry Fraser) LL Cecelia Ryland; *The Forty-Niners* (Freuler; John P. McCarthy) LL Betty Mack; *Galloping Thru* (Monogram; Lloyd Nosler) LL Betty Mack. **1933:** *When a Man Rides Alone* (Freuler; J.P. McGowan) LL Adele Lacy; *Clancy of the Mounted* (serial) (Universal; Ray Taylor) LL Jacqueline Wells; *Deadwood Pass* (Freuler; J.P. McGowan) LL Alice Dahl; *War on the Range* (Freuler; J.P. McGowan) LL Caryl Lincoln. **1934:** *Mystery Ranch* (Reliable; Ray

Bernard [B.B. Ray]) *LL* Roberta Gale; *Fighting Hero* (Reliable; Harry S. Webb) *LL* Renee Borden; *Terror of the Plains* (Reliable; Harry S. Webb) *LL* Roberta Gale. **1935:** *Unconquered Bandit* (Reliable; Harry S. Webb) *LL* Lillian Gilmore; *Tracy Rides* (Reliable; Harry S. Webb) *LL* Virginia Brown Faire; *The Silver Bullet* (Reliable; B.B. Ray) *LL* Jayne Regan; *Ridin Thru* (Reliable; Harry S. Webb) *LL* Ruth Hiatt; *Born to Battle* (Reliable; Harry S. Webb) *LL* Jean Carmen; *Coyote Trails* (Reliable; B.B. Ray) *SK* Ben Corbett, *LL* Helen Dahl; *The Laramie Kid* (Reliable; Harry S. Webb) *LL* Alberta Vaughn; *Rio Rattler* (Reliable; Franklin Shamray [B.B. Ray]) *LL* Marion Shilling; *Silent Valley* (Reliable; B.B. Ray) *LL* Nancy DeShon; *Trigger Tom* (Reliable; Henri Samuels [Harry S. Webb]) *SK* Al St. John, *LL* Bernadine Hayes. **1936:** *Fast Bullets* (Reliable; Henri Samuels [Harry S. Webb]) *LL* Margaret Nearing; *Ridin' On* (Reliable; B.B. Ray) *LL* Geraine Greear (Joan Barclay); *Roamin' Wild* (Reliable; B.B. Ray) *LL* Carol Wyndham; *Pinto Rustlers* (Reliable; Henri Samuels [Harry S. Webb]) *SK* Al St. John, *LL* Catherine Cotter; *Santa Fe Bound* (Reliable; Henri Samuels [Harry S. Webb]) *LL* Jeanne Martel, Dorothy Woods; *Rip Roarin' Buckaroo* (Victory; Robert Hill) *LL* Beth Marion; *The Phantom of the Range* (Victory; Robert Hill) *LL* Beth Marion, Soledad Jiminez. **1937:** *Cheyenne Rides Again* (Victory; Robert Hill) *LL* Lucille Brown, Carmen Laroux; *The Feud of the Trail* (Victory; Robert Hill) *LL* Harlene Wood; *Mystery Range* (Victory; Bob Hill); *Orphan of the Pecos* (Victory; Sam Katzman) *LL* Jeanne Martel; *Brothers of the West* (Victory; Sam Katzman) *LL* Lois Wilde, Dorothy Short; *Lost Ranch* (Victory; Sam Katzman) *LL* Jeanne Martel, Marjorie Beebe. **1941:** *Outlaws of the Cherokee Trail* (Republic; Les Orlebeck) *SK* 3 Mesquiteers, *LL* Lois Collier; *Gauchos of El Dorado* (Republic; Les Orlebeck) *SK* 3 Mesquiteers, *LL* Lois Collier; *West of Cimarron* (Republic; Les Orlebeck) *SK* 3 Mesquiteers, *LL* Lois Collier. **1942:** *Code of the Outlaw* (Republic; John English) *SK* 3 Mesquiteers, *LL* Melinda Leighton; *Raiders of the Range* (Republic; John English) *SK* 3 Mesquiteers, *LL* Lois Collier; *Westward Ho* (Republic; John English) *SK* 3 Mesquiteers, *LL* Lois Collier, Evelyn Brent; *The Phantom Plainsmen* (Republic; John English) *SK* 3 Mesquiteers, *LL* Lois Collier; *Shadows on the Sage* (Republic; Les Orlebeck) *SK* 3 Mesquiteers, *LL* Cheryl Walker; *Valley of Hunted Men* (Republic; John English) *SK* 3 Mesquiteers, *LL* Anna Marie Stewart. **1943:** *Thundering Trails* (Republic; Al Herman) *SK* 3 Mesquiteers, *LL* Nell O'Day; *Santa Fe Scouts* (Republic; Howard Bretherton) *SK* 3 Mesquiteers, *LL* Lois Collier; *Riders of the Rio Grande* (Republic; Howard Bretherton) *SK* 3 Mesquiteers, *LL* Lorraine Miller; *The Blocked Trail* (Republic; Elmer Clifton) *SK* 3 Mesquiteers, *LL* Helen Deverall. **1945:** *Sing Me a Song of Texas* (Columbia; Vernon Keays) *LL* Rosemary Lane.

Jimmy Wakely

Horse: Sunset
Sidekicks: Dub "Cannonball" Taylor, Lee "Lasses" White

Jimmy Wakely was born in Mineola, Arkansas, on February 16, 1914.
When he was a youngster, his family moved to Oklahoma where Jimmy
learned to play guitar and sing.

In 1937 he formed the Jimmy Wakely Trio with Johnny Bond and
Scotty Harrell and began performing on an Oklahoma City radio station.
Later they took their talents to the National Barn Dance. In 1938 they
signed with Decca Records.

Wakely made his film debut in 1939 in *The Saga of Death Valley,*
which starred Roy Rogers.

The trio was signed to be regulars on Gene Autry's Melody Ranch
radio show and began making onscreen music in Autry's films. They also
appeared in films starring Charles Starrett and Tex Ritter.

In 1944 Monogram Pictures signed Jimmy Wakely to star in his own
series of musical Westerns.

Beginning with *Song of the Range,* Wakely made 28 films for
Monogram between 1944 and 1949. His sidekick in the first 12 was Lee
"Lasses" White. White gave way to Cannonball Taylor, who rode with
Wakely for the remainder of the series.

Jimmy Wakely's biggest hit records were "Slipping Around" and Eddie
Dean's "One Has My Name, the Other Has My Heart."

In the early sixties he starred in his own nationally-syndicated television show.

Jimmy Wakely died of a heart attack on September 23, 1982.

Jimmy Wakely Filmography

1944: *Song of the Range* (Monogram; Wallace Fox) *SK* Lee "Lasses" White,
LL Kay Forrester. **1945:** *Springtime in Texas* (Monogram; Oliver Drake) *SK*
Lee "Lasses" White, *LL* Marie Harmon; *Saddle Serenade* (Monogram;
Oliver Drake) *SK* Lee "Lasses" White, *LL* Nancy Brinkman; *Riders of the
Dawn* (Monogram; Oliver Drake) *SK* Lee "Lasses" White, *LL* Phyllis Adair;
Lonesome Trail (Monogram; Oliver Drake) *SK* Lee "Lasses" White, *LL* Iris
Clive. **1946:** *Moon Over Montana* (Monogram; Oliver Drake) *SK* Lee
"Lasses" White, *LL* Jennifer Holt; *West of the Alamo* (Monogram; Oliver
Drake) *SK* Lee "Lasses" White, *LL* Iris Clive; *Trail to Mexico* (Monogram;
Oliver Drake) *SK* Lee "Lasses" White, *LL* Delores Castelli, Dora Del Rio;

Jimmy Wakely

Song of the Sierras (Monogram; Oliver Drake) SK Lee "Lasses" White, LL Jean Carlin, Iris Clive. **1947:** *Rainbow Over the Rockies* (Monogram; Oliver Drake) SK Lee "Lasses" White, LL Pat Starling; *Six Gun Serenade* (Monogram; Ford Beebe) SK Lee "Lasses" White; *Song of the Wasteland* (Monogram; Thomas Carr) SK Lee "Lasses" White, LL Dottye Brown; *Ridin' Down the Trail* (Monogram; Howard Bretherton) SK Cannonball Taylor, LL Beverly Jons. **1948:** *Song of the Drifter* (Monogram; Frank Wishbar) SK Cannonball Taylor, LL Mildred Coles; *Oklahoma Blues* (Monogram; Lambert Hillyer) SK Cannonball Taylor, LL Virginia Belmont; *The Rangers Ride* (Monogram; Derwin Abrahams) SK Cannonball

Taylor, *LL* Virginia Belmont; *Range Renegades* (Monogram; Lambert Hillyer) *SK* Cannonball Taylor, *LL* Jennifer Holt; *Cowboy Cavalier* (Monogram; Derwin Abrahams) *SK* Cannonball Taylor, *LL* Jan Bryant; *Partners of the Sunset* (Monogram; Lambert Hillyer) *SK* Cannonball Taylor, *LL* Christine Larson; *Silver Trails* (Monogram; Christy Cabanne) *SK* Cannonball Taylor, Whip Wilson, *LL* Christine Larson; *Outlaw Brand* (Monogram; Lambert Hillyer) *SK* Cannonball Taylor, *LL* Christine Larson, Kay Morley; *Courtin' Trouble* (Monogram; Ford Beebe) *SK* Cannonball Taylor, *LL* Virginia Belmont. **1949:** *Gun Runner* (Monogram; Lambert Hillyer) *SK* Cannonball Taylor, *LL* Mae Clark, Noel Neill; *Gun Law Justice* (Monogram; Lambert Hillyer) *SK* Cannonball Taylor, *LL* Jane Adams; *Across the Rio Grande* (Monogram; Oliver Drake) *SK* Cannonball Taylor, *LL* Reno Browne; *Brand of Fear* (Monogram; Oliver Drake) *SK* Cannonball Taylor, *LL* Gail Davis; *Roaring Westward* (Monogram; Oliver Drake) *SK* Cannonball Taylor, *LL* Lois Hall; *Lawless Code* (Monogram; Oliver Drake) *SK* Cannonball Taylor, *LL* Ellen Hall.

Wally Wales

Horse: Silver King
Sidekick: Buzz Barton

Silent screen and early B Western star Wally Wales was born Floyd Taliaferro Alderson on November 13, 1895, in Sheridan, Wyoming. He was raised on a ranch and later worked as a cowboy.

The year 1916 found him working as an extra in Tom Mix Westerns. In 1917 and 1918 he was part of the American Expeditionary Forces in France during World War I.

When he returned from the war he went back to work in films, gradually getting bigger and bigger parts.

In 1924 he was signed by Pathé for his own series of Westerns. They changed his name to Wally Wales with the release of his first film *Tearing Loose.* For the next several years Wales was one of Pathé's biggest box-office attractions.

When the sound era arrived, Wales began making films for the much smaller and lower-funded Big 4 Film Company. Beginning with *Canyon Hawks,* he made seven films in 1930 and 1931. He could also be found in films starring other Big 4 cowboys such as Buffalo Bill, Jr.

In 1934 he signed with Imperial Pictures. He did seven pictures in this series in which he rode a horse called Silver King, who had formerly been owned by the late silent film cowboy star Fred Thompson.

Wally Wales

In 1936 Wales changed his name to Hal Taliaferro and began to concentrate on character roles. As Taliaferro his first major role was as one of
the leads in the 1937 Republic serial *The Lone Ranger*. Taliaferro went on
to make scores of Westerns and other films before retiring in the late
1950s.

He passed away of pneumonia on February 12, 1980, back home in
Sheridan, Wyoming.

Wally Wales Filmography

1930: *Canyon Hawks* (Big 4; J.P. McGowan, Alan James) *SK* Buzz Barton,
LL Rene Borden; *Trails of Peril* (Big 4; Alan James) *LL* Virginia Brown
Faire; *Breed of the West* (Big 4; Alan James) *SK* Buzz Barton, *LL* Virginia
Brown Faire. **1931:** *Red Fork Range* (Big 4; Alan James) *LL* Ruth Mix; *Hell's*

Valley (Big 4; Alan James) *LL* Virginia Brown Faire; *Riders of the Cactus* (Big 4; David Kirkland) *SK* Buzz Barton, *LL* Lorraine Laval; *Flying Lariats* (Big 4; Alan James) *SK* Buzz Barton, *LL* Bonnie Gray. **1934:** *Potluck Pards* (Reliable; Bernard B. Ray) *SK* Ben Corbett, *LL* Josephine Hill; *Arizona Cyclone* (Imperial; Robert Emmett Tansey) *SK* Silver King, *LL* Karla Cowan; *Carrying the Mail* (Imperial; Robert Emmett Tansey) *SK* Silver King, *LL* Peggy Darling; *Desert Man* (Imperial; Robert Emmett Tansey) *SK* Silver King, *LL* Peggy Darling; *The Lone Rider* (Imperial; Robert Emmett Tansey) *SK* Silver King, *LL* Marla Bratton; *Pals of the West* (Imperial; Robert Emmett Tansey) *SK* Silver King, *LL* Dorothy Gritten; *The Sundown Trail* (Imperial; Robert Emmett Tansey) *SK* Silver King, *LL* Fay McKenzie; *West of the Law* (Imperial; Robert Emmett Tansey) *SK* Silver King, *LL* Marla Bratton.

James Warren

James Warren starred in a trio of B Westerns for RKO Studios in the mid forties. The films were based on the writings of Zane Grey.

Warren was born James Wittlig in Marietta, Ohio. He moved to New York to study and was making a comfortable living as a successful commercial artist when he was signed to an acting contract by MGM studios.

He did small parts at Metro for a couple of years before moving to RKO.

Following the Grey Westerns, he remained in the movies for a time before returning to his first love — art.

Recent reports have him a very successful artist in Hawaii.

James Warren Filmography

1945: *Wanderer of the Wasteland* (RKO; Edward Killy, Wallace Grissell) *SK* Richard Martin, *LL* Audrey Long. **1946:** *Sunset Pass* (RKO; William Berke) *LL* Jane Greer. **1947:** *Code of the West* (RKO; William Berke) *LL* Debra Alden.

James Warren and Jane Greer.

John Wayne

Horse: Duke

Movie fans know John Wayne for his performances in such Western epics as *Stagecoach, The Alamo, Rio Bravo, The Angel and the Badman* and scores of others including his Oscar-winning characterization of Marshal Rooster Cogburn in *True Grit.* What most folks don't know is that Wayne got his basic cowboy hero training in 39 B Westerns that he made in the 1930s.

John Wayne's onscreen performances over the years perpetuated an

John Wayne

upright, stalwart image that has become the epitome of the American hero.

His film career began inauspiciously enough. As a member of the University of Southern California Trojan football team Wayne, along with several of his teammates, was hired by a director to be an extra in the film *The Dropkick.*

When he was forced to set aside his athletic career due to a leg injury, Wayne got a job as a prop man and bit player at Fox Studios.

He formed a lifelong friendship with director John Ford while working on Ford's 1929 film *Salute.* In fact that friendship led to Wayne's securing his first lead role in Raul Walsh's 1930 epic *The Big Trail.*

In early 1932 Wayne was given featured parts in two Tim McCoy

John Wayne in one of his 39 B Western roles of the 1930s.

Westerns, *The Texas Cyclone* and *Two-Fisted Law*. Later that same year he was signed to star in his own series by Warner Bros. The Duke's first B Western was *Ride Him Cowboy*. It was released on August 21, 1932, and ran 56 minutes. This film also introduced John Wayne's four-legged B Western compadre, his horse "Duke." Wayne and Duke rode through six films for Warners before galloping over to Monogram Pictures in 1933.

Riders of Destiny was the first of Wayne's films at Monogram. The films, while released by Monogram, were actually produced by Paul Malvern's Lone Star Productions and were commonly called Lone Star Westerns. Wayne made 16 of these over a two-year span.

Wayne's Lone Star Westerns had some interesting points. His character in several of the films was Singin' Sandy. While Wayne rode along on horseback plunking a guitar and lip-syncing words, the voice was actually provided by soon-to-be-cowboy-star Smith Ballew.

A regular in the seriers was a pre–"Gabby" George Hayes, and many of the films were directed by Bob Steele's dad, R.N. Bradbury.

The series also produced one of the best of the B Westerns, *The Dawn Rider* in 1935.

When Monogram along with several other studios became Republic pictures, the new company signed Wayne to a contract. He starred in eight films, and then in 1938 he joined the Three Mesquiteers, replacing Bob Livingston as Stoney Brooke. Wayne made eight Mesquiteer films.

While working on the Mesquiteer series, Wayne was signed by his old pal John Ford to play the Ringo Kid in *Stagecoach.*

John Wayne was born Marion Michael Morrison in Winterset, Iowa, on May 26, 1907, and died on June 11, 1979. He made his last film, *The Shootist,* in 1976.

John Wayne Filmography

1932: *Ride Him Cowboy* (Warner Bros.; Fred Allen) SK Duke, LL Ruth Hall; *The Big Stampede* (Warner Bros.; Tenny Wright) SK Duke, LL Mae Madison; *Haunted Gold* (Warner Bros.; Mack Wright) SK Duke, LL Sheila Terry. **1933:** *The Telegraph Rail* (Warner Bros.; Tenny Wright) SK Duke, LL Marceline Day; *Somewhere in Sonora* (Warner Bros.; Mack V. Wright) SK Duke, LL Shirley Palmer; *The Man from Monterey* (Warner Bros.; Mack V. Wright) SK Duke, LL Ruth Hall; *Riders of Destiny* (Monogram; Robert N. Bradbury) SK Duke, LL Cecilia Parker; *Sagebrush Trail* (Monogram; Armand Schaefer) LL Nancy Shubert. **1934:** *The Lucky Texan* (Monogram; R.N. Bradbury) LL Barbara Sheldon; *West of the Divide* (Monogram; R.N. Bradbury) LL Virginia Brown Faire; *Blue Steel* (Monogram; R.N. Bradbury) LL Eleanor Hunt; *The Man from Utah* (Monogram; R.N. Bradbury) LL Polly Ann Young; *Randy Rides Alone* (Monogram; Harry Fraser) LL Alberta Vaughn; *The Star Packer* (Monogram; R.N. Bradbury) LL Verna Hillie; *The Trail Beyond* (Monogram; R.N. Bradbury) LL Verna Hillie, Iris Lancaster; *Lawless Frontier* (Monogram; R.N. Bradbury) LL Sheila Terry; *'Neath the Arizona Skies* (Monogram; Harry Fraser) LL Sheila Terry. **1935:** *Texas Terror* (Monogram; R.N. Bradbury) LL Lucille Browne; *Rainbow Valley* (Monogram; R.N. Bradbury) LL Lucille Browne; *The Desert Trail* (Monogram; Cullen Lewis) LL Mary Kornman, Carmen Laroux; *The Dawn Rider* (Monogram; R.N. Bradbury) LL Marion Burns; *Paradise Canyon* (Monogram; Carl Pierson) LL Marion Burns; *Westward Ho* (Republic; R.N. Bradbury) LL Sheila Mannors; *The New Frontier* (Republic; Carl Pierson) LL Muriel Evans, Mary MacLaren; *Lawless Range* (Republic; R.N. Bradbury) LL Sheila Mannors. **1936:** *The Oregon Trail* (Republic; Scott Pembroke) LL Ann Rutherford; *The Lawless Nineties* (Republic; Joseph Kane) LL Ann Rutherford; *King of the Pecos* (Republic; Joseph Kane) LL Muriel Evans; *The Lonely Trail* (Republic;

Joseph Kane) *LL* Ann Rutherford; *Winds of the Wasteland* (Republic; Mack Wright) *LL* Phyllis Fraser. **1937:** *Born to the West* (Paramount; Charles Barton) *SK* Johnny Mack Brown, *LL* Marsha Hunt. **1938:** *Pals of the Saddle* (Republic; George Sherman) *SK* 3 Mesquiteers, *LL* Doreen McKay; *Overland Stage Raiders* (Republic; George Sherman) *SK* 3 Mesquiteers, *LL* Louise Brooks; *Santa Fe Stampede* (Republic; George Sherman) *SK* 3 Mesquiteers, *LL* June Martel; *Red River Range* (Republic; George Sherman) *SK* 3 Mesquiteers, *LL* Polly Moran. **1939:** *The Night Riders* (Republic; George Sherman) *SK* 3 Mesquiteers, *LL* Doreen McKay, Ruth Rogers; *Three Texas Steers* (Republic; George Sherman) *SK* 3 Mesquiteers, *LL* Carole Landis, Colette Lyons; *Wyoming Outlaw* (Republic; George Sherman) *SK* 3 Mesquiteers, *LL* Adele Pearce, Katharine Kentworthy; *The New Frontier* (Republic; George Sherman) *SK* 3 Mesquiteers, *LL* Phyllis Isley.

Ted Wells

Lanky Ted Wells was a professional rodeo bronc-riding and calf-roping champion when he was signed by Universal Pictures in 1921.

He debuted the following year by starring in *Straight Shootin'* and gained a respectable legion of fans throughout the twenties in such films as *Border Wildcat, Desert Dust* and *Born to the Saddle.*

When the talkies arrived, Wells' career wound down and he retired from the movies.

He returned in 1935 for a pair of one-shot B's for Aywon and American, two small Poverty Row outfits, then once again retired.

Ted Wells Filmography

1935: *The Phantom Cowboy* (Aywon; Robert J. Horner) *LL* Edna Aslin; *Defying the Law* (American; Robert J. Horner) *LL* Edna Aslin.

Big Boy Williams

He stood way over six feet tall, weighed in excess of 200 pounds and was given his most appropriate "Big Boy" tag by his friend, the great Will Rogers.

Ted Wells

Big Boy was born Guinn Williams in Decatur, Texas, April 26, 1900, the son of a U.S. congressman.

He was an all-round athlete in high school and studied law for a spell at North Texas State.

His ability as a rodeo performer got him to Hollywood and he made his debut in Rogers' 1919 film *Almost a Husband.*

He began starring in his own Westerns and comedies in the early twenties.

In 1934 and 1935 he starred in his own B series for First Division and Beacon studios. An interesting point is that his film *Law of the 45's* introduced the Three Mesquiteers to movie audiences. He played Tucson Smith in that film and had the role of Lullaby in the classic B *Powdersmoke Range* the same year.

Big Boy Williams

In 1944 he served as Roy Rogers' sidekick "Teddy Bear" in two features, *Hands Across the Border* and *The Cowboy and the Senorita*.

Williams became one of Hollywood's busiest and most recognizable character actors. He played the part of Pete the Canvas Boss in the early TV series *Circus Boy*.

Big Boy Williams died of uremic poisoning on June 6, 1962, in Van Nuys, California.

Big Boy Williams Filmography

1934: *Cowboy Holiday* (Beacon; Bob Hill) *LL* Janet Chandler; *Thunder Over Texas* (Beacon; John Warner) *LL* Marion Shilling. **1935:** *Law of the 45's* (First Division; John P. McCarthy) *SK* Fuzzy St. John, *LL* Molly O'Day; *Big Boy Rides Again* (First Division; Al Herman) *LL* Connie Bergen; *Danger Trails* (First Division; Bob Hill) *LL* Marjorie Gordon; *Gun Play* (aka *Lucky Boots*) (First Division; Al Herman) *LL* Marion Shilling.

Jay Wilsey *see* Buffalo Bill, Jr.

Whip Wilson

Horse: Silver Bullet
Sidekicks: Andy Clyde, Fuzzy Knight

Fan reaction to his appearance in the 1948 Jimmy Wakely film *Silver Trails* got former rodeo performer and bullwhip master Whip Wilson his own series of Westerns with Monogram Pictures.

Beginning with *Crashing Thru* in 1949 Wilson made 22 films for the company over a two-year period, twelve of them with Andy Clyde as his trail partner and eight with Fuzzy Knight by his side.

There was no avoiding comparison between Wilson and the screen's other whip expert, Lash LaRue. While LaRue was the more famous of the two, due to his magnetic personality, Wilson made better films; basically because Monogram's production standards and budgets were a cut above those at PRC.

Wilson was born Charles Myers in Pecos, Texas, on June 16, 1919. He was a direct descendant of General George Armstrong Custer and became a rodeo cowboy as a teenager. In 1939 he won the title of Best All-Round Cowboy at the West Texas Rodeo.

Wilson joined the U.S. Marines during World War II and saw action at Guadalcanal. For his bravery and heroism he was awarded the Purple Heart.

When the war was over he resumed his rodeo career. He was spotted by a talent scout for Monogram, underwent the customary name change and was given a co-starring role in the Wakely film.

In 1952 he left the screen and returned to the rodeo circuit.

Whip Wilson passed away of a heart attack on October 23, 1964, at the age of 45.

Whip Wilson Filmography

1949: *Crashing Thru* (Monogram; Ray Taylor) *SK* Andy Clyde, *LL* Christine Larson; *Shadows of the West* (Monogram; Ray Taylor) *SK* Andy Clyde, *LL* Reno Browne; *Haunted Trails* (Monogram; Lambert Hillyer) *SK* Andy Clyde, *LL* Reno Browne; *Riders of the Dusk* (Monogram; Lambert Hillyer) *SK* Andy Clyde, *LL* Reno Browne; *Range Land* (Monogram; Lambert Hillyer) *SK* Andy Clyde, *LL* Reno Browne. **1950:** *Fence Riders* (Monogram; Wallace Fox) *SK* Andy Clyde, *LL* Reno Browne; *Gunslingers* (Monogram; Wallace Fox) *SK* Andy Clyde, *LL* Reno Browne; *Arizona Territory* (Monogram; Wallace Fox) *SK* Andy Clyde, *LL* Nancy Saunders;

Whip Wilson and Silver Bullet.

Silver Raiders (Monogram; Wallace Fox) *SK* Andy Clyde, *LL* Virginia Herrick; *Cherokee Uprising* (Monogram; Lewis Collins) *SK* Andy Clyde, *LL* Lois Hall; *Outlaws of Texas* (Monogram; Thomas Carr) *SK* Andy Clyde, *LL* Phyllis Coates. **1951:** *Abilene Trail* (Monogram; Lewis Collins) *SK* Andy Clyde, *LL* Noel Neill; *Wanted Dead or Alive* (Monogram; Thomas Carr) *SK* Fuzzy Knight, *LL* Christine McIntyre; *Canyon Raiders* (Monogram; Lewis Collins) *SK* Fuzzy Knight, *LL* Phyllis Coates; *Nevada Badmen* (Monogram; Lewis Collins) *SK* Fuzzy Knight, *LL* Phyllis Coates); *Stagecoach Driver* (Monogram; Lewis Collins) *SK* Fuzzy Knight, *LL* Gloria Winters; *Lawless Cowboys* (Monogram; Lewis Collins) *SK* Fuzzy Knight, *LL* Pamela Duncan; *Stage to Blue River* (Monogram; Lewis Collins) *SK* Fuzzy Knight, *LL* Phyllis Coates. **1952:** *Night Raiders* (Monogram; Howard Bretherton) *SK* Fuzzy Knight, *LL* Lois Hall; *The Gunman* (Monogram; Lewis Collins) *SK* Fuzzy Knight, *LL* Phyllis Coates; *Montana Incident* (Monogram; Lewis Collins) *LL* Noel Neill, Peggy Stewart; *Wyoming Roundup* (Monogram; Thomas Carr) *LL* Phyllis Coates.

THE
SIDEKICKS

Has Anybody Seen
That Ole Saddle Pal o' Mine

Next to his horse, his guitar, his lasso, and his six-gun, the B Western cowboy hero's best friend was his faithful sidekick who rode with him through thick and thin, tumbleweed and sagebrush, ambushes and Indian raids.

In most instances sidekicks supplied to the films what film critics and analysts have dubbed "comedy relief." However, an overall look at the B Western sidekicks reveals that they would tend to fall into four basic categories: comedy, juvenile, romantic and musical.

The most famous of the sidekicks were the comedians. This group included the best of the breed: Gabby Hayes, Smiley Burnette, Al "Fuzzy" St. John, Andy Clyde, Max Terhune, Raymond Hatton, Pat Buttram, Pat Brady, and a host of others.

While undoubtedly Hayes is the most famous of the sidekicks, the overall sidekick craze can be traced to Smiley Burnette. In 1935 Burnette began making a successful series of films with Gene Autry; and it soon became apparent that one of the main reasons for their box office appeal was the chemistry between Autry and the multitalented Burnette. Also in that era Hayes began his run in the Hopalong Cassidy series.

Because most of the performers in this category had backgrounds in vaudeville and radio they were also well adept at musical comedy.

The best remembered of the juvenile sidekicks is Bobby Blake who played Little Beaver in the Republic Pictures series of Red Ryder films.

Since most of the heroes were themselves romantic leading men, the corps of romantic sidekicks is very thin. The tops in this category would be Jimmy Ellison and Russ Hayden of the Hopalong Cassidy series, but both of them moved on to star in their own films. They would be followed by Richard Martin, Tim Holt's compadre.

The era of the singing cowboy also spawned an array of singing sidekicks. These included novelty performers like Burnette, Fuzzy Knight and Cannonball Taylor, talented vocalists like Ray Whitley, and musical groups like the Sons of the Pioneers, Foy Willing and the Riders of the Purple Sage and the immortal Bob Wills and His Texas Playboys. In fact it was in this mode that Jimmy Wakely got started in films.

In addition to being a musical backup and complement to the hero, groups like the Pioneers were a ready-made posse when it came time for the final showdown and shoot-out.

Aside from the aforementioned, groups like the Hoosier Hot Shots, the Light Crust Doughboys, Al Clauser and His Oklahoma Outlaws, the Pals of the Golden West, the Cass County Boys, Red Foley and His Saddle Pals, Walt Shrum and His Colorado Hillbillies, Wesley Tuttle and His Texas Stars, and Merle Travis and His Bronco Busters made appearances with various cowboys in B Westerns.

* * *

Arkansas Slim Andrews

Sidekick Handle: Arkansas

Arkansas, born Slim Andrews, and his mule Josephine rode through ten B Westerns with his good friend Tex Ritter. Ritter and Andrews had met in the late thirties when the latter was a member of a country and western troupe that played throughout the Midwest and the South.

When he moved to the West Coast he contacted Ritter and was given a contract by Monogram Pictures.

Andrews was an incredibly gifted musician and often performed as a one-man band, beginning his career playing tent shows and theaters around Arkansas and Louisiana in the 1920s. He specialized in comic and novelty songs and routines.

After his stint with Ritter, Andrews went on to make films with Tom Keene and Red Barry. He also had parts in several Gene Autry movies.

Andrews and Ritter remained friends long after their film partnership ended, touring together well into the 1950s.

In the early 1950s, Andrews hosted a popular children's TV show in Los Angeles. Today he continues to work in the medium and often makes appearances at Western film fairs and festivals.

Arkansas Slim Andrews Filmography

1940: *Rhythm of the Rio Grande* (H Tex Ritter); *Pals of the Silver Sage* (H Tex Ritter); *Cowboy from Sundown* (H Tex Ritter); *The Golden Trail* (H Tex Ritter); *Rainbow Over the Range* (H Tex Ritter); *Arizona Frontier* (H Tex Ritter); *Take Me Back to Oklahoma* (H Tex Ritter); *Rollin' Home to Texas* (H Tex Ritter). **1941:** *Ridin' the Cherokee Trail* (H Tex Ritter); *The Pioneers* (H Tex Ritter); Wanderers of the West (H Tom Keene); *Dynamite Canyon* (H Tom Keene); *The Driftin' Kid* (H Tom Keene); *Ridin' the Sunset Trail* (H Tom Keene). **1942:** *The Cyclone Kid* (H Don "Red" Barry); *The Sombrero Kid* (H Don "Red" Barry).

Roscoe Ates

Sidekick Handle: Soapy Jones

Fiddly, fumbly Roscoe Ates fidgeted his way through B Westerns as the comic relief for such heroic stalwarts as Tex Ritter, George O'Brien, Tom Keene and Eddie Dean.

Roscoe Ates

He is best remembered as Soapy Jones, Dean's sidekick in a series of 15 films produced by PRC between 1946 and 1948.

Ates was born in Mississippi on January 20, 1892, and began his entertainment career in vaudeville and silent films.

When the talkies came about, he appeared in Westerns like *Billy the Kid* (1930) with Johnny Mack Brown and slapstick comedies such as *Hold 'em Jail* (1932) with Wheeler and Woolsey.

He got his start as a sidekick in 1932 when RKO paired him with Tom Keene in five films. In the years between the Keene and the Dean series, he was in such notable films as *Alice in Wonderland, Gone with the Wind* and *Bad Men of Missouri.*

Ates also appeared in such B's as *Rancho Grande* with Gene Autry and *Robin Hood of the Pecos* with Roy Rogers.

He continued his film career until 1961, making his final screen appearance in *The Errand Boy* with Jerry Lewis in 1962.

Roscoe Ates died of lung cancer on March 1, 1962, in Hollywood, California.

Roscoe Ates Filmography

1932: *Rainbow Trail* (*H* George O'Brien); *Come on Danger* (*H* Tom Keene); *Renegades of the West* (*H* Tom Keene); *Scarlet River* (*H* Tom Keene). **1933:** *The Cheyenne Kid* (*H* Tom Keene). **1940:** *The Cowboy from Sundown* (*H* Tex Ritter). **1946:** *Colorado Serenade* (*H* Eddie Dean); *Driftin' River* (*H* Eddie Dean); *Tumbleweed Trail* (*H* Eddie Dean); *Stars Over Texas* (*H* Eddie Dean); *Wild West* (*H* Eddie Dean). **1947:** *Wild Country* (*H* Eddie Dean); *Range Beyond the Blue* (*H* Eddie Dean); *West to Glory* (*H* Eddie Dean); *Black Hills* (*H* Eddie Dean); *Shadow Valley* (*H* Eddie Dean). **1948:** *Check Your Guns* (*H* Eddie Dean); *Tornado Range* (*H* Eddie Dean); *The Westward Trail* (*H* Eddie Dean); *Hawk of Powder River* (*H* Eddie Dean); *The Tioga Kid* (*H* Eddie Dean).

Vince Barnett

Sidekick Handle: Kewpie

Actor/comedian Vince Barnett rode quickly across the Western screen in 1939 as sidekick to the singing cowgirl Dorothy Page in a trio of films.

Barnett was the son of noted stage actor Luke Barnett and was born in Pittsburgh, Pennsylvania, on July 4, 1902. He worked in vaudeville, legitimate theater and silent films early in his career. He continued to make films until the mid-1970s, and his credits include such films as *All Quiet on the Western Front* (1930), *A Star Is Born* (1937), *Kid Dynamite* (1943), *Mule Train* (1950) and *Dr. Goldfoot and the Bikini Machine* (1965).

Barnett died August 10, 1977, in Encino, California.

Vince Barnett Filmography

1939: *Water Rustlers* (*H* Dorothy Page); *Ride 'em Cowgirl* (*H* Dorothy Page); *The Singing Cowgirl* (*H* Dorothy Page).

Buzz Barton

Youthful Buzz Barton was born Billy Lamarr in Texas in 1914 and began performing in rodeos around Texas at the age of ten.

He won the title of Champion Trick Rider and Fancy Rider, and in 1926 he was signed to a contract by FBO Studios.

In 1927 Barton made his debut in a film called *The Boy Wonder.* He starred in ten more pictures for FBO in 1927 and 1928.

The films were action packed adventures which gave Barton a showcase for his excellent trick riding and roping skills. In 1929 when FBO became RKO, Barton made another four films before being dropped by the studio.

In 1930 he went to the independent Big Four and was assigned to co-star in a series of films with Wally Wales. He was also given one starring vehicle, *The Cyclone Kid* in 1931.

Barton had only bit parts over the next few years before Resolute teamed him with Rex Bell for four films in 1935.

He landed supporting roles in such B Westerns as *Powdersmoke Range* (1935) with Harry Carey, *Feud of the West* (1936) with Hoot Gibson and *Phantom Gold* (1938) with Jack Luden before retiring from the screen in 1938.

He returned to the screen in 1967 for a part in the film *In the Heat of the Night.*

Buzz Barton passed away on November 20, 1980, in St. Louis, Missouri.

Buzz Barton Filmography

1930: *Canyon Hawks (H* Wally Wales); *Breed of the West (H* Wally Wales). **1931:** *Riders of the Cactus (H* Wally Wales); *Flying Lariats (H* Wally Wales); *Wild West Whoopee (H* Jack Perrin). **1935:** *Fighting Pioneers (H* Rex Bell); *Gunfire (H* Rex Bell); *Saddle Aces (H* Rex Bell); *The Tonto Kid (H* Rex Bell).

Bobby Blake
"Little Beaver"

Bobby Blake, better known today as the critically acclaimed actor Robert Blake and star of TV's *Baretta* series, rode with Wild Bill Elliott and

Bobby Blake as Little Beaver.

Rocky Lane through 23 adventures as Little Beaver in Republic Pictures' highly successful Red Ryder films from 1944 to 1947.

He ranked alongside Gabby Hayes and Smiley Burnette when it came to sidekick popularity.

Blake was born Michael Gubitosi in Nutley, New Jersey, September 18, 1938.

When he was about a year old he became a member of MGM's popular Our Gang comedy troupe. He remained with Our Gang until the series folded in 1944 and made 41 of the comedy shorts. Immediately following the demise of the "Gang" he was signed to play Red Ryder's ridin' partner.

Over the years Blake has enjoyed a reputation as one of Hollywood's most talented actors and most ardent rebels.

He has been featured in films like *In Cold Blood* (1967), *Tell Them Willie Boy Is Here* (1969) and *Electra Glide in Blue* (1973).

Blake starred as the funkily philosophical street cop Tony Baretta on the ABC-TV series from 1975 to 1978. His sidekicks in the series were a cockatoo named Fred and a pimp named Rooster. Baretta's favorite catch phrase was "You can take dat to da' bank."

Blake had a short-lived series in 1985 called *Helltown* in which he portrayed a Baretta-like priest.

Bobby Blake Filmography

1944: *Tucson Raiders* (H Wild Bill Elliott); *Marshal of Reno* (H Wild Bill Elliott); *The San Antonio Kid* (H Wild Bill Elliott); *Cheyenne Wildcat* (H Wild Bill Elliott); *Vigilantes of Dodge City* (H Wild Bill Elliott); *Sheriff of Las Vegas* (H Wild Bill Elliott). **1945:** *The Great Stagecoach Robbery* (H Wild Bill Elliott); *Lone Texas Ranger* (H Wild Bill Elliott); *Phantom of the Plains* (H Wild Bill Elliott); *Marshal of Laredo* (H Wild Bill Elliott); *Colorado Pioneers* (H Wild Bill Elliott); *Wagon Wheels Westward* (H Wild Bill Elliott). **1946:** *California Gold Rush* (H Wild Bill Elliott); *Sun Valley Cyclone* (H Wild Bill Elliott); *Conquest of Cheyenne* (H Wild Bill Elliott); *Sheriff of Redwood Valley* (H Wild Bill Elliott); *Santa Fe Uprising* (H Rocky Lane); *Stagecoach to Denver* (H Rocky Lane). **1947:** *Vigilantes of Boomtown* (H Rocky Lane); *Homesteaders of Paradise Valley* (H Rocky Lane); *Oregon Trail Scouts* (H Rocky Lane); *Rustlers of Devil's Canyon* (H Rocky Lane); *Marshal of Cripple Creek* (H Rocky Lane).

Pat Brady

Sidekick Handle: Sparrow Biffle

Most Western fans best remember Pat Brady and his jeep Nelliebelle ridin' side by side with Roy Rogers & Trigger and Dale Evans & Buttermilk in the popular TV adventure series *The Roy Rogers Show* in the early 1950s.

Pat Brady (right) was Roy Rogers' sidekick in five B Westerns made in 1949 and 1950.

Brady's relationship with Rogers dated back to the 1930s. In fact, when Roy Rogers left the Sons of the Pioneers in 1937 to work in films, Brady took his place in the famous singing group.

He was born Robert Ellsworth Patrick Aloysious Brady on December 31, 1914, in Toledo, Ohio. His parents were in vaudeville and Pat began performing at the age of four.

Rogers and Brady met while both were playing clubs around California.

Brady rode and sang with the Pioneers in the series of films that they made with Charles Starrett from 1937 to 1941 before they rejoined Rogers for 40+ features.

World War II forced Brady out of the group. He served in France with the Third Army and collected two Purple Hearts for valor.

In 1949 Brady took over Rogers' sidekick duties from Andy Devine and made five films. When Rogers began production on the TV series, he chose Brady to play the comic relief.

When the show ended in 1957, Pat Brady rejoined the Sons of the Pioneers and remained with them until 1967. He moved to Colorado, where he operated a guest ranch.

Pat Brady passed away on February 27, 1972.

Pat Brady Filmography

1949: *Down Dakota Way* (H Roy Rogers); *The Golden Stallion* (H Roy Rogers). **1950:** *Bells of Coronado* (H Roy Rogers); *Twilight in the Sierras* (H Roy Rogers); *Trigger Jr.* (H Roy Rogers).

Rand Brooks

Sidekick Handle: Lucky Jenkins

Rand Brooks played Lucky Jenkins in the final dozen films of the Hopalong Cassidy series, assuming the role in 1946.

Prior to that his best known film role had been that of Scarlett O'Hara's wimpy first husband Charles Hamilton in the 1939 movie classic *Gone with the Wind.*

He had also appeared in *Babes in Arms* with Judy Garland and Mickey Rooney, *The Old Maid* with Bette Davis and George Brent and *Love Finds Andy Hardy* with Rooney, Garland and an extremely youthful Lana Turner.

Following the Cassidy series, Brooks continued his film work and appeared in the role of Corporal Boone in the early fifties TV adventure series *The Adventures of Rin Tin Tin.*

Rand Brooks Filmography

1946: *Fool's Gold* (H Hopalong Cassidy); *The Devil's Playground* (H Hopalong Cassidy); *Unexpected Guest* (H Hopalong Cassidy). **1947:** *Dangerous Venture* (H Hopalong Cassidy); *The Marauders* (H Hopalong Cassidy); *Hoppy's Holiday* (H Hopalong Cassidy). **1948:** *Silent Conflict* (H Hopalong Cassidy); *The Dead Don't Dream* (H Hopalong Cassidy);

Rand Brooks

Sinister Journey (H Hopalong Cassidy); *False Paradise* (H Hopalong Cassidy); *Borrowed Trouble* (H Hopalong Cassidy); *Strange Gamble* (H Hopalong Cassidy).

Smiley Burnette

Sidekick Handle: Frog Millhouse, Smiley

Lester Alvin Burnette was born in Summun, Illinois, on March 18, 1911. As a youngster he became interested in music and before he graduated from high school was proficient in the playing of around 50 different instruments.

Smiley Burnette (right) with Gene Autry (center) and Noah Beery, Sr., in Mexicali Rose *(Republic, 1939).*

He entered vaudeville as a one-man band and eventually entered radio at a 100-watt station where he was a veritable one-man operation. He was engineer, announcer, entertainer and musician. It was during this period that Burnette first met Gene Autry.

Autry was instrumental in getting Burnette on the National Barn Dance on WLS in Chicago. The chemistry between Autry and Burnette was immediately evident on the radio and in personal appearances around the country.

When Autry was signed by Mascot Pictures in 1934 to appear in films, he took his ready-made sidekick with him. The pair made their first appearances with Ken Maynard in the feature film *In Old Santa Fe* and in the serial *Mystery Mountain.*

In 1935 the studio starred Autry in his first film and serial called *The Phantom Empire.* The storyline featured Autry and Burnette (as Oscar) as radio performers in danger of losing their ranch and radio show to crooks and underground aliens. There was plenty of action and plenty of music and fun.

Later that year Mascot became Republic Pictures, and Autry was signed to star in a series of singing Westerns.

Autry and Burnette began their successful series of films with *Tumbling Tumbleweeds* which was released in September 1935.

The success of the Autry films led to Hollywood's singing cowboy mania, with studios scrambling to find anybody coordinated well enough to sing and ride a horse at the same time.

Burnette's popularity as a sidekick also started studios looking seriously at comedians and character actors to pair with their top cowboy stars. Previously, sidekicks had appeared infrequently and usually were relegated to holding the hero's horse while he battled the bad guys. But with the release of the Autry/Burnette films and the Hopalong Cassidy series (also beginning in 1935) suddenly sidekicks became serious business.

From 1935 until Autry enlisted in the service in 1942, Smiley and Gene made over 50 pictures together.

Burnette's popularity was illustrated by the fact that in 1940 he made the list of top ten box office cowboys. He was also given his own sidekick, Tadpole (Joe Stauch, Jr.), in several films.

Following Autry's exit, Republic paired Burnette with first Roy Rogers, then Eddie Dew, Bob Livingston and finally Sunset Carson. In the Carson films Burnette was given top billing.

In 1946 Smiley Burnette left Republic for Columbia Pictures, where he would co-star with Charles Starrett in 56 entries in the Durango Kid series. The Starrett/Burnette alliance lasted until 1952 when the series ended and Starrett retired from films.

In 1953 Burnette was reunited with his old pal Gene Autry for the last six B films of his career.

Burnette continued to be active in such activities as TV and personal appearances. He also made a successful series of TV commercials for Tube Rose snuff.

In 1963 Smiley Burnette came to prime-time TV as Charlie Pratt, engineer of the Hooterville Cannonball on *Petticoat Junction.*

The series was very successful and Burnette was still appearing in the role at the time of his death on February 16, 1967. He succumbed to leukemia.

Burnette was an extremely gifted musical performer. He composed over 300 songs and always performed novelty songs (with catchy titles like 'The Defective Detective from Brooklyn") in his films.

Smiley Burnette Filmography

1934: *In Old Santa Fe* (*H* Ken Maynard); *Mystery Mountain* (*H* Ken Maynard). **1935:** *Phantom Empire* (*H* Gene Autry); *Tumbling Tumbleweeds*

(*H* Gene Autry); *Melody Trail* (*H* Gene Autry); *Sagebrush Troubadour* (*H* Gene Autry); *Singing Vagabond* (*H* Gene Autry). **1936:** *Red River Valley* (*H* Gene Autry); *Comin' Round the Mountain* (*H* Gene Autry); *The Singing Cowboy* (*H* Gene Autry); *Guns and Guitars* (*H* Gene Autry); *The Border Patrolman* (*H* George O'Brien); *Oh, Susannah* (*H* Gene Autry); *Ride Ranger Ride* (*H* Gene Autry); *The Big Show* (*H* Gene Autry); *The Old Corral* (*H* Gene Autry). **1937:** *Roundup Time in Texas* (*H* Gene Autry); *Git Along Little Dogies* (*H* Gene Autry); *Rootin' Tootin' Rhythm* (*H* Gene Autry); *Yodelin Kid from Pine Ridge* (*H* Gene Autry); *Public Cowboy #1* (*H* Gene Autry); *Boots and Saddles* (*H* Gene Autry); *Manhattan Merry Go Round* (*H* Gene Autry); *Springtime in the Rockies* (*H* Gene Autry). **1938:** *The Old Barn Dance* (*H* Gene Autry); *Gold Mine in the Sky* (*H* Gene Autry); *Man from Music Mountain* (*H* Gene Autry); *Prairie Moon* (*H* Gene Autry); *Under Western Stars* (*H* Roy Rogers); *Billy the Kid Returns* (*H* Roy Rogers); *Rhythm of the Saddle* (*H* Gene Autry); *Western Jamboree* (*H* Gene Autry). **1939:** *Home on the Prairie* (*H* Gene Autry); *Mexicali Rose* (*H* Gene Autry); *Blue Montana Skies* (*H* Gene Autry); *Mountain Rhythm* (*H* Gene Autry); *Colorado Sunset* (*H* Gene Autry); *In Old Monterey* (*H* Gene Autry); *Rovin' Tumbleweeds* (*H* Gene Autry); *South of the Border* (*H* Gene Autry). **1940:** *Rancho Grande* (*H* Gene Autry); *Gaucho Serenade* (*H* Gene Autry); *Carolina Moon* (*H* Gene Autry); *Ride Tenderfoot Ride* (*H* Gene Autry). **1941:** *Ridin' on a Rainbow* (*H* Gene Autry); *Back in the Saddle* (*H* Gene Autry); *The Singing Hill* (*H* Gene Autry); *Sunset in Wyoming* (*H* Gene Autry); *Under Fiesta Stars* (*H* Gene Autry); *Down Mexico Way* (*H* Gene Autry); *Sierra Sue* (*H* Gene Autry). **1942:** *Cowboy Serenade* (*H* Gene Autry); *Heart of the Rio Grande* (*H* Gene Autry); *Home in Wyoming* (*H* Gene Autry); *Stardust on the Sage* (*H* Gene Autry); *Call of the Canyon* (*H* Gene Autry); *Bells of Capistrano* (*H* Gene Autry); *Heart of the Golden West* (*H* Roy Rogers). **1943:** *Idaho* (*H* Roy Rogers); *King of the Cowboys* (*H* Roy Rogers); *Silver Spurs* (*H* Roy Rogers); *Beyond the Last Frontier* (*H* Eddie Dew); *Raiders of Sunset Pass* (*H* Eddie Dew); *Pride of the Plains* (*H* Robert Livingston). **1944:** *Trail to Gunsight* (*H* Eddie Dew); *Beneath Western Skies* (*H* Robert Livingston); *The Laramie Trail* (*H* Robert Livingston); *Call of the Rockies* (*H* Sunset Carson); *Bordertown Trail* (*H* Sunset Carson); *Firebrands of Arizona* (*H* Sunset Carson). **1946:** *Roaring Rangers* (*H* Charles Starrett); *Gunning for Vengeance* (*H* Charles Starrett); *Galloping Thunder* (*H* Charles Starrett); *Two Fisted Stranger* (*H* Charles Starrett); *The Desert Horseman* (*H* Charles Starrett); *Heading West* (*H* Charles Starrett); *Land Rush* (*H* Charles Starrett); *Terror Trail* (*H* Charles Starrett); *Fighting Frontiersman* (*H* Charles Starrett). **1947:** *South of the*

Smiley Burnette alongside Roy Rogers (holding horse's reins) in Billy the Kid Returns *(Republic, 1938). Also pictured next to Burnette is Horace Murphy.*

The very talented Smiley Burnette upped the status of the sidekick with his appearances in Gene Autry's films.

Chisholm Trail (H Charles Starrett); The Lone Hand Texan (H Charles Starrett); West of Dodge City (H Charles Starrett); Law of the Canyon (H Charles Starrett); Prairie Raiders (H Charles Starrett); Stranger from Ponca City (H Charles Starrett); Riders of the Lone Star (H Charles Starrett); Buckaroo from Powder River (H Charles Starrett); Last Days of Boot Hill (H Charles Starrett); Six Gun Law (H Charles Starrett); Phantom Valley (H Charles Starrett). **1948:** West of Sonora (H Charles Starrett); Whirlwind Raiders (H Charles Starrett); Blazing Across the Pecos (H Charles Starrett); Trail to Laredo (H Charles Starrett); El Dorado Pass (H Charles Starrett); Quick on the Trigger (H Charles Starrett). **1949:** Challenge of the Range (H Charles Starrett); Desert Vigilante (H Charles Starrett); Laramie (H Charles Starrett); The Blazing Trail (H Charles Starrett); South of Death Valley (H Charles Starrett); Horsemen of the Sierras (H Charles Starrett); Bandits of

El Dorado (H Charles Starrett); *Renegades of the Sage* (H Charles Starrett).
1950: *Trail of the Rustlers* (H Charles Starrett); *Outcasts of Black Mesa* (H
Charles Starrett); *Texas Dynamo* (H Charles Starrett); *Streets of Ghost
Town* (H Charles Starrett); *Across the Badlands* (H Charles Starrett);
Raiders of Tomahawk Creek (H Charles Starrett); *Lightning Guns* (H
Charles Starrett); *Frontier Outpost* (H Charles Starrett). **1951:** *Whirlwind*
(H Gene Autry); *Prairie Roundup* (H Charles Starrett); *Ridin' the Outlaw
Trail* (H Charles Starrett); *Fort Savage Raiders* (H Charles Starrett); *Snake
River Desperadoes* (H Charles Starrett); *Bonanza Town* (H Charles Star-
rett); *Cyclone Fury* (H Charles Starrett); *Kid from Amarillo* (H Charles
Starrett); *Pecos River* (H Charles Starrett); *Smoky Canyon* (H Charles
Starrett). **1952:** *Hawk of Wild River* (H Charles Starrett); *The Rough
Tough West* (H Charles Starrett); *Junction City* (H Charles Starrett);
Laramie Mountains (H Charles Starrett); *Kid from Broken Gun* (H Charles
Starrett). **1953:** *Winning of the West* (H Gene Autry); *On Top of Old
Smoky* (H Gene Autry); *Goldtown Ghost Riders* (H Gene Autry); *Pack
Train* (H Gene Autry); *Saginaw Trail* (H Gene Autry); *Last of the Pony
Riders* (H Gene Autry).

Pat Buttram

Pat Buttram and Gene Autry were sidekicks in 17 films, sidekicks in
15 years of Melody Ranch radio shows, sidekicks in 80+ TV episodes of
The Gene Autry Show and sidekicks in real life.

Their relationship dated back to the early 1930s when both were performers on the National Barn Dance.

Buttram, born in Winston County, Alabama, was a master at country
humor and a master monologist.

His first film with Gene Autry was *The Strawberry Roan* in 1948. They
made films together until 1952, and the TV series ran on CBS from 1950 to
1954.

In 1965 Buttram assumed his best-known role, that of the connivin',
shifty, swindlin' Mr. Haney on the hit TV series *Green Acres*. The show ran
until 1971 and is still one of the most popular vehicles on the rerun
circuit.

Buttram often made personal appearances with Autry and was married to one of Gene's leading ladies, Sheila Ryan.

Today he continues to be active in the entertainment industry.

Pat Buttram

Pat Buttram Filmography

1948: *The Strawberry Roan* (H Gene Autry). **1949:** *Riders in the Sky* (H Gene Autry). **1950:** *Mule Train* (H Gene Autry); *Beyond the Purple Hills* (H Gene Autry); *Indian Territory* (H Gene Autry); *The Blazing Sun* (H Gene Autry). **1951:** *Gene Autry and the Mounties* (H Gene Autry); *Texans Never Cry* (H Gene Autry); *Silver Canyon* (H Gene Autry); *Hills of Utah* (H Gene Autry); *Valley of Fire* (H Gene Autry). **1952:** *The Old West* (H Gene Autry); *Night Stage to Galveston* (H Gene Autry); *Apache Country*

(*H* Gene Autry); *Barbed Wire* (*H* Gene Autry); *Wagon Team* (*H* Gene Autry); *Blue Canadian Rockies* (*H* Gene Autry).

Leo Carrillo

Sidekick Handle: Pancho

"Hey Ceesco I don' theenk we oughta went there — cause if we went there, there gonna be trouble, I theenk. . ." Cautious words from Pancho, the faithful but not too enthusiastic saddle pal of the Cisco Kid.

Leo Carrillo played Pancho to Duncan Renaldo's Cisco in five films and several dozen TV episodes in the late forties and early fifties. Their closing frame was always a jovial "Oh Cisco" — "Oh Pancho."

Carrillo was born Leo Antonio Carrillo on August 6, 1881, in Los Angeles; his great-grandfather had been California's first governor in the early 1800s. Carrillo began his career as a vaudeville actor and even appeared on Broadway in the early 1900s. He made his movie debut in the 1920s in silent comedy shorts, and his first full-length film was *Mister Antonio* in 1929.

He appeared in such notable films as *Villa Rides, Manhattan Melodrama,* and *The Barretts of Wimpole Street.*

He made Westerns like *Twenty Mule Team* (1940) and was in Universal's million dollar serial *Riders of Death Valley* (1941).

It is reported that Carrillo did not care to accept the role of Pancho, fearing that the character would be little more than the movies' stereotypical Mexican clown.

Carrillo died of cancer on September 6, 1961, in Santa Monica, California.

Leo Carrillo Filmography

1948: *The Valiant Hombre* (*H* Duncan Renaldo [Cisco Kid]). **1949:** *The Gay Amigo* (*H* Duncan Renaldo [Cisco Kid]); *The Daring Caballero* (*H* Duncan Renaldo [Cisco Kid]); *Satan's Cradle* (*H* Duncan Renaldo [Cisco Kid]). **1950:** *The Girl from San Lorenzo* (*H* Duncan Renaldo [Cisco Kid]).

Chief Thundercloud

Chief Thundercloud is best known for his portrayal of the Lone Ranger's faithful Indian companion Tonto in the highly successful Republic series *The Lone Ranger* (1938) and *The Lone Ranger Rides Again* (1939).

Thundercloud, real name Victor Daniels, was born in Muskogee, Oklahoma, on April 12, 1889. He began his career as a rodeo and wild West show performer and entered films in 1929 as a stuntman.

He appeared in many B Westerns such as *Rustler's Paradise* with Harry Carey and *For the Service* with Buck Jones, and several Western serials including *Wild West Days* (Johnny Mack Brown) and *Daredevils of the West* (Dick Foran), and major Western features like *The Plainsman,* starring Gary Cooper.

His stint as a B sidekick was a short one: In 1941 he co-starred with David Sharpe in *The Silver Stallion* and in 1944 he was brought in to punch up the sagging Trail Blazers series when Ken Maynard departed, but he too departed after two films.

In 1942 Monogram Pictures starred Thundercloud and fellow movie Indian chief Yowlachie in a film called *King of the Stallions* which was produced and directed by Tex Ritter's old producer Edward Finney.

The Chief died of cancer on November 30, 1955, in Ventura, California.

Chief Thundercloud Filmography

1938: *The Lone Ranger* (serial) (*H* Lee Powell). **1939:** *The Lone Ranger Rides Again* (serial) (*H* Robert Livingston). **1941:** *Silver Stallion* (*H* David Sharpe). **1944:** *Outlaw Trail* (*H* Trail Blazers); *Sonora Stagecoach* (*H* Trail Blazers).

Andy Clyde

Sidekick Handle: California Carlson

Master film funnyman Andy Clyde, in the guise of California Carlson, fought side by side with William "Hopalong Cassidy" Boyd in three dozen Cassidy adventures beginning with *Three Men from Texas* in 1940 until the series ended in 1948.

Chief Thundercloud played sidekick Tonto to Lee Powell's masked Lone Ranger in the Republic serial The Lone Ranger *(1938).*

When the Hoppy films gave way, Clyde signed on with Whip Wilson as sidekick for a dozen pictures.

Clyde was also a top star of comedy shorts. Between the years 1929 and 1956 he starred in nearly 150 features for first Sennett and later Columbia studios. His shorts rivaled those of the Three Stooges in popularity.

Clyde was born in Blairgowrie, Scotland, on March 25, 1892, the son of a theatrical producer. He made his stage debut as a child and arrived in America in 1912 to play the vaudeville circuit.

In 1919 he was signed to a contract by Mack Sennett, the leading comedy producer at the time.

By the mid-1920s Clyde was one of Sennett's top stars. He teamed with Billy Bevan in a slew of slapstick adventures. In 1929 he became the studio's first talkie star.

He was featured in such top full-length films as *Annie Oakley* with Barbara Stanwyck, *It's a Wonderful World* with Jimmy Stewart and *Abe Lincoln in Illinois* with Raymond Massey.

Andy Clyde

On television he played Grandpa McCoy's (Walter Brennan) good friend George McMichael on *The Real McCoys* and was seen as Mr. Culley on the *Lassie* series.

Clyde was one of the film world's true comedy legends. He passed away on May 18, 1967, in Los Angeles.

Andy Clyde Filmography

1940: *Three Men from Texas* (H Hopalong Cassidy). **1941:** *Doomed Caravan* (H Hopalong Cassidy); *In Old Colorado* (H Hopalong Cassidy); *Border Vigilantes* (H Hopalong Cassidy); *Pirates on Horseback* (H Hopalong Cassidy); *Wide Open Town* (H Hopalong Cassidy); *Riders of the Timberline* (H Hopalong Cassidy); *Twilight on the Trail* (H Hopalong Cassidy); *Stick to Your Guns* (H Hopalong Cassidy); *Outlaws of the Desert* (H Hopalong Cassidy); *Secrets of the Wasteland* (H Hopalong Cassidy). **1942:** *Undercover Man* (H Hopalong Cassidy). **1943:** *Hoppy Serves a Writ* (H Hopalong Cassidy); *Border Patrol* (H Hopalong Cassidy); *The Leather Burners* (H Hopalong Cassidy); *Colt Comrades* (H Hopalong Cassidy); *Bar 20* (H Hopalong Cassidy); *False Colors* (H Hopalong Cassidy); *Riders of the Deadline* (H Hopalong Cassidy); *Lost Canyon* (H Hopalong Cassidy). **1944:** *Texas Masquerade* (H Hopalong Cassidy); *Lumberjack* (H Hopalong Cassidy); *Mystery Man* (H Hopalong Cassidy); *Forty Thieves* (H Hopalong Cassidy). **1945:** *Song of the Prairie* (H Ken Curtis). **1946:** *Throw a Saddle on a Star* (H Ken Curtis); *The Texas Jamboree* (H Ken Curtis); *Fools Gold* (H Hopalong Cassidy); *Devil's Playground* (H Hopalong Cassidy). **1947:** *Unexpected Guest* (H Hopalong Cassidy); *Dangerous Venture* (H Hopalong Cassidy); *The Marauders* (H Hopalong Cassidy); *Hoppy's Holiday* (H Hopalong Cassidy). **1948:** *Silent Conflict* (H Hopalong Cassidy); *The Dead Don't Dream* (H Hopalong Cassidy); *Sinister Journey* (H Hopalong Cassidy); *Borrowed Trouble* (H Hopalong Cassidy); *False Paradise* (H Hopalong Cassidy); *Strange Gamble* (H Hopalong Cassidy). **1949:** *Crashing Thru* (H Whip Wilson); *Shadows of the West* (H Whip Wilson); *Haunted Trails* (H Whip Wilson); *Riders of the Dusk* (H Whip Wilson); *Range Land* (H Whip Wilson). **1950:** *Fence Riders* (H Whip Wilson); *Gunslingers* (H Whip Wilson); *Arizona Territory* (H Whip Wilson); *Silver Raiders* (H Whip Wilson); *Cherokee Uprising* (H Whip Wilson); *Outlaws of Texas* (H Whip Wilson). **1951:** *Abilene Trail* (H Whip Wilson).

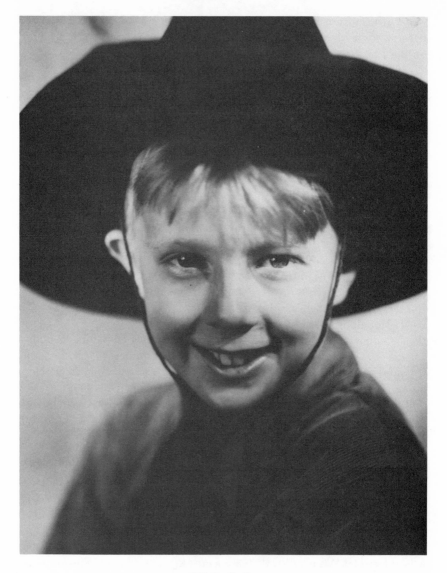

Bill Cody, Jr.

Bill Cody, Jr.

Bill Cody, Jr., the son of B Western film star Bill Cody, was a member of the Corps of Juvenile Actors who appeared in westerns in the 1930s. Other included Frankie Darro, Billy King and Buzz Henry.

Ben Corbett

He appeared in five films as sidekick with his dad, who had earlier used Andy Shuford as his young partner.

He also had a major supporting role in Johnny Mack Brown's 1937 serial *The Oregon Trail*.

Bill Cody, Jr. Filmography

1934: *Frontier Days* (H Bill Cody); *Border Guns* (H Bill Cody). **1935:** *The Vanishing Riders* (H Bill Cody); *The Reckless Buckaroo* (H Bill Cody). **1936:** *Outlaws of the Range* (H Bill Cody).

Ben Corbett

Ben Corbett appeared in scores of B Westerns as co-star, sidekick, villain, supporting player, bit player and stuntman.

He co-starred with Jack Perrin in 1933 and 1934 in a series of feature-length films and shorts called the Bud 'n' Ben Westerns. They combined Western action and comedy.

Corbett was born in 1892 in Hudson, Illinois, and entered the film industry around 1915 as a stuntman, soon doubling for such top stars as William Duncan and Antonio Moreno. He also was featured in such silent serials as *Lightning Bryce, The Riddle Rider* and *The Mystery Rider* and many Westerns in the twenties.

In 1939 Victory Pictures paired Ben with Tim McCoy for a series of six films.

Corbett continued to work in films until the mid-fifties.

He passed away on May 19, 1961, in Hollywood.

Ben Corbett Filmography

1932: *Partners* (H Tom Keene); *Saddle Buster* (H Tom Keene); *.45 Calibre Echo* (H Jack Perrin). **1933:** *Girl Trouble* (H Jack Perrin). **1934:** *Arizona Nights* (H Jack Perrin); *Rainbow Riders* (H Jack Perrin); *Ridin' Gents* (H Jack Perrin); *Pot Luck Pards* (H Wally Wales); *The Lone Bandit* (H Lane Chandler). **1935:** *Coyote Trails* (H Tom Tyler). **1936:** *Border Menace* (H Bill Cody). **1939:** *Code of the Cactus* (H Tim McCoy); *Texas Wildcats* (H Tim McCoy); *Outlaws' Paradise* (H Tim McCoy); *The Fighting Renegade* (H Tim McCoy); *Straight Shooter* (H Tim McCoy); *Trigger Fingers* (H Tim McCoy).

Art Davis

In 1935 Art Davis was a $14-a-week musician at a radio station in Dallas, Texas, when Gene Autry hired him as a backup singer and musician. This led to big parts in several Autry films.

In 1939 Davis changed his name to Larry Mason and made a Western called *The Adventures of the Masked Phantom* (a film few people had ever heard of until it was unearthed and shown on the Nashville Network's *Tumbleweed Theatre*).

In 1941 PRC gave Davis the chief supporting role in Tim McCoy's *The Texas Marshal.* Impressed by Davis's talent they signed him to do a series of films with his old radio buddy Bill "Cowboy Rambler" Boyd and Lee Powell. The trio starred in six films in 1942, but they were not well accepted at the box office and the project was scrapped.

Art Davis

Davis entered the navy where he served throughout World War II then returned to radio work.

He and his band the Rhythm Riders made a musical short, *A Cowboy's Holiday* in 1949.

Art Davis was born May 31, 1913, in Paradise, Texas.

Art Davis Filmography

1939: *Adventures of the Masked Phantom*. **1942:** *Texas Manhunt* (H Bill Boyd); *Raiders of the West* (H Bill Boyd); *Rolling Down the Great Divide* (H Bill Boyd); *Tumbleweed Trail* (H Bill Boyd); *Prairie Pals* (H Bill Boyd); *Along the Sundown Trail* (H Bill Boyd).

Rufe Davis

Sidekick Handle: Lullaby

Oklahoma-born (1914) Rufe Davis took over the role of Lullaby, the comic member of the Three Mesquiteers, in the 1940 film *Under the Texas Skies* and went on to make 14 films in the popular Republic series.

Davis was a vaudevillian and member of the National Barn Dance Troupe when he made his film debut in *The Big Broadcast of 1937*.

Following his role in the Mesquiteers films, Davis went back to doing radio work and making personal appearances with his old pal from the Barn Dance, Gene Autry.

In the early 1960s he played the role of Floyd, the engineer of the Hooterville Cannonball, on the TV series *Petticoat Junction*. His cab partner Charlie was played by old Frog Millhouse himself, Smiley Burnette.

Rufe Davis died December 13, 1974.

Rufe Davis Filmography

1940: *Under Texas Skies* (H Three Mesquiteers); *The Trail Blazers* (H Three Mesquiteers); *Lone Star Raiders* (H Three Mesquiteers). **1941:** *Prairie Pioneers* (H Three Mesquiteers); *Pals of the Pecos* (H Three Mesquiteers); *Saddle Mates* (H Three Mesquiteers); *Gangs of Sonora* (H Three Mesquiteers); *Outlaws of the Cherokee Trail* (H Three Mesquiteers); *Gauchos of El Dorado* (H Three Mesquiteers); *West of Cimarron* (H Three Mesquiteers). **1942:** *Code of the Outlaw* (H Three Mesquiteers); *Raiders of the Range* (H Three Mesquiteers); *Westward Ho* (H Three Mesquiteers); *The Phantom Plainsman* (H Three Mesquiteers).

Andy Devine

Andy Devine

Sidekick Handle: Cookie Bullfincher

The voice of 300+-pound Andy Devine was one of the most un-mistakable in motion picture and TV history. It brought to mind the possibility that at one time a demented surgeon may have removed his ton-sils with a bush hog.

Devine was noted for several of his onscreen portrayals: he was the gallows-bound retarded killer in the acclaimed 1932 Western *Law and Order;* he drove John Ford's 1939 *Stagecoach* which John Wayne rode disguised as the Ringo Kid; and last but not least, he was Jingles, the sidekick to Wild Bill Hickock (Guy Madison) who spent more time eating than he did catching crooks on TV and radio in the early fifties.

In 1947 and 1948 Devine played sidekick to Roy Rogers in nine Republic films. He most always was constable or deputy sheriff Cookie Bullfincher.

Devine was born October 7, 1905, in Flagstaff, Arizona. He attended Santa Clara College and was an excellent football player, and upon completion of his studies played pro football for a short spell. His athletic ability got him into the movies in 1926 as a bit player and extra. His roles grew gradually until he had featured roles in the 1930 film *The Spirit of Notre Dame* and in Tom Mix's *Destry Rides Again* (1932).

Some of his later films of note include *The Man Who Shot Liberty Valance, Around the World in 80 Days* and *It's a Mad, Mad, Mad, Mad World.*

Andy Devine passed away in Orange, California, of leukemia on February 18, 1977.

Andy Devine Filmography

1947: *Bells of San Angelo* (*H* Roy Rogers); *Springtime in the Sierras* (*H* Roy Rogers); *The Old Spanish Trail* (*H* Roy Rogers). **1948:** *The Gay Ranchero* (*H* Roy Rogers); *Under California Stars* (*H* Roy Rogers); *Eyes of Texas* (*H* Roy Rogers); *Night Time in Nevada* (*H* Roy Rogers); *Grand Canyon Trail* (*H* Roy Rogers); *The Far Frontier* (*H* Roy Rogers).

Jimmie Dodd

Sidekick Handle: Lullaby Joslin

Jimmie Dodd is best remembered as the chaperon and adult leader of TV's most famous group of talented kids, The Mickey Mouse Club. Beginning in 1955 Jimmie along with Darlene, Cubby, Karen, Cheryl, Annette and a host of others delighted youthful viewers five days a week with music, cartoons, adventure and general all-around fun. Over 300 shows were done.

Dodd played the part of Lullaby Joslin in the final six entries in the

Jimmie Dodd

popular Three Mesquiteers series for Republic films. Prior to the Mesquiteers series Dodd, a talented singer and songwriter, had spent most of his screen time doing B comedies like *Snuffy Smith*.

Following his Mesquiteers stint, he appeared in films such as *Keep 'em Sluggin'* with the East Side Kids and *Buck Privates Come Home* with Abbott and Costello.

Jimmie Dodd was born in Cincinnati, Ohio, in 1910 and passed away

November 10, 1964, in Honolulu, Hawaii, where he hosted a local television show.

Jimmie Dodd Filmography

1942: *Shadows of the Sage* (H Three Mesquiteers); *Valley of Hunted Men* (H Three Mesquiteers). **1943:** *Thundering Trails* (H Three Mesquiteers); *The Blocked Trail* (H Three Mesquiteers); *Santa Fe Scouts* (H Three Mesquiteers); *Riders of the Rio Grande* (H Three Mesquiteers).

Buddy Ebsen

Sidekick Handles: Happy Hooper, Muscles, Snooper

Buddy Ebsen, aka Georgie Russell, Davy Crockett's sidekick; aka Uncle Jed Clampett of *The Beverly Hillbillies;* aka Barnaby Jones, private detective, was the movie sidekick to the Arizona cowboy Rex Allen in five Republic films in 1950 and 1951.

Ebsen was born Christian Rudolph Ebsen in Belleville, Illinois, on April 2, 1908. He began in show business as a professional dancer and appeared in the famous Ziegfield Follies and on Broadway. His movie work began in the early 1930s in musicals such as *Banjo on My Knee, Broadway Melody of 1936* and *Broadway Melody of 1938.*

His most successful work has been in the world of television. *The Beverly Hillbillies* ran on CBS from 1962 to 1971 and is still in rerun. It was TV's top'rated show its first two seasons.

Barnaby Jones also had a long run, and the Davy Crockett series of films and TV shows caused a coonskin cap mania during the fifties.

Buddy Ebsen Filmography

1950: *Under Mexicali Stars* (H Rex Allen). **1951:** *Silver City Bonanza* (H Rex Allen); *Thunder in God's Country* (H Rex Allen); *Rodeo King and the Senorita* (H Rex Allen); *Utah Wagon Train* (H Rex Allen).

Cliff "Ukulele Ike" Edwards

Cliff Edwards was one of the top entertainers of the 1920s and 1930s. He was a singer, songwriter, musician, comedian and actor. He appeared in vaudeville, made hit records, had a radio show and made scores of films. He was also the well known voice of Walt Disney's Jiminy Crickett.

Edwards was born in Hannibal, Missouri, on June 14, 1895. He entered vaudeville and acquired the nickname "Ukulele Ike" while playing ukulele in a Chicago nightclub.

He entered films at the dawn of the sound era and appeared in musicals like *The Hollywood Revue of 1929* and *So This Is College.* He appeared in the Western *Montana Moon* in 1930 with Johnny Mack Brown. During the thirties he had parts in comedies like *Parlor, Bedroom and Bath* and *Dance, Fools, Dance.*

Cliff Edwards came to the B Western screen in 1941 when Columbia Pictures signed him to co-star with their number one cowboy, Charles Starrett. He made eight films before leaving for RKO and teaming up with Tim Holt for a half-dozen pictures made immediately before Holt entered the navy.

Following the Holt series, Edwards made a few more films and concentrated on radio.

In 1949 he starred in *The Cliff Edwards Show* on CBS-TV and was a regular on *The 54th Street Revue* that same year.

Among his best-selling records are such classics as "Fascinating Rhythm," "Sleepy Time Gal," "Toot Toot Tootsie," "When You Wish Upon a Star," and he was the first to record "Singin' in the Rain."

Ukulele Ike passed away on July 17, 1971, in Hollywood, California.

Cliff "Ukulele Ike" Edwards Filmography

1941: *Thunder Over the Prairie* (H Charles Starrett); *Prairie Stranger* (H Charles Starrett); *Riders of the Badlands* (H Charles Starrett). **1942:** *West of Tombstone* (H Charles Starrett); *Lawless Plainsmen* (H Charles Starrett); *Riders of the Northland* (H Charles Starrett); *Badmen of the Hills* (H Charles Starrett); *Overland to Deadwood* (H Charles Starrett); *Bandit Ranger* (H Tim Holt); *Pirates of the Prairie* (H Tim Holt). **1943:** *Fighting Frontier* (H Tim Holt); *Sagebrush Law* (H Tim Holt); *Avenging Rider* (H Tim Holt); *Red River Robin Hood* (H Tim Holt).

Alice Fleming

Sidekick Handle: Duchess

Alice Fleming played the Duchess, the feisty matron who ruled over the ranch that Red Ryder and Little Beaver called home. Fleming, best known for her stage and radio work, played the role in 16 films starring Wild Bill Elliott. Maude Pierce Allen had created the part in the 1940 serial *The Adventures of Red Ryder* starring Don Barry, and when Rocky Lane succeeded Elliott as Red the role of Duchess passed to Martha Wentworth.

Alice Fleming was born in 1882 and passed away on December 6, 1952, in New York City. She entered films in 1921. She made many silent films before concentrating on the legitimate theater.

She returned to film work in the early forties and appeared in such films as *Who Done It* (1942) with Abbott and Costello.

Alice Fleming Filmography

1944: *Tucson Raiders* (H Wild Bill Elliott); *The San Antonio Kid* (H Wild Bill Elliott); *Cheyenne Wildcat* (H Wild Bill Elliott); *Vigilantes of Dodge City* (H Wild Bill Elliott); *Sheriff of Las Vegas* (H Wild Bill Elliott). **1945:** *The Great Stagecoach Robbery* (H Wild Bill Elliott); *Lone Texas Ranger* (H Wild Bill Elliott); *Phantom of the Plains* (H Wild Bill Elliott); *Marshal of Laredo* (H Wild Bill Elliott); *Colorado Pioneers* (H Wild Bill Elliott); *Wagon Wheels Westward* (H Wild Bill Elliott). **1946:** *California Gold Rush* (H Wild Bill Elliott); *Sun Valley Cyclone* (H Wild Bill Elliott); *Conquest of Cheyenne* (H Wild Bill Elliott); *Sheriff of Redwood Valley* (H Wild Bill Elliott).

Martin Garralaga

Sidekick Handle: Pancho

Although Leo Carrillo made famous the role of Pancho, the Cisco Kid's saddlemate, it was Martin Garralaga who originated it in the 1945 film *The Cisco Kid Returns.*

Garralaga had been a popular character actor throughout the thirties and forties specializing in ethnic roles. He appeared in films like *Message to Garcia* and *For Whom the Bell Tolls*.

Although he appeared in seven Cisco films he only played Pancho in four; in fact, in *Beauty and the Bandit* he was one of the bad guys.

Martin Garralaga Filmography

1945: *The Cisco Kid Returns* (H Duncan Renaldo); *The Cisco Kid in Old New Mexico* (H Duncan Renaldo); *South of the Rio Grande* (H Duncan Renaldo). 1946: *The Gay Cavalier* (H Gilbert Roland); *South of Monterey* (H Gilbert Roland); *Beauty and the Bandit* (H Gilbert Roland). 1947: *Riding the California Trail* (H Gilbert Roland).

Tex Harding

Relatively unknown Tex Harding served as chief supporting player to Charles Starrett and Smiley Burnette in seven entries in the popular Durango Kid series for Columbia Pictures during the mid-forties. His role varied from film to film and he quickly disappeared from the screen.

Tex Harding Filmography

1945: *Return of the Durango Kid* (H Charles Starrett); *Blazing the Western Trail* (H Charles Starrett); *Outlaws of the Rockies* (H Charles Starrett); *Lawless Empire* (H Charles Starrett); *Texas Panhandle* (H Charles Starrett); *Both Barrels Blazing* (H Charles Starrett). 1946: *Frontier Gunlaw* (H Charles Starrett).

Harry Harvey

Harry Harvey took over as sidekick to the silvery-voiced Buckaroo Fred Scott from Al "Fuzzy" St. John in Scott's Spectrum Pictures series of films. His four films turned out to be the final four in the series.

Harvey was best known for his work in comedy shorts starring Leon Errol and Edgar Kennedy.

In the late forties and early fifties he was a supporting player in many TV Westerns like *The Lone Ranger.*

Harry Harvey Filmography

1939: *Code of the Fearless* (H Fred Scott); *In Old Montana* (H Fred Scott); *Two Gun Troubador* (H Fred Scott). **1940:** *Ridin' the Trail* (H Fred Scott).

Raymond Hatton

Sidekick Handles: Sandy Hopkins, Rusty Joslin

One of Western filmdom's most prolific sidekicks, Raymond William Hatton was born in Red Oak, Iowa, on July 7, 1887, and began working in films for Kalem Studios around 1911. A talented comedian, Hatton soon went to work for the famous silent laugh factory run by Mack Sennett.

In the mid-1920s he teamed up with Wallace Beery to make several highly successful comedy features.

Shortly after the advent of talking films, Hatton seemed to find his niche in the area of Westerns and adventure films by appearing in pictures like *The Rogue of the Rio Grande* (1930) with Myrna Loy, *Law and Order* (1932) with Walter Huston, *Hidden Gold* (1932) with Tom Mix and the 1933 serial *The Three Musketeers* starring young John Wayne.

By the mid-thirties his Western film career was going strong: he sidekicked Johnny Mack Brown in the 1935 serial *Rustlers of Red Dog* and made several films with Buster Crabbe. He also appeared in such top-rated chapter plays as *The Undersea Kingdom, The Vigilantes Are Coming,* and *Jungle Jim* during this time.

In 1938 Republic Pictures decided to make Ray the sidekick to their newest cowboy star, Roy Rogers. Beginning with *Come on Rogers,* Ray mounted a mule named Dinah and rode side by side with Roy and Trigger in four films.

The following year Republic signed Gabby Hayes to team with Rogers, deciding that Hatton would replace the departing Max Terhune in *The Three Mesquiteers* series. He played the role of Rusty Joslin (Terhune's character was called Lullaby Joslin) beginning with *The Wyoming Outlaw.* His tenure with the Mesquiteers lasted nine films.

In 1941 he left Republic for Monogram Studios to begin work on a newly created series of films, "The Rough Riders," which would team him with Western film legends Tim McCoy and Buck Jones.

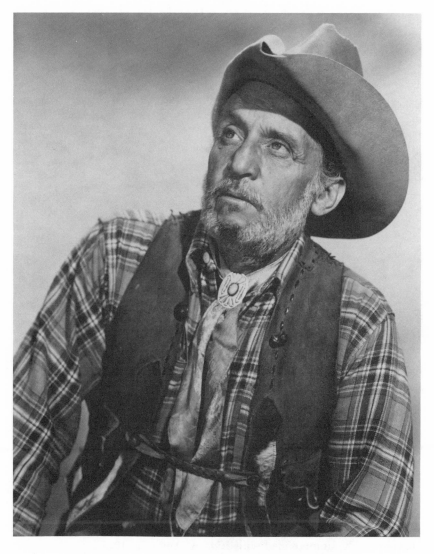

Raymond Hatton

This series created his best known sidekick character, Sandy Hopkins. The gist of The Rough Riders series was that three lawmen from varied corners of the West (Hatton from Texas, McCoy from Wyoming and Jones from Arizona) would come together and pool their bad guy catching talents to rid the West of a diabolical gang of outlaws.

Beginning with *Arizona Bound* in 1941, the trio rode through eight highly successful adventures.

From left: Buck Jones, Tim McCoy and Raymond Hatton starred in eight Rough Riders films.

McCoy departed before a ninth film could be produced. The film *Dawn on the Great Divide* was made, starring Jones and Hatton. It proved to be Buck Jones's last film.

In 1943 Monogram teamed Hatton with Johnny Mack Brown in the first of what was to be one of the longest partnerships in B Western history.

Over the next five years the pair would make 45 films together. In most every entry Hatton played Sandy Hopkins and Brown was Nevada Jack McKenzie. The union ended with *Hidden Danger* in 1948.

In 1950 Raymond Hatton had his last sidekick role in a half-dozen Lippert films that starred two former Hopalong Cassidy sidekicks, Jimmy Ellison and Russell Hayden.

Hatton continued to work in a variety of films including *Invasion of the Saucer Men*, *Shake, Rattle and Roll* and *Motorcycle Gang*. His last screen appearance was in the 1967 film *In Cold Blood* which starred Robert "Little Beaver" Blake.

A heart attack claimed the life of Raymond Hatton on October 21, 1971.

Raymond Hatton Filmography

1935: *Rustlers of Red Dog* (serial) (*H* Johnny Mack Brown); *Nevada* (*H* Buster Crabbe). **1936:** *Arizona Raiders* (*H* Buster Crabbe). **1938:** *Come on Rangers* (*H* Roy Rogers). **1939:** *Rough Riders Roundup* (*H* Roy Rogers); *Frontier Pony Express* (*H* Roy Rogers); *Wall Street Cowboy* (*H* Roy Rogers); *Wyoming Outlaw* (*H* 3 Mesquiteers); *New Frontier* (*H* 3 Mesquiteers); *The Kansas Terrors* (*H* 3 Mesquiteers); *Cowboys from Texas* (*H* 3 Mesquiteers). **1940:** *Heroes of the Saddle* (*H* 3 Mesquiteers); *Pioneers of the West* (*H* 3 Mesquiteers); *Covered Wagon Days* (*H* 3 Mesquiteers); *Rocky Mountain Rangers* (*H* 3 Mesquiteers); *Oklahoma Renegades* (*H* 3 Mesquiteers). **1941:** *Arizona Bound* (*H* Rough Riders); *Gunman from Bodie* (*H* Rough Riders); *Forbidden Trails* (*H* Rough Riders); *White Eagle* (serial) (*H* Buck Jones). **1942:** *Below the Border* (*H* Rough Riders); *Ghost Town Law* (*H* Rough Riders); *Down Texas Way* (*H* Rough Riders); *Riders of the West* (*H* Rough Riders); *West of the Law* (*H* Rough Riders); *Dawn on the Great Divide* (*H* Buck Jones). **1943:** *The Ghost Rider* (*H* Johnny Mack Brown); *Stranger from Pecos* (*H* Johnny Mack Brown); *Six Gun Gospel* (*H* Johnny Mack Brown); *Outlaws of Stampede Pass* (*H* Johnny Mack Brown); *Texas Kid* (*H* Johnny Mack Brown). **1944:** *Raiders of the Border* (*H* Johnny Mack Brown); *Partners of the Trail* (*H* Johnny Mack Brown); *Law Men* (*H* Johnny Mack Brown); *Range Law* (*H* Johnny Mack Brown); *West of the Rio Grande* (*H* Johnny Mack Brown); *Land of the Outlaws* (*H* Johnny Mack Brown); *Law of the Valley* (*H* Johnny Mack Brown); *Ghost Guns* (*H* Johnny Mack Brown). **1945:** *The Navajo Trail* (*H* Johnny Mack Brown); *Gun Smoke* (*H* Johnny Mack Brown); *Stranger from Santa Fe* (*H* Johnny Mack Brown); *Flame of the West* (*H* Johnny Mack Brown); *The Lost Trail* (*H* Johnny Mack Brown); *Frontier Feud* (*H* Johnny Mack Brown); *Border Bandits* (*H* Johnny Mack Brown); *Rhythm Roundup* (*H* Ken Curtis). **1946:** *Drifting Along* (*H* Johnny Mack Brown); *Haunted Mine* (*H* Johnny Mack Brown); *Under Arizona Skies* (*H* Johnny Mack Brown); *Gentleman from Texas* (*H* Johnny Mack Brown); *Trigger Fingers* (*H* Johnny Mack Brown); *Shadows on the Range* (*H* Johnny Mack Brown); *Silver Range* (*H* Johnny Mack Brown). **1947:** *Raiders of the South* (*H* Johnny Mack Brown); *Valley of Fear* (*H* Johnny Mack Brown); *Trailing Danger* (*H* Johnny Mack Brown); *Law of the Lawless* (*H* Johnny Mack Brown); *Law Comes to Gunsight* (*H* Johnny Mack Brown); *Code of the Saddle* (*H* Johnny Mack Brown); *Flashing Guns* (*H* Johnny Mack Brown); *Prairie Express* (*H* Johnny Mack Brown); *Gun Talk* (*H* Johnny Mack Brown). **1948:** *Overland Trails* (*H* Johnny Mack Brown); *Crossed Trails* (*H* Johnny Mack Brown); *Frontier Agent* (*H* Johnny Mack Brown); *Trigger Man* (*H* Johnny Mack Brown); *Back Trail* (*H* Johnny Mack Brown); *Fighting Ranger* (*H* Johnny Mack Brown); *Sheriff of Medicine Bow* (*H* Johnny Mack Brown); *Gunning for*

Justice (*H* Johnny Mack Brown); *Hidden Danger* (*H* Johnny Mack Brown). **1950:** *Hostile Country* (*H* Russ Hayden/James Ellison); *Marshal of Hedorado* (*H* Russ Hayden/James Ellison); *Colorado Ranger* (*H* Russ Hayden/James Ellison); *West of the Brazos* (*H* Russ Hayden/James Ellison); *Crooked River* (*H* Russ Hayden/James Ellison); *Fast on the Draw* (*H* Russ Hayden/James Ellison).

George "Gabby" Hayes

Sidekick Handle: Windy Haliday, Gabby Whitaker

Gabby Hayes ranks as the Western movies' all-time leading sidekick and as one of the most unique and distinct characters and personalities that Hollywood has ever produced. He appeared in excess of 130 Westerns, and in most he portrayed basically the same character: a crotchety old-timer whose disdain for "gal darn polecats" (outlaws) and "durn persnickety females" he made known to everyone in no uncertain terms. Hayes appeared with almost every major Western star at one time or another.

He is best noted as the sidekick of two of the movies' most successful cowboys, Roy Rogers and Hopalong Cassidy.

Hayes made 40 films with Rogers at various times between 1939 and 1946 and 22 with Cassidy during the period of 1935–39.

Gabby was born George Francis Hayes in Wellsville, New York, on May 7, 1885, and before coming to Hollywood he had logged a 25-year career in vaudeville.

He made his film debut in the 1929 film *The Rainbow Man*. His first meaty part came later that year when he played a reporter in the Pathé film *The Big News*. In 1931 Hayes began making Westerns with the likes of Bob Steele, Rex Bell, Tom Tyler, Hoot Gibson and Randolph Scott among others. In these films his roles ranged from bit parts to bad guys.

In 1933 he became a stock player in a series of Westerns produced by Paul Malvern's Lone Star Productions, released by Monogram Pictures and starring a young cowboy named John Wayne. He made 11 of these films. In 1935 Hayes became a part of the most successful series of B Westerns ever made — the Hopalong Cassidy series. In the first four entries of the series Hayes played characters called Windy, Ben, Spike and Shanghai. Beginning with film number five, *Three on the Trail*, his character Windy Haliday became a prominent figure in the series.

Republic Pictures offered a sizable contract to Hayes and his Windy character to leave the Cassidy series in 1939. Paramount, the producer of

George "Gabby" Hayes

the Cassidy films, took legal action prohibiting the use of the name Windy Haliday. So thus was born Gabby—the character and the monicker that Hayes would retain for the remainder of his life.

Republic paired Hayes with young Roy Rogers. Their first film together was *Southward Ho!* released in May 1939. Between 1939 and 1942 Rogers and Hayes turned out 27 films together. In 1943 the studio decided to match up Hayes and their latest acquisition, Wild Bill Elliott. The Elliott/ Hayes union lasted ten films before Hayes returned to Rogers' side in 1944 for two more years of sidekick duty.

In 1946 Gabby Hayes said goodbye to B Westerns to concentrate on major films.

He made his last film, *The Caribou Trail*, in 1950.

That same year *The Gabby Hayes Show* premiered on NBC-TV. The show featured Gabby and special guests like Roy Rogers telling tales of the old West, and it ran for two seasons.

Top: From left, William Boyd, Gabby Hayes and Russell Hayden in Texas Trail *(Paramount, 1937). Bottom: Hayes hams it up with Roy Rogers and the Sons of the Pioneers in* Lights of Old Santa Fe *(Republic, 1944).*

In 1954 when Buffalo Bob Smith suffered a heart attack, Hayes replaced him on the enormously popular *Howdy Doody Show.* Following that run, Gabby Hayes retired from show business in 1955.

The Westerns' most famous sidekick passed away on February 9, 1969, in Burbank, California.

George "Gabby" Hayes Filmography

1931: *God's Country and the Man* (H Tom Tyler); *The Nevada Buckaroo* (H Bob Steele); *Cavalier of the West* (H Harry Carey). **1932:** *Without Honors* (H Harry Carey); *Border Devils* (H Harry Carey); *Riders of the Desert* (H Bob Steele); *The Night Rider* (H Harry Carey); *Man from Hell's Edges* (H Bob Steele); *From Broadway to Cheyenne* (H Rex Bell); *Hidden Valley* (H Bob Steele); *Texas Buddies* (H Bob Steele); *The Boiling Point* (H Hoot Gibson); *Wild Horse Mesa* (H Randolph Scott); *The Fighting Champ* (H Bob Steele). **1933:** *Breed of the Border* (H Bob Steele); *The Gallant Fool* (H Bob Steele); *Crashing Broadway* (H Rex Bell); *The Fighting Texans* (H Rex Bell); *Galloping Romeo* (H Bob Steele); *The Rangers Code* (H Bob Steele); *The Fugitive* (H Rex Bell); *Riders of Destiny* (H John Wayne); *Trailing North* (H Bob Steele). **1934:** *The Lucky Texan* (H John Wayne); *West of the Divide* (H John Wayne); *Blue Steel* (H John Wayne); *The Man from Utah* (H John Wayne); *Randy Rides Alone* (H John Wayne); *The Star Packer* (H John Wayne); *The Man from Hell* (H Reb Russell); *Brand of Hate* (H Bob Steele); *In Old Santa Fe* (H Ken Maynard); *The Lawless Frontier* (H John Wayne); *'Neath the Arizona Skies* (H John Wayne). **1935:** *Texas Terror* (H John Wayne); *Rainbow Valley* (H John Wayne); *The Outlaw Tamer* (H Lane Chandler); *Justice of the Range* (H Tim McCoy); *Hopalong Cassidy* (H William Boyd); *The Throwback* (H Buck Jones); *Thunder Mountain* (H George O'Brien); *Smokey Smith* (H Bob Steele); *Tumbling Tumbleweeds* (H Gene Autry); *The Eagle's Brood* (H William Boyd [Hopalong Cassidy]); *Bar 20 Rides Again* (H William Boyd [Hopalong Cassidy]); *Swifty* (H Hoot Gibson). **1936:** *Silver Spurs* (H Buck Jones); *Valley of the Lawless* (H Johnny Mack Brown); *The Lawless Nineties* (H John Wayne); *Call of the Prairie* (H Hopalong Cassidy); *Song of the Trail* (H Kermit Maynard); *Three on the Trail* (H Hopalong Cassidy); *Heart of the West* (H Hopalong Cassidy); *Texas Rangers* (H Fred MacMurray); *Hopalong Cassidy Returns* (H Hopalong Cassidy); *Trail Dust* (H Hopalong Cassidy); *The Plainsman* (H Gary Cooper). **1937:** *Borderland* (H Hopalong Cassidy); *Hills of Old Wyoming* (H Hopalong Cassidy); *North of the Rio Grande* (H Hopalong Cassidy); *Rustlers Valley* (H Hopalong Cassidy); *Hopalong Rides Again* (H Hopalong Cassidy); *Texas Trail* (H Hopalong Cassidy). **1938:** *Heart of Arizona* (H Hopalong Cassidy); *Bar 20 Justice* (H

Hopalong Cassidy); *Pride of the West* (H Hopalong Cassidy); *In Old Mexico* (H Hopalong Cassidy); *The Frontiersman* (H Hopalong Cassidy). **1939:** *Sunset Trail* (H Hopalong Cassidy); *Silver on the Sage* (H Hopalong Cassidy); *Southward Ho* (H Roy Rogers); *In Old Caliente* (H Roy Rogers); *Renegade Trail* (H Hopalong Cassidy); *Wall Street Cowboy* (H Roy Rogers); *In Old Monterey* (H Gene Autry); *The Arizona Kid* (H Roy Rogers); *Saga of Death Valley* (H Roy Rogers); *Days of Jesse James* (H Roy Rogers). **1940:** *Young Buffalo Bill* (H Roy Rogers); *The Carson City Kid* (H Roy Rogers); *The Ranger and the Lady* (H Roy Rogers); *Colorado* (H Roy Rogers); *Young Bill Hickok* (H Roy Rogers); *Melody Ranch* (H Gene Autry); *The Border Legion* (H Roy Rogers). **1941:** *Robin Hood of the Pecos* (H Roy Rogers); *In Old Cheyenne* (H Roy Rogers); *Sheriff of Tombstone* (H Roy Rogers); *Nevada City* (H Roy Rogers); *Bad Man of Deadwood* (H Roy Rogers); *Jesse James at Bay* (H Roy Rogers); *Red River Valley* (H Roy Rogers). **1942:** *Man from Cheyenne* (H Roy Rogers); *South of Santa Fe* (H Roy Rogers); *Sunset on the Desert* (H Roy Rogers); *Romance on the Range* (H Roy Rogers); *Sons of the Pioneers* (H Roy Rogers); *Sunset Serenade* (H Roy Rogers); *Heart of the Golden West* (H Roy Rogers); *Ridin' Down the Canyon* (H Roy Rogers). **1943:** *Calling Wild Bill Elliott* (H Wild Bill Elliott); *The Man from Thunder River* (H Wild Bill Elliott); *Death Valley Manhunt* (H Wild Bill Elliott); *Bordertown Gunfighters* (H Wild Bill Elliott); *Wagon Tracks West* (H Wild Bill Elliott); *Overland Mail Robbery* (H Wild Bill Elliott). **1944:** *Mojave Firebrand* (H Wild Bill Elliott); *Hidden Valley Outlaws* (H Wild Bill Elliott); *Tucson Raiders* (H Wild Bill Elliott); *Marshal of Reno* (H Wild Bill Elliott); *Lights of Old Santa Fe* (H Roy Rogers); *Tall in the Saddle* (H John Wayne). **1945:** *Utah* (H Roy Rogers); *Bells of Rosarita* (H Roy Rogers); *The Man from Oklahoma* (H Roy Rogers); *Don't Fence Me In* (H Roy Rogers); *Along the Navajo Trail* (H Roy Rogers); *The Big Bonanza* (H Richard Arlen). **1946:** *Song of Arizona* (H Roy Rogers); *Rainbow Over Texas* (H Roy Rogers); *My Pal Trigger* (H Roy Rogers); *Under Nevada Skies* (H Roy Rogers); *Roll on Texas Moon* (H Roy Rogers); *Home in Oklahoma* (H Roy Rogers); *Heldorado* (H Roy Rogers); *Badman's Territory* (H Randolph Scott). **1947:** *Trail Street* (H Randolph Scott); *Wyoming* (H William Elliott). **1948:** *Albuquerque* (H Randolph Scott); *Return of the Badmen* (H Randolph Scott); *The Untamed Breed* (H Sonny Tufts). **1949:** *El Paso* (H John Payne). **1950:** *The Caribou Trail* (H Randolph Scott).

Sterling Holloway

Sidekick Handles: Nellie Bly, Droopy

In 1946 when Gene Autry returned from World War II to the Republic Pictures B Western wars, he chose as his sidekick wilty-voiced Sterling Holloway. His old saddle pal Smiley Burnette was successfully ridin' in tandem with Charles Starrett over at Columbia.

Starting with *Sioux City Sue,* Holloway played characters who were totally confused by the action around them and who appeared to be on the edge of a nervous breakdown. His best known character name was Nellie Bly. He served with Autry in Gene's final five pictures for Republic Studios.

As far as his overall career is concerned, Holloway is probably best known as various character voices in the Walt Disney cartoon features. He was the voice of the Cheshire Cat in *Alice in Wonderland,* the stork in *Dumbo* and the mouse in *Ben and Me.*

He had a recurring role in the fifties television series *The Life of Riley,* playing Riley's tentative neighbor Waldo Binney and was a regular on the 1964 CBS series *The Baileys of Balboa,* playing a scatterbrained sailor.

Sterling Holloway was born in Cedartown, Georgia, in 1905.

Sterling Holloway Filmography

1946: *Sioux City Sue* (*H* Gene Autry). **1947:** *Trail of San Antone* (*H* Gene Autry); *Twilight on the Rio Grande* (*H* Gene Autry); *Saddle Pals* (*H* Gene Autry); *Robin Hood of Texas* (*H* Gene Autry).

Olin Howlin

As far as being a B Western sidekick, Olin Howlin might best be described as a second-string sidekick. When one of the starting sidekicks was out, Republic Pictures brought in Howlin.

He made two films in 1945 with Sunset Carson after Smiley Burnette departed the Carson series and the studio, and in 1947 he bridged Roy Rogers' sidekick gap between Gabby Hayes and Andy Devine.

Howlin was born in Denver, Colorado, on February 10, 1896. He started his show biz career as a vaudeville comic and entered films in 1918. He made over fifty films in his career and was still active in the movie-making world at the time of his death on September 20, 1959.

Some of his films were *A Star Is Born* (1937), *Bringing Up Baby* (1938) and *The Blob* (1958).

Olin Howlin Filmography

1945: *Sheriff of Cimarron* (H Sunset Carson); *Santa Fe Saddlemates* (H Sunset Carson). 1947: *Apache Rose* (H Roy Rogers).

Arthur Hunnicutt

For four decades lanky Arthur Hunnicutt was a familiar face and voice in Western films. He specialized in playing grubby hillbillies and cantankerous mountain men. His portrayal of a mountain man in the 1952 film *The Big Sky* won him an Oscar nomination for Best Supporting Actor.

Hunnicutt also had major roles in such top Westerns as *Cat Ballou*, *The Tall T* and *Broken Arrow*.

Hunnicutt got his start in Westerns by playing sidekick to Charles Starrett in eight Columbia Pictures adventures in 1942 and 1943, beginning with *Riding Through Nevada*. His characterizations in those films molded his basic screen image.

Hunnicutt was born February 17, 1911, in Gravelly, Arkansas. He made his film debut in the 1942 film *Wildcat*.

He passed away September 27, 1979, in Woodland Hills, California.

Arthur Hunnicutt Filmography

1942: *Riding Through Nevada* (H Charles Starrett); *Pardon My Gun* (H Charles Starrett). 1943: *The Fighting Buckaroo* (H Charles Starrett); *Law of the Northwest* (H Charles Starrett); *Frontier Fury* (H Charles Starrett); *Robin Hood of the Range* (H Charles Starrett); *Hail to the Rangers* (H Charles Starrett); *Riding West* (H Charles Starrett).

Paul Hurst

Paul Hurst was the screen sidekick of Republic cowboy Monte Hale for 13 of the 19 films that Hale made.

Hurst enjoyed a wide and varied screen career. He was born in Tulare County, California, in 1888 and began work in the film industry during its infancy. By 1912 Hurst was working as an actor, screenwriter, producer and director. Hurst made dozens of silent films.

When the talkies arrived, Hurst found himself most in demand as a comedian. In the early thirties he starred in a series of comedy shorts as a semi–punch-drunk boxer.

Throughout the thirties and forties Hurst racked up a host of memorable film roles, including one of the leads in the 1939 Columbia comedy short *The Glove Slingers;* the frazzled streetcar conductor in the Our Gang short *Goin' Fishin';* the coldblooded hangman in *The Ox Bow Incident* and the selfish old-timer who is redeemed by John Wayne in *The Angel and the Badman.*

When the Hale series ended, Hurst continued to appear in films like John Wayne's 1952 flick, *Big Jim McLain.*

Paul Hurst committed suicide on February 27, 1953.

Paul Hurst Filmography

1947: *Under Colorado Skies* (*H* Monte Hale). 1948: *California Firebrand* (*H* Monte Hale); *Son of God's Country* (*H* Monte Hale). 1949: *Prince of the Plains* (*H* Monte Hale); *Law of the Golden West* (*H* Monte Hale); *Outcasts of the Trail* (*H* Monte Hale); *South of Rio* (*H* Monte Hale); *San Antone Ambush* (*H* Monte Hale); *Ranger of the Cherokee Strip* (*H* Monte Hale); *Pioneer Marshal* (*H* Monte Hale). 1950: *Vanishing Westerner* (*H* Monte Hale); *The Old Frontier* (*H* Monte Hale); *The Missourians* (*H* Monte Hale).

Chubby Johnson

Veteran charactor actor Chubby Johnson pinch-hit for Eddy Waller as Rocky Lane's sidekick in three films during 1951.

Chubby was born Charles Randolph Johnson in 1903 in Terre Haute, Indiana, and had worked in films, in radio and in the legitimate theater. His specialty was playing blustery old-timers. In later years he wrote a syndicated entertainment column.

Johnson passed away on October 31, 1974.

Chubby Johnson Filmography

1951: *Night Riders of Montana* (*H* Rocky Lane); *Wells Fargo Gunmaster* (*H* Rocky Lane); *Fort Dodge Stampede* (*H* Rocky Lane).

Gordon Jones

Sidekick Handles: Splinters McGonigle, I.Q.

Iowa-born Gordon Jones played simple but lovable Splinters McGonigle in a half-dozen Roy Rogers films in 1950 and 1951. He began as a secondary sidekick in the film *Trigger Jr.* and in his next outing, *Sunset in the West,* he replaced Pat Brady as Roy's main compadre.

Jones's first saddle pal part had been earlier in 1950 when he co-starred with Rex Allen in Allen's first film, *The Arizona Cowboy,* playing a character ironically called I.Q.

Gordon Jones had begun his film career in 1930 and over the years had been seen in such top-rated films as *My Sister Eileen, The Secret Life of Walter Mitty* and the 1940 serial *The Green Hornet.*

On TV Jones was a regular in series like *Ozzie and Harriet, The Ray Milland Show* and *So This Is Hollywood.*

Jones was born April 15, 1911, in Alden, Iowa, and passed away June 20, 1963, in Tarzana, California, the victim of a heart attack.

Gordon Jones Filmography

1950: *The Arizona Cowboy* (*H* Rex Allen); *Trigger Jr.* (*H* Roy Rogers); *Sunset in the West* (*H* Roy Rogers); *North of the Great Divide* (*H* Roy Rogers); *Trail of Robin Hood* (*H* Roy Rogers). **1951:** *Spoilers of the Plains* (*H* Roy Rogers); *Heart of the Rockies* (*H* Roy Rogers).

Guy Kibbee

Guy Kibbee was one of the most successful screen comedy actors of the thirties and forties. He appeared in all sorts of films; comedies like *Three Men on a Horse* (1936), musicals like *42nd Street* (1933) and *The Gold*

Diggers of 1933, and dramatic films such as *Taxi* (1932) and *Mr. Smith Goes to Washington* (1939).

Perhaps his best-remembered role was as the delightful lighthouse keeper in the 1936 Shirley Temple film *Captain January*.

In the mid-forties, Kibbee became part of the musical-comedy troupe that populated the Columbia-produced rhythm oaters that starred former Sons of the Pioneers Ken Curtis. Others in the ensemble included Andy Clyde, Carolina Cotton, and the Hoosier Hot Shots.

Kibbee was born Guy Bridges Kibbee on March 6, 1886, in El Paso, Texas, and died on May 24, 1956. His brother Milton Kibbee was also a successful screen actor in the thirties and forties.

Guy Kibbee Filmography

1946: *Cowboy Blues* (H Ken Curtis); *Singing on the Trail* (H Ken Curtis); *Lone Star Moonlight* (H Ken Curtis); *Over the Santa Fe Trail* (H Ken Curtis).

Brad King

Sidekick Handle: Johnny Nelson

Brad King replaced Russell Hayden as Hopalong Cassidy's youthful sidekick. He took on the role of Johnny Nelson in the 1941 series entry *Riders of the Timberline* and remained for five films.

He resurfaced in 1949 with co-star billing in a Western called *Trouble at Melody Mesa* which starred Cal Shrum.

Brad King Filmography

1941: *Riders of the Timberline* (H Hopalong Cassidy); *Stick to Your Guns* (H Hopalong Cassidy); *Outlaws of the Desert* (H Hopalong Cassidy); *Secrets of the Wasteland* (H Hopalong Cassidy); *Twilight on the Trail* (H Hopalong Cassidy).

Brad King

Jay Kirby

Sidekick Handle: Johnny Travers

In 1942 the production of the Hopalong Cassidy films shifted from Paramount to United Artists. The first UA-released picture was *Undercover Man.* The film featured William Boyd as Cassidy, Andy Clyde as California and newcomer Jay Kirby as Johnny "Breezy" Travers. After six films Kirby just rode away.

From left, William Boyd, Claudia Drake, George Reeves, Andy Clyde and Jay Kirby in Border Patrol (United Artists, 1943).

Jay Kirby Filmography

1942: Undercover Man (H Hopalong Cassidy). 1943: Hoppy Serves a Writ (H Hopalong Cassidy); Border Patrol (H Hopalong Cassidy); The Leather Burners (H Hopalong Cassidy); Colt Comrades (H Hopalong Cassidy); Lost Canyon (H Hopalong Cassidy).

Fuzzy Knight

John Forrest "Fuzzy" Knight was one of the most prolific and popular sidekicks that the B Western era produced.

In an 18-year span as a saddle pal, Knight appeared in over a hundred films with the cinema genre's top cowboy stars and always providing top-rank comedy relief.

He is best known for his Universal series with Johnny Mack Brown. Knight was born May 9, 1901, in Fairmont, West Virginia, and began his career as a tent show minstrel while a teenager. While excelling as a comic he was also a talented musician. Knight attended the University of West Virginia and upon graduation reentered show business as a vaudeville performer and musical/comedy player.

By the late twenties he had made it to Broadway and was appearing in shows like "Earl Carroll's Vanities."

Knight arrived in Hollywood in 1932, and his first notable role was in the 1933 Mae West film *She Done Him Wrong.*

He made his first sidekick appearances for Ambassador Pictures in three films starring Kermit Maynard in 1935 and 1936.

In 1936 he signed on with Universal Pictures and was paired with their singing cowboy Bob Baker for four films in 1937 and 1938.

Baker was demoted to supporting player when the company signed highly-rated cowboy Johnny Mack Brown. The Brown/Knight duo was one of filmdom's best known and best working cowboy/sidekick combinations. Beginning with *Desperate Trails* in 1939, Johnny and Fuzzy caught bad guys in 28 films between 1939 and 1943. Their best outings featured Johnny, Fuzzy and female co-star Nell O'Day.

When Johnny departed Universal for Monogram, the studio then co-starred Knight with a plethora of Western actors including Tex Ritter, Russell Hayden, Rod Cameron, Eddie Dew and, in seven films in 1945 and 1946, with a pre–Sky King Kirby Grant.

During the late forties Knight appeared in films like *The Egg and I* and *The Adventures of Gallant Bess.*

In 1950 he returned to a sidekick role along with another ex–Johnny Mack Brown compadre, Raymond Hatton, in a series of six hastily produced films starring Russ Hayden and Jimmy Ellison.

Next, Monogram Studios signed Knight to ride with Whip Wilson in eight pictures. He ended his career as a screen pal by co-starring with Wild Bill Elliott in four of the "super B" Westerns Elliott was making at the time.

In the 1950s he was a regular on Buster Crabbe's foreign legion adventure television series *The Adventures of Capt. Gallant.*

Fuzzy Knight continued his film career into the late 1960s. He passed away February 23, 1976, in Hollywood, California.

Fuzzy Knight Filmography

1935: *Trails of the Wild* (H Kermit Maynard). **1936:** *Song of the Trail* (H Kermit Maynard); *Wild Cat Trooper* (H Kermit Maynard); *Song of the Gringo* (H Tex Ritter). **1937:** *Courage of the West* (H Bob Baker). **1938:** *The Singing Outlaw* (H Bob Baker); *Border Wolves* (H Bob Baker); *The Last*

Fuzzy Knight

Stand (H Bob Baker); *Where the West Begins* (H Jack Randall). **1939:** *Desperate Trails* (H Johnny Mack Brown); *Oklahoma Frontier* (H Johnny Mack Brown); *Chip of the Flying U* (H Johnny Mack Brown). **1940:** *Riders of Pasco Basin* (H Johnny Mack Brown); *West of Carson City* (H Johnny Mack Brown); *Bad Man from Red Butte* (H Johnny Mack Brown); *Son of Roaring Dan* (H Johnny Mack Brown); *Ragtime Cowboy Joe* (H Johnny Mack Brown); *Law and Order* (H Johnny Mack Brown); *Pony Post* (H Johnny Mack Brown). **1941:** *Boss of Bullion City* (H Johnny Mack Brown); *Bury Me Not on the Lone Prairie* (H Johnny Mack Brown); *Law of the Range* (H Johnny Mack Brown); *Rawhide Rangers* (H Johnny Mack Brown); *Man from Montana* (H Johnny Mack Brown); *Masked Rider* (H Johnny Mack Brown); *Arizona Cyclone* (H Johnny Mack Brown); *Fighting Bill Fargo* (H Johnny Mack Brown). **1942:** *Stagecoach Buckaroo* (H Johnny Mack Brown); *The Silver Bullet* (H Johnny Mack Brown); *Boss of Hangtown Mesa* (H Johnny Mack Brown); *Deep in the Heart of Texas* (H Johnny Mack Brown); *Little Joe the Wrangler* (H Johnny Mack Brown); *The Old*

Chisholm Trail (H Johnny Mack Brown). **1943:** Tenting Tonight on the Old Campground (H Johnny Mack Brown); Cheyenne Roundup (H Johnny Mack Brown); Raiders of San Joaquin (H Johnny Mack Brown); Lone Star Trail (H Johnny Mack Brown); Arizona Trail (H Tex Ritter); Frontier Law (H Russell Hayden). **1944:** Marshal of Gunsmoke (H Tex Ritter); Oklahoma Raiders (H Tex Ritter); Boss of Boom Town (H Rod Cameron); Trigger Trail (H Rod Cameron); Riders of the Santa Fe (H Rod Cameron); The Old Texas Trail (H Rod Cameron); Trail to Gunsight (H Eddie Dew); The Cowboy and the Senorita (H Roy Rogers). **1945:** Beyond the Pecos (H Rod Cameron); Renegades of the Rio Grande (H Rod Cameron); Badmen of the Border (H Kirby Grant); Code of the Lawless (H Kirby Grant); Trail to Vengeance (H Kirby Grant). **1946:** Guntown (H Kirby Grant); Rustlers Roundup (H Kirby Grant); Lawless Breed (H Kirby Grant); Gunman's Code (H Kirby Grant). **1950:** Hills of Oklahoma (H Rex Allen); Hostile Country (H Russ Hayden, Jimmy Ellison); Marshal of Heldorado (H Russ Hayden, Jimmy Ellison); Colorado Ranger (H Russ Hayden, Jimmy Ellison); West of the Brazos (H Russ Hayden, Jimmy Ellison); Crooked River (H Russ Hayden, Jimmy Ellison); Fast on the Draw (H Russ Hayden, Jimmy Ellison). **1951:** Wanted Dead or Alive (H Whip Wilson); Canyon Raiders (H Whip Wilson); Nevada Badmen (H Whip Wilson); Stagecoach Driver (H Whip Wilson); Lawless Cowboys (H Whip Wilson); Stage to Blue River (H Whip Wilson). **1952:** Night Riders (H Whip Wilson); The Gunman (H Whip Wilson); Kansas Territory (H William Elliott); Fargo (H William Elliott). **1953:** Topeka (H William Elliott); Vigilante Terror (H William Elliott).

Pinky Lee

In television's early years the two most successful children's programs on the air were The Howdy Doody Show and The Pinky Lee Show.

Lee in his checkerboard suit and crayon box hat songs, did slapstick comedy and performed kids-level burlesque routines.

Lee got his start on TV in 1949 on a show called Hollywood Premiere. On April 5, 1950, NBC premiered The Pinky Lee Show live from Hollywood. The original Pinky Lee Show's run ended in November of 1950.

Early in 1951 Republic Pictures approached Lee to become the sidekick of their leading cowboy star Roy Rogers. Lee agreed and provided comedy antics for what were to be Roy Rogers' last three B Westerns: In Old Amarillo, South of Caliente and Pals of the Golden West.

Lee returned to TV in a series called Those Two which enjoyed a successful run from 1951 to 1953. Following the end of *Those Two* Lee began his popular run of Saturday morning kids' shows. These were jamborees of songs, games and joyful all-around silliness. But unfortunately illness caused Lee to give up the shows in 1955.

Though he returned to television in a series of ventures as late as the mid-1960s, he never attained super-popularity again.

Pinky Lee Filmography

1951: *In Old Amarillo* (H Roy Rogers); *South of Caliente* (H Roy Rogers); *Pals of the Golden West* (H Roy Rogers).

Emmett Lynn

Sidekick Handles: Whopper, Uncle Ezra, Buckskin

Goggle-eyed Emmett Lynn ranks as one of the funniest of the B Western sidekicks, but, alas, also one of the most forgettable. Lynn palled around with such top-notch Western stars as Tim Holt, Red Barry, Bill Elliott, Rocky Lane, Jim Bannon, and Monte Hale. On top of that he had supporting roles in films with Roy Rogers, Buster Crabbe, and others.

Lynn was born in Muscatine, Iowa, on February 14, 1897, and began working in films at Biograph Studios in 1913. He began his entertainment career as a burlesque comic.

His first sidekick stint was with Tim Holt at RKO Studios. The union lasted only four films in which he played a grizzly prevaricator aptly called Whopper. Next he went to work on a half-dozen films with Don "Red" Barry at Republic.

He preceded Roscoe Ates as Eddie Dean's saddle pal at PRC (playing Uncle Ezra) and appeared in Red Ryder films with both Wild Bill Elliott and Rocky Lane.

Emmett's last sidekick role was as Buckskin in the Eagle Lion Red Ryder series which starred Jim Bannon.

Aside from dozens of hoss operas, Lynn also appeared in such films as *The Ten Commandments* and *A Man Called Peter*.

He died of a heart attack on October 20, 1958, in Hollywood, California.

Emmett Lynn

Emmett Lynn Filmography

1940: *Wagon Train* (*H* Tim Holt); *The Fargo Kid* (*H* Tim Holt). **1941:** *Along the Rio Grande* (*H* Tim Holt); *Robbers of the Range* (*H* Tim Holt). **1942:** *Outlaws of Pine Ridge* (*H* Don "Red" Barry); *The Sundown Kid* (*H* Don "Red" Barry). **1943:** *Dead Man's Gulch* (*H* Don "Red" Barry); *Carson City Cyclone* (*H* Don "Red" Barry); *Days of Old Cheyenne* (*H* Don "Red" Barry). **1944:** *Outlaws of Santa Fe* (*H* Don "Red" Barry). **1945:** *Song of Old Wyoming* (*H* Eddie Dean); *Wagon Wheels Westward* (*H* Wild Bill Elliott). **1946:** *Romance of the West* (*H* Eddie Dean); *Caravan Trail* (*H* Eddie Dean); *Conquest of Cheyenne* (*H* Wild Bill Elliott); *Stagecoach to Denver* (*H* Rocky Lane); *Man from Rainbow Valley* (*H* Monte Hale). **1947:** *Rustlers of Devil's Canyon* (*H* Rocky Lane); *Oregon Trail Scouts* (*H* Rocky Lane). **1949:** *Ride Ryder Ride* (*H* Jim Bannon); *Roll Thunder Roll* (*H* Jim Bannon); *The Fighting Redhead* (*H* Jim Bannon); *Cowboy and the Prize Fighter* (*H* Jim Bannon).

Frank McGlynn, Jr.

Sidekick Handle: Red Connors

Frank McGlynn, Jr., played Hopalong Cassidy's pal Red Connors in the first and third films in the famous series. Red was an action sidekick; while Gabby Hayes handled the comedy, Jimmy Ellison, the romance, McGlynn was mostly around to help Cassidy clean out the bad guys.

He received equal sidekick billing in the ads for *Bar 20 Rides Again.*

McGlynn was the son of one of the film industry's pioneer actors, Frank McGlynn, Sr., who began acting in movies with the Edison Film Company in the early 1900s. McGlynn, Sr., was Buck Jones's sidekick Junglebob Morgan in the 1935 serial *The Roaring West.*

McGlynn, Jr., starred in a couple of RKO's Masquers Club comedy shorts in 1933.

Frank McGlynn, Jr. Filmography

1935: *Hopalong Cassidy* (*H* Hopalong Cassidy). **1936:** *Bar 20 Rides Again* (*H* Hopalong Cassidy).

Chris-Pin Martin

Rotund Chris-Pin Martin was one of the many character actors who populated Westerns (B's and A's) in the thirties and forties. He appeared in such top-flight features as *Stagecoach* with John Wayne and in low-budget B's like Jack Hoxie's 1933 *Outlaw Justice*.

Martin's role as the Cisco Kid's pal Gordito bridged the gap between A's and B's.

He first created the part in the 1931 film *The Cisco Kid*, a fine feature which starred Warner Baxter in the title role. In 1939 when Baxter once again starred as Cisco in *The Return of the Cisco Kid*, Martin was once again at his side. However in this film he was sort of a second sidekick, as Cesar Romero in the part of Lopez received second billing and was the basic action sidekick.

That same year when 20th Century–Fox decided to make a series of Cisco films, Baxter relinquished the lead and it was passed on to Romero, but Martin remained in his role throughout the six films which were released in 1940 and 1941. In 1947 Martin returned to the Cisco series, now being produced by Monogram, and rode beside Gilbert Roland for two films.

Martin was born Ysabel Poinciana Chris Martin Piaz in 1894 in Tucson, Arizona. Some of the other notable films in which he appeared include *The Mark of Zorro*, *The Ox Bow Incident* and *Ali Baba and the Forty Thieves*.

Martin died of a heart attack on June 27, 1953, in Los Angeles, California.

Chris-Pin Martin Filmography

1931: *The Cisco Kid* (*H* Warner Baxter). **1939:** *The Return of the Cisco Kid* (*H* Warner Baxter). **1940:** *The Cisco Kid and the Lady* (*H* Cesar Romero); *Viva Cisco Kid* (*H* Cesar Romero); *Lucky Cisco Kid* (*H* Cesar Romero); *The Gay Caballero* (*H* Cesar Romero). **1941:** *Romance of the Rio Grande* (*H* Cesar Romero); *Ride on Vaquero* (*H* Cesar Romero). **1947:** *Robin Hood of Monterey* (*H* Gilbert Roland); *King of the Bandits* (*H* Gilbert Roland).

Richard Martin

Sidekick Handle: Chito Rafferty

Washington State–born Richard Martin played Chito Jose Gonzalez Bustamonte Rafferty, the handsome, two-fisted, woman-chasing, English language–mangling sidekick of RKO's number one cowboy Tim Holt in 29 films between 1947 and 1952.

Martin's character was one of the best-developed sidekick parts that the B Western era produced — in a category with Smiley Burnette's Frog Millhouse and Gabby Hayes's Gabby Whitaker.

Martin was an RKO contract player who had appeared in all types of films (including Westerns) with Robert Mitchum and James Warren.

When Holt returned from his armed forces duty tour to resume his Western career, Martin was drafted to fill Tim's old sidekick Ray Whitley's boots.

The results were pleasing to the studio heads and to the fans who put down coins at the box office. When the series ended, Martin retired from the screen.

He was born December 12, 1917, in Spokane, Washington, and was raised in Los Angeles, California.

Richard Martin Filmography

1945: *Wanderer of the Wasteland* (*H* James Warren). **1947:** *Thunder Mountain* (*H* Tim Holt); *Under the Tonto Rim* (*H* Tim Holt); *Wild Horse Mesa* (*H* Tim Holt). **1948:** *Western Heritage* (*H* Tim Holt); *Guns of Hate* (*H* Tim Holt); *Arizona Ranger* (*H* Tim Holt); *Indian Agent* (*H* Tim Holt); *Gun Smugglers* (*H* Tim Holt). **1949:** *Brothers in the Saddle* (*H* Tim Holt); *Rustlers* (*H* Tim Holt); *Stagecoach Kid* (*H* Tim Holt); *Masked Raiders* (*H* Tim Holt); *Mysterious Desperado* (*H* Tim Holt). **1950:** *Riders of the Range* (*H* Tim Holt); *Dynamite Pass* (*H* Tim Holt); *Storm Over Wyoming* (*H* Tim Holt); *Rider from Tucson* (*H* Tim Holt); *Border Treasure* (*H* Tim Holt); *Rio Grande Patrol* (*H* Tim Holt). **1951:** *Law of the Badlands* (*H* Tim Holt); *Saddle Legion* (*H* Tim Holt); *Gun Play* (*H* Tim Holt); *Pistol Harvest* (*H* Tim Holt); *Hot Lead* (*H* Tim Holt); *Overland Telegraph* (*H* Tim Holt). **1952:** *Trail Guide* (*H* Tim Holt); *Road Agent* (*H* Tim Holt); *Target* (*H* Tim Holt); *Desert Passage* (*H* Tim Holt).

Frank Mitchell

Sidekick Handle: Cannonball

Frank Mitchell was a member of the highly successful comedy team of Mitchell and Durant who had appeared in such hit Broadway shows as"Earl Carroll's Vanities" and "George White's Scandal." Mitchell was a master of slapstick as well as an acrobat.

He replaced Dub Taylor in the role of Cannonball in seven B Westerns starring Wild Bill Elliott and Tex Ritter at Columbia Pictures in 1941 and 1942.

Earlier he had appeared in films like Shirley Temple's *Stand Up and Cheer.*

He and Durant eventually split and Mitchell continued working in films like *Scaramouche* and Red Skelton's *Neptune's Daughter.*

Frank Mitchell was born in New York City May 13, 1905.

Frank Mitchell Filmography

1941: *Roaring Frontier* (*H* Wild Bill Elliott). **1942:** *The Lone Star Vigilantes* (*H* Wild Bill Elliott); *Bullets for Bandits* (*H* Wild Bill Elliott); *North of the Rockies* (*H* Wild Bill Elliott); *The Devil's Trail* (*H* Wild Bill Elliott); *Prairie Gunsmoke* (*H* Wild Bill Elliott); *Vengeance of the West* (*H* Wild Bill Elliott).

Horace Murphy

Blustery Horace Murphy played sidekick to some of the best of the cowboy hero lot: Bob Steele, Johnny Mack Brown and Tex Ritter.

He is best known for the Ritter films in the late thirties in which he and Snub Pollard were often paired.

Murphy appeared in a ton of B Westerns. His best characterizations were those of pompous mayors or officials reduced to begging for help from a hero or being forced to pay tribute to a bandit.

Murphy was born May 3, 1880, in Tennessee and began working as a teenager on Mississippi River showboats, eventually working his way up to captain. He also worked in vaudeville and tent shows. At one time he was a show producer and theater owner. His film work began in the 1930s.

He passed away on January 20, 1975.

Horace Murphy Filmography

1936: *Undercover Man* (*H* Johnny Mack Brown); *Sundown Saunders* (*H* Bob Steele); *Too Much Beef* (*H* Rex Bell). **1937:** *Gambling Terror* (*H* Johnny Mack Brown); *Trail of Vengeance* (*H* Johnny Mack Brown); *Lawless Land* (*H* Johnny Mack Brown); *Bar Z Badman* (*H* Johnny Mack Brown); *Boot Hill Brigade* (*H* Johnny Mack Brown); *Lightnin' Crandall* (*H* Bob Steele); *Gun Lords of Stirrup Basin* (*H* Bob Steele); *Doomed at Sundown* (*H* Bob Steele); *The Red Rope* (*H* Bob Steele); *Colorado Kid* (*H* Bob Steele); *Stars Over Arizona* (*H* Jack Randall); *Arizona Days* (*H* Tex Ritter); *Trouble in Texas* (*H* Tex Ritter); *Sing Cowboy Sing* (*H* Tex Ritter); *Riders of the Rockies* (*H* Tex Ritter); *Mystery of the Hooded Horseman* (*H* Tex Ritter). **1938:** *Paroled to Die* (*H* Bob Steele); *Thunder in the Desert* (*H* Bob Steele); *Durango Valley Raiders* (*H* Bob Steele); *Tex Rides with the Boy Scouts* (*H* Tex Ritter); *Frontier Town* (*H* Tex Ritter); *Rollin' Plains* (*H* Tex Ritter); *Utah Trail* (*H* Tex Ritter); *Starlight Over Texas* (*H* Tex Ritter); *Where the Buffalo Roam* (*H* Tex Ritter); *Song of the Buckaroo* (*H* Tex Ritter). **1939:** *Sundown on the Prairie* (*H* Tex Ritter); *Rollin' Westward* (*H* Tex Ritter); *Down the Wyoming Trail* (*H* Tex Ritter).

Bob Nolan and the Sons of the Pioneers

The Sons of the Pioneers was formed by Bob Nolan, Leonard Slye and Tim Spencer in late 1933 in California.

The group was originally known as the Pioneer Trio. When they added Hugh and Karl Farr in 1934 they officially became the Sons of the Pioneers.

In 1936 the group caught the attention of Republic Pictures, who featured them in three Gene Autry films: *The Big Show, The Old Corral* and *The Old Barn Dance.*

Slye, who had changed his name to Dick Weston, left the group and signed with Republic to star in Westerns. This once again prompted a name change — this time to Roy Rogers. He was replaced in the group by Pat Brady.

In 1937, with the musical cowboy craze in full bloom, Columbia Pictures signed the group to co-star in a series of films with Charles Starrett. Beginning with *Old Wyoming Trail* the Sons of the Pioneers rode and sang with Starrett through 28 films before departing on a return trip to Republic in 1941.

Republic, having liked the way the Pioneers had supported Starrett, placed them in the same kind of role; this time behind their old compadre Roy Rogers. Their first film with Rogers was *The Red River Valley* and during the next seven years 38 more would follow.

Members of the group (especially Nolan, Brady and later Shug Fisher) were given featured roles in the films, and the group as a whole proved well-adept at comedy and action as well as musical sequences.

Following their stint in the Rogers films the group underwent major changes in 1949 when Nolan and Spencer quit. Spencer's replacement was former Columbia singing cowboy Ken Curtis.

The Sons of the Pioneers produced such legendary hit records as "Tumbling Tumbleweeds" and "Cool Water" and their melodic sound was unmistakable.

Bob Nolan was born in Canada in 1908 and passed away on June 16, 1980, in Newport Beach, California. The other original members, with the exception of Rogers, are all deceased. Tim Spencer was born in 1908 and died in 1974; Hugh Farr, born 1903, died in 1980; Karl Farr born 1909 and died in 1961; long-time member Lloyd Perryman born 1917, died in 1977; and Pat Brady born 1914, died in 1972.

Bob Nolan and the Sons of the Pioneers Filmography

1936: *The Big Show* (H Gene Autry); *The Old Corral* (H Gene Autry). **1937:** *The Old Wyoming Trail* (H Charles Starrett); *Outlaws of the Prairie* (H Charles Starrett). **1938:** *The Old Barn Dance* (H Gene Autry); *Cattle Raiders* (H Charles Starrett); *Call of the Rockies* (H Charles Starrett); *Law of the Plains* (H Charles Starrett); *West of Cheyenne* (H Charles Starrett); *South of Arizona* (H Charles Starrett); *The Colorado Trail* (H Charles Starrett); *West of the Santa Fe* (H Charles Starrett); *Rio Grande* (H Charles Starrett). **1939:** *The Thundering West* (H Charles Starrett); *Texas Stampede* (H Charles Starrett); *North of the Yukon* (H Charles Starrett); *Spoilers of the Range* (H Charles Starrett); *Western Caravans* (H Charles Starrett); *The Man from Sundown* (H Charles Starrett); *Riders of Black River* (H Charles Starrett); *Outpost of the Mounties* (H Charles Starrett); *The Stranger from Texas* (H Charles Starrett). **1940:** *Two Fisted Rangers* (H Charles Starrett); *Bullets for Rustlers* (H Charles Starrett); *Blazing Six Shooters* (H Charles Starrett); *Texas Stagecoach* (H Charles Starrett); *The Durango Kid* (H Charles Starrett); *West of Abilene* (H Charles Starrett); *Thundering Frontier* (H Charles Starrett). **1941:** *The Pinto Kid* (H Charles Starrett); *Outlaws of the Panhandle* (H Charles Starrett); *Red River Valley* (H Roy Rogers). **1942:** *The Man from Cheyenne* (H Roy Rogers); *South of Santa Fe* (H Roy Rogers); *Romance on the Range* (H Roy Rogers); *Sons of the Pioneers* (H Roy Rogers); *Sunset Serenade* (H Roy Rogers); *Heart of the*

Bob Nolan

Golden West (H Roy Rogers); *Ridin' Down the Canyon* (H Roy Rogers).
1943: *Idaho* (H Roy Rogers); *King of the Cowboys* (H Roy Rogers); *Song of Texas* (H Roy Rogers); *Silver Spurs* (H Roy Rogers); *The Man from Music Mountain* (H Roy Rogers). **1944:** *Hands Across the Border* (H Roy Rogers); *Cowboy and the Senorita* (H Roy Rogers); *Yellow Rose of Texas* (H Roy Rogers); *Song of Nevada* (H Roy Rogers); *San Fernando Valley* (H Roy Rogers); *Lights of Old Santa Fe* (H Roy Rogers). **1945:** *Utah* (H Roy

Rogers); *Bells of Rosarita* (H Roy Rogers); *The Man from Oklahoma* (H Roy Rogers); *Sunset in Eldorado* (H Roy Rogers); *Don't Fence Me In* (H Roy Rogers). **1946:** *Along the Navajo Trail* (H Roy Rogers); *Song of Arizona* (H Roy Rogers); *Rainbow Over Texas* (H Roy Rogers); *My Pal Trigger* (H Roy Rogers); *Under Nevada Skies* (H Roy Rogers); *Roll on Texas Moon* (H Roy Rogers); *Heldorado* (H Roy Rogers). **1947:** *Apache Rose* (H Roy Rogers); *Bells of San Angelo* (H Roy Rogers); *Springtime in the Sierras* (H Roy Rogers); *On the Old Spanish Trail* (H Roy Rogers). **1948:** *The Gay Ranchero* (H Roy Rogers); *Under California Stars* (H Roy Rogers); *Eyes of Texas* (H Roy Rogers); *Nighttime in Nevada* (H Roy Rogers).

Slim Pickens

Few movie fans can ever forget the sequence in Stanley Kubrick's 1964 film *Dr. Strangelove* in which Slim Pickens as a fanatically demented general rides an atomic bomb as it heads for the U.S.S.R. Mounted astride the bomb, Pickens whoops and tia yia yeas like a rodeo bronc rider just out of the chute.

That film made the veteran actor a household name after he had spent most of his career in Western films.

Pickens was born Louis B. Lindley, Jr., on June 29, 1919, in Kingsburg, California. He began riding horses almost before he could walk, and by his early teens he was a consistent and competent rodeo performer. It was during his rodeo days that he changed his name to Slim Pickens.

Pickens made his film debut in the 1946 feature *Smoky*, with Fred Mac-Murray, playing a rodeo cowboy.

Slim's parts were slim over the next few years, until Republic Pictures signed him to replace Buddy Ebsen as the sidekick to Rex Allen.

Beginning with *Colorado Sundown* in 1952 Slim and Rex teamed in 11 films over a two-year span. His character was always a kind of slow-witted, loudmouthed but well-meaning oaf.

Pickens went on to make many Westerns like *Major Dundee* (1965), *Rocky Mountain* (1950), and *Blazing Saddles* (1974).

He also made many TV appearances and was a regular on such series as *The Outlaws* (1964–62) playing a character called Slim, *Custer* (1967) playing California Joe and *Hee Haw* (1981–82).

Slim Pickens passed away on December 8, 1983.

Slim Pickens

Slim Pickens Filmography

1952: *Colorado Sundown* (H Rex Allen); *The Last Musketeer* (H Rex Allen); *Border Saddlemates* (H Rex Allen); *Old Oklahoma Plains* (H Rex Allen); *South Pacific Trails* (H Rex Allen). **1953:** *Old Overland Trail* (H Rex Allen); *Iron Mountain Trail* (H Rex Allen); *Down Laredo Way* (H Rex Allen); *Red River Shore* (H Rex Allen). **1954:** *Phantom Stallion* (H Rex Allen).

Snub Pollard

Mustachioed Snub Pollard was one of the original Keystone Cops, the slapstick madcap bunch that set the tone for movie comedy in the early 1900s.

Pollard was born Harold Frazer in Melbourne, Australia, in 1886. He came to this country as a vaudeville actor and began making films around 1914 with the screen's first cowboy star Broncho Billy Anderson.

He made scores of features and shorts during the silent era but when the sound era arrived Pollard, like many others, found work hard to come by and was relegated to bit parts.

His Western sidekick parts came in a dozen films starring Tex Ritter. He was often paired with blustery Horace Murphy.

Pollard was still active in films at the time of his death on January 19, 1962.

His last screen appearance was in *A Pocket Full of Miracles.*

Snub Pollard Filmography

1936: *Headin' for the Rio Grande* (H Tex Ritter). **1937:** *Arizona Days* (H Tex Ritter); *Hittin' the Trail* (H Tex Ritter); *Sing Cowboy Sing* (H Tex Ritter); *Riders of the Rockies* (H Tex Ritter). **1938:** *Tex Rides with the Boy Scouts* (H Tex Ritter); *Frontier Town* (H Tex Ritter); *Rollin' Plains* (H Tex Ritter); *Utah Trail* (H Tex Ritter); *Starlight Over Texas* (H Tex Ritter); *Where the Buffalo Roam* (H Tex Ritter); *Song of the Buckaroo* (H Tex Ritter).

Don Reynolds

Sidekick Handle: Little Beaver

Don Kay Reynolds, who also made films under the name Little Brown Jug, was the young actor chosen for the part of Little Beaver in the Jim Bannon series of Red Ryder films in 1949.

Following the series Reynolds continued to work in B Westerns, appearing in several Gene Autry films at Columbia.

Don Reynolds Filmography

1949: *Ride Ryder Ride* (*H* Jim Bannon); *Roll Thunder Roll* (*H* Jim Bannon); *The Fighting Redhead* (*H* Jim Bannon); *Cowboy and the Prizefighter* (*H* Jim Bannon).

Frank Rice

Frank Rice appeared in a slew of early B Westerns in all kinds of roles. His best sidekick efforts were with Ken Maynard, and their best work together was the 1933 film *The Phantom Thunderbolt*.

Rice was born Frank Thomas Rice in Muskegon, Michigan, on May 13, 1892, and began making films in the early 1920s. His appearances in silent films were mostly relegated to serials and Westerns. When the talkies arrived he continued to work in the same type of films.

Rice contracted hepatitis and died in the midst of his career on January 9, 1936, in Los Angeles, California.

Frank Rice Filmography

1930: *Fighting Legion* (*H* Ken Maynard); *Song of the Caballero* (*H* Ken Maynard). **1931:** *Freighters of Destiny* (*H* Tom Keene). **1932:** *Sunset Trail* (*H* Ken Maynard). **1933:** *Phantom Thunderbolt* (*H* Ken Maynard); *Fiddlin' Buckaroo* (*H* Ken Maynard). **1934:** *Losers End* (*H* Jack Perrin).

The Riders of the Purple Sage *see* **Foy Willing and the Riders of the Purple Sage**

Skeeter Bill Robbins

Lanky Skeeter Bill Robbins was an old rodeo pal of Hoot Gibson's, and the two began making films together in the early 1920s.

The two old saddle pals hitched up again in Gibson's series of films for Allied Pictures in 1931, with Skeeter appearing in eight of the movies.

Skeeter Bill's given name was Roy.

He was killed in an automobile crash on November 29, 1933.

Skeeter Bill Robbins

Skeeter Bill Robbins Filmography

1931: *Wild Horse* (H Hoot Gibson); *Hard Hombre* (H Hoot Gibson). **1932:** *The Local Bad Man* (H Hoot Gibson); *A Man's Land* (H Hoot Gibson); *The Cowboy Counselor* (H Hoot Gibson); *The Boiling Point* (H Hoot Gibson). **1933:** *Dude Bandit* (H Hoot Gibson); *The Fighting Parson* (H Hoot Gibson).

From left: William Boyd, Andy Clyde and Jimmy Rogers in Forty Thieves *(United Artists, 1944).*

Jimmy Rogers

Jimmy Rogers succeeded Brad King and Jay Kirby as the youthful third party in the familiar Hopalong Cassidy trio, but like the others Rogers only lasted a few films, six to be exact. His first was *False Colors* in 1943; his last, *Forty Thieves*, the following year.

The character he played was called Jimmy Rogers.

Rogers was the son of the great comic and philosopher Will Rogers. Before joining the Cassidy crew, he had starred in a series of short, light Western films for United Artists. These included *Dudes Are Pretty People* (1942), *Calaboose* (1943), and *Prairie Chickens* (1943). The films were all directed by Hal Roach, Jr., and co-starred Noah Beery, Jr.

Jimmy Rogers Filmography

1943: *False Colors* (H Hopalong Cassidy); *Riders of the Deadline* (H Hopalong Cassidy). **1944:** *Texas Masquerade* (H Hopalong Cassidy); *Lumber Jack* (H Hopalong Cassidy); *Mystery Man* (H Hopalong Cassidy); *Forty Thieves* (H Hopalong Cassidy).

Betsy King Ross

Betsy King Ross was a youthful rodeo performer and former national trick riding champion who appeared in Western films in the early 1930s. Her best-remembered role was as the female juvenile lead (Frankie Darro was the male) in Gene Autry's first starring film, the 1935 serial *The Phantom Empire*. She was also in the 1933 Johnny Mack Brown chapter play *Fighting with Kit Carson*.

Betsy King Ross Filmography

1933: *Smoke Lightning* (H Tom Keene); *Fighting with Kit Carson* (H Johnny Mack Brown). **1935:** *The Phantom Empire* (H Gene Autry).

Al St. John

Sidekick Handle: Fuzzy Q. Jones

If they rated B Western sidekicks on sheer comedic talents, Al "Fuzzy Q. Jones" St. John would win hands down.

St. John was a master of slapstick who could pratfall with the best of 'em, and his slight, bearded scruffly appearance made one chuckle just to look at him. His slightest move illicited a gutteral guffaw.

Fuzzy St. John was one of Western films' hardest working sidekicks, appearing in over one hundred films and at one point in 1942 was appearing in three different Western series starring different cowboys.

His most famous alter ego, the inimitable Fuzzy Q. Jones, was first created in the late thirties in a film series that starred Fred Scott, who was billed as the "Silvery Voiced Buckaroo."

Al St. John in a scene from one of his movies.

The bungling Jones was top hat at creating well meaning, but total chaos, and his words or actions almost always caused him to be pulled from the jaws of doom by whichever cowboy hero he was supposedly assisting at the time.

His best-remembered series of films were with Buster Crabbe and Lash LaRue. Both were produced by PRC Pictures.

His 35 films with Crabbe, produced between 1941 and 1946, were known as the Billy the Kid/Billy Carson series in which Crabbe played the famous gunslinger out to clean up the West. The series had originally begun

Al St. John

in 1940 with Bob Steele in the lead. The interesting thing about this series is that Fuzzy was always an integral part of the story and action. In several he could even be deemed as the protagonist of the plot.

When Crabbe quit PRC, the studio promoted Al "Lash" LaRue from supporting player to star and Fuzzy continued to assist Lash (in his character of Cheyenne) much the same way he did Buster Crabbe.

When PRC folded in 1948, St. John and LaRue went to Screen Guild and then to Western adventure films to make a total of 19 films in the series.

St. John was born on September 10, 1893, in Santa Ana, California. His parents were vaudeville performers and his uncle was the famous comedian Fatty Arbuckle.

At an early age he developed a talent for acrobatics and unicycle riding.

In 1914, producer Mack Sennett invited St. John to join his famous silent screen chaos creators, the Keystone Cops. In the mid-teens he teamed up with Arbuckle to produce and star in a series of comedies. Their off and on relationship lasted until Arbuckle's death.

He began making Westerns in the early 1930s, appearing in all sorts of roles from bit parts to sidekicks to an even occasional bad guy.

His career really got rolling in 1935 when he co-starred with Big Boy Williams in a film called *Law of the 45s*. The film served as the introduction of the Three Mesquiteers to B Western audiences.

His first regular stint as a sidekick began in 1937 at Spectrum Pictures with Fred Scott, and that marked the birth of Fuzzy Q. Jones. After seven films with Scott and a couple with Jack Randall, PRC signed him to ride with Bob Steele in the Billy the Kid series and also to assist George Houston in a series of Lone Rider films.

Steele was succeeded by Crabbe in one series while Houston gave way to Robert Livingston in the other. At the same time he was sidekicking Red Barry over at Republic Studios.

Following the completion of the LaRue films, St. John appeared at scores of county fairs and rodeos.

He passed away on January 31, 1963, after making a personal appearance in Vidalia, Georgia.

Al St. John Filmography

1930: *Oklahoma Cyclone* (H Bob Steele); *Land of Missing Men* (H Bob Steele). **1931:** *Son of the Plains* (H Bob Custer). **1935:** *Law of the 45s* (H Big Boy Williams); *Trigger Tom* (H Tom Tyler). **1936:** *Pinto Rustlers* (H Tom Tyler); *West of Nevada* (H Rex Bell). **1937:** *A Lawman Is Born* (H Johnny

Mack Brown); *Melody of the Plains* (H Fred Scott); *The Fighting Deputy* (H Fred Scott); *Moonlight on the Range* (H Fred Scott); *Roaming Cowboy* (H Fred Scott). **1938:** *Rangers Roundup* (H Fred Scott); *Knight of the Plains* (H Fred Scott); *Songs and Bullets* (H Fred Scott); *Frontier Scout* (H George Houston); *Gunsmoke Trail* (H Jack Randall). **1939:** *Oklahoma Terror* (H Jack Randall). **1940:** *Billy the Kid Outlawed* (H Bob Steele); *Billy the Kid in Texas* (H Bob Steele); *Billy the Kid's Gun Justice* (H Bob Steele); *Texas Terrors* (H Don "Red" Barry). **1941:** *Billy the Kid's Range War* (H Bob Steele); *Billy the Kid's Fighting Pals* (H Bob Steele); *Billy the Kid in Santa Fe* (H Bob Steele); *The Apache Kid* (H Don "Red" Barry); *Missouri Outlaw* (H Don "Red" Barry); *The Lone Rider Rides On* (H George Houston); *The Lone Rider Crosses the Rio* (H George Houston); *The Lone Rider in Ghost Town* (H George Houston); *Frontier Fury* (H George Houston); *The Lone Rider Ambushed* (H George Houston); *The Lone Rider Fights Back* (H George Houston); *Billy the Kid Wanted* (H Buster Crabbe); *Billy the Kid's Roundup* (H Buster Crabbe). **1942:** *Arizona Terror* (H Don "Red" Barry); *Stagecoach Express* (H Don "Red" Barry); *Jesse James Jr.* (H Don "Red" Barry); *The Lone Rider and the Bandit* (H George Houston); *The Lone Rider in Cheyenne* (H George Houston); *Texas Justice* (H George Houston); *Border Roundup* (H George Houston); *Outlaws of Boulder Pass* (H George Houston); *Overland Stagecoach* (H Robert Livingston); *Billy the Kid Trapped* (H Buster Crabbe); *Billy the Kid's Smoking Guns* (H Buster Crabbe); *Law and Order* (H Buster Crabbe); *Sheriff of Sage Valley* (H Buster Crabbe); *The Mysterious Rider* (H Buster Crabbe). **1943:** *Wild Horse Rustlers* (H Robert Livingston); *Death Rides the Plains* (H Robert Livingston); *Wolves of the Range* (H Robert Livingston); *Law of the Saddle* (H Robert Livingston); *Raiders of Red Gap* (H Robert Livingston); *The Kid Rides Again* (H Buster Crabbe); *Fugitive of the Plains* (H Buster Crabbe); *Western Cyclone* (H Buster Crabbe); *Cattle Stampede* (H Buster Crabbe); *The Renegade* (H Buster Crabbe); *Blazing Frontier* (H Buster Crabbe); *Devil Riders* (H Buster Crabbe); *Frontier Outlaws* (H Buster Crabbe). **1944:** *Thundering Gunslingers* (H Buster Crabbe); *Valley of Vengenace* (H Buster Crabbe); *The Drifter* (H Buster Crabbe); *Fuzzy Settles Down* (H Buster Crabbe); *Rustlers Hideout* (H Buster Crabbe); *Wild Horse Phantom* (H Buster Crabbe); *Oath of Vengenace* (H Buster Crabbe). **1945:** *His Brother's Ghost* (H Buster Crabbe); *Gangsters Den* (H Buster Crabbe); *Stagecoach Outlaws* (H Buster Crabbe); *Border Badmen* (H Buster Crabbe); *Fighting Bill Carson* (H Buster Crabbe); *Prairie Rustlers* (H Buster Crabbe). **1946:** *Lightning Raiders* (H Buster Crabbe); *Gentlemen with Guns* (H Buster Crabbe); *Terrors on Horseback* (H Buster Crabbe); *Ghost of Hidden Valley* (H Buster Crabbe); *Prairie Badmen* (H Buster Crabbe); *Overland Raiders* (H Buster Crabbe); *Outlaws of the Plains* (H Buster Crabbe). **1947:** *Law of the Lash* (H Lash LaRue); *Border Feud* (H Lash LaRue); *Pioneer Justice* (H

Lash LaRue); *Ghost Town Renegades* (H Lash LaRue); *Stage to Mesa City* (H Lash LaRue); *Return of the Lash* (H Lash LaRue); *Fighting Vigilantes* (H Lash LaRue); *Cheyenne Takes Over* (H Lash LaRue). **1948:** *Dead Man's Gold* (H Lash LaRue); *Mark of the Lash* (H Lash LaRue); *Frontier Revenge* (H Lash LaRue); *Outlaw Country* (H Lash LaRue). **1949:** *Son of Billy the Kid* (H Lash LaRue); *Son of a Badman* (H Lash LaRue). **1950:** *The Dalton's Women* (H Lash LaRue). **1951:** *King of the Bullwhip* (H Lash LaRue); *The Thundering Trail* (H Lash LaRue). **1952:** *The Black Lash* (H Lash LaRue); *Frontier Phantom* (H Lash LaRue).

Marin Sais

Sidekick Handle: the Duchess

Film veteran Marin Sais was the Duchess to Jim Bannon's Red Ryder and Don Kay Reynolds' Little Beaver in a series of four films released by Eagle Lion in 1949.

Sais, who had begun her film career around 1910, had appeared in supporting roles in dozens of B Westerns over the years, playing mostly Mexican matrons or crotchety old ranch owners in need of a hero.

She was born August 2, 1890, in San Raphael, California, and passed away December 31, 1972.

Marin Sais Filmography

1949: *Ride Ryder Ride* (H Jim Bannon); *Roll Thunder Roll* (H Jim Bannon); *The Fighting Redhead* (H Jim Bannon); *Cowboy and the Prizefighter* (H Jim Bannon).

Syd Saylor

Syd Saylor's movie trademark was his bobbing Adam's apple, and though he made many appearances as a cowboy sidekick, Westerns were just a small part of a screen career that included over one hundred films.

His place in the sidekick hall of fame is etched in part becuase he was one of the original Three Mesquiteers in the Republic series. Saylor created the role of Lullaby Joslin in the series' initial entry, *The Three Mesquiteers,* in 1936. But the head honchos at Republic were not plesed with his performance and replaced him with Max Terhune, who made the role famous.

Saylor also played saddle pal to Don Barry, Tex Ritter, George O'Brien, the Maynard brothers, Johnny Mack Brown, and in 1945–46 he had a four-film run with Bob Steele.

Saylor appeared in major films like *Abe Lincoln in Illinois, Union Pacific,* and *The Spirit of St. Louis.*

He is remembered for his roles in action serials like *Mystery Mountain* with Ken Maynard and *The Lost Jungle* with Clyde Beatty.

He was born Leo Sailor on March 24, 1895, in Chicago, Illinois, and began as a stage actor.

He entered films in the early 1920s and in 1926–27 starred in his own series of 54 comedy shorts. Although he made several Westerns during the silent era, it was in the early talking picture days that he began to get a lot of work in horse operas and cliff-hangers.

Syd Saylor died of a heart attack on December 21, 1962, in Hollywood, California.

Syd Saylor Filmography

1934: *When a Man Sees Red* (H Buck Jones); *Mystery Mountain* (serial) (H Ken Maynard); *The Dude Ranger* (H George O'Brien). **1935:** *Branded a Coward* (H Johnny Mack Brown); *Wilderness Mail* (H Kermit Maynard). **1936:** *The Three Mesquiteers* (H Three Mesquiteers); *Headin' for the Rio Grande* (H Tex Ritter). **1937:** *Arizona Days* (H Tex Ritter). **1941:** *Wyoming Wildcat* (H Don "Red" Barry). **1945:** *The Navajo Kid* (H Bob Steele). **1946:** *Six Gun Man* (H Bob Steele); *Ambush Trail* (H Bob Steele); *Thunder Town* (H Bob Steele).

Andy Shuford

One of the earliest hero/sidekick teams of the B Western era was the one composed of veteran cowboy star Bill Cody and youngster Andy Shuford. This duo dated back to 1931 with a series of films released by Monogram Pictures, the first being *Dugan of the Badlands.*

Shuford never provided comedy relief per se, but was there for a sort of "Aw gee Bill, you're a swell hero" atmosphere.

Syd Saylor

The chemistry between the two was good, with the good guy always protecting the kid and keeping him on the straight and narrow.

Andy Shuford Filmography

1931: *Dugan of the Badlands* (H Bill Cody); *The Montana Kid* (H Bill Cody); *Oklahoma Jim* (H Bill Cody). **1932:** *Ghost City* (H Bill Cody); *Mason of the Mounted* (H Bill Cody); *Law of the North* (H Bill Cody); *Texas Pioneers* (H Bill Cody); *Land of Wanted Men* (H Bill Cody).

Andy Shuford (in tub) with his partner Bill Cody. This pair made eight films together from 1931 to 1932 for Monogram.

The Sons of the Pioneers *see* **Bob Nolan and the Sons of the Pioneers**

Joe Stauch, Jr.

Sidekick Handle: Tadpole

Roly-poly Joe Stauch, Jr., was sorta sidekick to a sidekick. He played Tadpole, the tagalong and often nemesis of Frog Millhouse (Smiley Burnette), who was the saddle pal of Gene Autry.

Tadpole looked like a miniature Millhouse, complete with tattered turned up hat, checkerboard shirt and ringeye pony.

He was introduced in the 1941 film *Under Fiesta Stars* and appeared in five Autry/Burnette outings.

In 1944 Stauch reassumed the role in *Beneath Western Skies* featuring Burnette and Robert Livingston.

Part of their schtick was the fact that in matters of brains and money Tadpole could always outsmart Frog.

Joe Stauch, Jr. Filmography

1941: *Under Fiesta Stars* (H Gene Autry). 1942: *Heart of the Rio Grande* (H Gene Autry); *Home in Wyomin'* (H Gene Autry); *Call of the Canyon* (H Gene Autry); *Bells of Capistrano* (H Gene Autry). 1944: *Beneath Western Skies* (H Robert Livingston).

Dub Taylor

Sidekick Handle: Cannonball

Former vaudevillian Walter "Dub" Taylor is best known in B Western circles as "Cannonball," the musical/comedy sidekick of Jimmy Wakely in a series of 15 films for Monogram Pictures between 1947 and 1949.

Taylor began his sidekick duties and his "Cannonball" character back in 1939 in the film *Taming of the West* starring Wild Bill Elliott. Under contract at the time to Columbia Pictures, Taylor would be sidekick to Columbia's top cowboy stars over the next seven years. He did 13 films with Elliott, nine with Hopalong Cassidy's ex-pal Russ "Lucky" Hayden and from 1943 to 1946 a dozen with Charles Starrett.

Taylor was born in Richmond, Virginia, in 1909 but grew up in Oklahoma City, Oklahoma. He made his film debut in 1938 in *You Can't Take It with You* starring Jimmy Stewart. Over the years he developed into a well-recognized character actor appearing in such films as *Bonnie and Clyde, Bandalero,* and *Support Your Local Gunfighter.*

On television he was a regular on the series *Casey Jones* and *Please Don't Eat the Daisies.* He has been seen in tons of commercials.

His son Buck Taylor was seen in the part of Newly on *Gunsmoke.*

Taylor's best known trademark is his deep-fried Southern accent.

Dub Taylor

Dub Taylor Filmography

1939: *Taming of the West* (H Wild Bill Elliott). **1940:** *Pioneers of the Fron-
tier* (H Wild Bill Elliott); *Man from Tumbleweeds* (H Wild Bill Elliott);
Return of Wild Bill (H Wild Bill Elliott); *Prairie Schooners* (H Wild Bill
Elliott); *Beyond the Sacramento* (H Wild Bill Elliott); *Wildcat of Tucson* (H
Wild Bill Elliott). **1941:** *Across the Sierras* (H Wild Bill Elliott); *North from
the Lone Star* (H Wild Bill Elliott); *Hands Across the Rockies* (H Wild Bill
Elliott); *Return of Daniel Boone* (H Wild Bill Elliott); *Son of Davy Crockett*
(H Wild Bill Elliott); *King of Dodge City* (H Wild Bill Elliott). **1942:** *The
Lone Prairie* (H Russell Hayden); *Pardon My Gun* (H Russell Hayden);

Tornado in the Saddle (H Russell Hayden). **1943:** *Riders of the Northwest Mounted* (H Russell Hayden); *Saddle and Sagebrush* (H Russell Hayden); *Silver City Raiders* (H Russell Hayden); *Cowboy in the Clouds* (H Charles Starrett). **1944:** *The Vigilantes Ride* (H Russell Hayden); *Wyoming Hurricane* (H Russell Hayden); *Last Horseman* (H Russell Hayden); *Cowboy from Lonesome River* (H Charles Starrett); *Cyclone Prairie Ranger* (H Charles Starrett); *Saddle Leather Law* (H Charles Starrett). **1945:** *Rough Ridin' Justice* (H Charles Starrett); *Both Barrels Blazing* (H Charles Starrett); *Rustlers of the Badlands* (H Charles Starrett); *Blazing the Western Trail* (H Charles Starrett); *Outlaws of the Rockies* (H Charles Starrett); *Lawless Empire* (H Charles Starrett); *Texas Panhandle* (H Charles Starrett). **1946:** *Frontier Gun Law* (H Charles Starrett). **1947:** *Ridin' Down the Trail* (H Jimmy Wakely). **1948:** *Song of the Drifter* (H Jimmy Wakely); *Oklahoma Blues* (H Jimmy Wakely); *Rangers Ride* (H Jimmy Wakely); *Cowboy Cavalier* (H Jimmy Wakely); *Partners of the Sunset* (H Jimmy Wakely); *Silver Trails* (H Jimmy Wakely); *Outlaw Brand* (H Jimmy Wakely); *Courtin' Trouble* (H Jimmy Wakely). **1949:** *Gun Runner* (H Jimmy Wakely); *Gun Law Justice* (H Jimmy Wakely); *Across the Rio Grande* (H Jimmy Wakely); *Brand of Fear* (H Jimmy Wakely); *Roaring Westward* (H Jimmy Wakely); *Lawless Code* (H Jimmy Wakely).

Max Terhune

Sidekick Handles: Lullaby, Alibi

Max Terhune, best known as Lullaby Joslin of the Three Mesquiteeers, is another in the long list of B Western performers who got his start in films because of his friendship with Gene Autry. When Gene was one of the stars of the National Barn Dance radio show, Terhune was the show's emcee.

A talented ventriloquist, Terhune and his ever-present dummy Elmer ranked as one of the genre's top sidekicks.

He was born Robert Max Terhune in Franklin, Indiana, on February 12, 1891.

In addition to being an actor, comedian and ventriloquist, he was also a musician, magician and impressionist. Early in his adult life he worked as a blacksmith's helper and a minor league baseball player.

He entered the entertainment field in the 1920s and was associated with such top country and western acts as the Weaver Brothers and Elviry and the Hoosier Hot Shots. He joined the National Barn Dance in 1932 and that was when he met Autry and Smiley Burnette.

Max Terhune and Elmer.

In 1936 he appeared in two Autry films, *Ride Ranger Ride* and *The Big Show*.

That same year Republic Pictures launched its highly successful Three Mesquiteers series. Of the original trio (Bob Livingston, Crash Corrigan and Syd Saylor), the studio was pleased with everyone's work except Saylor's.

For the second film in the series, *Ghost Town Gold*, they replaced Saylor with Terhune in the role of Lullaby.

Lullaby and Elmer would make 21 Mesquiteer films before departing Republic in 1939.

The following year he joined ex–Mesquiteer Crash Corrigan and newcomer Dusty King in a new series of trio Westerns, *The Range Busters*, at Monogram. In these films he was called Alibi and retained Elmer and most of his Lullaby characteristics. After 24 films the series ended in 1943.

Terhune made frequent appearances in Westerns following the demise of the series and also toured with various country comedy acts.

In 1948 he returned to Monogram to replace Raymond Hatton as Johnny Mack Brown's sidekick for eight films.

He continued his film work and appeared in such A Westerns as *Rawhide* with Tyrone Power, *Giant* with Rock Hudson and *A King and Four Queens* with Clark Gable.

He died on June 5, 1973, in Cottonwood, Arizona, of a heart attack.

Max Terhune Filmography

1936: *Ride Ranger Ride* (H Gene Autry); *The Big Show* (H Gene Autry); *Ghost Town Gold* (H 3 Mesquiteers); *Roarin' Lead* (H 3 Mesquiteers). **1937:** *Riders of the Whistlin' Skull* (H 3 Mesquiteers); *Hit the Saddle* (H 3 Mesquiteers); *Gunsmoke Ranch* (H 3 Mesquiteers); *Come on Cowboys* (H 3 Mesquiteers); *Range Defenders* (H 3 Mesquiteers); *Heart of the Rockies* (H 3 Mesquiteers); *Trigger Trio* (H 3 Mesquiteers); *Wild Horse Rodeo* (H 3 Mesquiteers). **1938:** *The Purple Vigilantes* (H 3 Mesquiteers); *Call the Mesquiteers* (H 3 Mesquiteers); *Outlaws of Sonora* (H 3 Mesquiteers); *Riders of the Black Hills* (H 3 Mesquiteers); *Heroes of the Hills* (H 3 Mesquiteers); *Pals of the Saddle* (H 3 Mesquiteers); *Overland Stage Raiders* (H 3 Mesquiteers); *Santa Fe Stampede* (H 3 Mesquiteers); *Red River Range* (H 3 Mesquiteers). **1939:** *The Night Riders* (H 3 Mesquiteers); *Three Texas Steers* (H 3 Mesquiteers). **1940:** *The Range Busters* (H Range Busters); *Trailing Double Trouble* (H Range Busters); *West of Pinto Basin* (H Range Busters). **1941:** *Trail of the Silver Spurs* (H Range Busters); *The Kid's Last Ride* (H Range Busters); *Tumbledown Ranch in Arizona* (H Range Busters); *Wranglers Roost* (H Range Busters); *Fugitive Valley* (H Range Busters); *Saddle Mountain Roundup* (H Range Busters); *Tonto Basin Outlaws* (H Range Busters); *Underground Rustlers* (H Range Busters). **1942:** *Thunder River Feud* (H Range Busters); *Rock River Renegades* (H Range Busters); *Boot Hill Bandits* (H Range Busters); *Texas Troubleshooters* (H Range Busters); *Arizona Stagecoach* (H Range Busters); *Texas to Bataan* (H Range Busters); *Trail Riders* (H Range Busters). **1943:** *Two Fisted Justice* (H Range Busters); *Haunted Ranch* (H Range Busters); *Land of Hunted Men* (H Range Busters); *Cowboy Commandos* (H Range Busters); *Black Market Rustlers* (H Range Busters); *Bullets and Saddles* (H Range Busters). **1948:** *Range Justice* (H Johnny Mack Brown); *Sheriff of Medicine Bow* (H Johnny Mack Brown); *Gunning for Justice* (H Johnny Mack Brown); *Hidden Danger* (H Johnny Mack Brown). **1949:** *Law of the West* (H Johnny Mack Brown); *Trails End* (H Johnny Mack Brown); *West of Eldorado* (H Johnny Mack Brown); *Western Renegades* (H Johnny Mack Brown).

The Texas Playboys *see* Bob Wills and the Texas Playboys

Wally Vernon

Former vaudeville song and dance man and minstrel show performer Wally Vernon served as sidekick to Republic cowboys Don "Red" Barry and Rocky Lane during 1943 and 1944.

Vernon was born in New York City in 1904 and never made a film until the mid-1930s. In 1937 he signed on as a contract player with 20th Century–Fox Studios and appeared in films like *Alexander's Ragtime Band* with Tyrone Power and Betty Grable.

In 1949 he reunited with Barry for some "Super B's" at Lippert Pictures.

Wally Vernon was the victim of a hit and run accident and passed away on March 7, 1970, in Van Nuys, California.

Wally Vernon Filmography

1943: *Fugitive from Sonora* (H Don "Red" Barry); *Black Hills Express* (H Don "Red" Barry); *Man from the Rio Grande* (H Don "Red" Barry); *Canyon City* (H Don "Red" Barry); *California Joe* (H Don "Red" Barry). **1944:** *Outlaws of Santa Fe* (H Don "Red" Barry); *Silver City Kid* (H Rocky Lane); *Stagecoach to Monterey* (H Rocky Lane).

Eddy Waller

Sidekick Handle: Nugget Clark

For 32 films Eddy Waller played Nugget Clark, the sidekick of Allan "Rocky" Lane at Republic Pictures between 1947 and 1953.

The thing that set the Nugget character apart from the other sidekicks was the fact that while the character remained the same, his situation varied from film to film. In one situation he might be just Lane's saddle pal and in the next film he would be the troubled owner of a wagon freight company. Unlike some sidekicks who were just thrown in for comedy relief, Nugget was always an integral part of the story line. But no matter what

Wally Vernon

he did during the rest of the picture, at the end Nugget was always there
to help Rocky round up the bad guys.

Waller was born in Wisconsin in 1889. He made his film debut in the
1936 Bing Crosby film *Rhythm on the Range* and soon followed with parts
in such varied films as *Call the Mesquiteers,* with the Three Mesquiteers,
Geronimo with Preston Foster and the serial *The Great Adventures of Wild
Bill Hickok* which starred Wild Bill Elliott.

Following the Lane series he appeared in Westerns like *Man Without*

Eddy Waller

a Star with Kirk Douglas, and *Day of the Bad Man* with Fred MacMurray.

Waller was also one of early TV's better known sidekicks, appearing in *Steve Donovan — Western Marshal* as Rusty, the deputy to the title character who was played by Douglas Kennedy. He also played Redrock, the conductor on the train engineered by Casey Jones (Allen Hale, Jr.).

Waller retired from the screen in 1958 and passed away on August 20, 1977, in Los Angeles, California, of a stroke.

Eddy Waller Filmography

1947: *The Wild Frontier* (H Rocky Lane); *Bandits of Dark Canyon* (H Rocky Lane). **1948:** *Oklahoma Badlands* (H Rocky Lane); *The Bold Frontiersman* (H Rocky Lane); *Carson City Raiders* (H Rocky Lane); *Marshal of Amarillo* (H Rocky Lane); *Desperadoes of Dodge City* (H Rocky Lane); *The Denver Kid* (H Rocky Lane); *Sundown in Santa Fe* (H Rocky Lane); *Renegades of Sonora* (H Rocky Lane). **1949:** *Sheriff of Wichita* (H Rocky Lane); *Death Valley Gunfighter* (H Rocky Lane); *Frontier Marshal* (H Rocky Lane); *Wyoming Bandit* (H Rocky Lane); *Bandit King of Texas* (H Rocky Lane); *Navajo Trail Raiders* (H Rocky Lane); *Powder River Rustlers* (H Rocky Lane). **1950:** *Gunmen of Abilene* (H Rocky Lane); *Code of the Silver Sage* (H Rocky Lane); *Salt Lake Raiders* (H Rocky Lane); *Covered Wagon Raid* (H Rocky Lane); *Vigilante Hideout* (H Rocky Lane); *Frisco Tornado* (H Rocky Lane); *Rustlers on Horseback* (H Rocky Lane). **1952:** *Leadville Gunslinger* (H Rocky Lane); *Black Hills Ambush* (H Rocky Lane); *Thundering Caravans* (H Rocky Lane); *Desperadoes Outpost* (H Rocky Lane). **1953:** *Marshal of Cedar Rock* (H Rocky Lane); *Savage Frontier* (H Rocky Lane); *Bandits of the West* (H Rocky Lane); *El Paso Stampede* (H Rocky Lane).

Martha Wentworth

Sidekick Handle: the Duchess

Martha Wentworth appeared in the role of the Duchess in the seven Rocky Lane films of the successful Red Ryder series produced by Republic Pictures.

She was best known in entertainment circles for her work on radio where she was known as "the lady of 100 voices."

She had roles in films like *A Tree Grows in Brooklyn* and *Clancy Street Boys.*

In later years she would provide voices for such Walt Disney cartoon features as *The Sword and the Stone* and *One Hundred and One Dalmatians.*

Born in New York City, she passed away on March 8, 1974, in Sherman Oaks, California.

Martha Wentworth Filmography

1946: *Santa Fe Uprising* (H Rocky Lane); *Stagecoach to Denver* (H Rocky Lane). **1947:** *Vigilantes of Dodge City* (H Rocky Lane); *Homesteaders of Paradise Valley* (H Rocky Lane); *Oregon Trail Scouts* (H Rocky Lane); *Rustlers of Devil's Canyon* (H Rocky Lane); *Marshal of Cripple Creek* (H Rocky Lane).

Lee "Lasses" White

Sidekick Handle: Whopper, Lasses

Lee "Lasses" White was a veteran of over twenty years in show business before he made his first film in 1938. He had appeared in vaudeville and tent shows and headlined in his own minstrel show. He was also active in radio broadcasting.

Once he got involved in film work, he was mostly cast in comedies and B Westerns. Some of the B's in which he appeared were *Rovin' Tumbleweeds* with Gene Autry and *Oklahoma Renegades* with the Three Mesquiteers.

In 1941 RKO signed him to take Emmett Lynn's role as Tim Holt's comedy sidekick. His first film with Holt was *Cyclone on Horseback.* He also inherited RKO's stock sidekick character Whopper who had originated with Chill Wills back in 1938. After eight films with Holt, White moved on.

In 1944 he teamed up with Monogram's singing cowboy Jimmy Wakely. Their partnership lasted three years and a dozen films.

It might be noted that the Wakely/White duo often toured together, as did many of the hero/sidekick teams, and that the talented pair was among the best when it came to live stage performances.

White left the Wakely series in 1947 and was replaced by Dub "Cannonball" Taylor.

"Lasses" White was born in Wills Point, Texas, on August 28, 1888, and passed away on December 16, 1949.

Lee "Lasses" White Filmography

1941: *Cyclone on Horseback* (H Tim Holt); *Six Gun Gold* (H Tim Holt); *Bandit Trail* (H Tim Holt); *Dude Cowboy* (H Tim Holt). **1942:** *Riding the*

Lee "Lasses" White

Wind (H Tim Holt); *Land of the Open Range* (H Tim Holt); *Come on Danger* (H Tim Holt); *Thundering Hoofs* (H Tim Holt). **1944:** *Song of the Range* (H Jimmy Wakely). **1945:** *Springtime in Texas* (H Jimmy Wakely); *Saddle Serenade* (H Jimmy Wakely); *Riders of the Dawn* (H Jimmy Wakely); *Lonesome Trail* (H Jimmy Wakely). **1946:** *Moon Over Montana* (H Jimmy Wakely); *West of the Alamo* (H Jimmy Wakely); *Trail to Mexico* (H Jimmy Wakely); *Song of the Sierras* (H Jimmy Wakely). **1947:** *Rainbow Over the Rockies* (H Jimmy Wakely); *Six Gun Serenade* (H Jimmy Wakely); *Song of the Wasteland* (H Jimmy Wakely).

Ray Whitley

Georgia native Ray Whitley must be considered the chief enigma among the sidekick corps of the B Western era. The general consensus among film historians is that Whitley had far more looks, talent and charisma than many of the actors who were promoted by studios and starred in Western epics, yet Whitley never made it above the co-starring rung on the Western success ladder.

Whitley was an actor, singer and composer of over two hundred country and western songs, including Gene Autry's theme song "Back in the Saddle Again."

When the singing cowboy rage took hold in the mid-thirties, Whitley and his group the Six Bar Cowboys were signed to a contract by RKO Pictures. In 1937 the studio began starring Whitley in a group of Western musical shorts. Over the years he would make nearly two dozen of the 15-minute musical sagas.

In 1938 RKO teamed Whitley up with their number one cowboy star George O'Brien. Whitley and O'Brien made five films together in 1938 and 1939.

In 1940 the studio replaced O'Brien with young Tim Holt, the son of veteran actor Jack Holt. With Holt, Whitley was again alongside as saddle pal and chief musical relief. They made a dozen pictures as a team.

After leaving RKO Whitley continued to appear in B Westerns. In 1944–45 he appeared in a series of films starring Rod Cameron at Universal Studios.

Whitley was born in Georgia in 1902. He made his film debut in *Hopalong Cassidy Returns* in 1936.

He passed away on February 21, 1979.

Ray Whitley Filmography

1938: *Gun Law* (H George O'Brien); *Border G-Men* (H George O'Brien); *The Painted Desert* (H George O'Brien); *The Renegade Ranger* (H George O'Brien). **1939:** *Trouble in Sundown* (H George O'Brien). **1940:** *Wagon Train* (H Tim Holt); *The Fargo Kid* (H Tim Holt). **1941:** *Along the Rio Grande* (H Tim Holt); *Robbers of the Range* (H Tim Holt); *Cyclone on Horseback* (H Tim Holt); *Six Gun Gold* (H Tim Holt); *The Bandit Trail* (H Tim Holt); *Dude Cowboy* (H Tim Holt). **1942:** *Riding the Wind* (H Tim Holt); *Land of the Open Range* (H Tim Holt); *Come on Danger* (H Tim Holt); *Thundering Hoofs* (H Tim Holt). **1944:** *Boss of Boomtown* (H Rod Cameron); *Trigger Trail* (H Rod Cameron); *Riders of the Santa Fe* (H Rod

Ray Whitley

Cameron); *The Old Texas Trail* (*H* Rod Cameron). **1945:** *Beyond the Pecos* (*H* Rod Cameron); *Renegades of the Rio Grande* (*H* Rod Cameron).

Guy Wilkerson

Sidekick Handle: Panhandle Perkins

Lean and lanky Guy Wilkerson played the part of Panhandle Perkins in PRC's Texas Rangers series from 1942 until 1945.

In the 22 series films that he made, Wilkerson handled the comedy and left the heroics to such cowboys as Dave O'Brien, Tex Ritter and James Newill.

Wilkerson was born in Katy, Texas, in 1898 and like many other early movie actors, began his career in minstrel shows and vaudeville. He entered films in the 1930s, and before joining the Texas Rangers he appeared in such B Westerns as *The Yodelin' Kid from Pine Ridge* with Gene Autry and in major films like *Gone with the Wind* and *Sergeant York*.

When the Rangers series ended, Wilkerson continued to work in films and in radio where he was at one time the voice of Wild Bill Hickok.

He went on to appear in such top Westerns as *Man of the West* with Gary Cooper, *The Big Sky* with Kirk Douglas and *True Grit* with John Wayne.

Guy Wilkerson died of cancer on July 15, 1971.

Guy Wilkerson Filmography

1942: *The Rangers Take Over* (H Texas Rangers). **1943:** *Bad Men of Thunder Gap* (H Texas Rangers); *West of Texas* (H Texas Rangers); *Border Buckaroos* (H Texas Rangers); *Fighting Valley* (H Texas Rangers); *Trail of Terror* (H Texas Rangers); *Return of the Rangers* (H Texas Rangers); *Boss of Rawhide* (H Texas Rangers). **1944:** *Gunsmoke Mesa* (H Texas Rangers); *Outlaw Roundup* (H Texas Rangers); *Guns of the Law* (H Texas Rangers); *The Pinto Bandit* (H Texas Rangers); *Spook Town* (H Texas Rangers); *Brand of the Devil* (H Texas Rangers); *Gangsters of the Frontier* (H Texas Rangers); *Dead or Alive* (H Texas Rangers); *The Whispering Skull* (H Texas Rangers). **1945:** *Marked for Murder* (H Texas Rangers); *Enemy of the Law* (H Texas Rangers); *Three in the Saddle* (H Texas Rangers); *Frontier Fugitives* (H Texas Rangers); *Flaming Frontier* (H Texas Rangers).

Foy Willing and the Riders of the Purple Sage

Foy Willing and the Riders of the Purple Sage succeeded the Sons of the Pioneers as the stock musical group and ready-made posse of the Roy Rogers Westerns beginning with *Grand Canyon Trail* in 1948. The outfit would make 15 screen appearances with Rogers — 13 of them billed as the Riders of the Purple Sage and two under the banner of the Roy Rogers Riders.

Before their stint with Roy, they had been featured in such B Westerns as *Saddle Serenade* with Jimmy Wakely, *Throw a Saddle on a Star* with Ken Curtis and several Republic features with Monte Hale.

Willing usually played himself as did Bob Nolan.

Guy Wilkerson

Foy Willing was born in 1915 in Bosque County, Texas, and got started in show business as a radio singer.

He passed away on July 24, 1978, in Nashville, Tennessee.

Foy Willing and the Riders of the Purple Sage Filmography

1948: *Grand Canyon Trail* (H Roy Rogers); *The Far Frontier* (H Roy Rogers). **1949:** *Susanna Pass* (H Roy Rogers); *Down Dakota Way* (H Roy Rogers); *The Golden Stallion* (H Roy Rogers). **1950:** *Bells of Coronado* (H Roy Rogers); *Twilight in the Sierras* (H Roy Rogers); *Trigger Jr.* (H Roy Rogers); *Sunset in the West* (H Roy Rogers); *North of the Great Divide* (H Roy Rogers); *Trail of Robin Hood* (H Roy Rogers). **1951:** *Spoilers of the Plains* (H Roy Rogers); *Heart of the Rockies* (H Roy Rogers; **As Roy Rogers**

Riders: *In Old Amarillo* (H Roy Rogers); *South of Caliente* (H Roy Rogers).

Bob Wills and the Texas Playboys

The tag "country music legends" has never been more appropriately applied than when it is used to describe Bob Wills and the Texas Playboys. Wills and his group are vastly responsible for the popularity of the country dance music commonly known as Western swing. Wills is also responsible for such country and western classics as *San Antonio Rose, Take Me Back to Tulsa* and *The Steel Guitar Rag*.

Wills was born James Robert Wills in 1905 in Limestone County, Texas. His father was a fiddle player and as a youngster Wills began playing fiddle around Fort Worth. In the late 1920s he became part of a pioneer country and western group known as the Light Crust Doughboys (the name was taken from the sponsor of their radio show).

In 1933 Wills, his brother Johnny Lee and another member left the group and formed the Texas Playboys in Tulsa, Oklahoma. Over the next decade they would prove to be one of the country music scene's most popular attractions.

Bob Wills and the Texas Playboys made their film debut in the 1940 Tex Ritter Western *Take Me Back to Oklahoma.*

They were featured in a series of films starring Russell Hayden at Columbia Pictures from 1942 to 1944. When that series ended the studio continued to use them in films with Charles Starrett and Ken Curtis.

They also made a series of popular musical shorts in the mid-forties.

Aside from Wills the group featured Leon McAuliffe on steel guitar, Eldon Shamblin on guitar and Al Stricklin on piano. At one time the group grew to 22 pieces.

Bob Wills and the Texas Playboys continued to perform well into the 1960s.

Bob Wills died on May 13, 1975, in Fort Worth, Texas, of bronchial pneumonia.

Bob Wills and the Texas Playboys Filmography

1940: *Take Me Back to Oklahoma* (H Tex Ritter). **1942:** *Lone Prairie* (H Russell Hayden); *Tornado in the Saddle* (H Russell Hayden); *Riders of the*

Northwest Mounted (*H* Russell Hayden). **1943:** *Saddles and Sagebrush* (*H* Russell Hayden); *Silver City Raiders* (*H* Russell Hayden). **1944:** *The Vigilantes Ride* (*H* Russell Hayden); *Wyoming Hurricane* (*H* Russell Hayden); *Last Horseman* (*H* Russell Hayden). **1945:** *Blazing Western Trail* (*H* Charles Starrett); *Lawless Empire* (*H* Charles Starrett); *Rhythm Roundup* (*H* Ken Curtis).

Chill Wills

Sidekick Handle: Whopper Hatch

Raspy-voiced, Texas-drawlin' Chill Wills was one of the movies' best known character actors. He was right at home in the dozens of Westerns that he made.

Born in Seagoville, Texas, on July 18, 1903, Wills worked in vaudeville and burlesque early in his career. He made his film debut in the 1935 Hopalong Cassidy film *The Bar 20 Rides Again.*

In 1938 and 1939 he made six pictures as sidekick to George O'Brien for RKO Studios. He played a verbose liar appropriately called Whopper Hatch.

Later in 1939 he got a part in the Clark Gable film *Boomtown* and his career took off. Wills went on to appear in such varied films as *The Westerner* with Gary Cooper, *Tarzan's New York Adventure* with Johnny Weissmuller and *Giant* with Elizabeth Taylor, Rock Hudson and James Dean.

During the late forties and early fifties he was the voice of Francis the Talking Mule in a series of comedies starring Donald O'Connor.

He starred in two TV series: *Frontier Circus* in 1961–62 and *The Rounders* in 1966–67.

Chill Wills was still pursuing his acting career when he died on December 15, 1978.

Chill Wills Filmography

1938: *Lawless Valley* (*H* George O'Brien). **1939:** *Arizona Legion* (*H* George O'Brien); *Trouble in Sundown* (*H* George O'Brien); *Racketeers of the Range* (*H* George O'Brien); *Timber Stampede* (*H* George O'Brien).

Chill Wills

Britt Wood

Sidekick Handle: Speedy McGinnis

Drawly-voiced, slow-moving Britt Wood's character Speedy McGinnis filled the comedy sidekick gap between Gabby Hayes's Windy Haliday and Andy Clyde's California Carlson in the popular Hopalong Cassidy series.

Britt Wood

When Hayes quit the series to join up with Roy Rogers, producer Harry Sherman hired Wood to fill the void. However his tenure only lasted five films, beginning with *Range War* in 1939 and ending with *Stagecoach War* in 1940.

Wood, born in 1885, was a former vaudevillian who entered the movies around 1926.

Following his stint with Hoppy he went on to make B Westerns with several cowboys in mostly small roles.

Britt Wood passed away on April 13, 1965, in Hollywood, California.

Britt Wood Filmography

1939: *Range War* (*H* Hopalong Cassidy). **1940:** *Santa Fe Marshal* (*H* Hopalong Cassidy); *The Showdown* (*H* Hopalong Cassidy); *Hidden Gold* (*H* Hopalong Cassidy); *Stagecoach War* (*H* Hopalong Cassidy). **1942:** *Down Rio Grande Way* (*H* Charles Starrett).

Hank Worden

Tex Ritter had a whole passel of partners. In his films Tex rode with what seemed to be an army of sidekicks. For instance in his 1938 film *Tex Rides with the Boy Scouts* he had Snub Pollard, Horace Murphy and Heber Snow around, as well as a whole troop of boy scouts.

Heber Snow is better known as Hank Worden. Worden made nine films with Ritter beginning with *Hittin' the Trail* in 1937. In these films Worden's character appeared to be the predecessor or the prototype for Slim Andrews' Arkansas character in later Ritter films.

Worden went on to become a well known character actor in Westerns like *The Big Sky*, *Wagonmaster*, *Yellow Sky* and *Red River*.

Hank Worden Filmography

1937: *Hittin' the Trail* (*H* Tex Ritter); *Sing Cowboy Sing* (*H* Tex Ritter); *Riders of the Rockies* (*H* Tex Ritter); *Mystery of the Hooded Horseman* (*H* Tex Ritter). **1938:** *Tex Rides with the Boy Scouts* (*H* Tex Ritter); *Frontier Town* (*H* Tex Ritter); *Rollin' Plains* (*H* Tex Ritter). **1939:** *Sundown on the Prairie* (*H* Tex Ritter); *Rollin' Eastward* (*H* Tex Ritter).

Frank Yaconelli

Frank Yaconelli is one of the most underrated of the B Western sidekicks. Though he was Italian, he spent most of his career playing

Frank Yaconelli

Mexicans. His trademark was a unique speech pattern that bordered on the total butchery of the English language. In one film he could toss out more malaprops than the entire Harvard English department could repair in a week.

He appeared in several films with Ken Maynard in the early 1930s. From 1938 to 1940 he was paired with Jack Randall for seven films at Monogram and in 1941 and 1942 with Tom Keene at the same studio.

In 1946 and 1947 he appeared with Gilbert Roland in three Cisco Kid features.

Aside from Westerns, Yaconelli could be found in comedies like the

Marx Brothers' *A Night at the Opera* and *Abbott & Costello Meet Captain Kidd.*

Born in Italy on October 2, 1898, he entered silent films during the 1920s.

Frank Yaconelli died of lung cancer on November 19, 1964, in Los Angeles, California.

Frank Yaconelli Filmography

1929: *Señor Americano* (*H* Ken Maynard). **1933:** *Strawberry Roan* (*H* Ken Maynard). **1935:** *Lawless Rider* (*H* Ken Maynard). **1937:** *Wild West Days* (serial) (*H* Johnny Mack Brown). **1938:** *Wild Horse Canyon* (*H* Jack Randall). **1939:** *Drifting Westward* (*H* Jack Randall); *Trigger Smith* (*H* Jack Randall); *Across the Plains* (*H* Jack Randall). **1940:** *Pioneer Days* (*H* Jack Randall); *Wild Horse Range* (*H* Jack Randall). **1941:** *The Driftin' Kid* (*H* Tom Keene); *Ridin' the Sunset Trail* (*H* Tom Keene); *Lone Star Lawmen* (*H* Tom Keene). **1942:** *Western Mail* (*H* Tom Keene); *Arizona Roundup* (*H* Tom Keene); *Where Trails End* (*H* Tom Keene). **1946:** *South of Monterey* (*H* Gilbert Roland); *Beauty and the Bandit* (*H* Gilbert Roland). **1947:** *Riding the California Trail* (*H* Gilbert Roland).

THE
COWGIRLS

She Went Thataway:
Leading Ladies of the B Western Era

The lot of the B Western heroine was best summed up by Dale Evans when she once remarked that even though she was "the Queen of the West," Roy, Gabby Hayes and even Roy's horse Trigger got better billing in films than did she.

The stereotypical picture of a B Western cowgirl was that of a helpless schoolmarm strapped to a lit keg of dynamite, tied to a railroad track in the path of an oncoming train and screaming "Help! help!" in hopes that some gallant defender would hear her plaintive pleas in time to avoid certain disaster. That baleful profile of Western womanhood was more apropos to the serials of the twenties than it was to the B Western films. Still, all in all the heroine in a B ranked somewhere behind the hero, his horse, his sidekick, the outlaws, the sheriff, the Indians . . .

The fact is a bunch of B Westerns didn't even bother to have a leading lady.

With the exception of the early Hopalong Cassidy films and the films of Roy Rogers and Gene Autry, women's roles in six-gun sagas were pretty limited. The female lead was almost always the daughter of a wrongly accused or murdered man. Sometimes she would inherit a ranch, a stagecoach line or a newspaper that was the target of a greedy outlaw. What she basically did was smile while the hero sang or cringe in terror when he was in danger. Occasionally she would get a chance to ride for the law.

As far as onscreen romantic interludes were concerned, the code of the

305

Hollywood cowboy forbade his engaging in any blazing hot passion. Autry, Rogers and the rest of the warbling wranglers sang to the object of their affections; Hopalong Cassidy occasionally would let a girl borrow Topper to ride; and in the thirties Buck Jones got kinda huggy and kissy with a few of his leading ladies. But that was about it.

Of the hundreds of actresses who appeared in B Westerns at one time or another, Dale Evans is the only one to gain fame exclusively from the genre.

Many actreses used parts in B Westerns to pay the rent until better things came along. These included Rita Hayworth, Jennifer Jones, Lorraine Day, Gale Storm, Marge Champion, Ann Miller, Virginia Grey, Adele Mara, Martha Hyer, Jacqueline Wells, Louise Currie, Lois Collier and Evelyn Brent.

Roy and Dale were not the only duo that was paired up by studios. There was Charles Starrett and Iris Meredith, Red Barry and Lynne Merrick, Bill Elliott and Anne Jeffreys, Monte Hale and Adrian Booth, and Johnny Mack Brown and Nell O'Day.

Neither were Roy and Dale the only onscreen couple to tie the knot in real life. In the early thirties Hoot Gibson married his leading lady Sally Eilers and Tex Ritter got hitched to Dorothy Fay.

* * *

Betty Adams

aka: Julie Adams; Julia Adams

Betty Adams was the leading lady in a series of six Western adventures released by Lippert Pictures in 1950 starring two ex–Hopalong Cassidy sidekicks, Russ Hayden and Jimmy Ellison. The pictures all featured the same cast, and it was rumored that they were all filmed at once.

Betty Adams is better known as Julie Adams and Julia Adams. She is best remembered as the girl who was chased by *The Creature from the Black Lagoon* in the 1954 3-D horror flick.

Born Betty May Adams in Waterloo, Iowa, on October 17, 1928, she entered films in 1947 and appeared in films like *The Hollywood Story* with Richard Conte, *Slaughter on 10th Avenue* with Richard Egan and *Tickle Me* with Elvis Presley.

She has appeared on television as Jimmy Stewart's wife on *The Jimmy Stewart Show* (1971–72) and on the CBS daytime drama *Capitol.*

Betty (Julie) Adams Filmography

1950: *Hostile Country* (*H* Hayden/Ellison); *Marshal of Heldorado* (*H* Hayden/Ellison); *Colorado Ranger* (*H* Hayden/Ellison); *West of the Brazos* (*H* Hayden/Ellison); *Crooked River* (*H* Hayden/Ellison); *Fast on the Draw* (*H* Hayden/Ellison).

Jane "Poni" Adams

Jane Adams (born 1916) was a contract player at Universal Studios in the 1940s. She appeared in films like *The House of Dracula* (1945) and the serial *Lost City of the Jungle* (1946) with Russell Hayden.

When the studio decided to make musical/cowboy star Kirby Grant a singing cowboy, they made Adams his leading lady and gave her the "Poni" monicker to be more Western.

She later appeared with Johnny Mack Brown and Jimmy Wakely in some films at Monogram and was the heroine of the last Cisco Kid feature to be made, *The Girl from San Lorenzo.*

She was also featured in the 1949 Columbia serial *Batman and Robin.*

Jane "Poni" Adams

Jane "Poni" Adams Filmography

1945: *Code of the Lawless* (H Kirby Grant); *Trail to Vengeance* (H Kirby Grant). **1946:** *Rustlers Roundup* (H Kirby Grant); *Lawless Breed* (H Kirby Grant); *Gunman's Code* (H Kirby Grant). **1949:** *Western Renegades* (H Johnny Mack Brown); *Gun Law Justice* (H Jimmy Wakely). **1950:** *Law of the Panhandle* (H Johnny Mack Brown); *Outlaw Gold* (H Johnny Mack Brown); *Girl from San Lorenzo* (H Duncan Renaldo).

Joan Barclay

Joan Barclay

Minnesota-born beauty Joan Barclay was one of the top stars of B pictures in the 1930s and 1940s.

She was featured in serials like *The Shadow of Chinatown* (1936) with Bela Lugosi and *Blake of Scotland Yard* (1936) with Ralph "Dick Tracy" Byrd; comedies like *Flying Wild* (1941) and *Mr. Wise Guy* (1942), both with the East Side Kids; and mysteries like *The Falcon Out West* (1944) with Tom Conway.

She was also a very popular leading lady in B Westerns. Between 1936 and 1943 she appeared in over 20 with such stars as Hoot Gibson, Ken Maynard, Tim McCoy, Tim Holt, Bob Steele and others. Top of the line B Westerns in which she appeared include *The Purple Vigilantes* (1936) with the Three Mesquiteers and Tex Fletcher's lone starring effort, *Six-Gun Rhythm* in 1939.

She was born Geraine Greear in Minneapolis, Minnesota, on August 31, 1920, and became a fashion model while still a child.

She became a top model and was brought to Hollywood after she appeared on the cover of *Cosmopolitan* and caught a talent scout's eye.

In her heyday she stood 5′4″, weighed 110 lbs., had red hair and hazel eyes.

She was also a top sportswoman excelling in tennis and horsemanship, which made her right at home on the Hollywood range.

Joan Barclay Filmography

1936: *The Kid Ranger* (H Bob Steele); *Ridin' On* (H Tom Tyler); *Feud of the West* (H Hoot Gibson); *West of Nevada* (H Rex Bell); *The Glory Trail* (H Tom Keene); *Men of the Plains* (H Rex Bell); *Phantom Patrol* (H Kermit Maynard). **1937:** *The Trusted Outlaw* (H Bob Steele). **1938:** *The Singing Outlaw* (H Bob Baker); *The Purple Vigilantes* (H 3 Mesquiteers); *Whirlwind Horseman* (H Ken Maynard); *Two Gun Justice* (H Tim McCoy); *Lightning Carson Rides Again* (H Tim McCoy). **1939:** *Six-Gun Rhythm* (H Tex Fletcher); *Texas Wildcats* (H Tim McCoy); *Outlaws Paradise* (H Tim McCoy); *The Gentleman from Arizona*. **1941:** *Billy the Kid's Range War* (H Bob Steele). **1942:** *Billy the Kid's Smoking Guns* (H Buster Crabbe); *The Bandit Ranger* (H Tim Holt); *Sagebrush Law* (H Tim Holt).

Reno Blair

aka: Reno Browne

Reno (Nevada)–born Reno Blair, who also made films as Reno Browne, was Monogram Pictures' main Western leading lady of the late 1940s. She made a half dozen films each with the studio's main cowboys, Johnny Mack Brown and Whip Wilson, and also appeared with Jimmy Wakely.

She was hired by Monogram more for her riding ability than for her acting ability, and all of the films that she made in her career were Westerns with Monogram.

Her real name was Browne, but when she made films with Johnny Mack Brown, the studio changed it to Blair, then back to Browne for the other films.

At one time she was married to Western ace Lash LaRue.

Reno Blair Filmography

1946: *Under Arizona Skies* (*H* Johnny Mack Brown); *The Gentleman from Texas* (*H* Johnny Mack Brown). **1947:** *The Law Comes to Gunsight* (*H* Johnny Mack Brown); *Riders of the South* (*H* Johnny Mack Brown). **1948:** *Frontier Agent* (*H* Johnny Mack Brown). **1949:** *West of El Dorado* (*H* Johnny Mack Brown); *Across the Rio Grande* (*H* Jimmy Wakely); *Shadows of the West* (*H* Whip Wilson); *Haunted Trails* (*H* Whip Wilson); *Riders of the Dusk* (*H* Whip Wilson); *Range Land* (*H* Whip Wilson). **1950:** *Fence Riders* (*H* Whip Wilson); *Gunslingers* (*H* Whip Wilson).

Adrian Booth

aka: Lorna Gray

Adrian Booth came to be known as one of the serial queens of past decades. She appeared in a half dozen exciting Saturday afternoon chapter plays beginning with *Flying G-Men* in 1939.

Known early in her career as Lorna Gray, she also began to appear as leading lady in B Westerns with Charles Starrett and Roy Rogers. In 1940 she made her second serial for Columbia Pictures, *Deadwood Dick.*

In 1942 she became well known to serial audiences when she played the villainous Queen Vultura in the Republic thriller *The Perils of Nyoka.* She became a familiar face in Republic serials, being featured as the heroine of *Capt. America* (1944) and *Federal Operator 99* (1945).

In early 1946 she changed her name to Adrian Booth, but continued to work in serials. Republic starred her in their 1946 cliff-hanger, *The Daughter of Don Q.*

That year they also played onscreen matchmaker and hooked up Booth with their latest singing cowboy, Monte Hale. Booth and Hale made seven films together from 1946 to 1948.

She would also appear in several of the "super B's" made by William (formerly Wild Bill) Elliott.

Adrian Booth served as leading lady in such major oaters as *Brimstone* (1949), *Rock Island Trail* (1950) and *Oh, Susanna* (1951).

Adrian Booth Filmography

1939: *(as Lorna Gray) The Stranger from Texas* (*H* Charles Starrett. **1940:** *Bullets for Rustlers* (*H* Charles Starrett). **1942:** *Ridin' Down the Canyon* (*H*

Roy Rogers). (as Adrian Booth) **1946:** *Home on the Range* (*H* Monte Hale); *Man from Rainbow Valley* (*H* Monte Hale); *Out California Way* (*H* Monte Hale). **1947:** *Last Frontier Uprising* (*H* Monte Hale); *Along the Oregon Trail* (*H* Monte Hale); *Under Colorado Skies* (*H* Monte Hale). **1948:** *California Firebrand* (*H* Monte Hale); *The Gallant Legion* (*H* Wild Bill Elliott). **1949:** *The Last Bandit* (*H* Wild Bill Elliott). **1950:** *The Savage Horde* (*H* Wild Bill Elliott).

Lucille Brown

Lovely Lucille Brown was one of the B Western era's earliest successful leading ladies, appearing with stars like Tom Tyler, George O'Brien, Ken Maynard, Bob Steele and Bob Custer. She also holds the distinction of being Gene Autry's first leading lady.

She was quite a busy actress in the early 1930s and was high in demand for work in serials. Between 1931 and 1932 she made *Battling with Buffalo Bill* (with Tom Tyler and Rex Bell), *The Airmail Mystery* and *Danger Island.*

In 1934 she was the heroine of the Mascot serial *The Law of the Wild.* Although Bob Custer was listed as the star, the real stars were Rin-Tin-Tin Jr. and Rex, the Wild Horse.

Ms. Brown's film career lasted until the early 1950s.

She was born in Memphis, Tennessee, in 1907 and passed away on May 5, 1976, in Los Angeles, California.

Lucille Brown Filmography

1930: *Last of the Duanes* (*H* George O'Brien). **1931:** *Battling with Buffalo Bill* (*H* Tom Tyler). **1932:** *The Texan* (*H* Buffalo Bill, Jr.). **1933:** *King of the Arena* (*H* Ken Maynard). **1934:** *The Law of the Wild* (*H* Bob Custer); *Brand of Hate* (*H* Bob Steele). **1935:** *Texas Terror* (*H* John Wayne); *Rainbow Valley* (*H* John Wayne); *Western Frontier* (*H* Ken Maynard); *Tumbling Tumbleweeds* (*H* Gene Autry). **1936:** *The Crooked Trail* (*H* Johnny Mack Brown). **1937:** *Cheyenne Rides Again* (*H* Tom Tyler).

Adrian Booth

Rita Cansino

aka: Rita Hayworth

Margarita Carmen Cansino (born October 17, 1918, in New York City) is best known to moviegoers everywhere as Rita Hayworth, one of the screen's all-time sex symbols. But a long time before the celluloid temptress vented her sexy ways on the likes of Frank Sinatra and Cary Grant, she was charming B Western cowboys like Tex Ritter, Tom Keene, George O'Brien and the Three Mesquiteers.

Rita Cansino (later Rita Hayworth) and the Three Mesquiteers in Hit the Saddle *(1937).*

Rita began her show business career at the age of six and came to Hollywood in the mid-thirties. Her first parts were in B mysteries like *Charlie Chan in Panama* and *The Lone Wolf's Spy Hunt.*

She also appeared in several B Westerns, the best of which was the 1937 Republic Three Mesquiteers adventure hit, *Hit the Saddle,* in which she played a conniving senorita. One look at her and the Mesquiteers forgot about fighting bad guys and started fighting with each other.

Her career took off after a name change and a juicy part as a bored wife in the 1939 melodrama *Only Angels Have Wings* which starred Cary Grant and Jean Arthur.

She had the title role in *The Lady in Question* (1940) and was Fred Astaire's leading lady in the delightful *You'll Never Get Rich* in 1941.

Rita Hayworth's best known films include *Cover Girl* (1944), *Miss Sadie Thompson* (1953), *Salome* (1953), *Pal Joey* (with Sinatra, 1957), *Separate Tables* (1958) and *They Came to Cordura* (with Gary Cooper, 1959).

Rita Cansino Filmography

1936: *Rebellion* (H Tom Keene). **1937:** *Old Louisiana* (H Tom Keene); *Hit the Saddle* (H 3 Mesquiteers); *Trouble in Texas* (H Tex Ritter). **1938:** *Renegade Ranger* (H George O'Brien).

Jean Carmen

aka: Julia Thayer

Lovely Western leading lady Jean Carmen also made films under the name Julia Thayer. In fact as Thayer she had her best remembered Western film role: that of the alluring and mysterious Indian princess known only as the Rider in the 1937 Republic serial *The Painted Stallion*. Thanks to the Rider (who rode the painted stallion in the title), Hoot Gibson and Crash Corrigan were able to survive 12 chapters of danger.

The Oregon-born Ms. Carmen appeared in B's with Fred Scott, Renfrew of the Royal Mounted (James Newell), Bob Steele and Tom Tyler. Her parents were in the entertainment field and she began her acting career at the age of five.

Following her acting career which included stage, film and radio work, she became active in the production and writing end of the movie industry and is currently still active in those endeavors.

Jean Carmen Filmography

1935: *Born to Battle* (H Tom Tyler). **1937:** *The Painted Stallion* (serial) (H Hoot Gibson); *Gunsmoke Ranch* (H 3 Mesquiteers); *Arizona Gunfighter* (H Bob Steele). **1939:** *Smoky Trails* (H Bob Steele); *In Old Montana* (H Fred Scott); *Crashing Thru* (H James Newell).

Phyllis Coates

Phyllis Coates was one of the most popular actresses that the B picture era produced. She was extremely popular with fans and producers and appeared in dozens of low budget adventures, Westerns and comedies.

She co-starred in 15 B Westerns with heroes like Whip Wilson, Bill Elliott, Rocky Lane and Johnny Mack Brown.

Phyllis Coates

Coates may well be described as the Republic serial queen of the 1950s. She co-starred in *Jungle Drums of Africa* (1953) with Clayton "Lone Ranger" Moore and in *Gunfighters of the Northwest* (1954) with Jock "Range Rider, Yancey Derringer" Mahoney.

In 1955 Republic gave her the title role in its 12-chapter epic *Panther Girl of the Congo*.

From 1948 to 1954 she was the co-star of the popular "Joe McDoakes" comedy shorts produced by Warner Bros., playing star George O'Hanlon's wife. The director of the series was Richard Bare, to whom she was later married.

In 1954 she was one of the stars of the NBC-TV comedy series *The Duke*. She played the sexy girlfriend of the title character, a boxer played by Paul Gilbert.

Phyllis Coates Filmography

1950: *Outlaws of Texas* (H Whip Wilson). **1951:** *Canyon Raiders* (H Whip Wilson); *Nevada Badmen* (H Whip Wilson); *Stage to Blue River* (H Whip Wilson); *The Long Horn* (H Wild Bill Elliott); *Man from Sonora* (H Johnny Mack Brown); *Oklahoma Justice* (H Johnny Mack Brown). **1952:** *Canyon Ambush* (H Johnny Mack Brown); *The Gunman* (H Whip Wilson); *Wyoming Roundup* (H Whip Wilson); *Fargo* (H Wild Bill Elliott); *The Maverick* (H Wild Bill Elliott). **1953:** *Topeka* (H Wild Bill Elliott); *El Paso Stampede* (H Rocky Lane); *Marshal of Cedar Rock* (H Rocky Lane).

Carolina Cotton

Carolina Cotton was every bit the Southern belle that her lyrical name implied. She was under contract to Columbia Studios and was seen in B musical comedies.

She appeared in several of the studio's Westerns with Charles Starrett. In 1946 Columbia made her part of the stock cast in a series of hoedown style Westerns starring Ken Curtis.

She also appeared in several Columbia films with Gene Autry in the early fifties.

Carolina Cotton Filmography

1945: *Texas Panhandle* (H Charles Starrett); *Outlaws of the Rockies* (H Charles Starrett). **1946:** *Song of the Prairie* (H Ken Curtis); *Singing on the Trail* (H Ken Curtis); *That Texas Jamboree* (H Ken Curtis); *Cowboy Blues* (H Ken Curtis). **1949:** *Stallion Canyon* (H Ken Curtis). **1952:** *Apache Country* (H Gene Autry); *Blue Canadian Rockies* (H Gene Autry); *The Rough, Tough West* (H Charles Starrett).

Carolina Cotton

Gail Davis

Arkansas-born Gail Davis rates as one of the B Western era's top leading ladies. She made more films as the heroine of Gene Autry films as did any other actress. She also portrayed Annie Oakley in the early 1950s TV series, coincidentally produced by Autry's Flying A's Productions.

Gail Davis was born Betty Jean Grayson in Little Rock, Arkansas. She studied drama at Harcum Junior College in Bryn Mawr, Pennsylvania, and at the University of Texas before coming to Hollywood and making her screen debut in 1948.

She was soon in demand as a leading lady in B Western films. Her all–American features, Southern accent and natural affinity for riding contributed to her popularity in these roles.

She co-starred with all the top stars of the time. She appeared with Roy Rogers, Rocky Lane and Monte Hale at Republic, Jimmy Wakely and Johnny Mack Brown at Monogram and with Charles Starrett and Autry at

Gail Davis

Columbia. During the period between 1948 and 1953 Gail Davis appeared in 25 B Westerns.

When Gene's Flying A's Productions decided to add *The Annie Oakley Show, Range Rider* and *The Adventures of Champion,* Autry called on his favorite leading lady to fill the title role.

Production on the Oakley series began in April of 1953, and over 150 episodes were produced in the next five years. The show, sponsored by Bosco and Wonder Bread, was syndicated on over 200 stations in the United States and Canada. Each adventure-packed episode featured the exploits of sharpshooter Annie, her brother Tagg (Jimmy Hawkins) and deputy sheriff Lofty Craig (Brad Johnson).

Following the series run Davis continued to make guest appearances on TV shows like *The Andy Griffith Show*, where in one episode she played Thelma Lou's sharpshootin' cousin Karen who was pitted against sheriff Andy in a skeet shooting contest.

Gail Davis Filmography

1948: *The Far Frontier* (H Roy Rogers). **1949:** *Death Valley Gunfighter* (H Rocky Lane); *Frontier Marshal* (H Rocky Lane); *Law of the Golden West* (H Monte Hale); *Brand of Fear* (H Jimmy Wakely); *South of Death Valley* (H Charles Starrett/Durango Kid). **1950:** *Sons of New Mexico* (H Gene Autry); *Trail of the Rustlers* (H Charles Starrett/Durango Kid); *West of Wyoming* (H Johnny Mack Brown); *Six Gun Mesa* (H Johnny Mack Brown); *Cowtown* (H Gene Autry); *Indian Territory* (H Gene Autry). **1951:** *Texans Never Cry* (H Gene Autry); *Whirlwind* (H Gene Autry); *Silver Canyon* (H Gene Autry); *Yukon Manhunt* (H Kirby Grant); *Valley of Fire* (H Gene Autry); *Overland Telegraph* (H Tim Holt). **1952:** *The Old West* (H Gene Autry); *Wagon Train* (H Gene Autry); *Blue Candian Rockies* (H Gene Autry). **1953:** *Winning of the West* (H Gene Autry); *On Top of Old Smoky* (H Gene Autry); *Goldtown Ghost Riders* (H Gene Autry); *Pack Train* (H Gene Autry).

Jeff Donnell

Jeff Donnell was born (1921) Jean Marie Donnell in South Windham, Maine. She studied drama at Yale before moving to Hollywood in the early forties. Perky Jeff was a supporting player in many 1940s comedies like *A Night to Remember, The Boogie Man Will Get You* and *My Sister Eileen.*

In 1945 Columbia Pictures placed her as co-star and leading lady in a series of Westerns that featured Ken Curtis, the Hoosier Hot Shots, Carolina Cotton, Guy Kibbee and Andy Clyde.

Jeff Donnell is best known to television audiences as Alice, the much-maligned wife of "Lonesome" George Gobel on NBC-TV's *George Gobel Show* from 1954 to 1958.

Some of her other films include *The Fuller Brush Girl* and *Gidget Goes Hawaiian.*

Most recently Ms. Donnell was seen on the ABC soap opera, *General Hospital.*

Jeff Donnell

Jeff Donnell succumbed to a heart attack on April 11, 1988, in Hollywood, California.

Jeff Donnell Filmography

1945: *Song of the Prairie* (H Ken Curtis). **1946:** *Throw a Saddle on a Star* (H Ken Curtis); *That Texas Jamboree* (H Ken Curtis); *Cowboy Blues* (H Ken Curtis); *Singing on the Trail* (H Ken Curtis). **1949:** *Outcasts of the Trail* (H Monte Hale); *Stagecoach Kid* (H Tim Holt).

Penny Edwards

Penny Edwards

Penny Edwards pinch-hit for Dale Evans as Roy Rogers' leading lady in a half dozen films in 1951–1952.

She also made films with other Republic cowboys like Rex Allen and Rocky Lane.

Born in 1919, she entered films in the early 1940s and was seen in comedies such as *Let's Face It* (1943), *That Hagen Girl* (1947), and *Feudin', Fussin' 'n' Fightin'* in 1948.

Penny Edwards Filmography

1950: *Sunset in the West* (H Roy Rogers); *Trail of Robin Hood* (H Roy Rogers); *North of the Great Divide* (H Roy Rogers). **1951:** *Spoilers of the*

Plains (*H* Roy Rogers); *Heart of the Rockies* (*H* Roy Rogers); *In Old Amarillo* (*H* Roy Rogers); *Utah Wagon Train* (*H* Rex Allen). **1952:** *Captive of Billy the Kid* (*H* Rocky Lane).

Dale Evans

Dale Evans, Western filmdom's most famous leading lady, was born Frances Octavia Smith in Uvalde, Texas, on October 31, 1921. She was raised in Arkansas and began singing at the age of nine. At the age of 14 she eloped with her childhood sweetheart, but the marriage was a very short one.

Her first professional entertainment job was as a singer on a small radio station in Memphis, Tennessee.

While working at station WHAS in Louisville, Kentucky, the station's program director changed her name to Dale Evans. Following a stint at WFAA in Dallas, Texas, Dale served as a big band singer with the Jay Mills and Anson Weeks orchestras.

In 1942 she was granted a screen test by Paramount Studios, but nothing came of it.

Later that year she was signed by 20th Century–Fox, but in a year's time she was given only several bit parts.

She also worked as a vocalist on the Edgar Bergen/Charlie McCarthy Radio Show.

In 1943 she left Fox and was signed by Republic Pictures.

The studio used her in musicals like *Swing Your Partner* and comedies such as *Here Comes Elmer* (both 1943).

She got her first part in a Western in the role of a singer in the 1943 John Wayne film *In Old Oklahoma* (aka *War of the Wildcats*).

The following year the studio co-starred her with Roy Rogers in *The Cowboy and the Senorita*. Movie audiences went wild for Rogers, already a superstar, and his new leading lady, and they made four more films in 1944.

By 1945 the Rogers-Evans duo was the B Western's hottest ticket. That year Roy, Dale and Gabby Hayes teamed up to make their best film and one of the truly great and entertaining B Westerns ever made — *Don't Fence Me In.* In the film Dale plays a snoopy reporter out to uncover the true story behind the legend of supposedly long-dead outlaw (Gabby). The film has good music and great action.

Between 1944 and 1947 Roy and Dale made 20 films together.

After the death of Roy's wife in 1946 the onscreen romance blossomed

Dale Evans with her husband and leading man Roy Rogers, and Gabby Hayes.

into a real-life relationship, and on New Year's Eve, 1947, Roy Rogers and Dale Evans were married.

The marriage was not well looked on by the studio heads at Republic, who felt the public wouldn't appreciate a cowboy hero and his real-life wife on screen, and they promptly removed Dale from the film series and replaced her with first Jane Frazee, then others.

In 1949 Republic yielded to fan pressure, and in the film *Susanna Pass* Dale Evans returned as Roy's leading lady, making eight more films. With Roy being king of the cowboys, the Republic PR hypesters dubbed Dale Queen of the West.

Dale Evans ca. 1945.

In 1951 Roy and Dale turned their attention to television and began production on *The Roy Rogers Show*.

The show, which featured Dale and her horse Buttermilk, along with Roy and Trigger, Roy's dog Bullet and Pat Brady, debuted on NBC-TV in December of 1951 and ran until 1957.

In the early 1960s Dale and Roy hosted a one-hour variety show.

Dale has also authored several books and has been a frequent guest on talk shows, especially the religious-oriented variety.

Roy and Dale can be seen currently each week on the Nashville Network hosting *Happy Trails Theatre*, which features some of their best films.

Dale and Roy with Trigger, ca. 1949.

Dale Evans Filmography

1944: *The Cowboy and the Senorita* (H Roy Rogers); *The Yellow Rose of Texas* (H Roy Rogers); *Song of Nevada* (H Roy Rogers); *San Fernando Valley* (H Roy Rogers); *Lights of Old Santa Fe* (H Roy Rogers). **1945:** *Utah* (H Roy Rogers); *Bells of Rosarita* (H Roy Rogers); *The Man from Oklahoma* (H Roy Rogers); *Sunset in El Dorado* (H Roy Rogers); *Don't Fence Me In* (H Roy Rogers). **1946:** *Along the Navajo Trail* (H Roy Rogers); *Song of Arizona* (H Roy Rogers); *Rainbow Over Texas* (H Roy Rogers); *My Pal Trigger* (H Roy Rogers); *Roll on Texas Moon* (H Roy Rogers); *Home in Oklahoma* (H Roy Rogers); *Heldorado* (H Roy Rogers); *Under Nevada Skies* (H Roy Rogers). **1947:** *Apache Rose* (H Roy Rogers); *Bells of San Angelo* (H Roy Rogers). **1949:** *Susanna Pass* (H Roy Rogers); *Down Dakota Way* (H Roy Rogers); *The Golden Stallion* (H Roy Rogers). **1950:** *Bells of Coronado* (H Roy Rogers); *Twilight in the Sierras* (H Roy Rogers); *Trigger Jr.* (H Roy Rogers). **1951:** *South of Caliente* (H Roy Rogers); *Pals of the Golden West* (H Roy Rogers).

Muriel Evans

It seems as though every cowboy had his favorite cowgirl to protect from the bad guys. Roy had Dale, Johnny Mack Brown had Nell O'Day, Charles Starrett had Iris Meredith and Buck Jones had Minneapolis, Minnesota, native Muriel Evans.

Evans co-starred with Jones in seven features and serials in the mid-1930s. In their first screen appearance together, the 1935 Universal serial *The Roaring West*, Buck saved Muriel's ranch from the villainous clutches of Walter Miller; however, in *The Boss Rider of Gun Creek* she returned the favor by helping Buck clear himself of a murder charge.

When Buck was not around, Muriel had only the most stalwart of heroes at her beck and call; she made two films with Hopalong Cassidy, two with John Wayne and a like number with Tex Ritter.

Comedy buffs remember Muriel Evans as the favorite leading lady of one of the screen's all-time mirth masters — Charlie Chase. Beginning with *Young Ironside* in 1932, Muriel co-starred with the madcap Chase in nearly a dozen of his screwball comedy shorts for Hal Roach Studios.

Muriel Evans began her career at the age of 15 as an extra. She had roles in such memorable films as *Manhattan Melodrama* with William Powell, *Queen Christina* with Greta Garbo, *The Prizefighter and the Lady* with boxing legends Max Baer and Jack Dempsey, and *Mr. Deeds Goes to Town* with Gary Cooper.

Muriel Evans with (from left to right) William Desmond, Frank McGlynn, Sr. and Buck Jones in The Roaring West *(Universal, 1935).*

Muriel Evans Filmography

1935: *The Roaring West* (serial) (H Buck Jones); *The Throwback* (H Buck Jones); *The New Frontier* (H John Wayne). **1936:** *Silver Spurs* (H Buck Jones); *Call of the Prairie* (H Hopalong Cassidy); *King of the Pecos* (H John Wayne); *Three on the Trail* (H Hopalong Cassidy); *Boss Rider of Gun Creek* (H Buck Jones). **1937:** *Smoketree Range* (H Buck Jones); *Law for Tombstone* (H Buck Jones); *Boss of Lonely Valley* (H Buck Jones). **1939:** *Westbound Stage* (H Tex Ritter). **1940:** *Roll Wagons Roll* (H Tex Ritter).

Virginia Brown Faire

Virginia Brown Faire

Virginia Brown Faire, with striking dark hair and eyes, was one of the most beautiful of the B Western leading ladies. She was around at the dawn of the era and may well be called the "queen of Poverty Row," as most of her films were low-budget entries from obscure outfits like Big 4 and

Resolute. She was saved from dastardly dangers by cowboys like Wally Wales, Rex Lease, Ken Maynard and even John Wayne.

Faire won a Motion Picture Classic Fame and Fortune contest in 1919 and made her screen debut in 1921.

She appeared in such silent films as *Monte Cristo, Peter Pan* and *The Temptress*. She made over 50 films before retiring in the late 1930s.

She passed away on June 30, 1980, in Laguna Beach, California, at the age of 75.

Virginia Brown Faire Filmography

1930: *Trails of Peril* (H Wally Wales); *Breed of the West* (H Wally Wales). **1931:** *Hell's Valley* (H Wally Wales); *Alias the Badman* (H Ken Maynard); *The Sign of the Wolf* (H Rex Lease). **1932:** *Tex Takes a Holiday* (H Wallace McDonald). **1934:** *West of the Divide* (H John Wayne); *Rainbow Riders* (H Jack Perrin). **1935:** *Tracy Rides* (H Tom Tyler).

Dorothy Fay

Dorothy Fay was a popular leading lady in B Westerns starring Buck Jones, Bob Baker and Art Jarrett when she met and married Tex Ritter in 1938.

She and Tex made a trio of films together in 1939 and 1940.

After marriage she continued to work in films for a few years before retiring. The Ritters had two children, Thomas and John of *Three's Company* TV fame.

Dorothy Fay Filmography

1938: *The Stranger from Arizona* (H Buck Jones); *Law of the Texan* (H Buck Jones); *Prairie Justice* (H Bob Baker). **1939:** *Trigger Pals* (H Art Jarrett); *Sundown on the Prairie* (H Tex Ritter); *Rollin' Westward* (H Tex Ritter). **1940:** *Rainbow Over the Range* (H Tex Ritter). **1941:** *White Eagle* (serial) (H Buck Jones); *North from the Lone Star* (H Wild Bill Elliott).

Evelyn Finley

Although she was a competent actress and the leading lady of nearly a dozen B Western films, Evelyn Finley was best known for four decades as one of Hollywood's top stuntwomen. Over the years she has doubled for such stars as Elizabeth Taylor, Donna Reed, Judy Garland, Kim Novak, Gale Storm and Olivia de Havilland.

Evelyn was born in Douglas, Arizona, and raised on ranches in Arizona and New Mexico. By the time she was a teenager she was already an expert horsewoman.

She broke into films in 1936 when, while attending college in Albuquerque, she was hired as a double for Jean Parker in the film *The Texas Rangers.*

She made her debut as a Western leading lady in the 1940 Tex Ritter film *Arizona Frontier.* She also appeared in other Monogram Pictures productions with Tom Keene and the Range Busters. Finley also did stunt work on some of the Roy Rogers films at Republic.

Her career as a stuntwoman lasted well into the 1970s with work in films like *Across the Wide Missouri, Scaramouche, Elephant Walk, Swiss Family Robinson* and *Hush, Hush Sweet Charlotte.* She also worked on top-rated television shows like *The Lone Ranger, The Munsters, Wagon Train* and *The Virginian.*

Evelyn Finley Filmography

1940: *Arizona Frontier* (H Tex Ritter); *Dynamite Canyon* (H Tom Keene). **1942:** *Trail Riders* (H Range Busters). **1943:** *Cowboy Commandos* (H Range Busters); *Black Market Rustlers* (H Range Busters). **1944:** *Valley of Vengeance* (H Buster Crabbe); *Ghost Guns* (H Johnny Mack Brown); *Sundown Riders* (H Andy Clyde). **1945:** *Prairie Rustlers* (H Buster Crabbe). **1948:** *Sheriff of Medicine Bow* (H Johnny Mack Brown); *Gunning for Justice* (H Johnny Mack Brown).

Jane Frazee

When Roy Rogers and Dale Evans were married in 1947, the powers-that-be at Republic Studios decided they should no longer appear on screen together. Hired to replace Dale as Roy's leading lady was the former

Jane Frazee

musical comedy star Jane Frazee. Beginning with *Springtime in the Sierras* Jane and Roy were paired in five films.

Jane Frazee was born Mary Jane Freshe in Duluth, Minnesota, on July 19, 1918, and began performing with her sisters at the age of six. Later they appeared in vaudeville and nightclubs.

She made her screen debut in the 1940 musical *Melody and Moonlight.*

In 1941 she was signed by Universal Studios and that same year co-starred with Abbott and Costello in *Buck Privates.* She made other films like *Hellzapoppin'* with Olsen and Johnson and *Hi Ya' Chum* with the Ritz Brothers.

In the mid-forties she moved to Republic Pictures.

In 1954 she replaced Phyllis Coates as Joe McDoakes' wife in that popular series of comedy shorts. There she remained until the series ended in 1956.

She retired from the screen in the late fifties to concentrate on her real estate business.

Jane Frazee passed away on September 6, 1985, in Newport Beach, California.

Jane Frazee Filmography

1947: *Springtime in the Sierras* (H Roy Rogers); *On the Old Spanish Trail* (H Roy Rogers). **1948:** *The Gay Ranchero* (H Roy Rogers); *Under California Stars* (H Roy Rogers); *Grand Canyon Trail* (H Roy Rogers); *Last of the Wild Horses* (H James Ellison).

Doris Hill

Doris Hill made the transition from silent screen Western heroine to talking picture B Western leading lady. In 1930 she co-starred with Ken Maynard in two of the earliest B's, *Song of the Cabellero* and *Sons of the Saddle*. The plot of *Sons of the Saddle* had Ken falling in love with Doris and saving her father's ranch from an outlaw named Red Slade (Francis Ford).

Over the next few years she would star with Bob Steele, Lane Chandler, Hoot Gibson and Bill Cody.

In her silent screen years, along with westerns, Doris Hill was most often seen in mysteries and comedies.

Doris Hill Filmography

1930: *Song of the Caballero* (H Ken Maynard); *Sons of the Saddle* (H Ken Maynard). **1931:** *The Montana Kid* (H Bill Cody). **1932:** *Spirit of the West* (H Hoot Gibson); *Battling Buckaroo* (H Lane Chandler); *Texas Tornado* (H Lane Chandler). **1933:** *Galloping Romeo* (H Bob Steele); *The Rangers Code* (H Bob Steele); *Trailing North* (H Bob Steele). **1934:** *Ridin Gents* (H Jack Perrin).

Jennifer Holt

Jennifer Holt was the most prolific of the B Western era's leading ladies.

Between 1942 and 1948 Jennifer appeared in 38 western films. She made more Westerns than many cowboy stars did.

Jennifer, daughter of the famous actor Jack Holt and the younger sister of cowboy star Tim Holt, was born in Hollywood on November 10, 1920. When her parents were divorced in 1931, Jennifer left California with her mother and was educated in New York and Chile. In the mid-thirties she returned to Hollywood and studied acting under the well-known film character actress Madame Maria Ouspenskaya (remember the Wolf Man's mother?).

She made her film debut in the 1942 Hopalong Cassidy film *Stick to Your Guns,* using the name of Jacqueline Holt. Later that year she signed a contract with Universal Studios and became the leading lady to top cowboy stars Johnny Mack Brown and Tex Ritter in a series of nine films.

From there Holt went on to make films with B Westerns heroes like Russell Hayden, Eddie Dew, Rod Cameron, Hoot Gibson, Bob Steele, Eddie Dean, Ken Curtis, Jimmy Wakely and Lash LaRue.

Of all the films she made, the series at Universal with Ritter and Brown are considered the best.

Jennifer appeared in two action serials: *The Adventures of the Flying Cadet* in 1943, in which she was menaced by a villain called the Black Hangman, and the 1946 Columbia thriller *Hop Harrigan* which coincidentally starred William Blakewell, to whom she was married at one time.

She also was in two Abbott and Costello comedies, *Buck Privates* and *Pardon My Sarong.*

After she made her last Western in 1948, Holt went into the realm of children's television for a Chicago-produced series called *Uncle Mistletoe and Aunt Judy* (she was Aunt Judy).

Jennifer Holt was considered the perfect all-around Western heroine. She was attractive, a competent actress, an excellent horsewoman and a good singer.

She even played the head of an outlaw gang in the 1948 Eddie Dean film *The Hawk of Powder Valley.*

Though retired, she often makes appearances at Western film fairs.

Jennifer Holt

Jennifer Holt Filmography

1942: *Stick to Your Guns* (as Jacqueline Holt) (*H* Hopalong Cassidy); *The Silver Bullet* (*H* Johnny Mack Brown); *Deep in the Heart of Texas* (*H* Johnny Mack Brown, Tex Ritter); *Little Joe the Wrangler* (*H* Johnny Mack Brown, Tex Ritter); *The Old Chisholm Trail* (*H* Johnny Mack Brown, Tex Ritter). **1943:** *Tenting Tonight on the Old Campground* (*H* Johnny Mack Brown, Tex Ritter); *Cheyenne Roundup* (*H* Johnny Mack Brown, Tex Ritter); *Raiders of San Joaquin* (*H* Johnny Mack Brown, Tex Ritter); *Lone Star Trail* (*H* Johnny Mack Brown, Tex Ritter); *Frontier Law* (*H* Russell Hayden); *Raiders of Sunset Pass* (*H* Eddie Dew). **1944:** *Marshal of Gunsmoke* (*H* Johnny Mack Brown, Tex Ritter); *Oklahoma Raiders* (*H* Johnny Mack Brown, Tex Ritter); *Outlaw Trail* (*H* Hoot Gibson, Bob Steele); *Guns of the Law* (*H* Texas Ranger series); *Riders of the Santa Fe* (*H* Rod

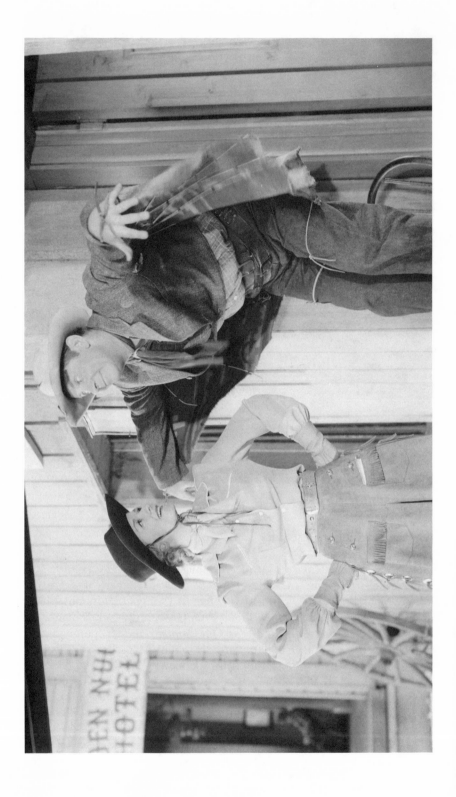

Cameron). **1945:** *Navajo Trail* (*H* Johnny Mack Brown); *Gunsmoke* (*H* Johnny Mack Brown); *The Lost Trail* (*H* Johnny Mack Brown); *Song of Old Wyoming* (*H* Eddie Dean); *Under Western Skies; Beyond the Pecos* (*H* Rod Cameron); *Renegades of the Rio Grande* (*H* Rod Cameron). **1946:** *Moon Over Montana* (*H* Jimmy Wakely); *Trigger Fingers* (*H* Johnny Mack Brown). **1947:** *Over the Santa Fe Trail* (*H* Ken Curtis); *Buffalo Bill Rides Again* (*H* Richard Arlen); *Pioneer Justice* (*H* Lash LaRue); *Ghost Town Renegades* (*H* Lash LaRue); *Fighting Vigilantes* (*H* Lash LaRue); *Where the North Begins* (*H* Russell Hayden); *Trail of the Mounties* (*H* Russell Hayden); *Shadow Valley* (*H* Eddie Dean). **1948:** *Stage to Mesa City* (*H* Lash LaRue); *Tornado Range* (*H* Eddie Dean); *The Tioga Kid* (*H* Eddie Dean); *Hawk of Powder Valley* (*H* Eddie Dean); *Range Renegades* (*H* Jimmy Wakely).

Lois January

Texas-born Lois January (1913) was one of the most popular of the B Western starlets of the mid-1930s. She co-starred in films with a variety of movie cowboys that ranged from superstars like Johnny Mack Brown, Tim McCoy and Bob Steele to more meagerly successful ones like Reb Russell. She worked for studios that ranged from giants like Republic and Universal to Poverty Row entities like Kent and Spectrum.

One of her best outings was in the 1937 Johnny Mack Brown film *Bar Z Bad Men*.

January began her entertainment career as a member of the dance team of January and May and worked in theatrical productions around southern California.

In the early thirties she was contracted to Universal Studios and had supporting roles in films such as *Embarrassing Moments* (1934) with Chester Morris and *One Rainy Afternoon* (1936) with Francis Lederer.

January continued to work in films, radio and the legitimate theater until the 1960s when she retired to work in public relations.

Lois January Filmography

1935: *Arizona Bad Man* (*H* Reb Russell). **1936:** *Border Caballero* (*H* Tim McCoy); *Lightnin' Bill Carson* (*H* Tim McCoy); *Rogue of the Range* (*H*

Jennifer Holt with Fuzzy Knight in one of the movies they made together.

Lois January

Johnny Mack Brown). **1937:** *Lightnin Crandall* (*H* Bob Steele); *Bar Z Bad Men* (*H* Johnny Mack Brown); *The Trusted Outlaw* (*H* Bob Steele); *The Red Rope* (*H* Bob Steele); *Courage of the West* (*H* Bob Baker); *The Roaming Cowboy* (*H* Fred Scott).

Anne Jeffreys

When Wild Bill Elliott made the move from Columbia to Republic Studios in 1943, the moguls at Republic made casting moves to ensure that his films would be top-rate. They gave him the legendary Gabby Hayes for a sidekick, and as leading lady he was given a delightful opera performer named Anne Jeffreys. Starting with *Calling Wild Bill Elliott*, Anne teamed with Elliott and Hayes in the first half dozen epics that he made for Republic.

Jeffreys was a popular B picture actress of the forties. She appeared in such varied films as *Zombies on Broadway* (1945), *Dillinger* (1945) and *I Married an Angel* (1942). She gave a good performance as a female outlaw reformed by Randolph Scott in *Return of the Badman* (1948) and co-starred with Ralph Byrd in two entries in the Dick Tracy series: *Dick Tracy Detective* (1945) and *Dick Tracy vs. Cueball* (1946).

In the early 1950s Jeffreys and her husband Robert Sterling starred as TV's most delightful ghosts, Marion and George Kirby on the series *Topper*. The show ran from 1953 to 1956.

In 1958 Anne and Robert starred in a short-lived ABC-TV series called *Love That Jill.*

Anne Jeffreys was born in Goldsboro, North Carolina on January 26, 1923.

Anne Jeffreys Filmography

1943: *Calling Wild Bill Elliott* (H Wild Bill Elliott); *Man from Thunder River* (H Wild Bill Elliott); *Wagon Tracks West* (H Wild Bill Elliott); *Overland Mail Robbery* (H Wild Bill Elliott); *Death Valley Manhunt* (H Wild Bill Elliott). **1944:** *Hidden Valley Outlaws* (H Wild Bill Elliott).

Mary Ellen Kay

Mary Ellen Kay was one of Republic Pictures' top starlets in the early 1950s. She co-starred in six Westerns with Rex Allen in 1951–52 and three with Rocky Lane.

She was also the heroine of the 1951 Republic serial *Government Agents vs. the Phantom Legion*, in which she helped Federal agents uncover a saboteur known only as the Voice.

Anne Jeffreys

She also appeared in B Westerns with Charles Starrett, Kirby Grant and Wild Bill Elliott.

Among her other screen appearances were in films such as *Tarzan and the Slave Girls, Francis in the Haunted House,* and *Vice Squad.*

Mary Ellen Kay Filmography

1950: *Streets of Ghost Town* (H Charles Starrett). **1951:** *Wells Fargo Gunmaster* (H Rocky Lane); *Fort Dodge Stampede* (H Rocky Lane); *Desert of*

Lost Men (*H* Rocky Lane); *Silver City Bonanza* (*H* Rex Allen); *Thunder in God's Country* (*H* Rex Allen); *Rodeo King and the Senorita* (*H* Rex Allen). **1952:** *Colorado Sundown* (*H* Rex Allen); *The Last Musketeer* (*H* Rex Allen); *Border Saddlemates* (*H* Rex Allen). **1953:** *Vigilante Terror* (*H* Wild Bill Elliott). **1954:** *Yukon Vengeance* (*H* Kirby Grant).

Mary Lee

Young Mary Lee was surely the cutest of the B Western gals.

During the late thirties and early forties she specialized in playing youthful but overly sophisticated cowgirls who always gave their big sisters a run for the featured cowboy's affections.

Beginning with *South of the Border* in 1939 she appeared in nine films with Gene Autry. In the Autry films she was often paired with lovely June Storey, and the two worked well together. Some of their little sister/big sister dialog was quite charming.

She appeared in a couple of films with Roy Rogers including *The Cowboy and the Senorita*, Roy and Dale's first film together.

Mary Lee Filmography

1939: *South of the Border* (*H* Gene Autry). **1940:** *Melody Ranch* (*H* Gene Autry); *Rancho Grande* (*H* Gene Autry); *Gaucho Serenade* (*H* Gene Autry); *Carolina Moon* (*H* Gene Autry); *Ride Tenderfoot Ride* (*H* Gene Autry). **1941:** *Ridin' on a Rainbow* (*H* Gene Autry); *Back in the Saddle* (*H* Gene Autry); *The Singing Hill* (*H* Gene Autry); *Meet Roy Rogers* (short) (*H* Roy Rogers). **1944:** *The Cowboy and the Senorita* (*H* Roy Rogers); *Song of Nevada* (*H* Roy Rogers).

Patti McCarty

Patti McCarty had the lion's share of leading lady parts in the B Western epics produced in the early-to-mid-1940s by PRC Studios.

Usually the roles were those of the stereotypically helpless sagebrush gal in dire need of a hero, and at PRC that usually meant Buster Crabbe or the Texas Rangers (James Newell, Dave O'Brien, Tex Ritter and Guy Wilkerson).

Mary Ellen Kay

McCarty made six films with Crabbe and half that number with the Rangers; all were made between 1943 and 1946.

Patti McCarty Filmography

1941: *Prairie Stranger* (H Charles Starrett). **1943:** *Fighting Valley* (H Texas Rangers); *Devil Riders* (H Buster Crabbe). **1944:** *Gunsmoke Mesa* (H Texas

Mary Lee

Rangers); *Gangsters of the Frontier* (H Texas Rangers); *Fuzzy Settles Down* (H Buster Crabbe); *Rustlers Hideout* (H Buster Crabbe). **1946:** *Terrors on Horseback* (H Buster Crabbe); *Overland Raiders* (H Buster Crabbe); *Outlaws of the Plains* (H Buster Crabbe).

Christine McIntyre

Although she made over 15 appearances as a leading lady in B Western films, gorgeous vocalist Christine McIntyre is best known as the Three Stooges' favorite leading lady. What Margaret Dumont was to the Marx Brothers, Christine was to the Stooges. Between 1944 and 1956 she appeared in over two dozen shorts with the tumultuous trio.

She was blessed with a beautiful operatic voice, which was the centerpiece of one of the Stooges' best and most famous films, *Micro-Phonies*, made in 1945.

She was also the charming villainess in another top Stooge comedy, *Hot Scots*, made in 1948. The sequence in which she and Moe Howard dance the Highland Fling is unforgettable.

Christine also made comedy shorts with Hugh Herbert, Vera Vague, Harry Langdon and Andy Clyde.

She made B Westerns with Whip Wilson, Buck Jones, Fred Scott and others, but she was especially one of the favorite leading ladies of Johnny Mack Brown in his Monogram series.

One of her most unusual roles was in the 1947 Brown film, *Land of the Lawless*, in which she played a saloon owner who heads up a gang of robbers.

Another highlight of her career is the fact that she appeared in Buck Jones's final film, *Dawn on the Great Divide*, completed shortly before Jones's untimely death.

Christine McIntyre Filmography

1938: *The Ranger's Round-up* (H Fred Scott). **1941:** *Gunman from Bodie* (H Rough Riders). **1942:** *Riders of the West* (H Rough Riders); *Rock River Renegades* (H Range Busters); *Dawn on the Great Divide* (H Buck Jones). **1943:** *The Stranger from Pecos* (H Johnny Mack Brown); *Border Buckaroos* (H Texas Rangers). **1944:** *West of the Rio Grande* (H Johnny Mack Brown); *Partners of the Trail* (H Johnny Mack Brown). **1945:** *Frontier Feud* (H Johnny Mack Brown). **1946:** *The Gentleman from Texas* (H Johnny Mack Brown). **1947:** *Gun Talk* (H Johnny Mack Brown); *Land of the Lawless* (H Johnny Mack Brown); *Valley of Fear* (H Johnny Mack Brown). **1951:** *Colorado Ambush* (H Johnny Mack Brown); *Wanted: Dead or Alive* (H Whip Wilson).

Christine McIntyre with Whip Wilson in Wanted: Dead or Alive *(Monogram, 1951).*

Betty Mack

Though she was an exceptionally talented vocalist, attractive Betty Mack made her mark on the movie scene in the area of B Westerns and comedy shorts in the early 1930s. In the period between 1931 and 1936, Betty Mack was surely one of Hollywood's busiest actresses in Western films. She co-starred with well-known cowboys like Tom Tyler and Harry Carey as well as lesser-known sagebrush stars like Fred Kohler and Reb Russell.

Betty, along with fellow Western heroine Muriel Evans, was the co-star of many Charlie Chase comedies during the same period, often showcasing her singing talent. She was often touted by critics for her subdued reactions to Chase's totally madcap antics, making such scenes all the more hilarious.

Betty Mack Filmography

1931: *God's Country and the Man* (H Tom Tyler); *Partners of the Trail* (H Tom Tyler); *Law of the Rio Grande* (H Bob Custer); *The Man from Death Valley* (H Tom Tyler); *Headin' for Trouble* (H Bob Custer). **1932:** *Scarlet Brand* (H Bob Custer); *The Forty Niners* (H Tom Tyler); *Galloping Thru* (H Tom Tyler). **1933:** *The Fighting Texans* (H Rex Bell). **1935:** *Outlaw Rule* (H Reb Russell); *The Last of the Clintons* (H Harry Carey); *The Reckless Buckaroo* (H Bill Cody); *Toll of the Desert* (H Fred Kohler, Jr.). **1936:** *Hair Trigger Casey* (H Jack Perrin); *Senor Jim* (H Conway Tearle).

Faye McKenzie

Faye McKenzie made her first Western when she was just an infant, but she is best known as Gene Autry's leading lady in five Republic films in 1941 and 1942.

Faye was born in Hollywood, California, in 1920. Her parents were actors in silent pictures, and she made her first screen appearance when she was only three months old.

She continued to work in films while she was growing up. In 1934 young Faye made her first B Western — the 1934 Superior Pictures release *Boss Cowboy* starring former silent film cowboy Buddy Roosevelt.

As a young actress she appeared in the A Western *When the Daltons Rode* in 1940. That same year she starred in *Death Rides the Sage* with an aging Ken Maynard.

The following year she made her first film with Gene Autry, *Down Mexico Way,* one of Gene's best-received releases. Four more quickly followed.

In 1944 she starred in a musical Western for Universal Studios, *The Singing Sheriff,* with popular big band leader Bob Crosby.

Faye appeared in such non–Westerns as *Remember Pearl Harbor* (1942) and *Murder in the Music Hall* (1946).

At one time she was married to 1950s screen actor Steve Cochran.

Faye McKenzie Filmography

1934: *Boss Cowboy* (H Buddy Roosevelt). **1940:** *Death Rides the Range* (H Ken Maynard). **1941:** *Down Mexico Way* (H Gene Autry); *Sierra Sue* (H Gene Autry). **1942:** *Cowboy Serenade* (H Gene Autry); *Heart of the Rio*

Faye McKenzie

Grande (H Gene Autry); *Home in Wyomin'* (H Gene Autry). **1944:** *The Singing Sheriff* (H Bob Crosby).

Blanche Mehaffey

aka: Janet Morgan

Blanche Mehaffey, who also made films under the name of Janet Morgan, was another of those early 1930s actresses who graced Poverty Row Westerns.

Born in Cincinnati, Ohio, on July 28, 1907, she entered films in 1924.

Throughout the 1920s she appeared in mostly melodramas, mysteries and of course Westerns.

Beginning in 1931 she began to make low budget Westerns with cowboys like Jack Perrin, Bill Cody, Rex Lease and Lane Chandler.

Blanche Mehaffey passed away on March 31, 1968, in Los Angeles.

Blanche Mehaffey Filmography

1931: *Sunrise Trail* (H Bob Steele); *Riders of the North* (H Bob Custer); *Dugan of the Badlands* (H Bill Cody). **1934:** *The Outlaw Tamer* (H Lane Chandler); *Border Guns* (H Bill Cody). **1935:** *The Cowboy and the Bandit* (H Rex Lease); *North of Arizona* (H Jack Perrin). **1936:** *Wildcat Saunders* (H Jack Perrin).

Iris Meredith

Mellow-eyed Iris Meredith (born 1916) was the Western and serial queen of Columbia Pictures in the late 1930s. She made two dozen B Westerns for the company between 1936 and 1941. Of those, 19 starred their number one cowboy Charles Starrett, four featured Wild Bill Elliott, and one was with Bob Allen.

She also made films with Johnny Mack Brown, Tex Ritter, Buster Crabbe, and the Texas Rangers.

Meredith was featured in three of Columbia's most exciting chapter plays, one of which was a Western starring Bill Elliott. In *Overland with Kit Carson* (1939) Iris portrayed the lovely Carmelita Gonzales, the daughter of a wealthy landowner who is rescued by Elliott from the vile clutches of one of serialdom's all-time greatest villains — the mysterious Peg Leg and his gang of cutthroats. She also portrayed the fiancée of the famous crimefighter, the Spider, in Columbia's 1938 serial *The Spider's Web* and was in the 1940 serial *The Green Archer.*

She co-starred with Elliott in one of his best films, *The Man from Tumbleweeds*, in 1940. This is considered to be one of the better B Westerns of the whole lot.

Iris Meredith began her career as a Goldwyn Girl, and one of her earliest film roles was in the 1938 Eddie Cantor film *Roman Scandals*, which also featured a young Lucille Ball.

Iris Meredith died January 22, 1980, in Los Angeles, California.

Iris Meredith Filmography

1936: *The Cowboy Star* (H Charles Starrett); *Rio Grande Ranger* (H Bob Allen). **1937:** *Trail of Vengeance* (H Johnny Mack Brown); *The Gambling Terror* (H Johnny Mack Brown); *A Lawman Is Born* (H Johnny Mack Brown); *Mystery of the Hooded Horseman* (H Tex Ritter); *Outlaws of the Prairie* (H Charles Starrett). **1938:** *Cattle Raiders* (H Charles Starrett); *Law of the Plains* (H Charles Starrett); *West of Cheyenne* (H Charles Starrett); *South of Arizona* (H Charles Starrett); *The Colorado Trail* (H Charles Starrett); *West of Santa Fe* (H Charles Starrett). **1939:** *The Thundering West* (H Charles Starrett); *Texas Stampede* (H Charles Starrett); *Spoilers of the Range* (H Charles Starrett); *Western Caravans* (H Charles Starrett); *The Man from Sundown* (H Charles Starrett); *Riders of Black River* (H Charles Starrett); *Overland with Kit Carson* (serial) (H Wild Bill Elliott); *Outpost of the Mounties* (H Charles Starrett); *Taming of the West* (H Wild Bill Elliott). **1940:** *Two Fisted Rangers* (H Charles Starrett); *Blazing Six Shooters* (H Charles Starrett); *The Man from Tumbleweeds* (H Wild Bill Elliott); *Texas Stagecoach* (H Charles Starrett); *The Return of Wild Bill* (H Wild Bill Elliott); *Thundering Frontier* (H Charles Starrett). **1941:** *Son of Davy Crockett* (H Wild Bill Elliott). **1942:** *The Rangers Take Over* (H Texas Rangers). **1943:** *The Kid Rides Again* (H Buster Crabbe).

Lynne Merrick

aka: Marilyn Merrick

Lovely Lynne Merrick was Don "Red" Barry's favorite leading lady in a series of Westerns for Republic Pictures. From 1941 to 1943 she made 16 pictures with Barry.

In 1940 Merrick had a part in Johnny Mack Brown's Universal Western *Ragtime Cowboy Joe.*

She appeared in Judy Canova's 1941 cornfield comedy *Sis Hopkins.* She also appeared in films under the name Marilyn Merrick.

Lynne Merrick Filmography

1940: *Ragtime Cowboy Joe* (H Johnny Mack Brown). **1941:** *Two Gun Sheriff* (H Don "Red" Barry); *Desert Bandit* (H Don "Red" Barry); *The Apache Kid* (H Don "Red" Barry); *Death Valley Outlaws* (H Don "Red"

Iris Meredith

Barry); *A Missouri Outlaw* (H Don "Red" Barry); *Kansas Cyclone* (H Don "Red" Barry). **1942:** *Arizona Terror* (H Don "Red" Barry); *Stagecoach Express* (H Don "Red" Barry); *Jesse James Jr.* (H Don "Red" Barry); *Cyclone Kid* (H Don "Red" Barry); *The Sombrero Kid* (H Don "Red" Barry); *Outlaws of Pine Ridge* (H Don "Red" Barry). **1943:** *Dead Man's Gulch* (H Don "Red" Barry); *Carson City Cyclone* (H Don "Red" Barry); *Days of Old Cheyenne* (H Don "Red" Barry); *Fugitive from Sonora* (H Don "Red" Barry).

Lynne Merrick

Gertrude Messinger

Along with being one of the B Western's most popular leading ladies of the early thirties, perky, dark-haired Gertrude "Gertie" Messinger was also a top-flight comedy actress.

She was one of the stars of a successful series of comedy shorts called

"The Boy Friends." In 1930–31 she made nine of the hilarious shorts which also starred former Our Gang kids Micky Daniels and Mary Kornman and future cowboy/stuntman David Sharpe.

In her Westerns (most of which were made between 1932 and 1936) she was protected from villains by the likes of Bob Steele, Gene Autry, Harry Carey, Bill Cody, and Lane Chandler.

Gertie was born into a show business family. Her mother was stage actress Josephine Messinger and her brother was Melvin "Buddy" Messinger, a silent screen comedian who in the mid-twenties starred in his own series of comedy shorts.

Gertie began her film career at a young age and appeared in well-known silents like *Penrod and Sam* (1923) and *The Jazz Age* (1929).

Gertrude Messinger Filmography

1932: *Riders of the Desert* (H Bob Steele); *Hidden Valley* (H Bob Steele); *Lawless Valley* (H Lane Chandler). **1935:** *Wagon Trail* (H Harry Carey); *Rustler's Paradise* (H Harry Carey); *Melody Trail* (H Gene Autry); *The Rider of the Land* (H Bob Steele). **1936:** *Aces Wild* (H Harry Carey); *Blazing Justice* (H Bill Cody). **1939:** *Feud of the Range* (H Bob Steele).

Betty Miles

Betty Miles was Monogram Pictures' top Western leading lady of the early forties.

Monogram paired the wholesome-looking Miles with the top stars Tom Keene (four films), Tex Ritter (one film) and Hoot Gibson and Ken Maynard in the Trail Blazers series (four films).

She also made films with Wild Bill Elliott and the Three Mesquiteers.

Betty was noted as one of the better horsewomen among the B Western leading lady corps.

Betty Miles Filmography

1941: *Wanderers of the West* (H Tom Keene); *The Driftin' Kid* (H Tom Keene); *Ridin' the Sunset Trail* (H Tom Keene); *Lone Star Lawmen* (H Tom Keene); *Ridin' the Cherokee Trail* (H Tex Ritter); *Return of Daniel Boone*

(*H* Wild Bill Elliott). **1943:** *Law of the Saddle* (*H* 3 Mesquiteers); *Wild Horse Stampede* (*H* Trail Blazers); *The Law Rides Again* (*H* Trail Blazers). **1944:** *Westward Bound* (*H* Trail Blazers); *Sonora Stagecoach* (*H* Trail Blazers).

Ruth Mix

Ruth Mix was the daughter of the legendary movie cowboy Tom Mix. Taught to ride and shoot as a youngster, she began getting parts in silent Westerns when she was still a teenager. She also appeared in stage productions on Broadway.

She made her B Western debut in the 1931 Big 4 production of *Red Fork Range* starring Wally Wales.

In 1935 she co-starred in four films with Rex Bell for Resolute Pictures.

In 1936 she was the leading lady in the Western serial *Custer's Last Stand* which starred Rex Lease.

She also appeared in two other chapter plays, *The Black Coin* and *The Clutching Hand*, both made in 1936.

Born in Dewey, Oklahoma, in 1912, Ruth Mix passed away on September 21, 1977.

Ruth Mix Filmography

1931: *Red Fork Range* (*H* Wally Wales). **1935:** *Fighting Pioneers* (*H* Rex Bell); *Saddle Aces* (*H* Rex Bell); *The Tonto Kid* (*H* Rex Bell); *Gunfire* (*H* Rex Bell). **1936:** *Custer's Last Stand* (serial) (*H* Rex Lease); *The Riding Avenger* (*H* Hoot Gibson).

Nell O'Day

Nell O'Day made B Westerns and one serial between 1940 and 1943. Hard ridin' was the way they described Nell, who was in essence more of a cowgirl than a leading lady. She could ride, rope and shoot right alongside the best of the Western heroes.

She is best known for the series of 12 cowboy pictures she made at Universal Studios from 1940 to 1942 with Johnny Mack Brown and Fuzzy Knight.

Nell O'Day

The series, which contained films like *Fighting Bill Fargo, Ragtime Cowboy Joe,* and *Bury Me Not on the Lone Prairie,* is considered one of the best B Western film series ever made; it also features Brown's best screen work.

The films not only gave Nell a chance to show off her athletic ability and horsewomanship, but also her singing voice. In the 1940 film *Law and Order* she crooned a little ditty entitled "Oklahoma's OK with Me."

Nell also appeared in Westerns with Tim Holt, the Three Mesquiteers, the Range Busters and the Texas Rangers.

Her first B Western was made back in 1933. It was called *Smoke Lightning* and starred George O'Brien.

During that period she was appearing as leading lady in a series of comedy shorts that starred Harry Langdon.

Nell made her lone serial appearance in the 1942 Columbia thriller *Perils of the Royal Mounted*.

Nell O'Day can also be seen in films such as *Never Give a Sucker an Even Break* (1941) with W.C. Fields, *The Mystery of Marie Rouget* (1942) and *The Road to Ruin* (1934).

Nell O'Day Filmography

1933: *Smoke Lightning* (H George O'Brien). **1940:** *Ragtime Cowboy Joe* (H Johnny Mack Brown); *Law and Order* (H Johnny Mack Brown); *Pony Post* (H Johnny Mack Brown). **1941:** *Boss of Bullion City* (H Johnny Mack Brown); *Bury Me Not on the Lone Prairie* (H Johnny Mack Brown); *Law of the Range* (H Johnny Mack Brown); *Rawhide Rangers* (H Johnny Mack Brown); *Man from Montana* (H Johnny Mack Brown); *The Masked Rider* (H Johnny Mack Brown); *Arizona Cyclone* (H Johnny Mack Brown); *Fighting Bill Fargo* (H Johnny Mack Brown). **1942:** *Stagecoach Buckaroo* (H Johnny Mack Brown); *Perils of the Royal Mounted* (serial) (H Robert Stevens); *Arizona Stagecoach* (H Range Busters); *Pirates of the Prairie* (H Tim Holt). **1943:** *Thundering Trails* (H 3 Mesquiteers); *Boss of Rawhide* (H Texas Rangers).

Cecilia Parker

Canadian-born Cecilia Parker was one of the best known and busiest action and adventure actresses of the talkies' first decade. She is best remembered for her roles in B Westerns, serials and as Andy Hardy's (Mickey Rooney) big sister in the Andy Hardy series.

Cecilia made 14 Westerns between 1932 and 1937 with cowboys like Buck Jones, John Wayne, Ken Maynard and George O'Brien. She was considered one of the most attractive heroines of the era.

In 1932 Cecilia was featured in two exciting Universal serials. The first, *The Jungle Mystery*, starred Western heroes Tom Tyler and Noah Beery, Jr., as big game hunters who help Cecilia find her long-lost brother. In the other, *The Lost Special*, she searched for a lost gold train.

She appeared with Clyde Beatty in his 1934 Mascot serial *The Lost Jungle*.

Beginning with *A Family Affair* in 1937, Cecilia Parker made 11 appearances as Marian Hardy, the older sister of Andy Hardy, whose main problems often rivaled Andy's girl troubles in the popular MGM series from 1937 to 1942.

In 1958 she returned in the role in a reunion film, *Andy Hardy Comes Home.*

Cecilia Parker was born April 26, 1915, in Fort William, Ontario, Canada, and began her entertainment career as a stage actress and dancer.

Aside from comedies, Westerns and serials, she appeared in films like *The Painted Veil* (1934) with Greta Garbo, *Ah, Wilderness!* (1935) with Rooney and Wallace Beery and *Naughty Marietta* (1935) with Nelson Eddy and Jeanette MacDonald.

Cecilia Parker Filmography

1932: *Mystery Ranch* (H George O'Brien); *Rainbow Trail* (H George O'Brien); *Tombstone Canyon* (H Ken Maynard). **1933:** *Rainbow Ranch* (H Rex Bell); *Unknown Valley* (H Buck Jones); *The Fugitive* (H Rex Bell); *The Trail Drive* (H Ken Maynard); *Riders of Destiny* (H John Wayne); *Gun Justice* (H Ken Maynard). **1934:** *The Man Trailer* (H Buck Jones); *Honor of the Range* (H Ken Maynard). **1937:** *Hollywood Cowboy* (H George O'Brien); *Roll Along Cowboy* (H Smith Ballew).

Shirley Patterson

Pretty Shirley Patterson appeared in 11 B Westerns between 1942 and 1947. She made four films with Charles Starrett at Columbia Pictures and a like number with Eddie Dean at PRC.

She was also in Westerns with Bill Elliott, Russ Hayden and Johnny Mack Brown.

In the 1943 serial *Batman* she played Batman's girlfriend. Patterson also had a part in *Between Two Women*, a 1944 entry in the popular Dr. Kildare series which starred Lionel Barrymore and Van Johnson.

Cecilia Parker

Shirley Patterson Filmography

1942: *North of the Rockies* (H Wild Bill Elliott); *Riders of the North Land* (H Charles Starrett); *Riding Through Nevada* (H Charles Starrett). **1943:** *Law of the Northwest* (H Charles Starrett); *The Texas Kid* (H Johnny Mack Brown). **1944:** *Riding West* (H Charles Starrett); *The Vigilantes Ride* (H

Russ Hayden). **1946:** *Driftin' River* (*H* Eddie Dean); *Tumbleweed Trail* (*H* Eddie Dean); *Stars Over Texas* (*H* Eddie Dean). **1947:** *Black Hills* (*H* Eddie Dean).

Sally Payne

Perky downhome comedienne Sally Payne is one of the most unforgettable ladies ever to grace the B Western screen. Sally wasn't so much of a glamorous leading lady as she ws a raucous sidekick gal. Her characters were loud, boisterous, funky, and usually ready to fight.

She appeared in ten Republic films starring Roy Rogers in the early forties, most often in roles like the one she played in the 1942 Rogers film *The Man from Cheyenne* in which she played Gale Storm's wild and woolly younger sister.

Her best scenes in the Rogers films came with Gabby Hayes. In fact, she reminds one of a female Gabby.

She also made two films with Gene Autry, *The Big Show* in 1936 and *The Man from Music Mountain* in 1938.

Sally's vast comedic talent was also showcased in the popular RKO series of Edgar Kennedy comedy shorts. In the 1941 short *Westward Ho-hum* Sally took over Florence Lake's role as Edgar's wife and remained in the role for a half dozen entries from 1941 to 1942.

Sally Payne Filmography

1936: *The Big Show* (*H* Gene Autry). **1938:** *The Man from Music Mountain* (*H* Gene Autry). **1940:** *Young Bill Hickok* (*H* Roy Rogers); *Rodeo Dough* (short) (*H* Roy Rogers, Gene Autry). **1941:** *Robin Hood of the Pecos* (*H* Roy Rogers); *In Old Cheyenne* (*H* Roy Rogers); *Sheriff of Tombstone* (*H* Roy Rogers); *Nevada City* (*H* Roy Rogers); *Bad Man of Deadwood* (*H* Roy Rogers); *Westward Ho-hum* (short) (*H* Edgar Kennedy); *Jesse James at Bay* (*H* Roy Rogers); *Red River Valley* (*H* Roy Rogers). **1942:** *Man from Cheyenne* (*H* Roy Rogers); *Romance on the Range* (*H* Roy Rogers).

Shirley Patterson

Sally Payne

Dorothy Revier

Sexy Dorothy Revier made the transition from silent screen Western heroine to talking picture Western heroine.

In the 1920s Revier, who made over 80 films in her career, was the leading lady to such early Western favorites as Jack Holt and Bill Fairbanks. During this period she and Holt were a popular screen duo who made a variety of films including *The Tigress* (1927), *The Warning* (1928), *Submarine* (1928), *The Donovan Affair* (1929) and *Vengeance* (1930). She was the villainess in Douglas Fairbank's 1929 swashbuckler, *The Iron Mask*.

In 1930 she starred in the Western *Call of the West*, the story of a show girl who marries a cowboy, and that same year she appeared with Walter Huston in *The Bad Man*.

Revier's best remembered B Westerns were made with Buck Jones. They first appeared in Jones's 1931 film *The Avenger*. Dorothy and Buck would make five screen appearances. She also made Westerns with Hopalong Cassidy and Rex Bell.

Coincidentally, the last film of her career was a Buck Jones Western, *The Cowboy and the Kid* (1936).

Dorothy Revier was born Doris Velegra in Oakland, California, on April 18, 1904. She made her screen debut in 1922.

Dorothy Revier Filmography

1931: *The Avenger* (H Buck Jones). **1932:** *Arm of the Law* (H Rex Bell). **1933:** *Thrill Hunter* (H Buck Jones). **1934:** *The Fighting Rangers* (H Buck Jones); *When a Man Sees Red* (H Buck Jones); *The Eagles Brood* (H Hopalong Cassidy). **1936:** *Cowboy and the Kid* (H Buck Jones).

Marjorie Reynolds

Marjorie Reynolds was born Marjorie Goodspeed on August 12, 1921, in Buhl, Idaho, and began her acting career as a child.

She made her first B Western in 1936 when, as a Universal Studios' contract player, she was assigned to be romanced by the company's newest singing cowboy sensation, Bob Baker. Paired with Baker and his sidekick Fuzzy Knight, she made five films.

Marjorie went on to appear in other Westerns with Tim Holt, Roy Rogers, George O'Brien, Buck Jones, Tex Ritter and others, making 14 oaters between 1938 and 1941.

During the 1940s she appeared in films like *Holiday Inn* (1942) with Bing Crosby, and *Star Spangled Rhythm* (1943), also with Crosby and Bob Hope.

From 1953 to 1958, Marjorie was seen as Peg Riley, the ever-tested and patient spouse of Chester A. Riley (William Bendix) on the top-rated NBC show *The Life of Riley*.

Marjorie Reynolds Filmography

1938: *The Black Bandit* (H Bob Baker); *Guilty Trails* (H Bob Baker); *The Last Stand* (H Bob Baker); *Western Trails* (H Bob Baker); *Overland Express* (H Buck Jones); *Six Shootin' Sheriff* (H Ken Maynard); *Man's Country* (H Jack Randall); *Tex Rides with the Boy Scouts* (H Tex Ritter). **1939:** *The Phantom Stage* (H Bob Baker); *The Racketeers of the Range* (H George O'Brien); *Timber Stampede* (H George O'Brien). **1941:** *Robin Hood of the Pecos* (H Roy Rogers); *Cyclone on Horseback* (H Tim Holt); *Dude Cowboy* (H Tim Holt).

Elaine Riley

Elaine Riley was married to Richard "Chito" Martin, Tim Holt's sidekick, and they appeared together in Holt's 1950 film *Rider from Tucson*.

Her most prominent B Western film roles were in the last entries in the Hopalong Cassidy series. She appeared in six of them, mostly as the romantic interest of Rand Brooks who played Lucky Jenkins.

Riley also made Westerns with Gene Autry and Rocky Lane.

She was featured in the 1948 mystery film *The Big Clock*.

Elaine Riley Filmography

1946: *The Devil's Playground* (H Hopalong Cassidy). **1947:** *Dangerous Venture* (H Hopalong Cassidy). **1948:** *Sinister Journey* (H Hopalong Cassidy); *False Paradise* (H Hopalong Cassidy); *Borrowed Trouble* (H Hopalong Cassidy); *Strange Gamble* (H Hopalong Cassidy). **1950:** *Rider from Tucson* (H Tim Holt). **1951:** *Hills of Utah* (H Gene Autry). **1952:** *Leadville Gunslinger* (H Rocky Lane).

Marjorie Reynolds

Lynne Roberts

aka: Mary Hart

In 1938 Lynne Roberts (born 1922) was a successful actress under contract to Republic Pictures. She had appeared in B Westerns with the Three Mesquiteers and had been the leading lady in two popular Republic serials,

Lynne Roberts

The Lone Ranger with Lee Powell and *Dick Tracy Returns* with Ralph Byrd.

Republic president Herbert Yates had always been a fan of the successful songwriting team of Rodgers and Hart; he thought that the names in tandem had a magical ring to them. He further decided that what Republic Pictures needed was a Rogers and Hart combo. He had his Rogers . . . Roy Rogers; he drafted Lynne Roberts to become his Hart. Her name was changed to Mary Hart, and in *Come on Rangers,* Roy's third film, they teamed up for the first time. In 1938 and 1939 Republic's version of Rogers and Hart made seven Westerns billed as "the Sweethearts of the West."

The Hart phase of Lynne's career ended when she left Republic Studios.

At 20th Century–Fox she made B Westerns with the Cisco Kid and a couple of Zane Grey features that starred George Montgomery.

Lynne returned to Republic in the mid-1940s. When Gene Autry returned from World War II, she appeared as his leading lady. One of her best roles was in the 1946 film *Sioux City Sue* in which she played a Hollywood talent scout who lures Gene to Hollywood to become what he thinks is a singing cowboy movie star. Instead he winds up as the voice for a guitar-strumming cartoon character who rides a slow-moving donkey. The result is he's ridiculed in his hometown. To quote one local towns-person, "They took Autry all the way to Hollywood to make a Jackass outa him."

She was reunited with Roy (this time under her real name) in *The Eyes of Texas* in 1948.

Among her screen appearances away from the celluloid sage were films like *Quiet Please Murder* (1942) with George Sanders and *The Blazing Forest* (1952) with John Payne.

Lynne Roberts Filmography

(as Lynne Roberts) **1937**: *Heart of the Rockies* (H 3 Mesquiteers). **1938**: *Call the Mesquiteers* (H 3 Mesquiteers); *The Lone Ranger* (serial) (H Lee Powell). **1941**: *Last of the Duanes* (H George Montgomery); *Romance of the Rio Grande* (H Cisco Kid); *Riders of the Purple Sage* (H George Montgomery). **1944**: *The Big Bonanza* (H Richard Arlen). **1946**: *Sioux City Sue* (H Gene Autry). **1947**: *Saddle Pals* (H Gene Autry); *Robin Hood of Texas* (H Gene Autry). **1948**: *Eyes of Texas* (H Roy Rogers); *The Timber Trail* (H Monte Hale). *(as Mary Hart)* **1938**: *Come on Rangers* (H Roy Rogers); *Shine on Harvest Moon* (H Roy Rogers); *Billy the Kid Returns* (H Roy Rogers). **1939**: *Rough Riders Roundup* (H Roy Rogers); *Frontier Pony Express* (H Roy Rogers); *Southward Ho* (H Roy Rogers); *In Old Caliente* (H Roy Rogers).

Claire Rochelle

Claire Rochelle made nearly a dozen B Westerns in the late thirties and early forties with some of the best of the breed of B Western cowboys: Buck Jones, Johnny Mack Brown, Bob Steele, Ken Maynard, Fred Scott and others.

Born in 1910, she died of cancer on May 23, 1981, in La Jolla, California.

Claire Rochelle Filmography

1936: *Empty Saddles* (*H* Buck Jones). **1937:** *Guns in the Dark* (*H* Johnny Mack Brown); *Boot Hill Brigade* (*H* Johnny Mack Brown); *Ridin the Lone Trail* (*H* Bob Steele). **1939:** *Riders of the Sage* (*H* Bob Steele); *El Diablo Rides* (*H* Bob Steele); *Code of the Fearless* (*H* Fred Scott); *Two Gun Troubador* (*H* Fred Scott). **1940:** *Lightning Strikes West* (*H* Ken Maynard); *The Kid from Santa Fe* (*H* Jack Randall). **1942:** *Texas Justice* (*H* George Houston).

Estelita Rodriguez

Republic Pictures billed Cuban-born Estelita Rodriguez as the Sensational Gypsy Bombshell when she debuted in the 1946 Roy Rogers film *Along the Navajo Trail.* Estelita appeared in nine of the Rogers films with Rex Allen and Wild Bill Elliott.

Fiery is the best way to describe Rodriguez's screen personality, whether it be in a red-hot Latin musical number or when she lost her Latin temper at the object of her romantic affection, which in several episodes was an unresponsive Pat Brady.

Estelita was born July 2, 1913, in Guanajay, Cuba, and worked in radio and nightclubs as well as in the movies.

She appeared in such varied films as *Mexicana* (1945), *The Cuban Fireball* (1951), *Tropical Heatwave* (1952), *Rio Bravo* (1959) and *Jesse James Meets Frankenstein's Daughter* (1966).

At one time she was married to actor Grant Withers.

Estelita Rodriguez passed away March 12, 1966.

Estelita Rodriguez

1946: *Along the Navajo Trail* (*H* Roy Rogers). **1947:** *The Old Spanish Trail* (*H* Roy Rogers). **1948:** *The Gay Ranchero* (*H* Roy Rogers); *In Old Los Angeles* (*H* Wild Bill Elliott). **1949:** *The Golden Stallion* (*H* Roy Rogers). **1950:** *Susanna Pass* (*H* Roy Rogers); *Twilight in the Sierras* (*H* Roy Rogers); *Sunset in the West* (*H* Roy Rogers). **1951:** *In Old Amarillo* (*H* Roy Rogers);

Estelita Rodriguez

Pals of the Golden West (H Roy Rogers). **1952:** *South Pacific Trail* (H Rex Allen).

Ann Rutherford

Ann Rutherford is best remembered as Polly Benedict, the much-maligned, oft-neglected, but ever-faithful girlfriend of Mickey Rooney in the Andy Hardy series of the late thirties and early forties. In almost every picture, the minute that Rooney got an eyeful of some sweet young thing (like a 16-year-old Judy Garland or a teenaged but already sexy Lana Turner) he fell deeply in love and unintentionally dumped on poor Polly. Beginning with *You're Only Young Once* in 1938, Ann portrayed Polly in 12 entries in the popular series, her last being *Andy Hardy's Double Life* in 1942.

As a B Western leading lady she made only seven appearances, but they were all in top-flight films. She made four with Gene Autry, all of which were early Autry vehicles which helped mold his successful career, and three with John Wayne before his joined the Three Mesquiteers at Republic Pictures.

Ann was born in Toronto, Canada, in 1920 and began performing in the theater as a child.

Among her film credits are *Gone with the Wind* (1939), *Pride and Prejudice* (1940), *The Secret Life of Walter Mitty* (1947) and *The Adventures of Don Juan* (1948).

Ann retired from the screen in the early 1950s; however she did reappear in *They Only Kill Their Masters* with James Garner in 1972.

Ann Rutherford Filmography

1935: *Melody Trail* (H Gene Autry); *Singing Vagabond* (H Gene Autry). **1936:** *Comin' Round the Mountain* (H Gene Autry); *The Oregon Trail* (H John Wayne); *The Lawless 90's* (H John Wayne); *Lonely Trail* (H John Wayne). **1937:** *Public Cowboy No. 1* (H Gene Autry).

Sheila Ryan

Although she made only a handful of B Westerns Sheila Ryan was one of the more popular of the genre's heroines, especially in her appearances with Gene Autry with whom she made four films.

She was also married to Gene's movie saddle pal Pat Buttram.

She co-starred with other cowboys like Roy Rogers, the Cisco Kid, George O'Brien and footballer-turned-hoss-opera-star John Kimbrough.

Ann Rutherford

To basically sum up Sheila Ryan's movie career, one could say that she was one of the top actresses of the whole B picture era. When she wasn't aiding cowboys, she could usually be found in the screen company of some of filmdom's better-known detectives such as the Lone Wolf *(The Lone Wolf in London, The Lone Wolf in Mexico)* and Philo Vance *(Philo Vance's Secret Mission)*.

She was also a favorite leading lady of Laurel and Hardy in the legendary comedy team's later film efforts. She appeared with them in *Great Guns* in 1941 and *A-Haunting We Will Go* in 1942.

Sheila Ryan in a scene from one of her movies.

Sheila Ryan was born Katherine Elizabeth McLaughlin on June 8, 1921, in Topeka, Kansas. She died of a lung ailment on November 4, 1975, in Woodland Hills, California.

Sheila Ryan Filmography

1940: *The Gay Caballero* (*H* Cesar Romero). 1942: *Lone Star Ranger* (*H* John Kimbrough). 1943: *Song of Texas* (*H* Roy Rogers). 1949: *The Cowboy and the Indians* (*H* Gene Autry). 1950: *Mule Team* (*H* Gene Autry). 1951: *Gold Raiders* (*H* George O'Brien). 1953: *On Top of Old Smoky* (*H* Gene Autry); *Pack Train* (*H* Gene Autry).

Billie Seward

Billie Seward was the main leading lady of Tim McCoy films in the mid-1930s. She appeared in several of the films he made for Columbia and Puritan Pictures.

Seward was basically a second feature or B picture actress appearing in films like *Charlie Chan at Treasure Island.*

Billie Seward Filmography

1935: *Land Beyond the Range* (*H* Tim McCoy); *The Revenge Rider* (*H* Tim McCoy); *Justice of the Range* (*H* Tim McCoy); *Riding Wild* (*H* Tim McCoy); *The Man from Guntown* (*H* Tim McCoy); *Trails of the Wild* (*H* Kermit Maynard).

Marion Shilling

Between 1931 and 1936 Marion Shilling was the leading lady in over a dozen B Westerns and sagebrush serials.

She appeared with the top action stars of the era including Buck Jones, Hoot Gibson, Tom Tyler, and Tom Keene and with lesser-known cowboys like Big Boy Williams, Rex Bell and Reb Russell. She also co-starred in the film *Fighting to Live* with Russell.

She was with Jones in his first serial for Universal Pictures, *The Red Rider*, in 1934. She was also in the 1936 chapter play *The Clutching Hand* where one of her co-stars was Ruth Mix.

Among her non–Western screen appearances were *Lord Byron on Broadway* (1930) and *The Keeper of the Bees* (1935).

Marion Shilling Filmography

1931: *The Sundown Trail* (H Tom Keene). **1932:** *A Man's Land* (H Hoot Gibson). **1934:** *Fighting to Live* (H Reb Russell); *The Red Rider* (serial) (H Buck Jones); *Thunder Over Texas* (H Big Boy Williams); *The Westerner* (H Tim McCoy). **1935:** *Stone of Silver Creek* (H Buck Jones); *Blazing Guns* (H Reb Russell); *Gun Play* (H Big Boy Williams); *Rio Rattler* (H Tom Tyler). **1936:** *The Idaho Kid* (H Rex Bell); *Romance Rides the Range* (H Fred Scott); *Cavalcade of the West* (H Hoot Gibson).

Dorothy Short

Dorothy Short was a busy actress during the decade from the mid-1930s to the mid-1940s. She appeared in the top-rated action serials *Call of the Savage* (1935) and *Capt. Midnight* (1941).

She was in comedy shorts like the Pete Smith Specialties and comedy action features such as *Spooks Run Wild* (1941) with Bela Lugosi and the Dead End Kids.

Though she made Westerns with cowboys like Tim McCoy, Ken Maynard, Tex Ritter and Jack Randall, her best B Western film role came in the 1938 Hopalong Cassidy feature *Heart of Arizona*. In that film she portrayed Jackie Starr, daughter of the notorious outlaw Belle Starr. She was in love with Lucky Jenkins, while her mama carried a torch for Cassidy. The film was one of the better Cassidy entries and showed why the Cassidy films offered better parts and more important roles for women than did other B's.

Dorothy Short Filmography

1938: *Heart of Arizona* (H Hopalong Cassidy); *Wild Horse Canyon* (H Jack Randall); *Where the Buffalo Roam* (H Tex Ritter). **1939:** *The Singing Cowgirl* (H Dorothy Page). **1940:** *Phantom Rancher* (H Ken Maynard);

Frontier Crusader (*H* Tim McCoy). **1941:** *Lone Rider Fights Back* (*H* George Houston). **1942:** *Bullets for Bandits* (*H* Wild Bill Elliott).

Louise Stanley

Between 1937 and 1940 Louise Stanley served as leading lady in 14 B Western films.

She made films with Bob Steele, Tex Ritter, Johnny Mack Brown and Renfrew of the Royal Mounted (James Newell), but she was the favorite leading lady of Monogram cowboy Jack Randall.

She was also Mrs. Jack Randall, and there abound stories that it was indeed Mrs. Randall who taught Mr. Randall how to ride a horse.

Stanley was featured in Johnny Mack Brown's 1939 Universal serial *The Oregon Trail.*

She was seen in films such as *Paid to Dance* (1937), *Personal Secretary* (1938) and in the delightful 1938 college musical *Start Cheering* which starred Jimmy Durante, the Three Stooges and cowboy star Charles Starrett.

Louise Stanley Filmography

1937: *Lawless Land* (*H* Johnny Mack Brown); *Gun Lords of Stirrup Basin* (*H* Bob Steele); *Sing, Cowboy, Sing* (*H* Tex Ritter); *Riders of the Rockies* (*H* Tex Ritter). **1938:** *Thunder in the Desert* (*H* Bob Steele); *Land of Fighting Men* (*H* Jack Randall); *Gunsmoke Trail* (*H* Jack Randall); *Durango Valley Raiders* (*H* Bob Steele); *Gun Packer* (*H* Jack Randall). **1939:** *The Oregon Trail* (serial) (*H* Johnny Mack Brown). **1940:** *Yukon Flight* (*H* James Newell [Renfrew]); *The Cheyenne Kid* (*H* Jack Randall); *Pinto Canyon* (*H* Bob Steele); *Land of the Six Guns* (*H* Jack Randall); *Sky Bandits* (*H* James Newell [Renfrew]). **1944:** *Wells Fargo Days* (short) (*H* Dennis Moore).

Eleanor Stewart

Eleanor Stewart was one of the most popular Western leading ladies of the late thirties and early forties.

She appeared with a wide and varied caliber of screen heroes that ranged from Hopalong Cassidy, Tex Ritter and Bob Steele to lesser-knowns like Jack Luden, Bob Custer and Bob Allen. She also appeared with Ken Maynard in the twilight of her career. The "Hoppys" were far and away her best Westerns.

Eleanor, who spent most of her career in B pictures, appeared in films like *Trapped by G-Men* (1937) and *Waterloo Bridge* (1940).

She was the heroine of the 1938 Republic serial *Fighting Devil Dogs* which starred Lee "the Lone Ranger" Powell.

Eleanor Stewart Filmography

1936: *Headin' for the Rio Grande* (H Tex Ritter). **1937:** *Arizona Days* (H Tex Ritter); *The Gun Ranger* (H Bob Steele); *Santa Fe Rides* (H Bob Custer); *The Rangers Step In* (H Bob Allen); *Where Trails Divide* (H Tom Keene). **1938:** *The Painted Trail* (H Tom Keene); *Rolling Caravans* (H Jack Luden); *Stagecoach Days* (H Jack Luden); *Mexicali Kid* (H Jack Randall). **1939:** *Flaming Lead* (H Ken Maynard). **1941:** *Riders of the Timberline* (H Hopalong Cassidy); *Pirates on Horseback* (H Hopalong Cassidy). **1944:** *Mystery Man* (H Hopalong Cassidy).

Peggy Stewart

Florida native Peggy Stewart made over two dozen cowboy features and four Western serials in her film career. Peggy rates as one of the genre's most popular heroines.

At Republic Pictures in the mid-forties she was featured in eight films with Sunset Carson as well as co-starring with other Republic stars like Rocky Lane, Wild Bill Elliott, Roy Rogers and Gene Autry.

After leaving Republic, she continued to make Westerns with the likes of Lash LaRue, Charles Starrett and Whip Wilson.

One interesting note is that Peggy appeared as leading lady to all three of the B Western's Red Ryders: Bill Elliott, Rocky Lane and Jim Bannon.

All of her serial appearances came at Republic. Her first was in *The Phantom Rider* in 1946, followed by *The Son of Zorro* in 1947, *Tex Granger* in 1948 and *Cody of the Pony Express* in 1950.

Peggy was born in West Palm Beach, Florida, and raised in Atlanta, Georgia, and southern California. She studied acting at the Pasadena Playhouse and made her screen debut in the 1937 super–Western *Wells*

Louise Stanley

Fargo. Aside from Westerns she appeared in films such as *The Little Tough Guys* (1938), *That Certain Age* (1938), *Little Tough Guys in Society* (1938) and *Back Street* (1941).

Eleanor Stewart with (from left to right) William Boyd, Jimmy Rogers and Forrest Taylor in Mystery Man *(1944).*

Her acting career continued into the 1970s with appearances on such popular TV shows as *Grizzly Adams* and *Quincy*.

Peggy often appears at film fairs and Western film conventions.

Peggy Stewart Filmography

1944: *Tucson Raiders* (H Wild Bill Elliott); *Silver City Kid* (H Rocky Lane); *Stagecoach to Monterey* (H Rocky Lane); *Cheyenne Wildcat* (H Bill Elliott [Red Ryder]); *Code of the Prairie* (H Sunset Carson); *Firebrands of Arizona* (H Sunset Carson); *Sheriff of Las Vegas* (H Bill Elliott [Red Ryder]). **1945:** *Utah* (H Roy Rogers); *Oregon Trail* (H Sunset Carson); *Bandits of the Bad Lands* (H Sunset Carson); *Marshal of Laredo* (H Bill Elliott [Red Ryder]); *Rough Riders of Cheyenne* (H Sunset Carson). **1946:** *The Phantom Rider* (serial) (H Robert Kent); *California Gold Rush* (H Bill Elliott [Red Ryder]); *Days of Buffalo Bill* (H Sunset Carson); *Alias Billy the Kid* (H Sunset Carson); *Red River Renegades* (H Sunset Carson); *Conquest of Cheyenne* (H

Peggy Stewart

Bill Elliott [Red Ryder]); *Sheriff of Redwood Valley* (H Bill Elliott [Red Ryder]); *Stagecoach to Denver* (H Rocky Lane [Red Ryder]). **1947:** *Son of Zorro* (serial) (H George Turner); *Trail to San Antone* (H Gene Autry); *Vigilantes of Boom Town* (H Rocky Lane [Red Ryder]); *Rustlers of Devils Canyon* (H Rocky Lane [Red Ryder]). **1948:** *Tex Granger* (serial) (H Robert Kellard); *Dead Man's Gold* (H Lash LaRue); *Frontier Revenge* (H Lash LaRue). **1949:** *Ride Ryder Ride* (H Jim Bannon [Red Ryder]); *The Fighting*

Redhead (H Jim Bannon [Red Ryder]); *The Desert Vigilante* (H Charles Starrett [Durango Kid]). **1950:** *Cody of the Pony Express* (serial) (H Jock O'Mahoney). **1952:** *The Black Lash* (H Lash LaRue); *Kansas Territory* (H Bill Elliott); *Montana Incident* (H Whip Wilson).

Linda Stirling

Linda Stirling was Republic Pictures' serial queen of the 1940s. She starred in some of the best action chapter plays ever made. Lovely Linda, villain Roy Barcroft and the amazing Republic stunt crew were some of the reasons that Republic turned out the top serials of the era.

In 1944 Linda starred in the first of her six Republic serials, a jungle epic titled *The Tiger Woman* in which she had the title role. Her co-star was soon-to-be top cowboy star Allen "Rocky" Lane. Next up was a Western adventure, *Zorro's Black Whip*, in which she played the Black Whip, a mysterious night rider who battled the bad guys with guns and bullwhips. This serial was a turnabout to most of its peers because in it the heroine kept saving the hero's (played by George Lewis) hide instead of vice versa.

In 1945 she made the best of her serials, a mystery thriller called *Manhunt of Mystery Island*. Throughout 15 exciting chapters Linda is menaced by one of the movies all-time great villains, Roy Barcroft as Captain Mephisto, the reincarnation of a sixteenth-century pirate with twentieth-century schemes and weapons. Two other mystery adventures followed, *The Purple Monster Strikes Again* (1945) and *The Crimson Ghost* in 1946.

Her final serial was a Western, *Jesse James Rides Again*, in 1947. Her co-stars were Clayton "the Lone Ranger" Moore as Jesse James, the hero, and Roy Barcroft as the main baddie.

Linda Stirling was also one of Republic's top B Western leading ladies. She appeared in nine Westerns, four with Sunset Carson, two with Rocky Lane and the remainder with Wild Bill Elliott in his Red Ryder series.

Her films with Carson were her best, and they included one of the best B Westerns ever made, *The Cherokee Flash*, in 1945. Their film *Santa Fe Saddlemates* also rates high.

She also appeared in films like *The Powers Girl* (1943) and *The Pretender* (1947).

Linda was married to Sloan Nibley, who authored many of Republic's serial and B Western scripts.

Linda Stirling

Linda Stirling Filmography

1944: *The San Antonio Kid* (H Bill Elliott [Red Ryder]); *Sheriff of Sundown* (H Rocky Lane); *Vigilantes of Dodge City* (H Bill Elliott [Red Ryder]); *Zorro's Black Whip* (serial) (H Title role). **1945:** *The Topeka Terror* (H Rocky Lane); *Sheriff of Cimarron* (H Sunset Carson); *Santa Fe Saddlemates* (H Sunset Carson); *The Cherokee Flash* (H Sunset Carson); *Wagon Wheels*

Linda Stirling and Sunset Carson. Stirling's films with Carson were her best.

Westward (H Bill Elliott [Red Ryder]). **1946:** *Rio Grande Raiders* (H Sunset Carson). **1947:** *Jesse James Rides Again* (serial) (H Clayton Moore).

June Storey

Sagebrush crooner Gene Autry serenaded lovely June Storey in ten films in 1939 and 1940, including some of his best films like *Colorado Sunset* and *South of the Border.*

June's character always seemed to have a tagalong friend, roommate or kid sister who was usually played by Barbara Pepper or Mary Lee.

Storey had begun making films in the mid-thirties and had appeared in films like *Girl's Dormitory* (1936), *In Old Chicago* (1938) and *Island in the Sky* (1938) before making her Western debut with Autry in *Home on the Range.*

After her stint as Gene's leading lady, June continued to appear in films like *The Lone Wolf Takes a Chance* (1941) and *The Strange Woman*

June Storey and Gene Autry. The pair made ten films together in 1939–40 for Republic Studios.

(1941). Later she would have a part in the critically-acclaimed film The Snake Pit (1948) which starred Olivia de Havilland.

June Storey Filmography

1939: *Home on the Range* (H Gene Autry); *Blue Montana Skies* (H Gene Autry); *Mountain Rhythm* (H Gene Autry); *Colorado Sunset* (H Gene Autry); *In Old Monterey* (H Gene Autry); *South of the Border* (H Gene Autry). **1940:** *Rancho Grande* (H Gene Autry); *Gaucho Serenade* (H Gene Autry); *Carolina Moon* (H Gene Autry); *Ride Tenderfoot Ride* (H Gene Autry). **1945:** *Song of the Prairie* (H Ken Curtis).

Virginia Vale

Virginia Vale

Virginia Vale was one of the most beautiful women to ever grace the Western screen. She was an RKO Studio contract player whose golden voice matched her beauty.

She co-starred with RKO's number one cowboy of the late thirties, George O'Brien, in six films.

Most of Virginia's Westerns were 15-minute musical shorts that starred Ray Whitley and his Six Bar Cowboys.

She was also in films like *You Can't Fool Your Wife, Millionaires in Prison* and *Crime Inc.*

Virginia Vale Filmography

1939: *Marshal of Mesa City* (H George O'Brien). **1940:** *Legion of the Lawless* (H George O'Brien); *Bullet Code* (H George O'Brien); *Prairie Law* (H George O'Brien); *Stage to Chino* (H George O'Brien); *Triple Justice* (H George O'Brien). **1941:** *Robbers of the Range* (H Tim Holt).

Luana Walters

When Gene Autry sang the words "Mexicali Rose keep smilin', I'll be coming back some sunny day" in his 1939 film *Mexicali Rose*, lovely Luana Walters was the gal he was singing to.

Between 1932 and 1942 Luana Walters was either rescued or romanced (or both) by almost every major B Western cowboy of the era. Tim McCoy, Buck Jones, Wild Bill Elliott, Charles Starrett and Autry were among the ones in whose films she served as leading lady.

Among the better films in which she appeared were the aforementioned *Mexicali Rose, The Durango Kid* in 1940 with Starrett and Tim McCoy's *Aces and Eights* in 1936.

On the other side of the coin, Walters was equally adept at playing villainesses, as witnessed by her role as the evil Fury Shark in the 1942 Columbia serial *Capt. Midnight.* For fifteen chapters Fury and her equally-evil father Ivan Shark, (James Craven) menaced the heroic combo of Dave O'Brien and Dorothy Short.

She had a semivillainous part in the 1936 serial *Shadow of Chinatown* and was the good girl in Republic's *Drums of Fu Manchu* in 1940.

Luana Walters appeared in a variety of films including *Miss Pinkerton* (1932) with Joan Blondell and *Algiers* (1938) with Charles Boyer.

Luana Walters Filmography

1932: *End of the Trail* (H Tim McCoy). **1933:** *Fighting Texans* (H Rex Bell). **1936:** *Ride 'em Cowboy* (H Buck Jones); *Aces and Eights* (H Tim McCoy). **1937:** *Under Strange Flags* (H Tom Keene). **1938:** *Where the West Begins* (H Jack Randall). **1939:** *Mexicali Rose* (H Gene Autry). **1940:** *Tulsa Kid* (H Don "Red" Barry); *The Durango Kid* (H Charles Starrett); *Return of Wild Bill* (H Wild Bill Elliott). **1941:** *Across the Sierras* (H Wild Bill Elliott); *Arizona Bound* (H Rough Riders). **1942:** *Lone Star Vigilantes* (H Wild Bill Elliott); *Down Texas Way* (H Rough Riders); *Thundering Hoofs* (H Tim

Joan Woodbury

Holt); *Lawless Plainsmen* (H Charles Starrett); *Bad Men of the Hills* (H
Charles Starrett).

Joan Woodbury

Lovely Joan Woodbury made over 70 feature films in her career, including ten B Westerns with some of America's best-known cowboy stars. She did films with Hopalong Cassidy, Roy Rogers, Tex Ritter, Tim McCoy, Johnny Mack Brown and Bob Steele.

She appeared in one of the better Cassidy films, *The Eagles Brood*, in 1935 and the following year in *Song of the Gringo* she was Tex Ritter's first leading lady.

Joan was also seen in B mysteries like *Charlie Chan on Broadway* (1937), *Confessions of Boston Blackie* (1941) and *The Whistler* (1944); and major films like *Algiers* (1938) and *The Ten Commandments* (1956).

Joan Woodbury starred in the 1945 Columbia serial *Brenda Starr, Reporter*.

She retired from films in 1960. At one time she was married to noted film actor Henry Wilcoxon.

Joan Woodbury Filmography

1935: *The Eagle's Brood* (H Hopalong Cassidy); *Bulldog Courage* (H Tim McCoy). **1936:** *The Lion's Den* (H Tim McCoy); *Song of the Gringo* (H Tex Ritter). **1937:** *The Luck of Roaring Camp*. **1941:** *In Old Cheyenne* (H Roy Rogers); *Ride on Vaquero* (H Cisco Kid). **1942:** *Sunset Serenade* (H Roy Rogers). **1945:** *Flame of the West* (H Johnny Mack Brown); *Northwest Trail* (H Bob Steele).

THE
BAD GUYS

Charlie King, Ace, Blackie and the Rest of the the Boys from Skull Bone Pass

They were called outlaws, bad guys, villains, gunslingers, desperadoes, owlhoots, varmints, bushwhackers, polecats, drygulchers, banditos and a hundred other less than flattering names.

They had names like Butch, Ace, Slick and Blackie.

They skulked about in places like Dark Canyon, El Dorado Pass, Black Horse Canyon, Circle Canyon, Hell Canyon, Devil's Canyon, Gunsmoke Mesa, Golden Gulch and Skull Bone Pass just waiting for a chance to swoop down upon and pillage, rob and plunder the peaceful denizens of such quaint Western hamlets as Cripple Creek, Ghost City, Gun Town, Stirrup Basin, Red Rock, Red Gap and the familiar Mesa City.

They were the bad men of the B Western movies, and without their ever-threatening presence the B would have stood for Borrrring.

You see, quite simply put, without a whole shebang of bad guys to battle, a cowboy hero was just another actor with a guitar and a couple of guns.

The onscreen life of a B Western bad man was not a glamorous one. While heroes sat around a roaring campfire singing love songs to a cowgirl, sometimes 15 or 20 bad guys were crowded into a one-room shack or cave playing poker and subsisting on coffee and beans. Heroes rode white stallions and golden palominos; bad guys rode the same old brown horses over and over again. Girls swooned when Roy and Gene rode by, but they slapped Roy Barcroft's face on sight. Villains were always second best. Heroes could outdraw 'em, outslug 'em and of course outsing 'em.

There also was no honor among celluloid thieves. While the gang languished in the hide-out, the boss was always snug in his bank, ranch house or saloon with the ill-gotten loot tucked away in his safe.

If a member of the gang was caught, you could bet the varmint would be plugged before he could spill the boss's name to the sheriff, and in the end the brains of the outfit always grabbed the cash and skedaddled.

B Western villains fell into two categories: the boss or "brains" heavies and the henchmen or action heavies. The latter were the saloon brawl and gunfight guys.

Another interesting note about B Western outlaws is this: In the thirties and early forties outlaw gangs were huge with large numbers of members, but by the end of the era they had dwindled to trios. Because of rising production costs, more owlhoots fell from the lead in some accountant's pencil than from the lead in a hero's six-shooter.

The actors who portrayed these sagebrush scoundrels were almost an exclusive fraternity unto themselves with the same faces appearing in picture after picture. Most were cast in countless Westerns in roles that ranged from the boss in one to a bit part in the next.

Most of them were veterans of the silent screen era, and most of their total screen careers were built around cowboy pictures and cliff-hangers. The best known of the corps — Roy Barcroft, Charles King, and Fred Kohler, Sr. — at most only attained a cult following, while others like Charles Middleton became well known because of roles in other vehicles.

The most famous actor to rise out of B Western villainy was Robert Mitchum, who began his film career battling Hopalong Cassidy in the early forties. Other familiar names like Joseph Sawyer, Ward Bond, Lon Chaney, Jr., Onslow Stevens, Morris Ankrum, Victor Jory and *Gunsmoke*'s Doc Adams (Milburn Stone) cut their movie teeth as B bad men.

While most of the villains in B Westerns were male, occasionally there was a female at the head of a band of crooks. The best remembered portrayals of gal gangleaders belong to Lynne Carver as the snooty society leader of modern-day cattle rustlers in Roy Rogers' 1942 film *The Man from Cheyenne* and Evelyn Brent's role as Lilli Marsh, who sacrificed herself for Hopalong Cassidy in the 1936 *Hopalong Cassidy Returns.*

Even top B leading ladies like Jennifer Holt and Christine McIntyre portrayed bad girls at one time or another.

B Western heels as a whole were in all actuality a very simplistic lot when compared to the megalomaniacal villains of, say, a James Bond film or even to Ming the Merciless. Very few indulged in grandiose schemes. Most were your basic blue collar bad guy who only wanted to steal some gold, have a beer, kiss a saloon girl and head for the border.

* * *

Ted Adams

Perennial Western player Ted Adams alternated between playing lawmen like the sheriff in Tex Fletcher's 1939 release *Six-Gun Rhythm* and gunslingers like Jim Trask in the 1936 Hopalong Cassidy adventure *Three on the Trail.*

Adams can be spotted in scores of films throughout the thirties and forties.

Like most B Western actors Adams made his share of serials, including *The Mysterious Pilot* (1937), *Holt of the Secret Service* (1941), *Daredevils of the West* (1943), *Dangers of the Canadian Mounted* (1948) and *King of the Rocket Men* (1949).

He was also seen in A Westerns like the 1941 version of *Billy the Kid* with Robert Taylor.

Ted Adams Filmography

1931: *God's Country and the Man* (H Tom Tyler); *Riders of the Plains* (H Tom Tyler); *The Ridin Fool* (H Bob Steele); *Cavalier of the West* (H Harry Carey). **1932:** *Ghost Valley* (H Tom Keene); *Beyond the Rockies* (H Tom Keene); *Battling Buckaroo* (H Lane Chandler). **1933:** *War on the Range* (H Tom Tyler). **1935:** *Hopalong Cassidy* (H Hopalong Cassidy); *His Fighting Blood* (H Kermit Maynard); *Lawless Borders* (H Bill Cody); *Gunfire* (H Rex Bell); *Toll of the Desert* (H Fred Kohler, Jr.). **1936:** *Border Caballero* (H Tim McCoy); *Desert Phantom* (H Johnny Mack Brown); *Three on the Trail* (H Hopalong Cassidy); *The Crooked Trail* (H Johnny Mack Brown); *Undercover Man* (H Johnny Mack Brown); *Trail Dust* (H Hopalong Cassidy). **1937:** *Lawless Land* (H Johnny Mack Brown); *Guns in the Dark* (H Johnny Mack Brown); *Smoketree Range* (H Buck Jones); *Arizona Gunfighter* (H Bob Steele); *Colorado Kid* (H Bob Steele). **1938:** *Gunsmoke Trail* (H Jack Randall); *Desert Patrol* (H Bob Steele); *Durango Valley Raiders* (H Bob Steele); *Pals of the Saddle* (H 3 Mesquiteers); *Lightning Carson Rides Again* (H Tim McCoy); *Six Gun Trail* (H Tim McCoy). **1939:** *Trigger Pals* (H Art Jarrett); *Six-Gun Rhythm* (H Tex Fletcher); *Code of the Cactus* (H Tim McCoy); *Texas Wildcats* (H Tim McCoy); *Outlaw's Paradise* (H Tim McCoy); *Mesquite Buckaroo* (H Bob Steele); *Three Texas Steers* (H 3 Mesquiteers); *Riders of the Sage* (H Bob Steele); *The Fighting Renegade* (H Tim McCoy); *The Pal from Texas* (H Bob Steele); *Fighting Mad* (H James Newell); *El Diablo Rides* (H Bob Steele); *Crashing Thru* (H James Newell); *Straight Shooter* (H Tim McCoy); *Trigger Fingers* (H Tim McCoy). **1940:** *Pioneer Days* (H Jack Randall); *Wild Horse Valley* (H Bob Steele);

Ted Adams

Phantom Rancher (H Ken Maynard); *Riders of Pasco Basin* (H Johnny Mack Brown); *Pinto Canyon* (H Bob Steele); *Gaucho Serenade* (H Gene Autry); *Riders from Nowhere* (H Jack Randall); *Frontier Crusader* (H Tim McCoy); *Sky Bandits* (H James Newill); *Billy the Kid Outlawed* (H Bob Steele); *Gun Code* (H Tim McCoy); *Law and Order* (H Johnny Mack Brown); *Billy the Kid's Gun Justice* (H Bob Steele). **1941:** *Billy the Kid's Range War* (H Bob Steele); *Frontier Fury* (H George Houston); *Lone Rider Ambushed* (H George Houston); *Fighting Bill Fargo* (H Johnny Mack Brown). **1942:** *Rolling Down the Great Divide* (H Bill Boyd); *Billy the Kid's Smoking Guns* (H Buster Crabbe); *Law and Order* (H Buster Crabbe); *Along the Sundown Trail* (H Bill Boyd); *The Mysterious Rider* (H Buster Crabbe); *Outlaws of Boulder Pass* (H George Houston); *Overland Stagecoach* (H Bob Livingston). **1943:** *The Kid Rides Again* (H Buster Crabbe); *Cattle Stampede* (H Buster Crabbe); *Hail to the Rangers* (H Charles Starrett). **1944:** *Saddle Leather Law* (H Charles Starrett). **1946:** *Under Arizona*

Skies (H Johnny Mack Brown); *The Gentleman from Texas* (H Johnny Mack Brown); *Red River Renegades* (H Sunset Carson); *Trigger Fingers* (H Johnny Mack Brown); *Shadows on the Range* (H Johnny Mack Brown); *Silver Range* (H Johnny Mack Brown). **1947:** *Raiders of the South* (H Johnny Mack Brown); *Valley of Fear* (H Johnny Mack Brown); *Song of the Wasteland* (H Jimmy Wakely); *Code of the Saddle* (H Johnny Mack Brown); *Flashing Guns* (H Johnny Mack Brown); *Buckaroo from Powder River* (H Charles Starrett); *Prairie Express* (H Johnny Mack Brown). **1948:** *Overland Trails* (H Johnny Mack Brown); *Crossed Trails* (H Johnny Mack Brown); *Frontier Agent* (H Johnny Mack Brown); *Back Trail* (H Johnny Mack Brown); *Sheriff of Medicine Bow* (H Johnny Mack Brown); *Gunning for Justice* (H Johnny Mack Brown); *Quick on the Trigger* (H Charles Starrett). **1949:** *Gun River* (H Jimmy Wakely); *Across the Rio Grande* (H Jimmy Wakely); *Haunted Trails* (H Whip Wilson). **1950:** *Hills of Oklahoma* (H Rex Allen); *Arizona Territory* (H Whip Wilson). **1951:** *Night Riders of Montana* (H Rocky Lane).

Richard Alexander

Overall in his screen career big Richard Alexander is probably best remembered for his role as Prince Barin, the powerful ally of Flash Gordon, in two of the three Flash Gordon serials, *Flash Gordon* in 1936 and *Flash Gordon's Trip to Mars* in 1938.

Alexander spent a good deal of his career playing B Western and serial bullies like El Lobo in the 1937 Republic serial *Zorro Rides Again*.

His forte was playing brutes and bushwhackers, never the brains of the outfit.

He appeared in B Westerns like *Forbidden Trails* with the Rough Riders and major films like *All Quiet on the Western Front, Law and Order* and *The Big Broadcast of 1936.*

Other cliff-hanger appearances included *The Law of the Wild, The Clutching Hand, S.O.S. Coast Guard* and *Sea Raiders.*

Richard Alexander Filmography

1930: *Lone Star Ranger* (H George O'Brien). **1931:** *Hurricane Horseman* (H Lane Chandler). **1932:** *The Sunset Trail* (H Ken Maynard); *One Man Law* (H Buck Jones); *Two Fisted Law* (H Tim McCoy); *Texas Badman* (H Tom Mix); *Daring Danger* (H Tim McCoy). **1933:** *The Fighting Code* (H Buck

Jones). **1934:** *Cowboy Holiday* (*H* Big Boy Williams). **1935:** *Cowboy and the Bandit* (*H* Rex Lease); *Riding Wild* (*H* Tim McCoy); *Coyote Trails* (*H* Tom Tyler); *Every Man's Law* (*H* Johnny Mack Brown); *Mystery Range* (*H* Tom Tyler); *Outlaws of the Prairie* (*H* Charles Starrett). **1938:** *Where the West Begins* (*H* Jack Randall); *On the Great White Trail* (*H* James Newill). **1939:** *Kansas Terrors* (*H* 3 Mesquiteers). **1940:** *Death Rides the Range* (*H* Ken Maynard); *Covered Wagon Days* (*H* 3 Mesquiteers); *Son of Roaring Dan* (*H* Johnny Mack Brown). **1941:** *Boss of Bullion City* (*H* Johnny Mack Brown); *Man from Montana* (*H* Johnny Mack Brown). **1942:** *Code of the Outlaw* (*H* 3 Mesquiteers).

Morris Ankrum

aka: Stephen Morris

Morris Ankrum was the chief bad guy in some of the best of the films in the Hopalong Cassidy series. He appeared in such Hoppys as *Hopalong Cassidy Returns* (1936), *Trail Dust* (1936), *Borderland* (1937), *Hills of Old Wyoming* (1937), *North of the Rio Grande* (1937), *Rustler's Valley* (1937), *Three Men from Texas* (1940), *Wide Open Town* (1941), *Doomed Caravan* (1941) and *Pirates on Horseback* (1941).

Ankrum's bad guy portrayals were some of the best ever in B Westerns, and several of his characters were unforgettable. He was the double-dealin' Blackie in *Hopalong Cassidy Returns,* rustler Tex Anderson in *Trail Dust,* the mysterious bandit leader the Lone Wolf in *North of the Rio Grande* and a villainous bandito known only as the Fox in *Borderland.*

Ankrum enjoyed a long and prosperous career as an actor (over 75 films) and as a director. Some of the films in which he appeared include *Thirty Seconds Over Tokyo* (1944), *Joan of Arc* (1948), *The Postman Always Rings Twice* (1946), *My Favorite Spy* (1951), *Vera Cruz* (1954) and *The Man with the X-Ray Eyes* (1963).

Morris Ankrum was born Morris Nussbaum on August 28, 1897, in Danville, Illinois, and he passed away on September 2, 1964, in Pasadena, California.

Morris Ankrum Filmography

1936: *Hopalong Cassidy Returns* (*H* Hopalong Cassidy); *Trail Dust* (*H* Hopalong Cassidy). **1937:** *Borderland* (*H* Hopalong Cassidy); *Hills of Old*

Richard Alexander's forte was playing brutes and bushwhackers (left). He is best remembered, however, for his portrayal of Prince Barin (right) as seen here in Flash Gordon's Trip to Mars *(1938).*

Wyoming (H Hopalong Cassidy); *North of the Rio Grande* (H Hopalong Cassidy); *Rustlers Valley* (H Hopalong Cassidy). **1940:** *Knights of the Range* (H Russell Hayden); *The Showdown* (H Hopalong Cassidy); *Three Men from Texas* (H Hopalong Cassidy); *Light of the Western Stars* (H Russell Hayden). **1941:** *In Old Colorado* (H Hopalong Cassidy); *Border Vigilantes* (H Hopalong Cassidy); *Wide Open Town* (H Hopalong Cassidy); *Doomed Caravan* (H Hopalong Cassidy); *Pirates on Horseback* (H Hopalong Cassidy); *Road Agent* (H Dick Foran); *The Bandit Trail* (H Tim Holt).

Roy Barcroft

When it comes to picking the best of the B Western baddies, Roy Barcroft gets the nod. Between his work in horse operas and serials Barcroft ranks as one of filmdom's all-time great villains.

For over a decade he was the lead heel at the Republic thrill factory, and in over 150 Westerns and numerous chapter plays he was the master of every kind of nefarious deed in the book.

Roy Barcroft

Roy Barcroft was born Howard H. Ravenscroft on September 7, 1902, in Crab Orchard, Nebraska, and made his screen debut in the 1932 Garbo film *Mata Hari*.

Barcroft made his first appearance in a serial as one of Bela Lugosi's henchmen in the 1937 Republic mystery serial *S.O.S. Coast Guard*. In 1939 he played Col. George Custer in Johnny Mack Brown's *The Oregon Trail* for Universal Pictures. That year he made *The Phantom Creeps* also for Universal. Barcroft made 31 serials, five of them Westerns.

His first role as the lead villain in a serial came in the 1944 adventure *Haunted Harbor* which was made by Republic.

His most memorable portrayal in a serial, possibly in his career, came in the 1946 mystery thriller *Manhunt of Mystery Island* which starred Republic's serial queen Linda Stirling. In it he played an eighteenth-century pirate, Captain Mephisto. In the story line, by the use of a "transformation chair" another villain (Kenne Duncan) was able to reincarnate himself as Mephisto to accomplish his evil work.

Roy Barcroft became a fixture in B Westerns by the late 1930s by appearing in scores of films with Hopalong Cassidy, Gene Autry, the Three Mesquiteers, Johnny Mack Brown, Buck Jones, Roy Rogers, Tim Holt and others, and almost always in the role of a bad guy. In late 1942 he signed an exclusive contract with Republic Pictures and began menacing the studio's corps of cowboy heroes that included Rogers, Don "Red" Barry, Wild Bill Elliott and later Sunset Carson, Rocky Lane and Monte Hale.

From 1944 until the end of the B Western era in 1954 Barcroft was the chief Republic villain.

Although he portrayed dozens of robbers, killers, rustlers and the like, a couple of his offbeat roles stand out: that of a mysterious, belligerent farmer whom everyone suspects as being the head of an outlaw gang (but he isn't, Surprise! Surprise!) in Rocky Lane's 1948 *Desperadoes of Dodge City*; and as the title character in Sunset Carson's superior 1945 Western *The Cherokee Flash*, a retired robber and Sunset's father, who is framed for murder.

Barcroft is at his evil best in *The Eyes of Texas*, a 1948 Roy Rogers adventure in which Barcroft and Nana Bryant as a crooked lawyer use a pack of wild dogs to murder those who stood in their way.

Besides the B's he also appeared in big production Westerns like *Man Without a Star*, *The Spoilers*, and *Bandolero*.

It must be noted that Roy Barcroft appeared in the final B Western, Wayne Morris's *Two Guns and a Badge* (1954).

Roy Barcroft was still active in film work at the time of his death on November 28, 1969, a victim a cancer.

Roy Barcroft Filmography

1938: *Heroes of the Hills* (H 3 Mesquiteers); *Stranger from Arizona* (H Buck Jones); *The Frontiersman* (H Hopalong Cassidy); *Flaming Frontiers* (H Johnny Mack Brown). **1939:** *Silver on the Sage* (H Hopalong Cassidy); *Mexicali Rose* (H Gene Autry); *The Renegade Trail* (H Hopalong Cassidy); *The Oregon Trail* (H Johnny Mack Brown); *Crashing Thru* (H James Newill). **1940:** *Winners of the West* (H Dick Foran); *Deadwood Dick* (serial) (*H* Don Douglas); *Rancho Grande* (*H* Gene Autry); *Hidden Gold* (*H* Hopalong Cassidy); *Yukon Flight* (*H* James Newill); *Stage to Chino* (*H* George O'Brien); *Ragtime Cowboy Joe* (*H* Johnny Mack Brown); *Trailing Double Trouble* (*H* Range Busters); *The Showdown* (*H* Hopalong Cassidy). **1941**: *Pals of the Pecos* (*H* 3 Mesquiteers); *The Bandit Trail* (*H* Tim Holt); *Wide Open Town* (*H* Hopalong Cassidy); *Jesse James at Bay* (*H* Roy Rogers); *Outlaws of the Cherokee Trail* (*H* 3 Mesquiteers); *The Masked Rider* (*H* Johnny Mack Brown); *West of Cimarron* (*H* 3 Mesquiteers); *King of the Texas Rangers* (*H* Slingin' Sammy Baugh); *Riders of Death Valley* (*H* Dick Foran); *Sheriff of Tombstone* (*H* Roy Rogers); *White Eagle* (*H* Buck Jones); *Riders of the Badlands* (*H* Charles Starrett). **1942**: *Valley of Vanishing Men* (*H* Wild Bill Elliott); *Lone Rider in Cheyenne* (*H* George Houston); *Northwest Rangers* (*H* James Craig); *Stardust on the Sage* (*H* Gene Autry); *Dawn on the Great Divide* (*H* Buck Jones); *Land of the Open Range* (*H* Tim Holt); *West of the Law* (*H* Rough Riders); *Romance on the Range* (*H* Roy Rogers); *Sunset on the Desert* (*H* Roy Rogers); *Below the Border* (*H* Rough Riders); *Pirates of the Prairie* (*H* Tim Holt). **1943**: *Hoppy Serves a Writ* (*H* Hopalong Cassidy); *False Colors* (*H* Hopalong Cassidy); *Man from the Rio Grande* (*H* Don Barry); *Cheyenne Roundup* (*H* Johnny Mack Brown); *Calling Wild Bill Elliott* (*H* Wild Bill Elliott); *Carson City Cyclone* (*H* Don Barry); *Stranger from Pecos* (*H* Johnny Mack Brown); *Border Town Gunfighters* (*H* Wild Bill Elliott); *Wagon Tracks West* (*H* Wild Bill Elliott); *Raiders of Sunset Pass* (*H* Eddie Dew); *The Old Chisholm Trail* (*H* Johnny Mack Brown); *Sagebrush Law* (*H* Tim Holt); *Idaho* (*H* Roy Rogers); *In Old Oklahoma* (*H* John Wayne); *Man from Music Mountain* (*H* Roy Rogers); *Overland Mail Robbery* (*H* Wild Bill Elliott); *Six Gun Gospel* (*H* Johnny Mack Brown). **1944**: *Tucson Raiders* (*H* Wild Bill Elliott); *Laramie Trail* (*H* Robert Livingston); *Hidden Valley Outlaws* (*H* Wild Bill Elliott); *Code of the Prairie* (*H* Sunset Carson); *Lights of Old Santa Fe* (*H* Roy Rogers); *Stagecoach to Monterey* (*H* Rocky Lane); *Firebrands of Arizona* (*H* Sunset Carson); *Sheriff of Sundown* (*H* Rocky Lane); *Cheyenne Wildcat* (*H* Wild Bill Elliott). **1945**: *Wagon Wheels Westward* (*H* Wild Bill Elliott); *Marshal of Laredo* (*H* Wild Bill Elliott); *Bells of Rosarita* (*H* Roy Rogers); *Sunset in El Diablo* (*H* Roy Rogers); *Dakota* (*H* John Wayne); *Along the Navajo Trail* (*H* Roy Rogers); *Santa Fe Saddlemates* (*H* Sunset Carson); *Lone Texas Ranger* (*H* Wild Bill Elliott); *Colorado Pioneers* (*H* Wild Bill Elliott); *Trail of Kit Carson* (*H* Rocky Lane); *Cherokee Flash* (*H* Sunset Carson); *Topeka Terror* (*H* Rocky Lane); *Corpus Christi Bandits* (*H* Rocky Lane). **1946**: *The Plainsman and the Lady* (*H* Wild Bill Elliott); *Home on the Range* (*H* Monte Hale); *Alias Billy the Kid* (*H* Sunset Carson); *Sun Valley Cyclone* (*H* Wild Bill Elliott); *My Pal Trigger* (*H* Roy Rogers); *Stagecoach to Denver* (*H* Rocky Lane). **1947**: *Oregon Trail Scouts* (*H* Rocky Lane); *Vigilantes of Boomtown* (*H* Rocky

Lane); *Rustlers of Devil's Canyon* (H Rocky Lane); *Springtime in the Sierras* (H Roy Rogers); *Wyoming* (H Wild Bill Elliott); *Marshal of Cripple Creek* (H Rocky Lane); *Along the Oregon Trail* (H Monte Hale); *The Wild Frontier* (H Rocky Lane); *Bandits of Dark Canyon* (H Rocky Lane); *Last Frontier Uprising* (H Monte Hale); *The Fabulous Texan* (H Wild Bill Elliott); *Jesse James Rides Again* (H Clayton Moore); *Son of Zorro* (serial) (H George Turner). **1948:** *Bold Frontiersman* (H Rocky Lane); *In Old Los Angeles* (H Wild Bill Elliott); *Oklahoma Badlands* (H Rocky Lane); *The Timber Trail* (H Monte Hale); *Eyes of Texas* (H Roy Rogers); *Grand Canyon Trail* (H Roy Rogers); *Renegades of Sonora* (H Rocky Lane); *Desperadoes of Dodge City* (H Rocky Lane); *Marshal of Amarillo* (H Rocky Lane); *Sundown at Santa Fe* (H Rocky Lane); *The Gallant Legion* (H Wild Bill Elliott); *The Far Frontier* (H Roy Rogers). **1949:** *Sheriff of Wichita* (H Rocky Lane); *Prince of the Plains* (H Monte Hale); *Frontier Marshal* (H Rocky Lane); *Law of the Golden West* (H Monte Hale); *Down Dakota Way* (H Roy Rogers); *San Antone Ambush* (H Monte Hale); *Ranger of the Cherokee Strip* (H Monte Hale); *Outcasts of the Trail* (H Monte Hale); *Powder River Rustlers* (H Rocky Lane); *Ghost of Zorro* (serial) (H Clayton Moore). **1950:** *Desperadoes of the West* (serial) (H Richard Powers); *Gunmen of Abilene* (H Rocky Lane); *James Brothers of Missouri* (serial) (H Keith Richards); *Pioneer Marshal* (H Monte Hale); *The Arizona Cowboy* (H Rex Allen); *The Vanishing Westerner* (H Monte Hale); *Code of the Silver Sage* (H Rocky Lane); *Salt Lake Raiders* (H Rocky Lane); *Vigilante Hideout* (H Rocky Lane); *Rustlers on Horseback* (H Rocky Lane); *The Missourians* (H Monte Hale); *Under Mexicali Skies* (H Rex Allen); *North of the Great Divide* (H Roy Rogers). **1951:** *Wells Fargo Gunmaster* (H Rocky Lane); *In Old Amarillo* (H Roy Rogers); *Night Riders of Montana* (H Rocky Lane); *The Dakota Kid* (H Rough Ridin' Kids); *Rodeo King and the Senorita* (H Rex Allen); *Fort Dodge Stampede* (H Rocky Lane); *Arizona Manhunt* (H Rough Ridin' Kids); *Utah Wagon Train* (H Rex Allen); *Pals of the Golden West* (H Roy Rogers); *Don Daredevil Rides Again* (H Ken Curtis). **1952:** *Leadville Gunslinger* (H Rocky Lane); *Border Saddlemates* (H Rex Allen); *Wild Horse Ambush* (H Rough Ridin' Kids); *Black Hills Ambush* (H Rocky Lane); *Thundering Caravans* (H Rocky Lane); *Old Oklahoma Plains* (H Rex Allen); *Desperadoes Outpost* (H Rocky Lane); *South Pacific Trail* (H Rex Allen); *Captive of Billy the Kid* (H Rocky Lane). **1953:** *Marshal of Cedar Creek* (H Rocky Lane); *Down Laredo Way* (H Rex Allen); *Iron Mountain Trail* (H Rex Allen); *Bandits of the West* (H Rocky Lane); *Savage Frontier* (H Rocky Lane); *Old Overland Trail* (H Rex Allen); *El Paso Stampede* (H Rocky Lane); *Shadows of Tombstone* (H Rex Allen). **1954:** *The Desperado* (H Wayne Morris); *Two Guns and a Badge* (H Wayne Morris); *The Man with the Steel Whip* (H Richard Simmons).

Trevor Bardette

Trevor Bardette's gallery of rogue portrayals ranged from one of serialdom's greatest all-time villains, the mysterious Pegleg in the 1939 Columbia cliff-hanger *Overland with Kit Carson*, to old man Clanton, the bitter patriarch of the notorious Clanton clan, leading his sons into the gunfight at the O.K. Corral on TV's *Life and Legend of Wyatt Earp*.

Bardette was well known in B Western circles for his roles as outlaw masterminds in the mid- to late 1940s, most often in Republic and Columbia films.

Bardette, born in 1902, made appearances in serials like *Winners of the West*, *The Secret Code* and *The Jungle Girl* in which he played a dual role.

He portrayed the role of Clanton from 1959 to 1961 on the popular Western series which starred Hugh O'Brian in the title role.

Bardette began making films in the mid-thirties and continued into the early seventies.

Among his many screen appearances include roles in *The Oklahoma Kid* (1939), *Charlie Chan at Treasure Island* (1939), *Abe Lincoln in Illinois* (1940), *The Big Sleep* (1946), *The Mating Game* (1959) and *McKenna's Gold* (1969).

He passed away on November 28, 1977.

Trevor Bardette Filmography

1937: *Borderland* (H Hopalong Cassidy). **1938:** *In Old Mexico* (H Hopalong Cassidy). **1940:** *Wagons Westward* (H Buck Jones); *Young Buffalo Bill* (H Roy Rogers). **1941:** *Romance of the Rio Grande* (H Cesar Romero); *Doomed Caravan* (H Hopalong Cassidy); *Red River Valley* (H Roy Rogers). **1947:** *The Last Roundup* (H Gene Autry); *Marshal of Cripple Creek* (H Rocky Lane). **1948:** *Sundown in Santa Fe* (H Rocky Lane); *Marshal of Amarillo* (H Rocky Lane). **1949:** *Renegades of the Sage* (H Charles Starrett); *Sheriff of Wichita* (H Rocky Lane); *The Wyoming Bandit* (H Rocky Lane); *San Antone Ambush* (H Monte Hale). **1950:** *Hills of Oklahoma*. **1951:** *Gene Autry and the Mounties* (H Gene Autry); *Fort Dodge Stampede* (H Rocky Lane). **1953:** *Bandits of the West* (H Rocky Lane); *Red River Shore* (H Rex Allen).

Noah Beery, Sr.

Noah Beery, Sr.'s, screen villainy dates all the way back to the era of silent film. He was Douglas Fairbanks' foe in the 1920 classic swashbuckler *The Mark of Zorro*.

He also appeared in such top-rated silent adventure films as *The Sea Wolf* (1920), *The Spoilers* (1923) and *Beau Geste* (1926).

His repertoire of Western scoundrels contained such villains as Marsden, whose gang of cutthroats tried to prevent the completion of the California-Yucatán Railroad in the 1937 Republic serial *Zorro Rides Again,* Red Ryder's notorious foe, Ace Hanlon, in *The Adventures of Red Ryder* starring Don "Red" Barry, and Barry's outlaw stepfather in *The Tulsa Kid,* one of Beery's best B Western characterizations.

Beery's aristocratic appearance made him a natural to play the head heavy who gave orders to legions of lawless brigands. But he was very adept at action sequences in which he attempted to do in many a cowboy hero himself.

Beery was the brother of the legendary film actor Wallace Beery and the father of the noted character actor Noah Beery, Jr. He was born January 17, 1884, in Kansas City, Missouri, and began his film career around 1918.

His career in talkies ranged from serials like *Fighting with Kit Carson* to Mae West's *She Done Him Wrong,* to B Westerns, to B comedies like *Clancy Street Boys* with the Dead End Kids.

Noah Beery, Sr., died of a heart attack on April 1, 1946, in Los Angeles, California.

Noah Beery, Sr. Filmography

1931: *Riders of the Purple Sage* (H George O'Brien). **1932:** *Cornered* (H Tim McCoy); *The Big Stampede* (H John Wayne). **1933:** *Rustlers Roundup* (H Tom Mix). **1934:** *The Trail Beyond* (H John Wayne). **1938:** *Panamints Bad Man* (H Smith Ballew). **1939:** *Mexicali Rose* (H Gene Autry). **1940:** *The Tulsa Kid* (H Don "Red" Barry); *Pioneers of the West* (H 3 Mesquiteers). **1941:** *A Missouri Outlaw* (H Don "Red" Barry). **1945:** *Sing Me a Song of Texas* (H Tom Tyler).

Noah Beery, Sr. (left) with Gene Autry in Mexicali Rose *(1939).*

Lane Bradford

You might say that Lane Bradford was a son of a gunslinger (celluloid type, that is). His father was master B baddie John Merton, and beginning in the mid-1940s Lane fell right into Pa's villainous footsteps.

Born in 1923, he entered films in 1946 and that same year appeared in Johnny Mack Brown's *Silver Range.* Over the next eight years he would appear with Brown, Lash LaRue, Roy Rogers, Monte Hale, Rocky Lane, Charles Starrett, Rex Allen and others.

He had permanent roles in serials including *The Adventures of Frank and Jesse James* (1948), *The James Brothers of Missouri* (1950), *Don Daredevil Rides Again* (1954), and *The Man with the Steel Whip* (1954).

Lane Bradford appeared in many early TV Westerns and in films like *The Conqueror* (1956), *The Lone Ranger and the Lost City of Gold* (1958), *Shenandoah* (1965) and *The Slender Thread* (1965).

He suffered a cerebral hemorrhage and died on June 7, 1973, in Honolulu, Hawaii.

Lane Bradford Filmography

1946: *Silver Range* (*H* Johnny Mack Brown). **1947:** *Ghost Town Renegades* (*H* Lash LaRue); *Black Hills* (*H* Eddie Dean); *Shadow Valley* (*H* Eddie Dean). **1948:** *Check Your Guns* (*H* Eddie Dean); *Dead Man's Gold* (*H* Lash LaRue). **1949:** *Roll Thunder Roll* (*H* Jim Bannon); *The Fighting Redhead* (*H* Jim Bannon). **1950:** *Bells of Coronado* (*H* Roy Rogers); *The Old Frontier* (*H* Monte Hale); *Frisco Tornado* (*H* Rocky Lane). **1951:** *Wanted Dead or Alive* (*H* Whip Wilson); *Stagecoach Driver* (*H* Whip Wilson); *Oklahoma Justice* (*H* Johnny Mack Brown); *Lawless Cowboys* (*H* Whip Wilson); *Stage to Blue River* (*H* Whip Wilson). **1952:** *Night Raiders* (*H* Whip Wilson); *Man from the Black Hills* (*H* Johnny Mack Brown); *The Gunman* (*H* Whip Wilson). **1953:** *Savage Frontier* (*H* Rocky Lane). **1954:** *49'ers* (*H* Wild Bill Eliott*).

Alan "Al" Bridge

Bad man Al Bridge's villainous screen career spanned the entire lifetime of the B Western era. He appeared in dozens of cowboy pictures.

Bridge was born in Pennsylvania on February 26, 1891, and he entered films at the dawn of the talkies.

His career was built mostly around Westerns, and he appeared in all types, from comedy oaters like *My Little Chickadee* with W.C. Fields and Mae West, to big production Westerns like *The Oklahoma Kid* with Cagney and Bogart, to serials such as *Mystery Mountain* (1934) with Ken Maynard, *Wild West Days* (1937) with Johnny Mack Brown, and Wild Bill Elliott's *The Great Adventures of Wild Bill Hickok* (1938).

In his B baddie roles he was equally at home playing a henchman or the brains of the outfit. Check his performance as the gunman, Kit, in John Wayne's *The New Frontier* (1935).

Al Bridge passed away December 27, 1957.

Alan "Al" Bridge Filmography

1931: *Rider of the Plains* (*H* Tom Tyler); *The Ridin' Fool* (*H* Bob Steele). **1932:** *The 49'ers* (*H* Tom Tyler); *Galloping Thru* (*H* Tom Tyler). **1933:** *When a Man Rides Alone* (*H* Tom Tyler); *Drum Taps* (*H* Ken Maynard); *Son of the Border* (*H* Tom Keene); *The Lone Avenger* (*H* Ken Maynard); *Cheyenne Kid* (*H* Tom Keene); *Fiddlin' Buckaroo* (*H* Ken Maynard);

Fighting Texans (H Rex Bell); *The Trail Drive* (H Ken Maynard). **1935:**
North of Arizona (H Jack Perrin); *Silent Valley* (H Tom Tyler). **1936:** *Fast
Bullets* (H Tom Tyler); *Lawless Nineties* (H John Wayne); *Call of the
Prairie* (H Hopalong Cassidy); *3 Mesquiteers* (H 3 Mesquiteers); *Dodge
City Trail* (H Charles Starrett). **1937:** *One Man Justice* (H Charles Starrett);
Border Land (H Hopalong Cassidy); *Western Gold* (H Smith Ballew); *Two
Gun Law* (H Charles Starrett). **1938:** *Two Gun Justice* (H Tim McCoy);
Colorado Trail (H Charles Starrett). **1939:** *Blue Montana Skies* (H Gene
Autry); *Man from Sundown* (H Charles Starrett). **1940:** *Blazing Six
Shooters* (H Charles Starrett). **1941:** *Law of the Range* (H Johnny Mack
Brown); *The Kid's Last Ride* (H Range Busters); *Fighting Bill Fargo* (H
Johnny Mack Brown). **1942:** *Bells of Capistrano* (H Gene Autry). **1946:** *My
Pal Trigger* (H Roy Rogers). **1947:** *Robin Hood of Texas* (H Gene Autry).
1949: *Trail of the Yukon* (H Kirby Grant). **1952:** *The Last Musketeer* (H Rex
Allen). **1953:** *Iron Mountain Trail* (H Rex Allen).

Yakima Canutt

Quite simply put, Enos Edward "Yakima" Canutt was Hollywood's all-
time greatest stuntman. In 1966 he was awarded a special Oscar for his con-
tributions to the stunt profession and for developing most of the safety
devices that stuntmen use today.

The highlight of his career came in 1959 when he staged the spectacular
chariot race sequence in the epic film *Ben Hur*, an undertaking which took
over two years of preparation. During his career he doubled for stars such
as John Wayne, Errol Flynn, Randolph Scott, Roy Rogers, Clark Gable,
Henry Fonda and Tyrone Power.

Canutt was born in Colfax, Washington, on November 29, 1896. He
learned his basic stuntman's craft while performing in the rodeos as a
young man. Like many other rodeo stars he soon found his way to
Hollywood.

In the early 1920s he starred in a series of Western films which were
characterized by above-average action sequences. At the beginning of the
sound era Canutt was a supporting player in low-budget Westerns starring cowboys like Wally Wales, Buffalo Bill, Jr., Jack Perrin and Lane
Chandler.

Several years later he became a regular in John Wayne's series of Lone
Star Westerns. Of the 16 films of the series, Canutt was in 15 of them, playing everything from Wayne's sidekick in one to the villain in another.

He continued to work as an actor and stuntman in B Westerns

Yakima Canutt

throughout the thirties. He also appeared in serials like *Battling with Buffalo Bill* (1931), *The Black Coin* (1936), *The Clutching Hand* (1936), *The Vigilantes Are Coming* (1936) and *The Painted Stallion* (1937).

He staged the Indian attacks in John Ford's 1939 film *Stagecoach* and performed many of the dangerous horse falls that dot the sequences.

In the 1940s Yakima Canutt became involved in directing. He worked in this capacity in Westerns like *The Sheriff of Cimarron* in 1945 and

Oklahoma Badmen in 1948. He also co-directed four serials for Republic Pictures: *Manhunt of Mystery Island* (1945), *The Adventures of Frank and Jesse James, G-Men Never Forget* and *Dangers of the Canadian Mounted* (all 1948).

He took his nickname from Washington's Yakima Valley.

Yakima Canutt passed away on May 24, 1986, in North Hollywood, California.

Yakima Canutt Filmography

1930: *Firebrand Jordan* (*H* Lane Chandler); *Ridin' Law* (*H* Jack Perrin); *Bar L Ranch* (*H* Buffalo Bill, Jr.); *Canyon Hawks* (*H* Wally Wales); *The Cheyenne Kid* (*H* Buffalo Bill, Jr). **1931:** *Westward Bound* (*H* Buffalo Bill, Jr.); *Pueblo Terror* (*H* Buffalo Bill, Jr.); *Hurricane Horseman* (*H* Lane Chandler); *Two Fisted Justice* (*H* Tom Tyler). **1932:** *Riders of the Golden Gulch* (*H* Buffalo Bill, Jr.); *The Cheyenne Cyclone* (*H* Lane Chandler); *Law and Lawless* (*H* Jack Hoxie); *Battling Buckaroo* (*H* Lane Chandler); *Guns for Hire* (*H* Lane Chandler); *The Texan* (*H* Buffalo Bill, Jr.); *Texas Tornado* (*H* Lane Chandler). **1933:** *The Telegraph Trail* (*H* John Wayne); *The Fighting Texans* (*H* Rex Bell). **1934:** *The Lucky Texan* (*H* John Wayne); *West of the Divide* (*H* John Wayne); *Blue Steel* (*H* John Wayne); *The Man from Utah* (*H* John Wayne); *Randy Rides Alone* (*H* John Wayne); *The Star Packer* (*H* John Wayne); *The Man from Hell* (*H* Reb Russell); *Fighting Through* (*H* Reb Russell); *Lawless Frontier* (*H* John Wayne); *'Neath the Arizona Skies* (*H* John Wayne); *Carrying the Mail* (*H* Wally Wales); *Desert Man* (*H* Wally Wales); *Pals of the West* (*H* Wally Wales). **1935:** *Texas Terror* (*H* John Wayne); *Outlaw Rule* (*H* Reb Russell); *Cyclone of the Saddle* (*H* Rex Lease); *Pals of the Range* (*H* Rex Lease); *The Dawn Rider* (*H* John Wayne); *Paradise Canyon* (*H* John Wayne); *Branded a Coward* (*H* Johnny Mack Brown); *Westward Ho* (*H* John Wayne); *Lawless Range* (*H* John Wayne); *Rough Riding Ranger* (*H* Rex Lease). **1936:** *The Oregon Trail* (*H* John Wayne); *King of the Pecos* (*H* John Wayne); *The Lonely Trail* (*H* John Wayne); *Winds of the Wasteland* (*H* John Wayne); *Wild Cat Trooper* (*H* Kermit Maynard); *Ghost Town Gold* (*H* 3 Mesquiteers); *Roarin' Lead* (*H* 3 Mesquiteers). **1937:** *Riders of the Whistling Skull* (*H* 3 Mesquiteers); *Hit the Saddle* (*H* 3 Mesquiteers); *Trouble in Texas* (*H* Tex Ritter); *Gunsmoke Ranch* (*H* 3 Mesquiteers); *Come on Cowboys* (*H* 3 Mesquiteers); *Range Defenders* (*H* 3 Mesquiteers); *Riders of the Rockies* (*H* Tex Ritter); *Riders of the Dawn* (*H* Jack Randall); *Heart of the Rockies* (*H* 3 Mesquiteers); *Prairie Thunder* (*H* Dick Foran). **1938:** *Overland Stage Raiders* (*H* 3 Mesquiteers); *Santa Fe Stampede* (*H* 3 Mesquiteers). **1939:** *The Night Riders* (*H* 3 Mesquiteers); *Wyoming Outlaw* (*H* 3 Mesquiteers); *Cowboys from Texas*

(*H* 3 Mesquiteers). **1940:** *Pioneers of the West* (*H* 3 Mesquiteers); *Ghost Valley Raiders* (*H* Don Barry); *The Carson City Kid* (*H* Roy Rogers); *The Ranger and the Lady* (*H* Roy Rogers); *Under Texas Skies* (*H* 3 Mesquiteers); *Frontier Vengeance* (*H* Don Barry). **1941:** *Prairie Pioneers* (*H* 3 Mesquiteers); *Nevada City* (*H* Roy Rogers); *Kansas Cyclone* (*H* Don Barry); *Bad Man of Deadwood* (*H* Roy Rogers); *Gauchos of El Dorado* (*H* 3 Mesquiteers). **1942:** *Shadows on the Sage* (*H* 3 Mesquiteers). **1943:** *Santa Fe Scouts* (*H* 3 Mesquiteers); *Song of Texas* (*H* Roy Rogers).

Ed Cassidy

Ed Cassidy split his B Western screen time between playing sheriffs and scoundrels, and was quite adept at both.

He appeared in films like *Tex Rides with the Big Scouts* (1937) with Tex Ritter, *The Purple Vigilantes* (1938) with the Three Mesquiteers and *Cassidy of the Bar 20* (1938) with William Boyd.

Cassidy was in the serials *Deadwood Dick, Manhunt of Mystery Island* and *Jesse James Rides Again.*

In the forties he was featured in films with cowboy stars like Buster Crabbe, Rocky Lane, Charles Starrett and others.

He usually would play a mid-level heavy, somewhere under the brains and the chief action heavy.

Born in 1893, he passed away January 19, 1968.

Ed Cassidy Filmography

1935: *The Courageous Avenger* (*H* Johnny Mack Brown); *No Man's Range* (*H* Bob Steele); *The Pecos Kid* (*H* Fred Kohler, Jr.); *The Reckless Buckaroo* (*H* Bill Cody); *Toll of the Desert* (*H* Fred Kohler, Jr.). **1936:** *Aces Wild* (*H* Harry Carey); *Valley of the Lawless* (*H* Johnny Mack Brown); *Roarin' Guns* (*H* Tim McCoy); *Ghost Town* (*H* Harry Carey); *Feud of the West* (*H* Hoot Gibson); *Winds of the Wasteland* (*H* John Wayne); *The Idaho Kid* (*H* Rex Bell); *Brand of the Outlaws* (*H* Bob Steele); *Santa Fe Bound* (*H* Tom Tyler); *Undercover Man* (*H* Johnny Mack Brown); *Men of the Plains* (*H* Rex Bell); *Cavalry* (*H* Bob Steele); *Vengeance of Rannah* (*H* Bob Custer); *Law and Lead* (*H* Rex Bell); *Gun Grit* (*H* Jack Perrin); *Hair Trigger Casey* (*H* Jack Perrin); *Sundown Saunders* (*H* Bob Steele). **1937:** *Cheyenne Rides Again* (*H* Tom Tyler); *Santa Fe Rides* (*H* Bob Custer); *The Silver Trail* (*H* Rex Lease); *Hit the Saddle* (*H* 3 Mesquiteers); *Hittin' the Trail* (*H* Tex

Ritter); *Lawless Land* (*H* Johnny Mack Brown); *Borderland* (*H* Hopalong Cassidy); *Come on Cowboys* (*H* 3 Mesquiteers); *Arizona Days* (*H* Tex Ritter). **1938:** *Tex Rides with the Boy Scouts* (*H* Tex Ritter); *Border Wolves* (*H* Bob Baker); *Outlaw Express* (*H* Bob Baker); *Frontier Town* (*H* Tex Ritter); *The Purple Vigilantes* (*H* 3 Mesquiteers); *Man from Music Mountain* (*H* Gene Autry); *Cassidy of the Bar 20* (*H* Hopalong Cassidy); *Rawhide* (*H* Smith Ballew); *The Mexicali Kid* (*H* Jack Randall); *Starlight Over Texas* (*H* Tex Ritter); *Wild Horse Canyon* (*H* Jack Randall). **1939:** *Silver on the Sage* (*H* Hopalong Cassidy); *Rovin' Tumbleweeds* (*H* Gene Autry); *Desperate Trails* (*H* Johnny Mack Brown); *Cowboys from Texas* (*H* 3 Mesquiteers). **1940:** *Riders of the Pasco Basin* (*H* Johnny Mack Brown); *Ragtime Cowboy Joe* (*H* Johnny Mack Brown); *Gaucho Serenade* (*H* Gene Autry). **1941:** *Wide Open Town* (*H* Hopalong Cassidy); *Robbers of the Range* (*H* Tim Holt); *Ridin' on a Rainbow* (*H* Gene Autry); *Bury Me Not on the Lone Prairie* (*H* Johnny Mack Brown). **1942:** *Stardust on the Sage* (*H* Gene Autry); *Pirates of the Prairie* (*H* Tim Holt). **1943:** *Thundering Trails* (*H* 3 Mesquiteers); *Cowboy in the Clouds* (*H* Charles Starrett); *The Avenging Rider* (*H* Tim Holt); *Boss of Rawhide* (*H* Texas Rangers). **1944:** *Brand of the Devil* (*H* Texas Rangers); *Frontier Outlaws* (*H* Buster Crabbe); *Fuzzy Settles Down* (*H* Buster Crabbe); *The Pinto Bandit* (*H* Texas Rangers); *Saddle Leather Law* (*H* Charles Starrett); *Rustlers Hideout* (*H* Buster Crabbe); *Trigger Law* (*H* Gibson/Steele); *Tucson Raiders* (*H* Wild Bill Elliott). **1945:** *Marked for Murder* (*H* Texas Rangers); *The Navajo Trail* (*H* Johnny Mack Brown); *Corpus Christi Bandits* (*H* Rocky Lane); *The Gangster's Den* (*H* Buster Crabbe); *Sheriff of Cimarron* (*H* Sunset Carson); *Stagecoach Outlaws* (*H* Buster Crabbe); *Sunset in El Dorado* (*H* Roy Rogers); *Three in the Saddle* (*H* Texas Rangers); *The Navajo Kid* (*H* Bob Steele). **1946:** *Alias Billy the Kid* (*H* Sunset Carson); *Ambush Trail* (*H* Bob Steele); *Trigger Fingers* (*H* Johnny Mack Brown); *Days of Buffalo Bill* (*H* Sunset Carson); *The El Paso Kid* (*H* Sunset Carson); *Prairie Badmen* (*H* Buster Crabbe); *Roaring Rangers* (*H* Charles Starrett); *Roll on Texas Moon* (*H* Roy Rogers); *Sun Valley Cyclone* (*H* Wild Bill Elliott); *Stagecoach to Denver* (*H* Rocky Lane). **1947:** *Homesteaders of Paradise Valley* (*H* Rocky Lane); *Oregon Trail Scouts* (*H* Rocky Lane); *Valley of Fear* (*H* Johnny Mack Brown); *Border Feud* (*H* Lash LaRue). **1948:** *Bold Frontiersman* (*H* Rocky Lane); *Desperadoes of Dodge City* (*H* Rocky Lane). **1950:** *Fence Riders* (*H* Whip Wilson); *Trail of Robin Hood* (*H* Roy Rogers). **1951:** *Buckaroo Sheriff of Texas* (*H* Rough Ridin' Kids). **1952:** *Desperadoes Outpost* (*H* Rocky Lane); *Black Hills Ambush* (*H* Rocky Lane); *Night Raiders* (*H* Whip Wilson).

George Chesebro

It was his natural scowl that led George Chesebro to appear in more than 200 B Westerns, mostly as an action villain. In fact he was one of the genre's most prolific bad men.

Chesebro's specialty was playing members of outlaw gangs — just plain old everyday unfinessed robbers, rustlers, louts and drygulchers.

Throughout the thirties and forties it was as though low-budget-fare studios like PRC, Monogram, Superior or Reliable couldn't make a Western without George taking a poke or a potshot at the hero.

In the latter forties Chesebro turned to being "the Boss" bad guy, and his best screen role came as the brains behind a gang of robbers in Lash LaRue's 1947 film *Cheyenne Takes Over*.

Chesebro was born in Minneapolis, Minnesota, on July 29, 1888, and entered films in the early 1900s.

Early on in his film career Chesebro became a featured player in silent serials such as *The Lost City*, *The Diamond Queen* and *The Hope Diamond Mystery*. He appeared in a variety of films, from Westerns to comedies throughout the silent era.

Along with the ton of Westerns that he made, Chesebro appeared in many of the classic Saturday afternoon serials of the thirties and forties, including *The Adventures of Wild Bill Hickok*, *Daredevils of the Red Circle*, *Mandrake the Magician*, *S.O.S. Coast Guard* and *The Adventures of Frank and Jesse James*.

George Chesebro succumbed to arteriosclerosis on May 28, 1959, in Hermosa Beach, California.

George Chesebro Filmography

1931: *Wild West Whoopee* (H Jack Perrin); *The Kid from Arizona* (H Jack Perrin); *The Sheriff's Secret* (H Jack Perrin); *Lariats and Sixshooters* (H Jack Perrin). **1932:** *Mark of the Spur* (H Bob Custer); *Lucky Larrigan* (H Rex Bell); *The Fighting Champ* (H Bob Steele); *Tombstone Canyon* (H Ken Maynard); *Forty-Five Calibre Echo* (H Jack Perrin). **1934:** *Pot Luck Pards* (H Wally Wales); *Mystery Ranch* (H Tom Tyler); *Rawhide Mail* (H Jack Perrin); *Fighting Hero* (H Tom Tyler); *Ridin' Gents* (H Jack Perrin); *Fighting Trooper* (H Kermit Maynard); *In Old Santa Fe* (H Ken Maynard); *Border Guns* (H Bill Cody); *The Border Menace* (H Bill Cody); *Boss Cowboy* (H Buddy Roosevelt). **1935:** *Unconquered Bandit* (H Tom Tyler); *Tracy Rides* (H Tom Tyler); *Cowboy and the Bandit* (H Rex Lease); *Cyclone of the Saddle* (H Rex Lease); *Pals of the Range* (H Rex Lease); *The*

Silver Bullet (*H* Tom Tyler); *Man from Guntown* (*H* Tim McCoy); *Tumbling Tumbleweeds* (*H* Gene Autry); *Gallant Defender* (*H* Charles Starrett); *Born to Battle* (*H* Tom Tyler); *Coyote Trails* (*H* Tom Tyler); *Danger Trails* (*H* Big Boy Williams); *Defying the Law* (*H* Ted Wells); *Fighting Caballero* (*H* Rex Lease); *The Laramie Kid* (*H* Tom Tyler); *North of Arizona* (*H* Jack Perrin); *The Phantom Cowboy* (*H* Ted Wells); *Rough Riding Ranger* (*H* Rex Lease); *Silent Valley* (*H* Tom Tyler); *Toll of the Desert* (*H* Fred Kohler, Jr.); *Western Racketeers* (*H* Bill Cody); *Wild Mustang* (*H* Harry Carey); *Wolf Riders* (*H* Jack Perrin). **1936:** *The Mysterious Avenger* (*H* Charles Starrett); *The Lawless Nineties* (*H* John Wayne); *Lucky Terror* (*H* Hoot Gibson); *Red River Valley* (*H* Gene Autry); *Roamin' Wild* (*H* Tom Tyler); *Pinto Rustlers* (*H* Tom Tyler); *Code of the Range* (*H* Charles Starrett); *The Big Show* (*H* Gene Autry); *Roarin' Lead* (*H* 3 Mesquiteers); *Dodge City Trail* (*H* Charles Starrett). **1937:** *Westbound Mail* (*H* Charles Starrett); *Borderland* (*H* Hopalong Cassidy); *Two Gun Law* (*H* Charles Starrett); *Hills of Old Wyoming* (*H* Hopalong Cassidy); *Two Fisted Sheriff* (*H* Charles Starrett); *Empty Holsters* (*H* Dick Foran); *Devils Saddle Legion* (*H* Dick Foran); *Prairie Thunder* (*H* Dick Foran); *The Old Wyoming Trail* (*H* Charles Starrett); *Springtime in the Rockies* (*H* Gene Autry); *Outlaws of the Prairie* (*H* Charles Starrett); *The Roaming Cowboy* (*H* Fred Scott). **1938:** *The Purple Vigilantes* (*H* 3 Mesquiteers); *Cattle Raiders* (*H* Charles Starrett); *Outlaws of Sonora* (*H* 3 Mesquiteers); *Law of the Plains* (*H* Charles Starrett); *Starlight Over Texas* (*H* Tex Ritter); *Mexicali Kid* (*H* Jack Randall); *Lawless Valley* (*H* George O'Brien); *Santa Fe Stampede* (*H* 3 Mesquiteers). **1939:** *Song of the Buckaroo* (*H* Tex Ritter); *Smoky Trails* (*H* Bob Steele); *Rough Riders Roundup* (*H* Roy Rogers); *Southward Ho* (*H* Roy Rogers); *The Man from Sundown* (*H* Charles Starrett); *Wall Street Cowboy* (*H* Roy Rogers); *New Frontier* (*H* 3 Mesquiteers); *Riders of Black River* (*H* Charles Starrett); *Stranger from Texas* (*H* Charles Starrett). **1940:** *Pioneer Days* (*H* Jack Randall); *Pioneers of the Frontier* (*H* Wild Bill Elliott); *The Cheyenne Kid* (*H* Jack Randall); *Pioneers of the West* (*H* 3 Mesquiteers); *Pinto Canyon* (*H* Bob Steele); *Land of the Six Guns* (*H* Jack Randall); *The Kid from Santa Fe* (*H* Jack Randall); *Texas Stagecoach* (*H* Charles Starrett); *Riders from Nowhere* (*H* Jack Randall); *Frontier Crusader* (*H* Tim McCoy); *Wild Horse Range* (*H* Jack Randall); *Lightning Strikes West* (*H* Ken Maynard); *Gun Code* (*H* Tim McCoy); *West of Pinto Basin* (*H* Range Busters). **1941:** *Trail of the Silver Spurs* (*H* Range Busters); *Billy the Kid's Fighting Pals* (*H* Bob Steele); *Lone Rider in Ghost Town* (*H* George Houston); *The Pioneers* (*H* Tex Ritter); *Wranglers Roost* (*H* Range Busters); *The Medico of Painted Springs* (*H* Charles Starrett); *Lone Rider Ambushed* (*H* George Houston). **1942:** *Lone Star Vigilantes* (*H* Wild Bill Elliott); *Thunder River Feud* (*H* Range Busters); *Billy the Kid Trapped* (*H* Buster Crabbe); *Jesse James Jr.* (*H* Don Barry); *Boot Hill Bandits* (*H* Range

Busters); *Rolling Down the Great Divide* (H Bill Boyd); *Tumbleweed Trail* (H Bill Boyd). **1943:** *Two Fisted Justice* (H Range Busters); *Death Rides the Plains* (H Bob Livingston); *Fugitive of the Plains* (H Buster Crabbe); *Black Market Rustlers* (H Range Busters); *The Renegade* (H Buster Crabbe); *Boss of Rawhide* (H Texas Rangers). **1944:** *The Drifter* (H Buster Crabbe); *Arizona Whirlwind* (H Trail Blazers); *Thundering Gunslingers* (H Buster Crabbe). **1945:** *Sheriff of Cimarron* (H Sunset Carson); *Rough Ridin' Justice* (H Charles Starrett); *Santa Fe Saddlemates* (H Sunset Carson); *Gangsters Den* (H Buster Crabbe); *Trail of Kit Carson* (H Rocky Lane); *Outlaws of the Rockies* (H Charles Starrett); *Marshal of Laredo* (H Wild Bill Elliott); *Lawless Empire* (H Charles Starrett); *Texas Panhandle* (H Charles Starrett). **1946:** *Days of Buffalo Bill* (H Sunset Carson); *Gunning for Vengeance* (H Charles Starrett); *Gentlemen with Guns* (H Buster Crabbe); *Sun Valley Cyclone* (H Wild Bill Elliott); *Two Fisted Stranger* (H Charles Starrett); *Land Rush* (H Charles Starrett); *Terror Trail* (H Charles Starrett); *Fighting Frontiersman* (H Charles Starrett); *Stagecoach to Denver* (H Rocky Lane). **1947:** *The Lone Hand Texan* (H Charles Starrett); *Vigilantes of Boomtown* (H Rocky Lane); *Over the Santa Fe Trail* (H Ken Curtis); *West of Dodge City* (H Charles Starrett); *Wyoming* (H Bill Elliott); *Song of the Wasteland* (H Jimmy Wakely); *Riders of the Lone Star* (H Charles Starrett); *Law of the Canyon* (H Charles Starrett); *Black Hills* (H Eddie Dean); *Return of the Lash* (H Lash LaRue); *Fighting Vigilantes* (H Lash LaRue); *Cheyenne Takes Over* (H Lash LaRue); *Stage to Mesa City* (H Lash LaRue); *Homesteaders of Paradise Valley* (H Rocky Lane). **1948:** *Tornado Range* (H Eddie Dean); *Check Your Guns* (H Eddie Dean); *West of Sonora* (H Charles Starrett). **1949:** *Death Valley Gunfighter* (H Rocky Lane); *Desert Vigilante* (H Charles Starrett); *Challenge of the Range* (H Charles Starrett); *Renegades of the Sage* (H Charles Starrett); *Horsemen of the Sierras* (H Charles Starrett). **1950:** *Gunslingers* (H Whip Wilson); *Gunmen of Abilene* (H Rocky Lane); *Salt Lake Raiders* (H Rocky Lane); *Texas Dynamo* (H Charles Starrett); *Streets of Ghost Town* (H Charles Starrett); *West of the Brazos* (H Ellison/Hayden); *Marshal of Heldorado* (H Ellison/Hayden); *Colorado Ranger* (H Ellison/Hayden); *Fast on the Draw* (H Ellison/Hayden); *Lightning Guns* (H Charles Starrett); *Trail of Robin Hood* (H Roy Rogers); *Frisco Tornado* (H Rocky Lane). **1951:** *Night Riders of Montana* (H Rocky Lane); *Snake River Desperadoes* (H Charles Starrett); *Kid from Amarillo* (H Charles Starrett).

Dick Curtis

Dick Curtis rates as one of the Western genre's top bad men. He was Columbia Pictures' ace bad man of the late thirties and forties and was well known for his villainous portrayals opposite Charles Starrett and Wild Bill Elliott.

The studio's main bad guys were Curtis and Kenneth MacDonald. While MacDonald was effective as a "brains" bad guy, the larger, well-built Curtis was a physically menacing force to be dealt with. His films, especially with Elliott, usually contained at least one well-staged brawl between Curtis and the hero.

Curtis was born May 11, 1902, in Newport, Kentucky, and made his film debut in the 1918 feature *The Unpardonable Sin* as an extra.

He had a role in the original version of *King Kong* (1933) and by the mid-thirties was becoming a familiar face in B Westerns like *The Lion's Den* (1935) with Tim McCoy and Kermit Maynard's *Wildcat Trooper* (1936).

He signed on with Columbia in 1938 and immediately locked up with Starrett in films like *The Colorado Trail* (1938) and Elliott in *Taming of the West* (1939).

He was also put to work in Columbia serials like *Mandrake the Magician, Overland with Kit Carson, Flying G-Men* and *Terry and the Pirates*.

Curtis showed a tremendous flair for slapstick, as attested to his many appearances in Columbia comedy shorts with Andy Clyde and especially the Three Stooges. Curtis is the villain in the Stooges' 1946 short *Three Troubledoers*, which is a great parody of B Westerns.

Dick Curtis passed away on January 3, 1952.

Dick Curtis Filmography

1935: *Wilderness Mail* (H Kermit Maynard); *Western Courage* (H Ken Maynard). **1936:** *Wildcat Trooper* (H Kermit Maynard); *The Lion's Den* (H Tim McCoy); *The Crooked Trail* (H Johnny Mack Brown); *Ghost Patrol* (H Tim McCoy); *The Traitor* (H Tim McCoy); *Phantom Patrol* (H Kermit Maynard). **1937:** *The Singing Buckaroo* (H Fred Scott); *Valley of Terror* (H Kermit Maynard); *The Gambling Terror* (H Johnny Mack Brown); *Trail of Vengeance* (H Johnny Mack Brown); *Bar Z Bad Men* (H Johnny Mack Brown); *Guns in the Dark* (H Johnny Mack Brown); *Boot Hill Brigade* (H Johnny Mack Brown); *Old Wyoming Trail* (H Charles Starrett); *Outlaws of the Prairie* (H Charles Starrett); *Moonlight on the Prairie* (H Fred Scott). **1938:** *Cattle Raiders* (H Charles Starrett); *Rawhide* (H Smith Ballew); *Call of the Rockies* (H Charles Starrett); *Law of the Plains* (H Charles Starrett);

Dick Curtis

West of Cheyenne (H Charles Starrett); *West of Santa Fe* (H Charles Starrett); *Rio Grande* (H Charles Starrett). **1939:** *The Thundering West* (H Charles Starrett); *Spoilers of the Range* (H Charles Starrett); *Western Caravans* (H Charles Starrett); *Riders of Black River* (H Charles Starrett); *Outpost of the Mounted* (H Charles Starrett); *Taming of the West* (H Charles Starrett); *The Stranger from Texas* (H Charles Starrett). **1940:** *Two Fisted Rangers* (H Charles Starrett); *Pioneers of the Frontier* (H Wild Bill

Elliott); *Bullets for Rustlers* (H Charles Starrett); *Blazing Six Shooters* (H Charles Starrett); *Texas Stagecoach* (H Charles Starrett). **1941:** *Across the Sierras* (H Wild Bill Elliott); *Stick to Your Guns* (H Hopalong Cassidy); *Arizona Cyclone* (H Johnny Mack Brown). **1942:** *Pardon My Gun* (H Charles Starrett). **1943:** *Cowboy in the Clouds* (H Charles Starrett). **1945:** *Song of the Prairie* (H Ken Curtis). **1946:** *California Gold Rush* (H Wild Bill Elliott); *Santa Fe Uprising* (H Rocky Lane). **1949:** *Navajo Trail Raiders* (H Rocky Lane).

Kenne Duncan

Stunt ace Kenne Duncan was one of the B Western's most active "action" heavies. He was an excellent athlete and horseman and at one time was being groomed by Republic Pictures for the slot as their number one villain, a role that was eventually given to Roy Barcroft.

Duncan was born Kenneth Duncan MacLachlan on February 17, 1902, in Chatham, Ontario, Canada, and was at one time a professional jockey. He entered films in the late 1920s and by the late thirties had become a well-recognized stock player in serial Westerns and adventure films.

He appeared in over a dozen serials including *Flash Gordon's Trip to Mars, The Adventures of Captain Marvel, King of the Texas Rangers, The Perils of Nyoka,* and *The Phantom Rider.*

He made dozens of Westerns, mostly for Republic, menacing such heroes as Roy Rogers, Wild Bill Elliott and Gene Autry.

Other films in which he appeared include *Buck Privates* with Abbott and Costello.

Kenne Duncan fell victim to a fatal stroke on February 5, 1972.

Kenne Duncan Filmography

1938: *Six Gun Trail* (H Tim McCoy). **1939:** *Man from Texas* (H Tex Ritter); *Trigger Fingers* (H Tim McCoy). **1940:** *Texas Renegades* (H Tim McCoy); *Murder on the Yukon* (H James Newill); *Pinto Canyon* (H Bob Steele); *The Kid from Santa Fe* (H Jack Randall); *Billy the Kid Outlawed* (H Bob Steele); *Roll Wagons Roll* (H Tex Ritter); *Arizona Gang Busters* (H Tim McCoy); *Billy the Kid's Gun Justice* (H Bob Steele). **1941:** *Dynamite Canyon* (H Tom Keene); *Riding the Sunset Trail* (H Tom Keene). **1942:** *Westward Ho* (H 3 Mesquiteers); *Texas to Bataan* (H Range Busters); *Outlaws of Boulder Pass* (H George Houston); *Sundown Kid* (H Don Barry). **1943:** *The Avenging*

Rider (*H* Tim Holt); *Fugitive from Sonora* (*H* Don Barry); *Man from the Rio Grande* (*H* Don Barry). **1944:** *Beneath Western Skies* (*H* Bob Livingston); *Outlaws of Santa Fe* (*H* Don Barry); *Hidden Valley Outlaws* (*H* Wild Bill Elliott); *Marshal of Reno* (*H* Wild Bill Elliott); *Cheyenne Wild Cat* (*H* Wild Bill Elliott); *Sheriff of Sundown* (*H* Rocky Lane); *Sheriff of Las Vegas* (*H* Wild Bill Elliott). **1945:** *Corpus Christi Bandits* (*H* Rocky Lane); *Santa Fe Saddlemates* (*H* Sunset Carson); *Bells of Rosarita* (*H* Roy Rogers); *Oregon Trail* (*H* Sunset Carson); *Rough Riders of Cheyenne* (*H* Sunset Carson). **1946:** *California Gold Rush* (*H* Wild Bill Elliott); *Sun Valley Cyclone* (*H* Wild Bill Elliott); *Man from Rainbow Valley* (*H* Monte Hale); *My Pal Trigger* (*H* Roy Rogers); *Red River Renegades* (*H* Sunset Carson); *Conquest of Cheyenne* (*H* Wild Bill Elliott). **1949:** *Gun Runner* (*H* Jimmy Wakely); *Law of the West* (*H* Johnny Mack Brown); *Across the Rio Grande* (*H* Jimmy Wakely); *West of El Dorado* (*H* Johnny Mack Brown). **1950:** *Code of the Silver Sage* (*H* Rocky Lane). **1951:** *Whirlwind* (*H* Gene Autry). **1953:** *On Top of Old Smoky* (*H* Gene Autry).

Earl Dwire

Craggy-faced Earl Dwire is one of the best remembered B Western ruffians of the 1930s. He was a stock player in John Wayne's Lone Star Westerns in the early thirties and in Tex Ritter's Grand National features.

One of his best roles was in Wayne's 1934 film *The Lawless Frontier* in which he played a half-breed bushwhacker named Zanti. The story revolves around Wayne's efforts to avenge his parents' deaths at the hands of Zanti and his gang.

Dwire was born in 1884 and passed away on January 16, 1940.

He was also in films like *Angels with Dirty Faces* (1938), the hilarious *His Girl Friday* (1940) and the cliff-hanger *Flash Gordon Conquers the Universe* (1940).

Earl Dwire Filmography

1932: *Law of the West* (*H* Bob Steele); *Man from Hell's Edges* (*H* Bob Steele); *Son of Oklahoma* (*H* Bob Steele). **1933:** *Galloping Romeo* (*H* Bob Steele); *Riders of Destiny* (*H* John Wayne). **1934:** *Lucky Texan* (*H* John Wayne); *West of the Divide* (*H* John Wayne); *Man from Utah* (*H* John Wayne); *Randy Rides Alone* (*H* John Wayne); *The Star Packer* (*H* John

Wayne); *The Trail Beyond* (*H* John Wayne); *Lawless Frontier* (*H* John Wayne). **1935:** *Wagon Trail* (*H* Harry Carey); *Fighting Pioneers* (*H* Rex Bell); *Justice of the Range* (*H* Tim McCoy); *Courageous Defender* (*H* Johnny Mack Brown); *Big Calibre* (*H* Bob Steele); *Alias John Law* (*H* Bob Steele); *Born to Battle* (*H* Tom Tyler); *The Pecos Kid* (*H* Fred Kohler, Jr.); *Saddle Aces* (*H* Rex Bell); *Toll of the Desert* (*H* Fred Kohler, Jr.); *Tombstone Terror* (*H* Bob Steele). **1936:** *The Kid Ranger* (*H* Bob Steele); *Ridin' On* (*H* Tom Tyler); *Pinto Rustlers* (*H* Tom Tyler); *Roaming Wild* (*H* Tom Tyler); *Law and Lead* (*H* Rex Bell); *Song of the Gringo* (*H* Tex Ritter); *Headin' for the Rio Grande* (*H* Tex Ritter); *Wild Cat Saunders* (*H* Jack Perrin); *Sundown Saunders* (*H* Bob Steele); *Desert Justice* (*H* Jack Perrin); *Gun Grit* (*H* Jack Perrin). **1937:** *The Gun Ranger* (*H* Bob Steele); *The Gambling Terror* (*H* Johnny Mack Brown); *Trouble in Texas* (*H* Tex Ritter); *Git Along Little Dogies* (*H* Gene Autry); *Hittin' the Trail* (*H* Tex Ritter); *The Trusted Outlaw* (*H* Bob Steele); *Riders of the Rockies* (*H* Tex Ritter); *Doomed at Sundown* (*H* Bob Steele); *Riders of the Dawn* (*H* Jack Randall); *Mystery of the Hooded Horseman* (*H* Tex Ritter); *Danger Valley* (*H* Jack Randall); *Hell Town* (*H* John Wayne); *Romance of the Rockies* (*H* Tom Keene). **1938:** *The Purple Vigilantes* (*H* 3 Mesquiteers); *Under Western Stars* (*H* Roy Rogers); *The Old Barn Dance* (*H* Gene Autry); *Two Gun Justice* (*H* Tim McCoy); *Man from Music Mountain* (*H* Gene Autry); *Six Shootin' Sheriff* (*H* Ken Maynard); *Gold Mine in the Sky* (*H* Gene Autry). **1939:** *The Arizona Kid* (*H* Roy Rogers).

Al Ferguson

Al Ferguson was born April 19, 1888, in Rosslarre, Ireland. He made his screen debut in 1910. By the 1920s he was a familiar face as a villain in Westerns and serials.

These roles carried Ferguson into the sound era, and he was cast as baddies in such early serials as *The Lightning Express* (1930), *The Hurricane Express* (1932), *Tailspin Tommy* (1934) and *Flash Gordon* (1936).

He also menaced B Western heroes like Bob Steele in *Near the Rainbow's End* (1930), Wally Wales in *Red Fork Range* (1931) and Tim McCoy in *One Way Trail* (1931).

In the late thirties Ferguson could be seen usually as a henchman in Hopalong Cassidy films like *North of the Rio Grande* and *Rustler's Valley*. In the former he played a crooked deputy sheriff who killed Hoppy's brother and naturally was killed in turn by Cassidy.

Al Ferguson

He also appeared in films like *Showboat* (1936), *The Road to Utopia* (1945) and *Son of Paleface* (1952).

Al Ferguson passed away December 4, 1971.

Al Ferguson Filmography

1930: *Near the Rainbow's End* (H Bob Steele). **1931:** *Red Fork Range* (H Wally Wales); *Pueblo Terror* (H Buffalo Bill, Jr.); *One Way Trail* (H Tim

McCoy). **1934:** *Arizona Nights* (*H* Jack Perrin). **1935:** *Desert Trail* (*H* John Wayne); *The Laramie Kid* (*H* Tom Tyler). **1936:** *Roamin' Wild* (*H* Tom Tyler). **1937:** *North of the Rio Grande* (*H* Hopalong Cassidy); *Rustler's Valley* (*H* Hopalong Cassidy). **1939:** *Frontiers of '49* (*H* Wild Bill Elliott). **1944:** *Riders of Santa Fe* (*H* Rod Cameron). **1945:** *Beyond the Pecos* (*H* Rod Cameron).

William Haade

Big Bill Haade spent most of his cowboy film career playing second-banana bad men like his character Ed in the 1942 Roy Rogers film *The Man from Cheyenne.* Ed carried out the orders of a scheming ranch owner played by Lynn Carver who headed up a busy gang of cattle thieves.

Because of his size his characters usually were handy with their fists — as well as their guns — and usually tangled with the film's hero in a barroom or bunkhouse brawl.

Haade was born in New York City on March 3, 1903. He began appearing on the screen in the mid-1930s.

Among his films are *Kid Galahad* (1937) with Humphrey Bogart, *The Grapes of Wrath* (1940) and *Sergeant York* (1941).

Appearances in above–B Westerns included films like *Union Pacific* (1939), *Northwest Mounted Police* (1940), and *Rancho Notorious*(1952).

Bill Haade passed away November 15, 1966.

William Haade Filmography

1941: *Pirates on Horseback* (*H* Hopalong Cassidy). **1942:** *Man from Cheyenne* (*H* Roy Rogers); *Heart of the Rio Grande* (*H* Gene Autry). **1944:** *Sheriff of Las Vegas* (*H* Wild Bill Elliott). **1945:** *Phantom of the Plains* (*H* Wild Bill Elliott). **1948:** *Last of the Wild Horses* (*H* James Ellison). **1949:** *The Wyoming Bandit* (*H* Rocky Lane). **1950:** *The Old Frontier* (*H* Monte Hale). **1951:** *Buckaroo Sheriff of Texas* (*H* Rough Ridin' Kids). **1953:** *Red River Shore* (*H* Rex Allen).

Karl Hackett

In his decade-long career (1937–1947) as a B Western bad man, Karl Hackett fluctuated between being a brains and an action heavy.

He appeared in films like *Tex Rides with the Boy Scouts* with Tex Ritter, *Chip of the Flying U* with Johnny Mack Brown, *Sons of the Pioneers* with Roy Rogers and *Bordertown Gunfighters* with Wild Bill Elliott.

Born in 1893, Hackett's film career consisted almost solely of B Westerns. He died in Los Angeles, California on October 24, 1948.

Karl Hackett Filmography

1935: *Bulldog Courage* (H Tim McCoy). **1936:** *Roarin' Guns* (H Tim McCoy); *Desert Phantom* (H Johnny Mack Brown); *Lightnin' Bill Carson* (H Tim McCoy); *The Traitor* (H Tim McCoy); *Law and Lead* (H Rex Bell). **1937:** *Borderland* (H Hopalong Cassidy); *Trail of Vengeance* (H Johnny Mack Brown); *Gun Lords of Stirrup Basin* (H Bob Steele); *Sing, Cowboy, Sing* (H Tex Ritter); *Border Phantom* (H Bob Steele); *Texas Trail* (H Hopalong Cassidy); *Colorado Kid* (H Bob Steele). **1938:** *Tex Rides with the Boy Scouts* (H Tex Ritter); *Paroled to Die* (H Bob Steele); *The Ranger's Roundup* (H Fred Scott); *Frontier Town* (H Tex Ritter); *The Feud Maker* (H Bob Steele); *Phantom Ranger* (H Tim McCoy); *Rollin' Plains* (H Tex Ritter); *Utah Trail* (H Tex Ritter); *Durango Valley Raiders* (H Bob Steele); *Starlight Over Texas* (H Tex Ritter); *Lightning Carson Rides Again* (H Tim McCoy); *Six-Gun Trail* (H Tim McCoy). **1939:** *Sundown on the Prairie* (H Tex Ritter); *Chip of the Flying U* (H Johnny Mack Brown); *Yukon Flight* (H James Newill); *Murder on the Yukon* (H James Newill); *Take Me Back to Oklahoma* (H Tex Ritter); *Billy the Kid's Gun Justice* (H Bob Steele). **1941:** *The Lone Rider Rides On* (H George Houston); *Boss of Bullion City* (H Johnny Mack Brown); *Billy the Kid's Range War* (H Bob Steele); *Lone Rider in Ghost Town* (H George Houston); *Billy the Kid in Santa Fe* (H Bob Steele); *Texas Marshal* (H Tim McCoy); *The Lone Rider in Frontier Fury* (H George Houston); *Bad Man of Deadwood* (H Roy Rogers); *Jesse James at Bay* (H Roy Rogers); *Lone Rider in Cheyenne* (H George Houston). **1942:** *Jesse James Jr.* (H Don Barry); *Rolling Down the Great Divide* (H Bill Boyd); *Come on Danger* (H Tim Holt); *Tumbleweed Trail* (H Bill Boyd); *Prairie Pals* (H Bill Boyd). **1943:** *The Kid Rides Again* (H Buster Crabbe); *Wild Horse Rustlers* (H Bob Livingston); *Sage Brush Law* (H Tim Holt); *Fugitive of the Plains* (H Buster Crabbe); *Death Rides the Plains* (H Bob Livingston); *The Avenging Rider* (H Tim Holt); *Wolves of the Range* (H Bob Livingston); *Lost Canyon* (H Hopalong Cassidy); *California Joe* (H Don

Barry). **1944:** *Tucson Raiders* (H Wild Bill Elliott); *Sonora Stagecoach* (H Trail Blazers); *Mojave Firebrand* (H Wild Bill Elliott); *Arizona Whirlwind* (H Trail Blazers); *Thundering Gunslingers* (H Buster Crabbe); *Pinto Bandit* (H Texas Rangers); *Brand of the Devil* (H Texas Rangers). **1945:** *His Brother's Ghost* (H Buster Crabbe); *Rustlers of the Badlands* (H Charles Starrett); *Prairie Rustlers* (H Buster Crabbe). **1946:** *Lightning Raiders* (H Buster Crabbe); *Lawless Breed* (H Kirby Grant); *Gentlemen with Guns* (H Buster Crabbe); *Terrors on Horseback* (H Buster Crabbe); *Outlaw of the Plains* (H Buster Crabbe); *Gunman's Code* (H Kirby Grant).

Myron Healey

Myron Healey was one of the busiest of the B bad men in the late forties and early fifties. A lot of his parts were similar to his role of Cameo Crogan, a crooked gambler and boss of a gang of landgrabbers in Whip Wilson's 1950 film *Fence Riders*. He could also be found in films such as *Trail of the Rustlers* with Charles Starrett, *Hidden Danger* with Johnny Mack Brown and *Fargo* with Wild Bill Elliott.

Healey was also a perennial cliff-hanger player appearing in *The Roar of the Iron Horse* for Columbia Pictures in 1951 as a villain, and as the hero of *The Panther Girl of the Congo* for Republic in 1955.

Healey was often seen as an outlaw on such early TV Westerns as *The Lone Ranger, Annie Oakley, The Cisco Kid* and *Wyatt Earp*.

Mr. Healey still works occasionally as an actor.

Myron Healey Filmography

1948: *Hidden Danger* (H Johnny Mack Brown). **1949:** *Gun Law Justice* (H Jimmy Wakely); *Trail's End* (H Johnny Mack Brown); *Brand of Fear* (H Jimmy Wakely); *Western Renegades* (H Johnny Mack Brown); *Riders of the Dusk* (H Whip Wilson). **1950:** *Fence Riders* (H Whip Wilson); *West of Wyoming* (H Johnny Mack Brown); *Over the Border* (H Johnny Mack Brown); *Salt Lake Raiders* (H Rocky Lane). **1951:** *Night Riders of Montana* (H Rocky Lane); *Montana Desperado* (H Johnny Mack Brown); *Bonanza Town* (H Charles Starrett). **1952:** *The Kid from Broken Gun* (H Charles Starrett); *Desperadoes' Outpost* (H Rocky Lane); *The Maverick* (H Wild Bill Elliott). **1953:** *Texas Bad Man* (H Wayne Morris).

Karl Hackett

Earle Hodgins

Fast-talking Earle Hodgins was the B Western's leading character actor. In one film he might be seen as a cattle rustler, in another as the sheriff, and in another a shifty snake oil salesman or the professor of a medicine show. On occasion he even played an Indian. No matter what the part, Hodgins' easily-recognized rapid-fire delivery of lines always reminded one of a cross between a tent evangelist and a Southern politician at campaign time.

Hodgins appeared in an endless array of roles in such B's as *The Cyclone Ranger* with Bill Cody, *Guns and Guitars* with Gene Autry, *Borderland* with William Boyd as Hopalong Cassidy and *Tenting Tonight on the Old Camp Ground* with Johnny Mack Brown.

Hodgins, who displayed a tremendous knack for comedy, was featured in farces like *My Favorite Wife* with Cary Grant, *Keep 'em Flying* with Abbott and Costello and *Jiggs and Maggie in Jackpotjitters.*

Earle Hodgins was born in 1899 and succumbed to a heart attack April 14, 1964, in Hollywood.

Earle Hodgins Filmography

1935: *The Texas Rambler* (*H* Bill Cody); *Paradise Canyon* (*H* John Wayne); *Cyclone Ranger* (*H* Bill Cody). **1936:** *Border Caballero* (*H* Tim McCoy); *The Singing Cowboy* (*H* Gene Autry); *Aces and Eights* (*H* Tim McCoy); *Oh, Susanna* (*H* Gene Autry); *Ghost Town Gold* (*H* 3 Mesquiteers); *Guns and Guitars* (*H* Gene Autry). **1937:** *Border Land* (*H* Hopalong Cassidy); *Trail of Vengeance* (*H* Johnny Mack Brown); *Hills of Old Wyoming* (*H* Hopalong Cassidy); *Roundup Time in Texas* (*H* Gene Autry); *Smoketree Range* (*H* Buck Jones); *A Lawman Is Born* (*H* Johnny Mack Brown); *Range Defenders* (*H* 3 Mesquiteers); *Law for Tombstone* (*H* Buck Jones); *Texas Trail* (*H* Hopalong Cassidy); *Headin' East* (*H* Buck Jones). **1938:** *The Purple Vigilantes* (*H* 3 Mesquiteers); *The Old Barn Dance* (*H* Gene Autry); *The Ranger's Roundup* (*H* Fred Scott); *Call the Mesquiteers* (*H* 3 Mesquiteers); *The Last Stand* (*H* Bob Baker); *Under Western Stars* (*H* Roy Rogers); *Pride of the West* (*H* Hopalong Cassidy); *Lawless Valley* (*H* George O'Brien). **1939:** *Home on the Prairie* (*H* Gene Autry); *Range War* (*H* Hopalong Cassidy). **1940:** *Santa Fe Marshal* (*H* Hopalong Cassidy); *Range Busters* (*H* Range Busters); *Under Texas Skies* (*H* 3 Mesquiteers); *Law and Order* (*H* Johnny Mack Brown); *Bad Man from Red Butte* (*H* Johnny Mack Brown). **1941:** *Fighting Bill Fargo* (*H* Johnny Mack Brown); *Sierra Sue* (*H* Gene Autry). **1942:** *Call of the Canyon* (*H* Gene Autry); *Undercover Man* (*H* Hopalong Cassidy); *Deep in the Heart of Texas* (*H* Johnny Mack Brown); *The Old Chisholm Trail* (*H* Johnny Mack Brown). **1943:** *Riders of the Deadline* (*H* Hopalong Cassidy); *False Colors* (*H* Hopalong Cassidy); *Tenting Tonight on the Old Campground* (*H* Johnny Mack Brown); *The Avenging Rider* (*H* Tim Holt); *Colt Comrades* (*H* Hopalong Cassidy); *Bar 20* (*H* Hopalong Cassidy); *Lone Star Trail* (*H* Johnny Mack Brown); *Hoppy Serves a Writ* (*H* Hopalong Cassidy). **1944:** *Hidden Valley Outlaws* (*H* Wild Bill Elliott); *Firebrands of Arizona* (*H* Sunset Carson); *San Antonio Kid* (*H* Wild Bill Elliott). **1945:** *The Topeka Terror* (*H* Rocky Lane). **1946:** *Gun Town* (*H* Kirby Grant); *Devil's Playground* (*H* Hopalong Cassidy);

Earle Hodgins

Fool's Gold (H Hopalong Cassidy); *Rustler's Roundup* (H Kirby Grant).
1947: *Unexpected Guest* (H Hopalong Cassidy); *Oregon Trail Scouts* (H
Rocky Lane); *Vigilantes of Boomtown* (H Rocky Lane). **1948:** *Silent Conflict* (H Hopalong Cassidy); *Old Los Angeles* (H Wild Bill Elliott). **1949:**
Sheriff of Wichita (H Rocky Lane).

Jack Ingram

Windy City native (born 1903) Jack Ingram entered films in 1929 as a stuntman. In the mid-thirties he began to hit his stride as a henchman and gangster in horse operas and cliff-hangers. He made in excess of two dozen serials that ranged from mysteries and adventures like *Dick Tracy Returns* (he played Slasher, one of Pa Stark's [Charles Middleton] sons), *The Perils of Nyoka* and *Manhunt of Mystery Island*, to Westerns which included *Zorro Rides Again*, *King of the Texas Rangers*, *The Valley of Vanishing Men*, *The Scarlet Horseman* and *Cody of the Pony Express*.

In B Westerns Ingram was usually cast as an action heavy and occasionally a lawman. His most prolific period was during the 1940s. He continued to make film appearances into the late 1950s.

Jack Ingram suffered a fatal heart attack on February 20, 1969, in Canoga Park, California.

Aside from being a prevalent actor in B Westerns, Ingram also owned a ranch on which many were filmed.

Jack Ingram Filmography

1938: *Western Trails* (H Bob Baker); *Riders of the Black Hills* (H 3 Mesquiteers); *Frontier Scout* (H George Houston). **1939:** *Two Gun Troubador* (H Fred Scott); *Lone Star Pioneers* (H Wild Bill Elliott); *Wall Street Cowboy* (H Roy Rogers). **1940:** *Ghost Valley Raiders* (H Don BArry); *One Man's Land* (H Don Barry); *The Carson City Kid* (H Roy Rogers). **1941:** *Prairie Pioneers* (H 3 Mesquiteers); *Sheriff of Tombstone* (H Roy Rogers); *Nevada City* (H Roy Rogers); *The Lone Rider Ambushed* (H George Houston). **1942:** *Man from Cheyenne* (H Roy Rogers); *Arizona Roundup* (H Tom Keene). **1943:** *Fugitive of the Plains* (H Buster Crabbe); *West of Texas* (H Texas Rangers); *Raiders of San Joaquin* (H Johnny Mack Brown); *Border Buckaroos* (H Texas Rangers); *Arizona Trail* (H Tex Ritter); *Frontier Law* (H Russell Hayden); *The Devil Riders* (H Buster Crabbe). **1944:** *Gunsmoke Mesa* (H Texas Rangers); *Outlaw Roundup* (H Texas Rangers); *Oklahoma Raiders* (H Tex Ritter). **1945:** *Bandits of the Badlands* (H Sunset Carson); *Enemy of the Law* (H Texas Rangers); *Flame of the West* (H Johnny Mack Brown); *Saddle Serenade* (H Jimmy Wakely); *Sheriff of Cimarron* (H Sunset Carson); *Stranger from Santa Fe* (H Johnny Mack Brown); *Frontier Fugitives* (H Texas Rangers). **1946:** *Moon Over Montana* (H Jimmy Wakely). **1947:** *Pioneer Justice* (H Lash LaRue); *South of the Chisholm Trail* (H Charles Starrett); *Ghost Town Renegades* (H Lash LaRue). **1948:** *The Strawberry Roan* (H Gene Autry). **1949:** *Law of the West* (H Johnny Mack Brown).

I. Stanford Jolley

I. Stanford Jolley was born in Elizabeth, New Jersey, in 1900 and entered films in 1935. Before coming to Hollywood he had worked in his family's circus, on the radio and on the legitimate stage.

He became one of the best B Western bad men of the 1940s, appearing in films with such cowboys as Tex Ritter, Buck Jones, Tim McCoy, Bob Livingston, Bob Steele, the Texas Rangers, Whip Wilson and Rocky Lane.

Jolley also appeared in serials such as *The Crimson Ghost, Daughter of Don Q, The Adventures of Frank and Jesse James, Dangers of the Royal Mounted, King of the Rocket Men* and *Don Daredevil Rides Again.*

B Western roles that fell his way were usually as a bandit or cattle rustler, but he also played the parts of sheriffs, stagecoach drivers and the like.

While most of his career was spent in B pictures, he could also be found in top-rated films like *The Long Hot Summer* with Paul Newman and Joanne Woodward.

He passed away December 7, 1978.

I. Stanford Jolley Filmography

1942: *Boot Hill Bandits* (H Range Busters); *The Sombrero Kid* (H Don Barry); *Border Roundup* (H George Houston); *Outlaws of Boulder Pass* (H George Houston); *The Rangers Take Over* (H Texas Rangers). **1943:** *The Kid Rides Again* (H Buster Crabbe); *Bad Men of Thunder Gap* (H Texas Rangers); *Death Rides the Plains* (H Bob Livingston); *Wolves of the Range* (H Bob Livingston); *Blazing Frontier* (H Buster Crabbe); *Frontier Law* (H Russell Hayden). **1944:** *Outlaw Roundup* (H Texas Rangers); *Oklahoma Raiders* (H Tex Ritter). **1945:** *Outlaws of the Rockies* (H Charles Starrett); *Fighting Bill Carson* (H Buster Crabbe). **1946:** *Ambush Trail* (H Bob Steele); *Terrors on Horseback* (H Buster Crabbe); *Two-Fisted Stranger* (H Charles Starrett); *'Neath Canadian Skies* (H Russell Hayden); *Silver Range* (H Johnny Mack Brown). **1947:** *Wild Country* (H Eddie Dean); *West of Dodge City* (H Charles Starrett); *Land of the Lawless* (H Johnny Mack Brown); *Prairie Express* (H Johnny Mack Brown). **1948:** *Check Your Guns* (H Eddie Dean); *Oklahoma Blues* (H Jimmy Wakely); *The Fighting Ranger* (H Johnny Mack Brown); *Gunning for Justice* (H Johnny Mack Brown). **1949:** *Gun Law Justice* (H Jimmy Wakely); *Haunted Trails* (H Whip Wilson). **1950:** *Fast on the Draw* (H Jimmy Ellison); *Trigger Jr.* (H Roy Rogers). **1951:** *Canyon Raiders* (H Whip Wilson); *Oklahoma Justice* (H Johnny Mack

Brown); *Lawless Cowboys* (H Whip Wilson). **1952:** *Waco* (H Wild Bill Elliott); *The Gunman* (H Whip Wilson).

Victor Jory

Victor Jory's place in motion picture villaindom's hall of shame was secured by his portrayals of such blackguards as Injun Joe in the *Adventures of Tom Sawyer* in 1938 and the greedy carpetbagger in *Gone with the Wind* the following year.

During the early 1940s Jory was the main menace of one of the Western's all-time great heroes ... Hopalong Cassidy. In action-packed thrillers such as *Border Vigilantes, Wide Open Town, Hoppy Serves a Writ, The Leather Burners* and *Colt Comrades* lawbreaker Jory and good guy Cassidy locked horns, with Cassidy always coming up with the winning hand. Jory was usually the "boss" heavy, the same kind of part that Morris Ankrum performed in the Cassidy films during the late thirties.

Jory, born in 1902, began his career as a stage actor in the mid-1920s. He made his film debut in 1932 in a film called *Sailor's Luck.*

Some of his screen appearances include *Valley of the Kings* in 1954, *The Miracle Worker* in 1963 and *Cheyenne Autumn* in 1964.

In 1940 Jory starred in a pair of mystery cliff-hangers for Columbia Pictures, *The Green Archer* and *The Shadow.*

Victory Jory Filmography

1940: *Knights of the Range* (H Russell Hayden); *The Light of Western Stars* (H Russell Hayden). **1941:** *Border Vigilantes* (H Hopalong Cassidy); *Wide Open Town* (H Hopalong Cassidy); *Riders of the Timberline* (H Hopalong Cassidy). **1943:** *Hoppy Serves a Writ* (H Hopalong Cassidy); *The Leather Burners* (H Hopalong Cassidy); *Colt Comrades* (H Hopalong Cassidy); *Bar 20* (H Hopalong Cassidy).

Charles King

Cowboy legend Tex Ritter once remarked in an interview that he must have killed Charlie King 50 times. In fact there weren't many B Western heroes who didn't finish off King a few times.

Victor Jory is taken into custody by William Boyd in Bar 20 *(1943).*

King was a burly bad guy whose face featured an ever-present black mustache. He specialized in playing rustlers and banditos who were usually called "Slick" or "Blackie." King hardly ever played the brains of the outfit; most always he was the gunslick sent out to do the good guy in. Just like he tried to do to Tex in the 1937 film *Trouble in Texas.*

King was born in 1899 and made his film debut in the early 1920s. Early in his career he began getting parts in Westerns and serials, a trend which carried over into talking pictures in the thirties.

It is hard to imagine anyone making a B Western in the thirties and forties without Charlie King being in it. He made in excess of a hundred, in parts that ranged from chief villain to just one of the gang.

Charles King also made a slew of serials beginning with John Wayne's *Hurricane Express* in 1932. While most of his cliff-hanger work was in Westerns like *The Painted Stallion* (1937), *Zorro's Fighting Legion* (1939), *Deadwood Dick* (1940) and *White Eagle* (1941), he also appeared in mystery serials like *The Iron Claw* in 1941. He was the villainous trader Jake Rayne in the 1945 Columbia chapter play *Jungle Raiders* and was the sidekick of George "Superman" Reeves in the *Adventures of Sir Galahad* in 1949.

In some of his later Western features King displayed a fantastic flair for comedy. This can be especially observed in several of the PRC films that he made with Buster Crabbe and Fuzzy St. John.

Charles King passed away May 7, 1957.

Charles King Filmography

1930: *Oklahoma Cyclone* (H Bob Steele); *The Dawn Trail* (H Buck Jones); *Fighting Thru* (H Ken Maynard). **1931:** *The Two-Gun Man* (H Ken Maynard); *Alias the Bad Man* (H Ken Maynard); *The Arizona Terror* (H Ken Maynard); *Range Law* (H Ken Maynard); *Branded Men* (H Ken Maynard); *The Pocatello Kid* (H Ken Maynard). **1932:** *Ghost City* (H Bill Cody); *The Gay Buckaroo* (H Hoot Gibson); *Vanishing Men* (H Tom Tyler); *A Man's Land* (H Hoot Gibson); *Honor of the Mounted* (H Tom Tyler); *Between Fighting Men* (H Ken Maynard); *The Man from Arizona* (H Rex Bell); *Young Blood* (H Bob Steele); *The Fighting Champ* (H Bob Steele). **1933:** *Son of the Border* (H Tom Keene); *The Lone Avenger* (H Ken Maynard); *Crashing Broadway* (H Rex Bell); *The Fighting Parson* (H Hoot Gibson); *The Strawberry Roan* (H Ken Maynard). **1934:** *Mystery Ranch* (H Tom Tyler); *The Fighting Trooper* (H Kermit Maynard); *Northern Frontier* (H Kermit Maynard); *The Silver Bullet* (H Tom Tyler); *The Red Blood of Courage* (H Kermit Maynard); *Outlawed Guns* (H Buck Jones); *Tumbling Tumbleweeds* (H Gene Autry); *His Fighting Blood* (H Kermit Maynard); *The Ivory-Handled Gun* (H Buck Jones); *Born to Battle* (H Tom Tyler); *Courage of the North* (H John Preston); *Silent Valley* (H Tom Tyler); *Trail of Terror* (H Bob Steele). **1936:** *Sunset of Power* (H Buck Jones); *Valley of the Lawless* (H Johnny Mack Brown); *The Kid Ranger* (H Bob Steele); *The Lawless Nineties* (H John Wayne); *Red River Valley* (H Gene Autry); *Desert Phantom* (H Johnny Mack Brown); *O'Malley of the Mounted* (H George O'Brien); *Last of the Warrens* (H Bob Steele); *The Law Rides* (H Bob Steele); *The Crooked Trail* (H Johnny Mack Brown); *The Idaho Kid* (H Rex Bell); *Brand of the Outlaws* (H Bob Steele); *Santa Fe Bound* (H Tom Tyler); *Men of the Plains* (H Rex Bell); *Rip Roarin' Buckaroo* (H Tom Tyler); *Phantom of the Range* (H Tom Tyler); *Headin' for the Rio Grande* (H Tex Ritter); *Guns and Guitars* (H Gene Autry); *Sundown Saunders* (H Bob Steele).

Charles King

1937: *The Gambling Terror* (H Johnny Mack Brown); *Trouble in Texas* (H Tex Ritter); *Lightnin' Crandall* (H Bob Steele); *Hittin' the Trail* (H Tex Ritter); *The Trusted Outlaw* (H Bob Steele); *Sing Cowboy Sing* (H Tex Ritter); *Rootin' Tootin' Rhythm* (H Gene Autry); *Smoketree Range* (H Buck Jones); *Riders of the Rockies* (H Tex Ritter); *The Red Rope* (H Bob Steele); *The Mystery of the Hooded Horseman* (H Tex Ritter); *God's Country and the Man* (H Tom Keene); *Black Aces* (H Buck Jones); *Ridin' the Lone Trail* (H Bob Steele); *The Fighting Deputy* (H Fred Scott). **1938:** *Tex Rides with the Boy Scouts* (H Tex Ritter); *Frontier Town* (H Tex Ritter); *Thunder in the Desert* (H Bob Steele); *Song and Bullets* (H Fred Scott); *Phantom Ranger* (H Tim McCoy); *Gold Mine in the Sky* (H Gene Autry); *Man's Country* (H Jack Randall); *Rollin' Plains* (H Tex Ritter); *On the Great White Trail* (H James Newill); *Utah Trail* (H Tex Ritter); *Starlight Over Texas* (H Tex Ritter); *Where the Buffalo Roam* (H Tex Ritter); *Gun Packer* (H Jack Randall); *Wild Horse Canyon* (H Jack Randall); *Songs and Saddles* (H Gene

Austin). **1939:** *Song of the Buckaroo* (*H* Tex Ritter); *Trigger Pals* (*H* Art Jarrett); *Feud of the Range* (*H* Bob Steele); *Frontiers of '49* (*H* Wild Bill Elliott); *Sundown on the Prairie* (*H* Tex Ritter); *Rollin' Westward* (*H* Tex Ritter); *Lone Star Pioneers* (*H* Wild Bill Elliott); *Frontier Pony Express* (*H* Roy Rogers); *The Law Comes to Texas* (*H* Wild Bill Elliott); *Mesquite Buckaroo* (*H* Bob Steele); *Down the Wyoming Trail* (*H* Tex Ritter); *Riders of the Frontier* (*H* Tex Ritter); *Cowboys from Texas* (*H* 3 Mesquiteers); *South of the Border* (*H* Gene Autry). **1940:** *Death Rides the Range* (*H* Ken Maynard); *The Cheyenne Kid* (*H* Jack Randall); *West of Carson City* (*H* Johnny Mack Brown); *Riders from Nowhere* (*H* Jack Randall); *Wild Horse Range* (*H* Jack Randall); *Lightning Strikes West* (*H* Ken Maynard); *Roll Wagons Roll* (*H* Tex Ritter); *Billy the Kid in Texas* (*H* Bob Steele); *Billy the Kid's Gun Justice* (*H* Bob Steele). **1941:** *Billy the Kid's Range War* (*H* Bob Steele); *The Lone Rider Crosses the Rio* (*H* George Houston); *Outlaws of the Rio Grande* (*H* Tim McCoy); *Billy the Kid's Fighting Pals* (*H* Bob Steele); *Lone Rider in Ghost Town* (*H* George Houston); *Law of the Range* (*H* Johnny Mack Brown); *Billy the Kid in Santa Fe* (*H* Bob Steele); *The Lone Rider Ambushed* (*H* George Houston); *The Apache Kid* (*H* Don Barry); *The Gunman from Bodie* (*H* Rough Riders); *Billy the Kid Wanted* (*H* Buster Crabbe); *Roaring Frontiers* (*H* Wild Bill Elliott); *Lone Rider Fights Back* (*H* George Houston); *Lone Star Lawmen* (*H* Tom Keene); *Billy the Kid's Roundup* (*H* Buster Crabbe); *Forbidden Trails* (*H* Rough Riders). **1942:** *Below the Border* (*H* Rough Riders); *Raiders of the West* (*H* Bill "Cowboy Rambler" Boyd); *Ghost Town Law* (*H* Rough Riders); *Where Trails End* (*H* Tom Keene); *Boot Hill Bandits* (*H* Range Busters); *Tumbleweed Trail* (*H* Bill Boyd); *Law and Order* (*H* Buster Crabbe); *Riders of the West* (*H* Rough Riders); *Arizona Stagecoach* (*H* Range Busters); *Prairie Pals* (*H* Bill Boyd); *Border Roundup* (*H* George Houston); *Along the Sundown Trail* (*H* Bill Boyd); *Sheriff of Sage Valley* (*H* Buster Crabbe); *Pirates of the Prairie* (*H* Tim Holt); *Outlaws of Boulder Pass* (*H* George Houston); *Trail Riders* (*H* Range Busters); *Overland Stagecoach* (*H* Bob Livingston); *The Rangers Take Over* (*H* Texas Rangers). **1943:** *Two Fisted Justice* (*H* Range Busters); *The Kid Rides Again* (*H* Buster Crabbe); *Haunted Ranch* (*H* Range Busters); *Land of Hunted Men* (*H* Range Busters); *The Ghost Rider* (*H* Johnny Mack Brown); *Calling Wild Bill Elliott* (*H* Wild Bill Elliott); *Western Cyclone* (*H* Buster Crabbe); *Border Buckaroos* (*H* Texas Rangers); *The Stranger from Pecos* (*H* Johnny Mack Brown); *Fighting Valley* (*H* Texas Rangers); *Cattle Stampede* (*H* Buster Crabbe); *Raiders of Red Gap* (*H* Bob Livingston); *Bordertown Gunfighters* (*H* Wild Bill Elliott); *Blazing Guns* (*H* Trail Blazers); *Outlaws of Stampede Pass* (*H* Johnny Mack Brown); *Return of the Rangers* (*H* Texas Rangers); *Boss of Rawhide* (*H* Texas Rangers); *Death Valley Rangers* (*H* Trail Blazers); *Cowboy in the Clouds* (*H* Charles Starrett). **1944:** *Outlaw Roundup* (*H* Texas Rangers);

Arizona Whirlwind (H Trail Blazers); *Frontier Outlaws* (H Buster Crabbe); *Thundering Gunslingers* (H Buster Crabbe); *Guns of the Law* (H Texas Rangers); *Outlaw Trail* (H Trail Blazers); *The Pinto Bandit* (H Texas Rangers); *Valley of Vengeance* (H Buster Crabbe); *Spook Town* (H Texas Rangers); *Fuzzy Settles Down* (H Buster Crabbe); *Brand of the Devil* (H Texas Rangers); *Rustlers' Hideout* (H Buster Crabbe); *Land of the Outlaws* (H Johnny Mack Brown); *Gangsters of the Frontier* (H Texas Rangers); *Code of the Prairie* (H Sunset Carson); *Law of the Valley* (H Johnny Mack Brown); *Dead or Alive* (H Texas Rangers); *Oath of Vengeance* (H Buster Crabbe). **1945:** *The Navajo Trail* (H Johnny Mack Brown); *His Brother's Ghost* (H Buster Crabbe); *Marked for Murder* (H Texas Rangers); *Shadows of Death* (H Buster Crabbe); *Enemy of the Law* (H Texas Rangers); *Both Barrels Blazing* (H Charles Starrett); *Gangsters' Den* (H Buster Crabbe); *Three in the Saddle* (H Texas Rangers); *Frontier Fugitives* (H Texas Rangers); *Border Bad Men* (H Buster Crabbe); *Flaming Bullets* (H Texas Rangers); *Fighting Bill Carson* (H Buster Crabbe); *Frontier Feud* (H Johnny Mack Brown). **1946:** *Ambush Trail* (H Bob Steele); *Thunder Town* (H Bob Steele); *The Caravan Trail* (H Eddie Dean); *Ghost of Hidden Valley* (H Buster Crabbe); *Colorado Serenade* (H Eddie Dean); *Prairie Badmen* (H Buster Crabbe); *Lawless Breed* (H Kirby Grant); *Outlaws of the Plains* (H Buster Crabbe). **1947:** *Law of the Lash* (H Lash LaRue).

Fred Kohler, Sr.

Burly Fred Kohler, Sr., made a career out of trying to bushwhack and dismember legendary cowboy heroes like Buck Jones, Ken Maynard and Tom Mix in the early days of the B Western era.

There was little finesse to the villainy of Kohler's characters; most were your basic evil brute. With his size and sinister air Kohler emitted a strong and violent screen presence.

Born in Kansas City, Missouri, on April 20, 1889, Kohler worked vaudeville before making his film debut in 1911 in a film called *Code of Honor*. Right from the onset of his career most of the roles he got were those of villains in Westerns and serials.

In 1924 Kohler was chosen to play the part of the lead action heavy in John Ford's Western classic *The Iron Horse*. As the savage Indian leader "Two Fingers," Kohler battled hero George O'Brien tooth and tomahawk throughout the epic.

His performance led to his becoming the top Western bad guy of the silent era. He appeared with Tom Mix in the 1925 version of *The Riders of the Purple Sage*, one of the most highly touted Westerns ever made.

Fred Kohler, Sr.

In the early thirties Kohler was the stock B Western bad guy at Universal Studios. He battled the best good guys that the lot had to offer: Ken Maynard in films like *The Fiddlin' Buckaroo,* Tom Mix in *Texas Badman* and *Riders of Death Valley* and Buck Jones in *Border Brigands.*

He also appeared in films with Reb Russell, Roy Rogers and Kermit Maynard among others.

Kohler made only two sound era serials, both in which he portrayed evildoers. In the 1933 Mascot serial *Wolf Dog* he played Frankie Darro's brutish stepfather, and in his best chapter play he was General Jason Burr who, if not for the heroic efforts of Bob Livingston, would have sold California to the Rusians in the Republic thriller *The Vigilantes Are Coming.*

He was also the bad guy in the Three Stooges 1935 comedy/Western short "Horse Collars."

Kohler was a huge man. He stood 6' 2" and weighed around 200 pounds. He had several fingers missing from one hand due to a hunting accident.

His son Fred Kohler, Jr., became an actor and had a brief splash as a cowboy hero before turning to celluloid villainy in the late thirties and forties.

Fred Kohler, Sr., died of a heart attack on October 8, 1938, in Los Angeles, California.

Fred Kohler, Sr. Filmography

1932: *Rider of Death Valley* (H Tom Mix); *Texas Badman* (H Tom Mix). **1933:** *Fiddlin' Buckaroo* (H Ken Maynard). **1934:** *Honor of the Range* (H Ken Maynard); *The Man from Hell* (H Reb Russell). **1935:** *Wilderness Mail* (H Kermit Maynard); *Border Brigands* (H Buck Jones); *Lightning Triggers* (H Reb Russell); *Trail's End* (H Conway Tearle). **1936:** *For the Service* (H Buck Jones); *Heart of the West* (H Hopalong Cassidy); *Arizona Mahoney* (H Buster Crabbe). **1938:** *Billy the Kid Returns* (H Roy Rogers); *Lawless Valley* (H George O'Brien).

Bob Kortman

Some B Western writers and afficionados consider Bob Kortman the ugliest and most sinister in appearance of all the genre's bad men.

The gaunt-faced Kortman's career as a Western villain lasted from the silent era to the mid-forties.

His roles were almost always that of henchman, usually the third or fourth member of an outlaw gang. However, on occasion this did vary, as in the 1933 Ken Maynard circus Western *King of the Arena* in which Kortman played Bargoff, a villainous cossack.

He was born Robert F. Kortman in Philadelphia, Pennsylvania on Christmas Eve, 1887. He began making films in the early 1900s. Kortman must be considered one of the earliest of the screen's Western villains, because in several of his silent films he menaced the movies' first cowboy hero, Broncho Billy Anderson.

Along with the several B Westerns which he made, Kortman also appeared in Western cliff-hangers like *The Miracle Rider* with Tom Mix in 1935, *Mystery Mountain* with Ken Maynard, *The Vigilantes Are Coming* with Robert Livingston, *Wild West Days* with Johnny Mack Brown and *The Adventures of Red Ryder* with Don "Red" Barry. *Wild West Days* was a real change of pace for Kortman, as he played sidekick to Brown.

Bob Kortman could also be seen in A Westerns like *Cimarron* in 1931 and *Whispering Smith* in 1948.

He passed away March 13, 1967, of cancer in Long Beach, California.

Bob Kortman Filmography

1931: *Branded* (H Buck Jones). **1932:** *The Fighting Fool* (H Tim McCoy); *Cornered* (H Tim McCoy); *Come on Tarzan* (H Ken Maynard); *Gold* (H Jack Hoxie); *White Eagle* (H Buck Jones). **1933:** *Terror Trail* (H Tom Mix); *The Phantom Thunderbolt* (H Ken Maynard); *King of the Arena* (H Ken Maynard); *The Fiddlin' Buckaroo* (H Ken Maynard); *Rainbow Ranch* (H Rex Bell); *The Fugitive* (H Rex Bell); *The Trail Drive* (H Ken Maynard). **1934:** *Smoking Guns* (H Ken Maynard). **1935:** *Branded a Coward* (H Johnny Mack Brown); *The Ivory Handled Gun* (H Buck Jones); *Swifty* (H Hoot Gibson); *Wild Mustang* (H Harry Carey). **1936:** *Song of the Saddle* (H Dick Foran); *Feud of the West* (H Hoot Gibson); *The Lonely Trail* (H John Wayne); *Winds of the Wasteland* (H John Wayne); *Brand of the Outlaws* (H Bob Steele); *Heroes of the Range* (H Ken Maynard); *Romance Rides the Range* (H Fred Scott); *Ghost Town Gold* (H 3 Mesquiteers). **1937:** *Ranger Courage* (H Bob Allen); *Sand Flow* (H Buck Jones); *Smoke Tree Range* (H Buck Jones); *The Rangers Step In* (H Bob Allen); *Texas Trail* (H Hopalong Cassidy); *Black Aces* (H Buck Jones). **1938:** *West of Rainbow's End* (H Tim McCoy); *Stagecoach Days* (H Jack Luden); *The Renegade Ranger* (H George O'Brien); *Law of the Texan* (H Buck Jones). **1939:** *Arizona Legion* (H George O'Brien); *Timber Stampede* (H George O'Brien); *Oklahoma Frontier* (H Johnny Mack Brown); *Renegade Trail* (H Hopalong Cassidy). **1940:** *Law and Order* (H Johnny Mack Brown). **1941:** *Fugitive Valley* (H Range Busters). **1942:** *The Sundown Kid* (H Don Barry). **1943:** *The Avenging Rider* (H Tim Holt); *Black Hills Express* (H Don Barry). **1944:** *Forty Thieves* (H Hopalong Cassidy); *Wyoming Hurricane* (H Russell Hayden); *The Vigilantes Ride* (H Russell Hayden); *Call of the Rockies* (H Sunset Carson); *The Pinto Bandit* (H Texas Rangers); *Guns of the Law* (H

Bob Kortman

Texas Rangers); *Saddle Leather Law* (H Charles Starrett). **1946:** *Frontier Gun Law* (H Charles Starrett); *Gunning for Vengeance* (H Charles Starrett).

Frank Lacteen

With his unique facial features and thickly accented voice, Asian-born Frank Lacteen spent most of his five-decade screen career playing foreign spies, witch doctors, medicine men and other assorted weird characters.

He appeared in more than ten serials, both silent and talking, including *The Fortieth Door* (1924), *The Hawk of the Hills* (1927), *Heroes of the West* (1932), *Tarzan the Fearless* (1933), *The Mysterious Pilot* (1937) and *Don Winslow of the Navy* (1942).

His most memorable cliff-hanger role came in the 1941 Republic serial *The Jungle Girl*. As the wicked witch doctor Shamba, Lacteen used innumerable booby traps and the like to try and barbeque Frances Gifford, who had the title role.

Lacteen's B Western roles were often lawless half-breeds like the one he played in the 1940 Hopalong Cassidy adventure *Stagecoach War*.

He was born August 29, 1894, in Kubber-Ilias, Asia Minor, and began making films around 1915.

His career stretched until the mid-1960s.

Frank Lacteen died July 8, 1968.

Frank Lacteen Filmography

1932: *Texas Pioneers* (H Bill Cody); *Land of Wanted Men* (H Bill Cody). **1933:** *Treason* (H Buck Jones); *Rustlers' Roundup* (H Tom Mix). **1936:** *Comin' Round the Mountain* (H Gene Autry). **1937:** *Left Handed Law* (H Buck Jones). **1939:** *Kansas Terrors* (H 3 Mesquiteers). **1940:** *Stagecoach War* (H Hopalong Cassidy). **1947:** *Oregon Trail Scouts* (H Rocky Lane); *The Cowboy and the Indians* (H Gene Autry). **1950:** *Indian Territory* (H Gene Autry).

Ethan Laidlaw

Ethan Laidlaw was a familiar face among the B Western bad guy corps of the thirties and forties. He was most often a henchman villain.

Laidlaw was born November 25, 1899, in Butte, Montana, and entered films in 1923.

Laidlaw appeared in such B Westerns as *Powdersmoke Range* with Harry Carey, *Border G-Man* with George O'Brien and *Marshal of Gunsmoke* with Tex Ritter.

He appeared in two Three Stooges Western parodies, *Goofs and Saddles* and *Three Troubledoers.*

Laidlaw had roles in major films like *Joan of Arc* and *The Ten Commandments.*

Ethan Laidlaw died May 25, 1963.

Ethan Laidlaw Filmography

1931: *Dugan of the Badlands* (H Bill Cody); *Fighting Marshal* (H Tim McCoy). **1934:** *Rainbow Riders* (H Jack Perrin). **1935:** *Fighting Shadows* (H Tim McCoy); *Powdersmoke Range* (H Harry Carey). **1937:** *One Man Justice* (H Charles Starrett). **1938:** *Border G-Man* (H George O'Brien); *Rhythm of the Saddle* (H Gene Autry). **1939:** *Home on the Prairie* (H Gene Autry); *Night Riders* (H 3 Mesquiteers); *Three Texas Steers* (H 3 Mesquiteers); *Western Caravans* (H Charles Starrett); *Cowboys from Texas* (H 3 Mesquiteers). **1940:** *Son of Roaring Dan* (H Johnny Mack Brown); *The Tulsa Kid* (H Don "Red" Barry); *Wagon Train* (H Tim Holt); *Stage to Chino* (H George O'Brien); *Law and Order* (H Johnny Mack Brown). **1941:** *Law of the Range* (H Johnny Mack Brown). **1942:** *Lone Star Vigilantes* (H Wild Bill Elliott); *Stagecoach Express* (H Don "Red" Barry); *Cowboy Serenade* (H Gene Autry); *Riding Through Nevada* (H Charles Starrett). **1943:** *Border Buckaroos* (H Texas Rangers). **1944:** *Marshal of Gunsmoke* (H Tex Ritter); *Oklahoma Raiders* (H Tex Ritter). **1945:** *Lawless Empire* (H Charles Starrett); *Blazing the Western Trail* (H Charles Starrett). **1946:** *Rustlers' Roundup* (H Kirby Grant). **1947:** *Buckaroo from Powder River* (H Charles Starrett); *Six Gun Law* (H Charles Starrett).

Tom London

Someone once estimated that in his 60-year career as an actor, Tom London appeared in between 700 and 800 films in every kind of role imaginable.

Westerns were home for London. When he was ten years old, he appeared in what is credited with being the first Western ever made, **The Great Train Robbery** (1903). During the silent era his fortes were Westerns and serials, and he became an expert at playing well-heeled evildoers.

Tom easily made the transition to talking pictures. He showed his scalawag talents in such early B Westerns as *Firebrand Jordan* with Lane Chandler (1930) and *Under Texas Skies* with Bob Custer (1930). He was

Ethan Laidlaw

cast as the lead villain in the 1931 serial *Spell of the Circus*, and he battled
football legend Red Grange in his cliff-hanger *The Galloping Ghost*.

Throughout the thirties and forties London was one of the busiest of
the B Western stock players. He was almost always cast as a rustler or robber, occasionally as a sheriff.

Among the Western serials in which he appeared are *Clancy of the
Mounted* (1933), *The Miracle Rider* (1935), *The Lone Ranger* (1938), *The
Valley of Vanishing Men* (1942), *Zorro's Black Whip* (1944) and *Jesse James
Rides Again* (1947).

He appeared in Westerns with virtually every star in the genre. London was in some of Gene Autry's better efforts like *Tumbling Tumbleweeds* (1935), *Guns and Guitars* (1936) and *Melody Ranch* (1940). He served as a sort of semisidekick to Sunset Carson in several films in the mid-forties.

Tom London was born Leonard Clapham on August 24, 1893, in Louisville, Kentucky. He was still a busy actor at the time of his death on December 5, 1963.

Tom London Filmography

1930: *Firebrand Jordan* (*H* Lane Chandler); *Under Texas Skies* (*H* Bob Custer). **1931:** *Westward Bound* (*H* Buffalo Bill, Jr.); *Trails of the Golden West* (*H* Buffalo Bill, Jr.); *The Two Gun Man* (*H* Ken Maynard); *Lightnin' Smith Returns* (*H* Buddy Roosevelt); *The Arizona Terror* (*H* Ken Maynard); *Range Law* (*H* Ken Maynard). **1932:** *Without Honors* (*H* Harry Carey); *Honor of the Mounted* (*H* Tom Tyler); *Beyond the Rockies* (*H* Tom Keene); *Gold* (*H* Jack Hoxie); *Hidden Valley* (*H* Bob Steele); *The Boiling Point* (*H* Hoot Gibson). **1933:** *The Fugitive* (*H* Rex Bell). **1934:** *Mystery Ranch* (*H* Tom Tyler); *Fighting Hero* (*H* Tom Tyler); *The Prescott Kid* (*H* Tim McCoy); *The Cactus Kid* (*H* Jack Perrin). **1935:** *Justice of the Range* (*H* Tim McCoy); *Tumbling Tumbleweeds* (*H* Gene Autry); *Last of the Clintons* (*H* Harry Carey); *The Sagebrush Troubador* (*H* Gene Autry); *Gallant Defender* (*H* Charles Starrett); *Courage of the North* (*H* John Preston); *Gun Play* (*H* Big Boy Williams); *Rio Rattler* (*H* Tom Tyler); *Timber Terrors* (*H* John Preston); *Toll of the Desert* (*H* Fred Kohler, Jr.). **1936:** *The Lawless Nineties* (*H* John Wayne); *O'Malley of the Mounted* (*H* George O'Brien); *The Border Patrolman* (*H* George O'Brien); *Avenging Waters* (*H* Ken Maynard); *Rio Grande Ranger* (*H* Bob Allen); *Guns and Guitars* (*H* Gene Autry); *Wildcat Saunders* (*H* Jack Perrin). **1937:** *Bar Z Bad Men* (*H* Johnny Mack Brown); *Law of the Ranger* (*H* Bob Allen); *Reckless Ranger* (*H* Bob Allen); *Western Gold* (*H* Smith Ballew); *Courage of the West* (*H* Bob Baker). **1938:** *Outlaws of Sonora* (*H* 3 Mesquiteers); *Phantom Ranger* (*H* Tim McCoy); *Six Shootin' Sheriff* (*H* Ken Maynard); *Riders of the Black Hills* (*H* 3 Mesquiteers); *Prairie Moon* (*H* Gene Autry); *Guilty Trail* (*H* Bob Baker); *Rhythm of the Saddle* (*H* Gene Autry); *Santa Fe Stampede* (*H* 3 Mesquiteers). **1939:** *Song of the Buckaroo* (*H* Tex Ritter); *Rollin' Westward* (*H* Tex Ritter); *Mexicali Rose* (*H* Gene Autry); *North of the Yukon* (*H* Charles Starrett); *The Night Riders* (*H* 3 Mesquiteers); *Man from Texas* (*H* Tex Ritter); *Southward Ho* (*H* Roy Rogers); *Mountain Rhythm* (*H* Gene Autry); *Timber Stampede* (*H* George O'Brien); *Flaming Lead* (*H* Ken Maynard); *Westbound Stage* (*H* Tex Ritter). **1940:** *Ghost Valley Raiders* (*H*

Don Barry); *Phantom Rancher* (*H* Ken Maynard); *Covered Wagon Days* (*H* 3 Mesquiteers); *Gaucho Serenade* (*H* Gene Autry); *The Kid from Santa Fe* (*H* Jack Randall); *Riders from Nowhere* (*H* Jack Randall); *Roll Wagons Roll* (*H* Tex Ritter); *Trailing Double Trouble* (*H* Range Busters); *Wild Horse Range* (*H* Jack Randall); *Stage to Chino* (*H* George O'Brien); *Melody Ranch* (*H* Gene Autry); *Lone Star Raiders* (*H* 3 Mesquiteers). **1941:** *The Lone Rider Rides On* (*H* George Houston); *Across the Sierras* (*H* Wild Bill Elliott); *Dude Cowboy* (*H* Tim Holt); *Robbers of the Range* (*H* Tim Holt); *Pals of the Pecos* (*H* 3 Mesquiteers); *Twilight on the Trail* (*H* Hopalong Cassidy); *Ridin' on a Rainbow* (*H* Gene Autry); *Stick to Your Guns* (*H* Hopalong Cassidy); *Fugitive Valley* (*H* Range Busters). **1942:** *Land of the Open Range* (*H* Tim Holt); *West of Tombstone* (*H* Charles Starrett); *Stardust on the Sage* (*H* Gene Autry); *Down Texas Way* (*H* Rough Riders); *Arizona Terrors* (*H* Don Barry); *Ghost Town Law* (*H* Rough Riders); *Cowboy Serenade* (*H* Gene Autry); *Sons of the Pioneers* (*H* Roy Rogers); *Shadows on the Sage* (*H* 3 Mesquiteers). **1943:** *Tenting Tonight on the Old Campground* (*H* Johnny Mack Brown); *Wild Horse Stampede* (*H* Trail Blazers); *False Colors* (*H* Hopalong Cassidy); *Hail to the Rangers* (*H* Charles Starrett); *Wagon Tracks West* (*H* Wild Bill Elliott); *Fighting Frontier* (*H* Tim Holt). **1944:** *Yellow Rose of Texas* (*H* Roy Rogers); *Sheriff of Sundown* (*H* Rocky Lane); *Code of the Prairie* (*H* Sunset Carson); *Beneath Western Skies* (*H* Robert Livingston); *San Antonio Kid* (*H* Wild Bill Elliott); *Hidden Valley Outlaws* (*H* Wild Bill Elliott); *Vigilantes of Dodge City* (*H* Wild Bill Elliott); *Stagecoach to Monterey* (*H* Rocky Lane); *Firebrands of Arizona* (*H* Sunset Carson); *Cheyenne Wildcat* (*H* Wild Bill Elliott). **1945:** *Colorado Pioneers* (*H* Wild Bill Elliott); *Don't Fence Me In* (*H* Roy Rogers); *Sunset in El Dorado* (*H* Roy Rogers); *Corpus Christi Bandits* (*H* Rocky Lane); *Marshal of Laredo* (*H* Wild Bill Elliott); *The Cherokee Flash* (*H* Sunset Carson); *Trail of Kit Carson* (*H* Rocky Lane); *Rough Riders of Cheyenne* (*H* Sunset Carson); *The Topeka Terror* (*H* Rocky Lane); *Sheriff of Cimarron* (*H* Sunset Carson). **1946:** *Sheriff of Redwood Valley* (*H* Wild Bill Elliott); *Days of Buffalo Bill* (*H* Sunset Carson); *Out California Way* (*H* Monte Hale); *California Gold Rush* (*H* Wild Bill Elliott); *Alias Billy the Kid* (*H* Sunset Carson); *Roll on Texas Moon* (*H* Roy Rogers); *Rio Grande Raiders* (*H* Sunset Carson); *Man from Rainbow Valley* (*H* Monte Hale); *Red River Renegades* (*H* Sunset Carson); *Santa Fe Uprising* (*H* Rocky Lane). **1947:** *Wyoming* (*H* Bill Elliott); *Last Frontier Uprising* (*H* Monte Hale); *Homesteaders of Paradise Valley* (*H* Rocky Lane); *Saddle Pals* (*H* Gene Autry); *Marshal of Cripple Creek* (*H* Rocky Lane); *Rustlers of Devil's Canyon* (*H* Rocky Lane); *Along the Oregon Trail* (*H* Monte Hale); *The Wild Frontier* (*H* Rocky Lane); *Under Colorado Skies* (*H* Monte Hale). **1948:** *Mark of the Lash* (*H* Lash LaRue); *Marshal of Amarillo* (*H* Rocky Lane). **1949:** *Brand of Fear* (*H* Jimmy Wakely); *Riders in the Sky* (*H* Gene

Autry); *Frontier Investigator* (H Rocky Lane); *South of Rio* (H Monte Hale); *San Antone Ambush* (H Monte Hale). **1950:** *The Old Frontier* (H Monte Hale). **1951:** *Rough Riders of Durango* (H Rocky Lane). **1952:** *The Old West* (H Gene Autry); *Blue Canadian Rockies* (H Gene Autry); *Apache Country* (H Gene Autry). **1953:** *Pack Train* (H Gene Autry).

Francis McDonald

Francis McDonald was one of the best known of the B Western "brains" bad buys. Perhaps his role as Hammond, a respected citizen who secretly headed up a band of killers, in the 1944 Republic serial *Zorro's Black Whip* was a shining example of the type of role in which McDonald excelled. His characters were noted for maintaining a legitimate front while sending out a Roy Barcroft or a George Chesebro to do their dirty work.

McDonald had a long and prolific career which began in silent films around 1918 and lasted into the mid-1960s.

Along with dozens of B Westerns, he appeared in A Westerns like *Union Pacific,* serials like *Wild West Days* and *Mystery of the Riverboat* and films like Greta Garbo's msterpiece *Anna Karenina.*

McDonald was born in Bowling Green, Kentucky, on August 22, 1891, and passed away September 18, 1968.

Francis McDonald Filmography

1932: *Honor of the Mounted* (H Tom Tyler); *Texas Buddies* (H Bob Steele). **1933:** *Terror Trail* (H Tom Mix). **1938:** *Gun Law* (H George O'Brien). **1939:** *Range War* (H Hopalong Cassidy). **1940:** *The Carson City Kid* (H Roy Rogers). **1943:** *Bar 20* (H Hopalong Cassidy). **1944:** *Texas Masquerade* (H Hopalong Cassidy); *Cheyenne Wildcat* (H Wild Bill Elliott); *Lumberjack* (H Hopalong Cassidy); *Mystery Man* (H Hopalong Cassidy). **1945:** *Great Stagecoach Robbery* (H Wild Bill Elliott); *South of the Rio Grande* (H Duncan Renaldo); *Corpus Christi Bandits* (H Rocky Lane); *Bad Men of the Border* (H Kirby Grant). **1946:** *My Pal Trigger* (H Roy Rogers); *Roll on Texas Moon* (H Roy Rogers). **1947:** *Saddle Pals* (H Gene Autry). **1948:** *Bold Frontiersman* (H Rocky Lane); *The Dead Don't Dream* (H Hopalong Cassidy); *Strange Gamble* (H Hopalong Cassidy). **1949:** *Brothers in the Saddle* (H Tim Holt); *Son of a Badman* (H Lash LaRue); *Powder River Rustlers* (H Rocky Lane). **1951:** *Gene Autry and the Mounties* (H Gene Autry).

Kenneth Macdonald

Kenneth MacDonald was Columbia Pictures' villain for all seasons from 1939 until the late 1940s. He menaced everyone at the studio from cowboys like Wild Bill Elliott and Charles Starrett to comedy kings the Three Stooges.

MacDonald made a half dozen–plus appearances in Columbia cliff-hangers as a henchman in *Mandrake the Magician, Overland with Kit Carson, The Desert Hawk* and *The Black Arrow* and was the villainous mastermind in serials like *Perils of the Royal Mounted, The Valley of Vanishing Men* and *The Phantom*.

His wrongdoing efforts were challenged by Starrett in films like *Spoilers of the Range* (1939), *Outposts of the Mounties* (1939), *Texas Stagecoach* (1940) and *The Durango Kid* (1940). Elliott and MacDonald locked horns in films such as *The Taming of the West* (1939) and *Wildcat of Tucson* (1940).

In the late forties he appeared in several Three Stooges comedies, usually as a gangster.

MacDonald was most at home playing a crooked gambler or the brains of an outlaw gang.

He was born in Portland, Indiana, in 1901.

Kenneth Macdonald Filmography

1939: *Spoilers of the Range* (*H* Charles Starrett); *Outpost of the Mounties* (*H* Charles Starrett). **1940:** *Two-Fisted Rangers* (*H* Charles Starrett); *Bullets for Rustlers* (*H* Charles Starrett); *Texas Stagecoach* (*H* Charles Starrett); *The Durango Kid* (*H* Charles Starrett); *Frontier Vengeance* (*H* Don Barry); *Wildcat of Tucson* (*H* Wild Bill Elliott). **1941:** *Hands Across the Rockies* (*H* Wild Bill Elliott); *Son of Davy Crockett* (*H* Wild Bill Elliott). **1942:** *Riders of the Northland* (*H* Charles Starrett). **1943:** *Robin Hood of the Range* (*H* Charles Starrett); *Six Gun Gospel* (*H* Johnny Mack Brown). **1944:** *Pride of the Plains* (*H* Bob Livingston); *Cowboy from Lonesome River* (*H* Charles Starrett). **1945:** *The Lost Trail* (*H* Johnny Mack Brown). **1948:** *Frontier Agent* (*H* Johnny Mack Brown).

Leroy Mason

Dapper Leroy Mason was one of the best "brains" bad men of the B Westerns. He excelled in playing crooked gamblers, crooked bankers, crooked politicians, crooked freight agents, . . . crooked anything. He was always the man with the plan to steal the gold, the ranch, the stagecoach line, the entire West, etc.

Typical of Mason's B Western roles was his part in Monte Hale's 1946 adventure *Home on the Range* in which Mason, as a scheming rancher, teamed up with superbaddie Roy Barcroft to steal valuable land from a wildlife preserve. To achieve their end they use a killer bear to destroy nearby cattle and turn the local folk against the preserve. However, the hard fightin' Hale thwarts the plot, and Mason falls victim to his own bear by the film's end.

Mason became a Western hero in the 1941 Monogram film *The Silver Stallion* in which he was part of a trio of good guys with stuntman David Sharpe and Chief Thundercloud.

Leroy Mason was also a frequent serial scoundrel. He made his first chapter play appearance in *The Last Frontier* in 1932. Roles in thrillers like *The Jungle Menace*, *Federal Operator 99*, *King of the Forest Rangers*, and *Jesse James Rides Again* made him well known to serial fans. Republic Pictures tabbed him as the lead villain in their serials *The Painted Stallion*, *The Tiger Woman*, *The Daughter of Don Q* and *The Phantom Rider*.

Mason was born in Larimore, North Dakota, in 1903 and entered films in the mid-twenties at Fox Studios.

He died October 13, 1947, in Los Angeles, California. Among his posthumous screen appearances was a role in Roy Rogers' *The Gay Ranchero* in 1948.

Leroy Mason Filmography

1932: *Mason of the Mounted* (H Bill Cody); *Texas Pioneers* (H Bill Cody). **1934:** *The Dude Ranger* (H George O'Brien); *The Fighting Trooper* (H Kermit Maynard); *When a Man Sees Red* (H Buck Jones). **1935:** *Texas Terror* (H John Wayne); *Northern Frontier* (H Kermit Maynard). **1936:** *Comin' Round the Mountain* (H Gene Autry); *Border Patrolman* (H George O'Brien). **1937:** *Yodelin' Kid from Pine Ridge* (H Gene Autry); *Western Gold* (H Smith Ballew). **1938:** *The Painted Trail* (H Tom Keene); *Outlaw Express* (H Bob Baker); *Gold Mine in the Sky* (H Gene Autry); *Heroes of the Hills* (H 3 Mesquiteers); *West of Santa Fe* (H Charles Starrett); *Rhythm of the Saddle* (H Gene Autry); *Santa Fe Stampede* (H 3 Mesquiteers). **1939:**

Mexicali Rose (H Gene Autry); Wyoming Outlaw (H 3 Mesquiteers); New Frontier (H 3 Mesquiteers). **1940:** Ghost Valley Raiders (H Don Barry); Rocky Mountain Rangers (H 3 Mesquiteers); The Range Busters (H Range Busters); Triple Justice (H George O'Brien). **1941:** Robbers of the Range (H Tim Holt); Silver Stallion (H [starring role]); Six Gun Gold (H Tim Holt); The Apache Kid (H Don Barry). **1942:** The Silver Bullet (H Johnny Mack Brown). **1944:** Beneath Western Skies (H Bob Livingston); Hidden Valley Outlaws (H Wild Bill Elliott); Marshal of Reno (H Wild Bill Elliott); The Mojave Firebrand (H Wild Bill Elliott); Vigilantes of Dodge City (H Wild Bill Elliott). **1946:** Heldorado (H Wild Bill Elliott); My Pal Trigger (H Roy Rogers); Sioux City Sue (H Gene Autry). **1947:** Under Colorado Skies (H Monte Hale). **1948:** California Firebrand (H Monte Hale); The Gay Ranchero (H Roy Rogers).

John Merton

Handsome John Merton was always convincing as any type of bad guy, from the cunning brains to a sulking backshooter. He appeared in such varied films as The Eagle's Brood and Bar 20 Rides Again with Hopalong Cassidy, Aces and Eights with Tim McCoy, The Colorado Kid with Bob Steele, The Three Mesquiteers with the Three Mesquiteers, Billy the Kid's Smoking Guns and Cheyenne Takes Over with Lash LaRue, and Melody Ranch with Gene Autry.

Merton was also featured in over a dozen cliff-hangers, including The Vigilantes Are Coming, Dick Tracy Returns, Zorro's Fighting Legion, White Eagle, Zorro's Black Whip, The Lone Ranger, and Hop Harrigan.

He was born John Merton LaVarre in 1901 and entered films in the early thirties. His son Lane Bradford was also a B Western villain.

John Merton suffered a fatal heart attack on September 19, 1959, in Los Angeles, California.

John Merton Filmography

1935: The Eagle's Brood (H Hopalong Cassidy); Hopalong Cassidy (H Hopalong Cassidy); Bar 20 Rides Again (H Hopalong Cassidy). **1936:** Border Caballero (H Tim McCoy); Call of the Prairie (H Hopalong Cassidy); Lightnin' Bill Carson (H Tim McCoy); Aces and Eights (H Tim McCoy); Wild Cat Trooper (H Kermit Maynard); The Crooked Trail (H Johnny Mack Brown); The Lion's Den (H Tim McCoy). **1937:** The Gun

John Merton

Ranger (H Bob Steele); *The Law Commands* (H Tom Keene); *Law of the Ranger* (H Bob Allen); *The Rangers Step In* (H Bob Allen); *Galloping Dynamite* (H Kermit Maynard); *Roaring Six Guns* (H Kermit Maynard); *Colorado Kid* (H Bob Steele). **1938:** *Two Gun Justice* (H Tim McCoy); *Knight of the Plains* (H Fred Scott); *Phantom Ranger* (H Tim McCoy); *Gunsmoke Trail* (H Jack Randall); *Where the Buffalo Roam* (H Tex Ritter). **1939:** *Code of the Fearless* (H Fred Scott); *In Old Montana* (H Fred Scott); *Renegade Trail* (H Hopalong Cassidy). **1940:** *Covered Wagon Days* (H 3 Mesquiteers); *Frontier Crusader* (H Tim McCoy); *Lone Star Raiders* (H 3 Mesquiteers); *Melody Ranch* (H Gene Autry); *The Trail Blazers* (H 3 Mesquiteers). **1941:** *Under Fiesta Stars* (H Gene Autry). **1942:** *Billy the Kid's Smoking Guns* (H Buster Crabbe); *Law and Order* (H Buster Crabbe); *Prairie Pals* (H Bill Boyd); *Mysterious Rider* (H Buster Crabbe). **1944:** *Mystery Man* (H Hopalong Cassidy); *Texas Masquerade* (H Hopalong Cassidy). **1947:** *Cheyenne Takes Over* (H Lash LaRue). **1949:** *Riders of the Dusk* (H Whip Wilson); *Western Renegades* (H Johnny Mack Brown). **1950:** *Arizona Territory* (H Whip Wilson); *Fence Riders* (H Whip Wilson);

West of Wyoming (H Johnny Mack Brown). **1951:** *Silver Canyon* (H Gene Autry); *Man from Sonora* (H Johnny Mack Brown). **1952:** *The Old West* (H Gene Autry); *Blue Canadian Rockies* (H Gene Autry).

Charles Middleton

Kentucky-born Charles Middleton rates as one of the top movie villains of all time basically on the strength of one role: that of Ming the Merciless, Emperor of Mongo, in the trio of popular Flash Gordon serials made between 1936 and 1940. Actually the selection of Middleton for the part of the evil ruler was one of Hollywood's casting masterpieces.

Middleton was born October 3, 1879, in Elizabethtown, Kentucky, and began his career in vaudeville as part of an act called Middleton and Spellmeyer. Spellmeyer was Leora Spellmeyer, whom he later married.

He made his screen debut in 1927. By 1936 he had appeared in dozens of films including top-rated ones like *Alexander Hamilton* (1931), *I Am a Fugitive from a Chain Gang* (1932) and *Duck Soup* (1933) with the Marx Brothers. Still, all in all, he had been mostly relegated to mid-level gangster and horse thief roles when he got the casting call for the part of Ming in the 1936 Universal serial *Flash Gordon*. The 13-chapter epic which starred Buster Crabbe was one of the most successful cliff-hangers of the era and begot two successful sequels: *Flash Gordon's Trip to Mars* in 1938 and *Flash Gordon Conquers the Universe* in 1940.

The trilogy of episodic thrillers detailed the efforts of the heroic cartoon hero Gordon to put an end to Ming's nefarious schemes to destroy the earth. Flash and Ming battled each other throughout 40 action-filled chapters until finally Gordon destroyed Ming and his henchcrew (we think!) by crashing a spaceship loaded with explosive solarite into his tower hideout in the final episode of *Flash Gordon Conquers the Universe*.

Middleton was a master serial villain. Among his other standout portrayals in cliff-hangers were Pa Stark in *Dick Tracy Returns*, the mysterious 39013 in *Daredevils of the Red Circle* and the clever mastermind in Tom Mix's *The Miracle Rider*.

In B Westerns Middleton appeared with Gene Autry, Buck Jones, Hopalong Cassidy, Charles Starrett and others.

He was also in A Westerns like *The Texas Rangers* in 1936, *Virginia City* in 1940 and *Western Union* in 1941.

He was still busy making films at the time of his death on April 22, 1949.

Charles Middleton

Charles Middleton Filmography

1932: *Mystery Ranch* (H George O'Brien). **1935:** *Square Shooter* (H Tim McCoy); *Hopalong Cassidy* (H Hopalong Cassidy). **1936:** *Sunset of Power* (H Buck Jones); *Song of the Saddle* (H Dick Foran); *Empty Saddles* (H Buck Jones). **1937:** *Two Gun Law* (H Charles Starrett); *Hollywood Cowboy* (H George O'Brien); *Yodelin' Kid from Pine Ridge* (H Gene Autry). **1939:**

Wyoming Outlaw (H 3 Mesquiteers); Cowboys from Texas (H 3 Mesquiteers). 1949: The Last Bandit (H Bill Elliott).

Walter Miller

Actor Walter Miller went from being a top-rate silent serial hero to being a top-rate sound serial and B Western heel. He made his first film in 1912.

During the 1920s the dashing Miller's daredevil exploits saved damsels in distress from countless dangers in such cliff-hangers as Leatherstocking (1924), The House Without a Key (1926), The Fighting Marine (1926), Hawk of the Hills (1927) and Queen of the North Woods (1929).

The sound era saw a change of hats for Miller. In 1930 and 1931 he was the hero of two Mascot cliff-hangers, The Lone Defender and King of the Wild. However, in 1931 he made the first of many appearances for Universal Pictures as their number one stock serial bad man in the film Danger Island. He would play similar roles in Universal chapter plays like Tailspin Tommy in 1934, Call of the Savage in 1935 and Rustlers of Red Dog also in 1935.

Western serial fans remember Miller as Buck Jones's chief menace in a trio of episodic actioners: Gordon of Ghost City (1933), The Red Rider (1934) and The Roaring West (1935).

He also did villainous turns in serials for Columbia (The Secret of Treasure Island, 1938) and Republic (Dick Tracy's G-Men, 1939).

The 1930s saw Miller flourish as a B Western bad man, especially in Universal Westerns. He appeared with Buck Jones in Rocky Rhodes (1934) and Boss of Lonely Valley (1937), and with Ken Maynard in Gun Justice (1934) and Smoking Guns (1934).

Away from Universal he appeared in Westerns like Hopalong Cassidy's Heart of the West in 1936, Maynard's The Fugitive Sheriff also in 1936 and George O'Brien's Bullet Code (1940).

Walter Corwin Miller was born in Dayton, Ohio, on March 9, 1892, and died March 30, 1940, in Los Angeles, California.

Walter Miller Filmography

1931: Hurricane Horseman (H Lane Chandler). 1932: Ghost City (H Bill Cody); Ridin' for Justice (H Buck Jones). 1933: Gun Justice (H Ken Maynard). 1934: Smoking Guns (H Ken Maynard); Rocky Rhodes (H Buck

Jones); *The Fighting Trooper* (*H* Kermit Maynard). **1935:** *Ivory Handled Gun* (*H* Buck Jones). **1936:** *Heart of the West* (*H* Hopalong Cassidy); *Ghost Patrol* (*H* Tim McCoy); *The Fugitive Sheriff* (*H* Ken Maynard). **1937:** *Ranger Courage* (*H* Bob Allen); *Border Cafe* (*H* Harry Carey); *Boss of Lonely Valley* (*H* Buck Jones); *Wild Horse Rodeo* (*H* 3 Mesquiteers). **1938:** *Lawless Valley* (*H* George O'Brien). **1939:** *Home on the Prairie* (*H* Gene Autry); *Bullet Code* (*H* George O'Brien).

Wheeler Oakman

Typical of Wheeler Oakman's B Western bad guy roles was his part in the classic B *In Old Santa Fe* (1934) in which he played a crook who tried to con Ken Maynard out of his beloved horse Tarzan.

The Virginia-born (1890) Oakman was one of the best cowboy picture villains of the 1930s. He plied his wares in many of Tim McCoy's Columbia features in the early part of the decade, films like *Man of Action, Silent Men,* and *Rusty Rides Alone* (all made in 1933).

He would later appear with McCoy in films like *The Man from Guntown* (1935) and *Aces and Eights* (1936).

Oakman was also in a slew of serials, usually as chief villain or one of his top henchmen. Among his chapter play appearances were *The Airmail Mystery* (1932), *The Lost Jungle* (1934), *The Phantom Empire* (1935), *Darkest Africa* (1936), *Buck Rogers* (1939), and *Brenda Starr, Reporter* (1945).

Oakman made his screen debut in 1913 and was in such silent films as *The Spoilers* (1914), *The Son of the Wolf* (1922) and *Fangs of Justice* (1926). Most of his sound pictures were Westerns, serials, or B adventures.

He died March 19, 1949, in Van Nuys, California.

Wheeler Oakman Filmography

1930: *Roaring Ranch* (*H* Hoot Gibson). **1932:** *Texas Cyclone* (*H* Tim McCoy); *The Riding Tornado* (*H* Tim McCoy); *Two Fisted Law* (*H* Tim McCoy); *The Western Code* (*H* Tim McCoy); *End of the Trail* (*H* Tim McCoy). **1933:** *Man of Action* (*H* Tim McCoy); *Silent Men* (*H* Tim McCoy); *The Sundown Rider* (*H* Buck Jones). **1934:** *Frontier Days* (*H* Bill Cody). **1935:** *Square Shooter* (*H* Tim McCoy); *Code of the Mounted* (*H* Kermit Maynard); *Trail of the Wild* (*H* Kermit Maynard); *Man from Guntown* (*H* Tim McCoy); *Timber War* (*H* Kermit Maynard); *Undercover Man*

(H Charles Starrett). **1936:** *The Mysterious Avenger* (H Charles Starrett); *Song of the Trail* (H Kermit Maynard); *Roaring Guns* (H Tim McCoy); *Aces and Eights* (H Tim McCoy); *Ghost Patrol* (H Tim McCoy). **1938:** *Code of the Rangers* (H Tim McCoy). **1939:** *In Old Montana* (H Fred Scott). **1943:** *The Fighting Buckaroo* (H Charles Starrett); *Saddles and Sagebrush* (H Russell Hayden). **1944:** *Sundown Valley* (H Charles Starrett); *Riding West* (H Charles Starrett). **1945:** *Rough Riding Justice* (H Charles Starrett).

Bud Osborne

Lennie "Bud" Osborne made his first film for the Thomas Ince Company in 1915. Throughout the silent film era he was cast primarily in Westerns, serials and adventure films.

He appeared in close to 100 B Westerns beginning in 1930, and his career lasted the full extent of the genre. He played villains, lawmen and everything in-between. He appeared with virtually every top cowboy star, and among the top B's in which he appeared are *The Outlaw Deputy* with Tim McCoy, *The Yodelin' Kid from Pine Ridge* with Gene Autry, *Robbers of the Range* with Tim Holt and *The Cherokee Flash* with Sunset Carson.

He was in many serials including *The Vigilantes Are Coming, Tailspin Tommy, Gordon of Ghost City* and *The Adventures of Frank Merriwell.*

Bud Osborne was born July 20, 1881, in Knox County, Texas, and died in Hollywood on February 2, 1964.

Bud Osborne Filmography

1930: *Call of the Desert* (H Tom Tyler); *Canyon of Missing Men* (H Tom Tyler); *The Apache Kid's Escape* (H Jack Perrin). **1931:** *Red Fork Range* (H Wally Wales). **1932:** *Mark of the Spur* (H Bob Custer); *Riding Tornado* (H Tim McCoy); *Western Code* (H Tim McCoy); *Come on Danger* (H Tom Keene); *Flaming Guns* (H Tom Mix). **1934:** *The Prescott Kid* (H Tim McCoy). **1935:** *Outlaw Deputy* (H Tim McCoy); *Riding Thru* (H Tom Tyler). **1936:** *Treachery Rides the Range* (H Dick Foran).

Bud Osborne

Marshall Reed

Marshall Reed was one of the B Western's premier action heavies during the mid-forties and early fifties.

He was especially visible in films made by Republic and Monogram Pictures which starred the likes of Johnny Mack Brown, Whip Wilson and Rocky Lane.

Marshall Reed (right) with Whip Wilson.

He was most at home playing crooked gamblers and blacksmiths.

In 1954 Reed starred in the 15-chapter Columbia serial *Riding with Buffalo Bill,* which was one of the last serials made. He also appeared in chapter plays like *Haunted Harbor, The Ghost of Zorro, Pirates of the High Seas, The James Brothers of Missouri* and *Gunfighters of the Northwest.*

Reed was born in Englewood, Colorado, on May 28, 1917. He entered films in the early forties.

From 1954 to 1959 he was featured as Inspector Fred Asher on the CBS-TV detective action series *The Lineup.*

Marshall Reed was also active in film production, direction and script-writing.

He passed away April 15, 1980, in Los Angeles, California.

Marshall Reed Filmography

1943: *The Texas Kid* (*H* Johnny Mack Brown). **1944:** *Range Law* (*H* Johnny Mack Brown); *Gangsters of the Frontier* (*H* Texas Rangers); *Law of the Valley* (*H* Johnny Mack Brown); *Ghost Guns* (*H* Johnny Mack Brown). **1946:** *Drifting Along* (*H* Johnny Mack Brown); *The Gentleman from Texas* (*H* Johnny Mack Brown); *Shadows of the Range* (*H* Johnny Mack Brown). **1947:** *Riders of the South* (*H* Johnny Mack Brown); *West of Dodge City* (*H* Charles Starrett); *Land of the Lawless* (*H* Johnny Mack Brown); *Stage to Mesa City* (*H* Lash LaRue); *Prairie Express* (*H* Johnny Mack Brown); *Fighting Vigilantes* (*H* Lash LaRue); *Cheyenne Takes Over* (*H* Lash LaRue). **1948:** *Song of the Drifter* (*H* Jimmy Wakely); *Overland Trails* (*H* Johnny Mack Brown); *Tornado Range* (*H* Eddie Dean); *Hawk of Powder River* (*H* Eddie Dean); *The Rangers Ride* (*H* Jimmy Wakely); *Trigger Man* (*H* Johnny Mack Brown); *Back Trail* (*H* Johnny Mack Brown); *The Fighting Ranger* (*H* Johnny Mack Brown); *Partners of the Sunset* (*H* Jimmy Wakely); *Mark of the Lash* (*H* Lash LaRue); *Courtin' Trouble* (*H* Jimmy Wakely); *Hidden Danger* (*H* Johnny Mack Brown). **1949:** *Gun Runner* (*H* Jimmy Wakely); *Law of the West* (*H* Johnny Mack Brown); *West of El Dorado* (*H* Johnny Mack Brown); *Brand of Fear* (*H* Jimmy Wakely); *Roaring Westward* (*H* Jimmy Wakely); *Riders of the Dusk* (*H* Whip Wilson); *The Cowboy and the Prize Fighter* (*H* Jim Bannon). **1950:** *Six Gun Mesa* (*H* Johnny Mack Brown); *Rider from Tucson* (*H* Tim Holt); *Covered Wagon Raid* (*H* Rocky Lane); *Silver Raiders* (*H* Whip Wilson); *Law of the Panhandle* (*H* Johnny Mack Brown); *Cherokee Uprising* (*H* Whip Wilson); *Outlaw Gold* (*H* Johnny Mack Brown). **1951:** *Abilene Trail* (*H* Whip Wilson); *Night Riders of Montana* (*H* Rocky Lane); *Canyon Raiders* (*H* Whip Wilson); *Nevada Bad Men* (*H* Whip Wilson); *Gunplay* (*H* Tim Holt); *Whistling Hills* (*H* Johnny Mack Brown); *Texas Lawmen* (*H* Johnny Mack Brown). **1952:** *Texas City* (*H* Johnny Mack Brown); *Laramie Mountains* (*H* Charles Starrett); *Canyon Ambush* (*H* Johnny Mack Brown).

Warner Richmond

Lantern-jawed Warner Richmond was one of the earliest of the B Western villains, a role which he carried over from the silent film era. All in all he is one of screendom's most underrated bad men. For instance, his evil performance in the 1931 version of *Huckleberry Finn* is classical.

He was also a popular villain in early serials. He played Sharkey, Clyde Beatty's devious assistant, in *The Lost Jungle* (1934), and the evil underground conspirator in Gene Autry's first starring vehicle, The Phantom Empire (1935).

One of his best performances in a B Western was in the 1935 John Wayne adventure, *The New Frontier*. He portrayed a backshootin' gambler named Ace Holmes who was such a double-crosser that one of his own men finally did him in. He was also in Tex Ritter's first film, *Song of the Gringo* (1936).

Richmond was born in Culpepper County, Virginia, on January 11, 1895, and entered films in 1916.

In the early thirties he appeared in such top films as the aforementioned *Huckleberry Finn*, Johnny Mack Brown's classic Western *Billy the Kid* and C.B. De Mille's *This Day and Age*.

Warner Richmond died June 19, 1948, in Los Angeles, California.

Warner Richmond Filmography

1933: *Life in the Raw* (H George O'Brien). **1935:** *The New Frontier* (H John Wayne); *The Singing Vagabond* (H Gene Autry); *The Courageous Avenger* (H Johnny Mack Brown); *Smokey Smith* (H Bob Steele). **1936:** *Song of the Gringo* (H Tex Ritter); *Headin' for the Rio Grande* (H Tex Ritter). **1937:** *Trail of Vengeance* (H Johnny Mack Brown); *Doomed at Sundown* (H Bob Steele); *Riders of the Dawn* (H Jack Randall); *Stars Over Arizona* (H Jack Randall); *Where Trails Divide* (H Tom Keene); *A Lawman Is Born* (H Johnny Mack Brown). **1938:** *Six Shootin' Sheriff* (H Ken Maynard); *Prairie Moon* (H Gene Autry); *Wild Horse Canyon* (H Jack Randall). **1940:** *Rhythm of the Rio Grande* (H Tex Ritter); *Pals of the Silver Sage* (H Tex Ritter); *The Golden Trail* (H Tex Ritter); *Rainbow Over the Range* (H Tex Ritter). **1946:** *Colorado Serenade* (H Eddie Dean).

Jack Rockwell

A familiar face throughout the B Western era, Jack Rockwell appeared in over 100 of the genre films. He specialized in playing outlaw henchmen and sheriffs.

Rockwell's most important supporting roles came in the early thirties vehicles of Ken Maynard.

He appeared in such excellent Westerns as *Range Law, Whistlin' Dan, Come on Tarzan* and *Wheels of Destiny.*
Throughout the thirties and forties Jack Rockwell supported all the top cowboy stars including Hopalong Cassidy, Roy Rogers and Gene Autry. He also appeared in Western serials like *The Adventures of Red Ryder.*
Jack Rockwell worked in B Westerns until his death on March 10, 1947.

Jack Rockwell Filmography

1930: *Lucky Larkin* (H Ken Maynard); *The Utah Kid* (H Rex Lease). **1931:** *The Arizona Terror* (H Ken Maynard); *Range Law* (H Ken Maynard); *Branded Men* (H Ken Maynard); *The Pocatello Kid* (H Ken Maynard). **1932:** *The Sunset Trail* (H Ken Maynard); *Texas Gunfighter* (H Ken Maynard); *Hell Fire Austin* (H Ken Maynard); *Whistlin' Dan* (H Ken Maynard); *Come on Tarzan* (H Ken Maynard); *Outlaw Justice* (H Jack Hoxie); *Between Fighting Men* (H Ken Maynard); *Guns for Hire* (H Lane Chandler). **1933:** *When a Man Rides Alone* (H Tom Tyler); *The Lone Avenger* (H Ken Maynard); *The Fiddlin' Buckaroo* (H Ken Maynard); *Strawberry Roan* (H Ken Maynard); *Fargo Express* (H Ken Maynard); *Gun Justice* (H Ken Maynard). **1934:** *The Lucky Texan* (H John Wayne); *Wheels of Destiny* (H Ken Maynard); *The Man from Hell* (H Reb Russell); *In Old Santa Fe* (H Ken Maynard); *Lawless Frontier* (H John Wayne); *'Neath the Arizona Skies* (H John Wayne). **1935:** *Law Beyond the Range* (H Tim McCoy); *Justice of the Range* (H Tim McCoy); *Ridin' Wild* (H Tim McCoy); *Man from Guntown* (H Tim McCoy); *Tumbling Tumbleweeds* (H Gene Autry); *Gallant Defender* (H Charles Starrett); *Bulldog Courage* (H Tim McCoy); *No Man's Range* (H Bob Steele); *The Tonto Kid* (H Bob Steele). **1936:** *The Mysterious Avenger* (H Charles Starrett); *Valley of the Lawless* (H Johnny Mack Brown); *Roarin' Guns* (H Tim McCoy); *Lucky Terror* (H Hoot Gibson); *Rogue of the Range* (H Johnny Mack Brown); *Winds of the Wastelands* (H John Wayne); *The Law Rides* (H Bob Steele); *Brand of the Outlaws* (H Bob Steele); *Heroes of the Range* (H Ken Maynard); *The Traitor* (H Tim McCoy); *The Big Show* (H Gene Autry); *Guns and Guitars* (H Gene Autry); *Sundown Saunders* (H Bob Steele). **1937:** *Hittin' the Trail* (H Tex Ritter); *Bar Z Bad Men* (H Johnny Mack Brown); *Reckless Ranger* (H Bob Allen); *Range Defenders* (H 3 Mesquiteers); *Riders of the Rockies* (H Tex Ritter); *The Red Rope* (H Bob Steele); *The Rangers Step In* (H Bob Allen); *Stars Over Arizona* (H Jack Randall); *Springtime in the Rockies* (H Gene Autry); *Texas Trail* (H Hopalong Cassidy); *Outlaws of the Prairie* (H Charles Starrett). **1938:** *Rolling Caravans* (H Jack Luden); *Under Western Stars* (H Roy Rogers); *Law* *of the Plains* (H Charles Starrett); *Western Trails* (H Bob Baker); *Black Bandit* (H Bob Baker); *Guilty Trail* (H Bob Baker); *Prairie Justice* (H Bob Baker); *Shine on Harvest Moon* (H Roy Rogers). **1939:** *Sunset Trail* (H Hopalong Cassidy); *Rough Riders Roundup* (H Roy Rogers); *Silver on the Sage* (H Hopalong Cassidy); *Renegade Trail* (H Hopalong Cassidy); *Days of Jesse James* (H Roy Rogers); *The Stranger from Texas* (H Charles Starrett). **1940:** *Santa Fe Marshal* (H Hopalong Cassidy); *Bullets for Rustlers* (H Charles Starrett); *Hidden Gold* (H Hopalong Cassidy); *The Carson City Kid* (H Roy Rogers); *Stagecoach War* (H Hopalong Cassidy); *The Durango Kid* (H Charles Starrett); *Pony Post* (H Johnny Mack Brown). **1941:** *The Pinto Kid* (H Charles Starrett); *Bury Me Not on the Lone Prairie* (H Johnny Mack Brown); *Border Vigilantes* (H Hopalong Cassidy); *Sheriff of Tombstone* (H Roy Rogers); *Rawhide Rangers* (H Johnny Mack Brown); *Wide Open Town* (H Hopalong Cassidy); *King of Dodge City* (H Wild Bill Elliott); *Bad Man of Deadwood* (H Roy Rogers); *Twilight on the Trail* (H Hopalong Cassidy); *Jesse James at Bay* (H Roy Rogers); *Secrets of the Wasteland* (H Hopalong Cassidy); *Red River Valley* (H Roy Rogers). **1942:** *Man from Cheyenne* (H Roy Rogers); *Below the Border* (H Rough Riders); *Bandit Ranger* (H Tim Holt); *Undercover Man* (H Hopalong Cassidy). **1943:** *Fighting Frontier* (H Tim Holt); *Dead Man's Gulch* (H Don Barry); *Black Hills Express* (H Don Barry); *The Renegade* (H Buster Crabbe); *Beyond the Last Frontier* (H Eddie Dew); *Overland Mail Robbery* (H Wild Bill Elliott); *Raiders of Sunset Pass* (H Eddie Dew). **1944:** *The Vigilantes Ride* (H Russell Hayden); *Law Men* (H Johnny Mack Brown); *Lumberjack* (H Hopalong Cassidy); *Mystery Man* (H Hopalong Cassidy); *Forty Thieves* (H Hopalong Cassidy); *West of the Rio Grande* (H Johnny Mack Brown). **1945:** *Rough Ridin' Justice* (H Charles Starrett); *Beyond the Pecos* (H Rod Cameron); *Outlaws of the Rockies* (H Charles Starrett); *Rough Riders of Cheyenne* (H Sunset Carson); *Lawless Empire* (H Charles Starrett); *Frontier Feud* (H Johnny Mack Brown). **1946:** *Drifting Along* (H Johnny Mack Brown); *Frontier Gun Law* (H Charles Starrett); *Roaring Rangers* (H Charles Starrett); *Under Arizona Skies* (H Johnny Mack Brown); *Two Fisted Stranger* (H Charles Starrett); *The Gentleman from Texas* (H Johnny Mack Brown).

Charles Stevens

Charles Stevens was the grandson of the legendary Apache warrior Geronimo, and stereotypically most of his Western screen career was spent playing Indians on the warpath.

One of his best roles during the B Western era was actually in the 1942 Universal serial *Overland Mail.* He played a maniacal half-breed called Puma.

Stevens was born May 20, 1893, in Solomanville, Arizona, and made his film debut in D.W. Griffith's epic *The Birth of a Nation* (1915). During the silent era he was noted for his roles in adventure films such as *The Thief of Bagdad* in which he actually played six different roles. He was also a fixture in the swashbuckling films of Douglas Fairbanks, Sr.

Along with many B Western appearances, he was in big production oaters like *My Darling Clementine* (1946) and *The Big Trail* (1930).

Other sound era appearances were in such varied films as *The Mummy's Curse* (1944) and *Killer Leopards* (1954).

Charles Stevens began his career in vaudeville and wild West shows. He passed away in Hollywood on August 22, 1964.

Charles Stevens Filmography

1932: *South of the Rio Grande* (H Buck Jones); *Mystery Ranch* (H George O'Brien). **1933:** *Drum Taps* (H Ken Maynard); *The California Trail* (H Buck Jones). **1936:** *The Bold Caballero* (H Bob Livingston); *Aces and Eights* (H Tim McCoy). **1938:** *The Renegade Ranger* (H George O'Brien). **1939:** *Desperate Trails* (H Johnny Mack Brown). **1940:** *Wagons Westward* (H Buck Jones). **1944:** *Marked Trails* (H Hoot Gibson). **1945:** *South of the Rio Grande* (H Duncan Renaldo). **1946:** *Border Bandits* (H Johnny Mack Brown). **1949:** *Roll Thunder Roll* (H Jim Bannon); *The Cowboy and the Indians* (H Gene Autry); *The Showdown* (H Wild Bill Elliott). **1950:** *Indian Territory* (H Gene Autry).

Glenn Strange

Millions of TV viewers know Glenn Strange as Sam, Miss Kitty's faithful bartender in Dodge City's Long Branch Saloon. But in the three decades before he assumed the role in 1962, Strange had enjoyed a reputation as a multifaceted movie villain. For Universal Studios he made several appearances as the Frankenstein monster in such films as *The House of Frankenstein* (1944), *House of Dracula* (1945) and *Abbott and Costello Meet Frankenstein* (1948).

He had roles in cliff-hangers like *The Hurricane Express* (Mascot, 1932), *The Lone Ranger Rides Again* (Republic 1939) and *The Riders of Death Valley* (Universal, 1941).

Charles Stevens

Most of Strange's B Western career was spent playing gunslingers like Bat in singing cowboy Bob Baker's 1939 film *Honor of the West* and Saunders in Hopalong Cassidy's *Pride of the West* (1938). He was a fixture in the early entries of the Cassidy series and appeared in B Westerns for Universal, RKO, Republic and PRC, among others.

He was born George Glenn Strange in New Mexico on August 16, 1899. Before he entered films as a stuntman, he had been a rodeo performer and a professional pugilist.

Glenn Strange

Glenn Strange died of cancer on September 20, 1973, in Burbank, California.

Glenn Strange Filmography

1931: *Border Law* (H Buck Jones); *Range Feud* (H Buck Jones). **1932:** *McKenna of the Mounted* (H Buck Jones). **1935:** *Lawless Range* (H John

Wayne); *Moonlight on the Prairie* (*H* Dick Foran). **1936:** *Trailin' West* (*H* Dick Foran); *California Mail* (*H* Dick Foran). **1937:** *Land Beyond the Law* (*H* Dick Foran); *Devil's Saddle Legion* (*H* Dick Foran). **1938:** *The Singing Outlaw* (*H* Bob Baker); *Border Wolves* (*H* Bob Baker); *The Last Stand* (*H* Bob Baker); *Whirlwind Horseman* (*H* Ken Maynard); *Pride of the West* (*H* Hopalong Cassidy); *In Old Mexico* (*H* Hopalong Cassidy); *California Frontier* (*H* Buck Jones); *Ghost Town Riders* (*H* Bob Baker). **1939:** *Arizona Legion* (*H* George O'Brien); *The Phantom Stage* (*H* Bob Baker); *Sunset Trail* (*H* Hopalong Cassidy); *Across the Plains* (*H* Jack Randall); *Oklahoma Terror* (*H* Jack Randall); *Law of the Pampas* (*H* Hopalong Cassidy); *Overland Mail* (*H* Jack Randall); *The Fighting Gringo* (*H* George O'Brien). **1940:** *Pioneer Days* (*H* Jack Randall); *Rhythm of the Rio Grande* (*H* Tex Ritter); *Covered Wagon Trails* (*H* Jack Randall); *Land of the Six Guns* (*H* Jack Randall); *Triple Justice* (*H* George O'Brien); *Wagon Train* (*H* Tim Holt); *Three Men from Texas* (*H* Hopalong Cassidy). **1941:** *The Kid's Last Ride* (*H* Range Busters); *In Old Colorado* (*H* Hopalong Cassidy); *Fugitive Valley* (*H* Range Busters); *The Bandit Trail* (*H* Tim Holt); *The Driftin' Kid* (*H* Tom Keene). **1942:** *The Lone Rider and the Bandit* (*H* George Houston); *Stagecoach Buckaroo* (*H* Johnny Mack Brown); *Billy the Kid Trapped* (*H* Buster Crabbe); *Rolling Down the Great Divide* (*H* Bill Boyd); *Down Texas Way* (*H* Rough Riders); *Come on Danger* (*H* Tim Holt); *Texas Troubleshooters* (*H* Range Busters); *The Bandit Ranger* (*H* Tim Holt); *Little Joe the Wrangler* (*H* Johnny Mack Brown); *Overland Stagecoach* (*H* Bob Livingston). **1943:** *The Kid Rides Again* (*H* Buster Crabbe); *Haunted Ranch* (*H* Range Busters); *Wild Horse Stampede* (*H* Trail Blazers); *Black Market Rustlers* (*H* Range Busters); *False Colors* (*H* Hopalong Cassidy); *Return of the Rangers* (*H* Texas Rangers); *Arizona Trail* (*H* Tex Ritter). **1944:** *Silver City Kid* (*H* Rocky Lane); *Forty Thieves* (*H* Hopalong Cassidy); *Sonora Stagecoach* (*H* Trail Blazers); *Trail to Gunsight* (*H* Eddie Dew); *San Antonio Kid* (*H* Wild Bill Elliott). **1945:** *Renegades of the Rio Grande* (*H* Rod Cameron). **1948:** *The Far Frontier* (*H* Roy Rogers); *Silver Trails* (*H* Jimmy Wakely). **1949:** *Roll, Thunder, Roll* (*H* Jim Bannon).

Forrest Taylor

Forrest Taylor was a well known character actor and "brains" heavy throughout the B Western era. He began making films around 1915. During the late forties he was a featured player in Republic Westerns and serials. Born in 1884, Taylor passed away February 19, 1965.

Forrest Taylor Filmography

1933: *Riders of Destiny* (*H* John Wayne). **1935:** *Rider of the Law* (*H* Bob Steele); *Courageous Avenger* (*H* Johnny Mack Brown); *Between Men* (*H* Johnny Mack Brown). **1936:** *Too Much Beef* (*H* Rex Bell); *West of Nevada* (*H* Rex Bell); *Men of the Plains* (*H* Rex Bell); *Headin' for the Rio Grande* (*H* Tex Ritter). **1937:** *Mystery of the Hooded Horseman* (*H* Tex Ritter); *Arizona Days* (*H* Tex Ritter); *Riders of the Dawn* (*H* Jack Randall). **1938:** *Heroes of the Hills* (*H* 3 Mesquiteers); *The Painted Trail* (*H* Tom Keene); *Outlaw Express* (*H* Bob Baker); *Gun Packer* (*H* Jack Randall); *Black Bandit* (*H* Bob Baker); *Law of the Texan* (*H* Buck Jones); *Lightning Carson Rides Again* (*H* Tim McCoy). **1939:** *Riders of Black River* (*H* Charles Starrett); *Rovin' Tumbleweeds* (*H* Gene Autry); *Chip of the Flying U* (*H* Johnny Mack Brown); *Straight Shooters* (*H* Tim McCoy). **1940:** *Rhythm of the Rio Grande* (*H* Tex Ritter); *Wild Horse Range* (*H* Jack Randall); *Frontier Crusader* (*H* Tim McCoy); *West of Abilene* (*H* Charles Starrett); *The Durango Kid* (*H* Charles Starrett); *Kid from Santa Fe* (*H* Jack Randall); *Trailing Double Trouble* (*H* Range Busters). **1941:** *Ridin' on a Rainbow* (*H* Gene Autry); *Billy the Kid's Fighting Pals* (*H* Bob Steele); *Wrangler's Roost* (*H* Range Busters); *Ridin' on the Cherokee Trail* (*H* Tex Ritter). **1942:** *Lone Star Vigilantes* (*H* Wild Bill Elliott); *Cowboy Serenade* (*H* Gene Autry); *Home in Wyomin'* (*H* Gene Autry); *Sons of the Pioneers* (*H* Roy Rogers); *The Rangers Take Over* (*H* Texas Rangers). **1943:** *Thundering Trails* (*H* 3 Mesquiteers); *Fighting Buckaroo* (*H* Charles Starrett); *Silver Spurs* (*H* Roy Rogers). **1944:** *Mystery Man* (*H* Hopalong Cassidy); *Song of Nevada* (*H* Roy Rogers); *Sundown Valley* (*H* Charles Starrett); *The Last Horseman* (*H* Russ Hayden); *Sonora Stagecoach* (*H* Trail Blazers); *Mojave Firebrand* (*H* Wild Bill Elliott); *Cyclone Prairie Rangers* (*H* Charles Starrett). **1945:** *Texas Panhandle* (*H* Charles Starrett). **1946:** *The Caravan Trail* (*H* Eddie Dean); *Colorado Serenade* (*H* Eddie Dean); *Santa Fe Uprising* (*H* Rocky Lane); *Stagecoach to Denver* (*H* Rocky Lane). **1947:** *Rustlers of Devil's Canyon* (*H* Rocky Lane); *Along the Oregon Trail* (*H* Monte Hale); *Stranger from Ponca City* (*H* Charles Starrett); *Buckaroo from Powder River* (*H* Charles Starrett). **1949:** *Navajo Trail Riders* (*H* Rocky Lane); *Death Valley Gunfighter* (*H* Rocky Lane); *Fighting Redhead* (*H* Jim Bannon); *The Cowboy and the Prizefighter* (*H* Jim Bannon). **1950:** *Cherokee Uprising* (*H* Whip Wilson); *Rustlers on Horseback* (*H* Rocky Lane). **1951:** *Prairie Roundup* (*H* Charles Starrett); *Wells Fargo Gunmaster* (*H* Rocky Lane); *Blazing Bullets* (*H* Johnny Mack Brown). **1952:** *Border Saddlemates* (*H* Rex Allen).

Charles "Slim" Whitaker

Slim Whitaker spent most of his film career as a supporting player in Western movies, silent and sound, A and B. He was equally at home playing a bandit, a sheriff or a buffoon. Actually he had all the credentials to become a B Western sidekick, but that never happened to any extent.

He made films with virtually all the top cowboy stars: Gene Autry, Wild Bill Elliott, Ken Maynard, George O'Brien, Buster Crabbe and John Wayne.

Slim was born Charles Orbie Whitaker on July 29, 1893, and passed away on June 27, 1960, of a heart attack.

Charles "Slim" Whitaker Filmography

1930: *The Fighting Legion* (H Ken Maynard); *Oklahoma Cyclone* (H Bob Steele); *Shadow Ranch* (H Buck Jones). **1931:** *Desert Vengeance* (H Buck Jones); *The Avenger* (H Buck Jones); *Lightnin' Smith Returns* (H Buddy Roosevelt); *The One Way Trail* (H Tim McCoy); *Freighters of Destiny* (H Tom Keene); *Branded Men* (H Ken Maynard). **1932:** *The Sunset Trail* (H Ken Maynard); *Man from New Mexico* (H Tom Tyler); *Ghost Valley* (H Tom Keene); *Come on Tarzan* (H Ken Maynard); *Haunted Gold* (H John Wayne); *Flaming Guns* (H Tom Mix). **1933:** *Drum Taps* (H Ken Maynard); *Somewhere in Sonora* (H John Wayne); *Deadwood Pass* (H Tom Tyler); *Trouble Busters* (H Jack Hoxie); *The Trail Drive* (H Ken Maynard); *War on the Range* (H Tom Tyler). **1934:** *Honor of the Range* (H Ken Maynard); *Smoking Guns* (H Ken Maynard); *Ridin' Gents* (H Jack Perrin); *The Man from Hell* (H Reb Russell); *Fighting Through* (H Reb Russell); *The Prescott Kid* (H Tim McCoy); *The Westerner* (H Tim McCoy); *The Lone Bandit* (H Lane Chandler); *Terror of the Plains* (H Tom Tyler). **1935:** *Unconquered Bandit* (H Tom Tyler); *Range Warfare* (H Reb Russell); *Rustler's Paradise* (H Harry Carey); *The Silver Bullet* (H Tom Tyler); *Western Frontier* (H Ken Maynard); *Tumbling Tumbleweeds* (H Gene Autry); *Lawless Range* (H John Wayne); *Last of the Clintons* (H Harry Carey); *Gallant Defender* (H Charles Starrett); *Lawless Riders* (H Ken Maynard); *Heir to Trouble* (H Ken Maynard); *Arizona Badman* (H Reb Russell); *Blazing Guns* (H Reb Russell); *Border Vengeance* (H Reb Russell); *Coyote Trails* (H Tom Tyler); *Rio Rattler* (H Tom Tyler). **1936:** *Bold Caballero* (H Bob Livingston); *Fast Bullets* (H Tom Tyler); *Ridin' On* (H Tom Tyler); *Rogue of the Range* (H Johnny Mack Brown); *Every Man's Law* (H Johnny Mack Brown); *The Riding Avenger* (H Hoot Gibson); *Ghost Patrol* (H Tim McCoy); *Santa Fe Bound* (H Tom Tyler); *The Fugitive Sheriff* (H Ken Maynard); *The Big*

Show (*H* Gene Autry); *Song of the Gringo* (*H* Tex Ritter); *Rio Grande Ranger* (*H* Bob Allen). **1937:** *Santa Fe Rides* (*H* Bob Custer); *Border Land* (*H* Hopalong Cassidy); *The Silver Trail* (*H* Rex Lease); *Melody of the Plains* (*H* Fred Scott); *Roundup Time in Texas* (*H* Gene Autry); *Law of the Ranger* (*H* Bob Allen); *Reckless Ranger* (*H* Bob Allen); *Orphan of the Pecos* (*H* Tom Tyler); *Lost Ranch* (*H* Tom Tyler); *Roaring Six Guns* (*H* Kermit Maynard); *Law for Tombstone* (*H* Buck Jones); *The Old Wyoming Trail* (*H* Charles Starrett). **1938:** *Rolling Caravans* (*H* Jack Luden); *Rawhide* (*H* Smith Ballew); *Under Western Stars* (*H* Roy Rogers); *Gunsmoke Trail* (*H* Jack Randall); *Stagecoach Days* (*H* Jack Luden); *Pioneer Trail* (*H* Jack Luden); *Phantom Gold* (*H* Jack Luden); *Overland Stage Raiders* (*H* 3 Mesquiteers); *In Early Arizona* (*H* Wild Bill Elliott). **1939:** *Frontiers of '49* (*H* Wild Bill Elliott); *Code of the Cactus* (*H* Tim McCoy); *Texas Wildcats* (*H* Tim McCoy); *The Law Comes to Texas* (*H* Wild Bill Elliott); *The Fighting Gringo* (*H* George O'Brien); *South of the Border* (*H* Gene Autry). **1940:** *Rancho Grande* (*H* Gene Autry); *Bullet Code* (*H* George O'Brien); *Prairie Law* (*H* George O'Brien); *Ride Tenderfoot Ride* (*H* Gene Autry); *Billy the Kid in Texas* (*H* Bob Steele); *Young Bill Hickok* (*H* Roy Rogers). **1941:** *Along the Rio Grande* (*H* Tim Holt); *Bury Me Not on the Lone Prairie* (*H* Johnny Mack Brown); *Law of the Range* (*H* Johnny Mack Brown); *Six Gun Gold* (*H* Tim Holt); *Arizona Bound* (*H* Rough Riders); *Cyclone on Horseback* (*H* Tim Holt). **1942:** *The Silver Bullet* (*H* Johnny Mack Brown); *Billy the Kid's Smoking Guns* (*H* Buster Crabbe); *The Mysterious Rider* (*H* Buster Crabbe). **1943:** *Fighting Frontier* (*H* Tim Holt). **1944:** *Marshal of Gunsmoke* (*H* Tex Ritter); *Oklahoma Raiders* (*H* Tex Ritter); *The Laramie Trail* (*H* Bob Livingston). **1946:** *Overland Riders* (*H* Buster Crabbe); *Outlaw of the Plains* (*H* Buster Crabbe). **1947:** *Law of the Lash* (*H* Lash LaRue). **1948:** *The Westward Trail* (*H* Eddie Dean). **1949:** *Masked Raiders* (*H* Tim Holt). **1951:** *Law of the Badlands* (*H* Tim Holt).

Harry Woods

During his four-decade career as a Western bad man, it is hard to find a cowboy hero that Harry Woods didn't try to bushwhack.

Gene Autry, Roy Rogers, Wild Bill Elliott, Johnny Mack Brown, Charles Starrett, John Wayne, Tim Holt, Tex Ritter and a whole corral full of other B Western do-gooders were the intended victims of Woods' cinematic skullduggery.

The slick, dapper mustachioed Woods was one of the B Western's best remembered "brains" heavies. He was expert at playing crooked lawyers, bankers, ranchers, saloon owners, real estate agents, miners as well as plain ole bank robbers and cattle rustlers.

Born Harry Lewis Woods, Sr., in 1888, he began his film career in the early 1920s. He appeared in a series of high action chapter plays with serial queen Ruth Roland as well as in early Western serials like *Wolves of the Trail* and *The Steel Trail*.

He became a well known stock player in serials and Westerns during the twenties and when the B Western era dawned Woods was in demand as a villain.

Some of the better B's that he appeared in include *Days of Jesse James* with Roy Rogers, *Flame of the West* with Johnny Mack Brown, *The Lawless Nineties* with John Wayne and Buck Jones' final film, *Dawn on the Great Divide*.

Along with the dozens of Westerns that he had roles in, Woods was a familiar face to serial viewers, appearing in thrillers like *The Adventures of Rex and Rinty*, *Rustlers of Red Dog*, *The Phantom Rider* and the 1935 cliff-hanger *Call of the Savage* in which he played good guy Noah Beery, Jr.'s sidekick.

Woods had roles in A Westerns like *Union Pacific* with Joel McRae, *My Darling Clementine* with Henry Fonda and *Rancho Notorious* with Marlene Dietrich.

He also appeared in films such as the Marx Brothers' *Monkey Business*, Mae West's *Belle of the Nineties*, *I Am a Fugitive from a Chain Gang* and *The Ten Commandments*.

Harry Woods died in Los Angeles, California, on December 28, 1968.

Harry Woods Filmography

1930: *'Neath Western Skies* (H Tom Tyler); *Pardon My Gun* (H Tom Keene); *Men Without Law* (H Buck Jones). **1931:** *West of Cheyenne* (H Tom Tyler); *The Texas Ranger* (H Buck Jones); *In Old Cheyenne* (H Rex Lease); *The Range Feud* (H Buck Jones). **1932:** *Texas Gunfighter* (H Ken Maynard); *Haunted Gold* (H John Wayne). **1935:** *Heir to Trouble* (H Ken Maynard); *When a Man's a Man* (H George O'Brien); *Gallant Defender* (H Charles Starrett). **1936:** *The Lawless Nineties* (H John Wayne); *Heroes of the Range* (H Ken Maynard). **1937:** *Courage of the West* (H Bob Baker); *Land Beyond the Law* (H Dick Foran); *Range Defenders* (H 3 Mesquiteers). **1938:** *Hawaiian Buckaroo* (H Smith Ballew); *Come on Rangers* (H Roy Rogers); *Panamint's Bad Man* (H Smith Ballew). **1939:** *Blue Montana Skies* (H Gene Autry). **1940:** *Bullet Code* (H George O'Brien); *West of Carson City* (H Johnny Mack Brown); *Ranger and the Lady* (H Roy Rogers).

Harry Woods

1941: *Sheriff of Tombstone* (H Roy Rogers). **1942:** *Romance on the Range* (H Roy Rogers); *Down Texas Way* (H Rough Riders); *Riders of the West* (H Rough Riders); *Deep in the Heart of Texas* (H Johnny Mack Brown); *West of the Law* (H Rough Riders); *Dawn on the Great Divide* (H Buck Jones). **1943:** *Outlaws of Stampede Pass* (H Johnny Mack Brown); *Cheyenne Roundup* (H Johnny Mack Brown); *Ghost Rider* (H Johnny Mack Brown); *Border Town Gunfighters* (H Wild Bill Elliott); *Beyond the Last*

Frontier (*H* Eddie Dew). **1944:** *Call of the Rockies* (*H* Sunset Carson); *Marshal of Gunsmoke* (*H* Tex Ritter). **1945:** *Wanderer of the Wasteland* (*H* James Warren). **1946:** *South of Monterey* (*H* Gilbert Roland). **1947:** *Wyoming* (*H* Bill Elliott); *Code of the West* (*H* James Warren). **1948:** *Western Heritage* (*H* Tim Holt); *Gallant Legion* (*H* Bill Elliott); *Indian Agent* (*H* Tim Holt).

Miscellaneous Players

Thumbnail Sketches of Familiar Faces
from The B Western Era

Ernie Adams. Diminutive bad guy of the thirties and forties. Specialized in playing sneaky thieves, gangsters and backshooters. Born in 1885, he began making films around 1918. Though he made dozens of B's, his best Western roles were in Mascot serials like *The Law of the Wild* and *The Miracle Rider.* Died November 26, 1947.

Gene Alsace. Also known as Rocky Camron. Usually seen as a deputy sheriff or a leading lady's falsely accused or about-to-be-bushwhacked brother.

Budd Buster. One of the B Western's most prolific supporting players. Usually played "old-timers." Occasionally played a bad guy. Began in B's in the mid-thirties and worked in them until the end of the era. Also made films under the name of George Selk. Born June 14, 1891; died December 22, 1965, in Los Angeles.

Tristram Coffin. Well known actor of the B picture era. Though he usually played hoods and gangsters, he was often seen as a villain in Republic Westerns in the forties. Was also cast by the same studio as a heel in serials like *The Perils of Nyoka.* Starred in the early TV Western series *Twenty-Six Men.*

Sugar Dawn. Juvenile who appeared in films with Tom Keene and Tex Ritter for Monogram Studios in the early forties.

Denver Dixon. The names Denver Dixon and Art Mix belonged to New Zealand–born actor, writer, producer and director Victor Adamson. Adamson produced and starred in several silent and sound Westerns using both names. He also produced Westerns (super–low-budget type) which starred an actor named George Kesterson, whom he billed as Art Mix.

Terry Frost. Most often seen shooting it out with Johnny Mack Brown and other late era B Western heroes. Forte was playing henchmen.

Bud Geary. Most noted for his work as an action heavy in nearly a dozen cliff-hangers. Was a B Western henchman and stuntman. Died as a result of injuries received in a car wreck on February 22, 1946.

Riley Hill. Familiar action heavy seen mostly in Monogram productions of the late forties and early fifties with Johnny Mack Brown, Jimmy Wakely and Whip Wilson.

Reed Howes. Western matinee and serial idol during the silent film years. In the thirties he was relegated to playing villains and other supporting characters in B Westerns. His best role of the genre was the outlaw brother of the girl that John Wayne loved in *Dawn Rider* in 1935. Born July 5, 1900, in Washington, D.C.; died August 6, 1964.

Pierce Lyden. Perennial bad guy foe of Johnny Mack Brown and Whip Wilson at Monogram Pictures in the late forties and early fifties. Was also a stuntman.

J.P. McGowan. Was a jack-of-all-trades in the early days of the B Western. He served as director for such early genre outings as *Under Texas Skies* with Bob Custer, *Canyon of Missing Men* with Tom Tyler and *Near the Rainbow's End* with Bob Steele. He also was a writer and producer, as well as being a supporting player and an occasional bad guy. He entered film work in 1909. Born in Australia in 1880; died March 26, 1952.

Lafe McKee. Probably the genre's top supporting player of the 1930s. Appeared in over 50 B Westerns during that decade in every kind of role imaginable. Born Lafayette Stocking McKee on January 23, 1872; died August 10, 1959.

Clayton Moore. Best known to Western fans as TV's Lone Ranger, Moore was the star of Republic cliff-hangers like *The Perils of Nyoka, Jesse James Rides Again, The Adventures of Frank and Jesse James* and *G-Men Never Forget.* He was also a featured supporting player in several of their Westerns with stars like Rocky Lane.

Jacques O'Mahoney. Better known as Jock Mahoney, movie Tarzan and TV star of *Range Rider* and *Yancey Derringer.* In the late forties and early fifties he was a Columbia contract player featured in serials, Three Stooges comedies and several B Westerns with Gene Autry.

Sarah Padden. Specialized in playing fiesty matrons. Began her screen career during the silent days. Good comedy relief player. Died December 4, 1967.

Lee Roberts. Best remembered as playing gunslingers in features with the Monogram cowboys of the forties. Good henchman with a surly air.

Roy Stewart. After beginning a film career in 1913 Stewart became a star of Western films in the days of the silent film, but with the advent of sound he fell to playing supporting roles and bit parts in early B's. Born October 17, 1889, and suffered a fatal heart attack on April 26, 1933.

Robert Walker. Well known actor of the silent screen; became one of the B Western's first bad guys. Battled cowboys like Buck Jones and Harry Carey. Born June 1888; died March 1954.

Twinkle Watts. Delightful juvenile featured in Republic films with Don "Red" Barry and Rocky Lane.

B Western Film Series Filmographies

Billy the Kid Filmography

1940: *Billy the Kid Outlawed* (PRC; Peter Stewart [Sam Newfield]) *CB* Bob Steele; *Billy the Kid in Texas* (PRC; Peter Stewart [Sam Newfield]) *CB* Bob Steele; *Billy the Kid's Gun Justice* (PRC; Peter Stewart [Sam Newfield]) *CB* Bob Steele. **1941:** *Billy the Kid's Range War* (PRC; Peter Stewart [Sam Newfield]) *CB* Bob Steele; *Billy the Kid's Fighting Pals* (PRC; Sherman Scott) *CB* Bob Steele; *Billy the Kid in Santa Fe (PRC; Sherman Scott) CB* Bob Steele; *Billy the Kid Wanted (PRC; Sherman Scott) CB* Buster Crabbe; *Billy the Kid's Roundup (PRC; Sherman Scott) CB* Buster Crabbe. **1942:** *Billy the Kid Trapped (PRC; Sherman Scott) CB* Buster Crabbe; *Billy the Kid's Smokin' Guns (PRC; Sherman Scott) CB* Buster Crabbe; *Law and Order (PRC; Sherman Scott) CB* Buster Crabbe; *Mysterious Rider (PRC; Sherman Scott) CB* Buster Crabbe; *Sheriff of Sage Valley (PRC; Sherman Scott) CB* Buster Crabbe. **1943:** *The Kid Rides Again (PRC; Sherman Scott) CB* Buster Crabbe; *Fugitive of the Plains (PRC; Sam Newfield) CB* Buster Crabbe; *Western Cyclone (PRC; Sam Newfield) CB* Buster Crabbe; *The Renegade (PRC; Sam Newfield) CB* Buster Crabbe; *Cattle Stampede (PRC; Sam Newfield) CB* Buster Crabbe; *Blazing Frontier (PRC; Sam Newfield) CB* Buster Crabbe.

The Cisco Kid Filmography

1929: *In Old Arizona* (Fox; Raoul Walsh, Irving Cummings) *CB* Warner Baxter, *LL* Dorothy Burgess, Soledad Jiminez. **1931:** *The Cisco Kid* (Fox; Irving Cummings) *CB* Warner Baxter, Chris Pin Martin, *LL* Conchita Montenegro, Nora Lane. **1939:** *The Return of the Cisco Kid* (20th Century–Fox; Herbert I. Leeds) *CB* Warner Baxter, Chris Pin Martin, *LL* Lynn Bari, Soledad Jiminez; *The Cisco Kid and the Lady* (20th Century–Fox; Herbert I. Leeds) *CB* Cesar Romero, Chris Pin Martin, *LL* Marjorie Weaver, Virginia Field. **1940:** *Viva Cisco Kid* (20th Century–Fox; Norman Foster) *CB* Cesar Romero, Chris Pin Martin, *LL* Jean Rogers; *Lucky Cisco Kid* (20th Century–Fox; H. Bruce Humberstone) *CB* Cesar Romero, Chris Pin Martin, *LL* Mary Beth Hughes, Evelyn Venable; *The Gay Caballero* (20th Century–Fox; Otto Brower) *CB* Cesar Romero, Chris Pin Martin, *LL* Sheila Ryan, Janet Beecher. **1941:** *Romance of the Rio Grande* (20th Century–Fox; Herbert I. Leeds) *CB* Cesar Romero, Chris Pin Martin, *LL* Patricia Morrison, Lynne Roberts; *Ride on Vaquero* (20th Century–Fox) *CB* Cesar Romero, Chris Pin Martin, *LL* Mary Beth Hughes, Lynne Roberts, Joan Woodbury. **1945:** *The Cisco Kid Returns* (Monogram; John P. McCarthy) *CB* Duncan Renaldo, Martin Garralaga, *LL* Cecilia Callejo, Vicky Lane, Jan Wiley; *The Cisco Kid in Old Mexico* (Monogram; Phil Rosen) *CB* Duncan Renaldo, Martin Garralaga, *LL* Gwen Kenyon, Aurora Roche; *South of the Rio Grande* (Monogram; Lambert Hillyer) *CB* Duncan Renaldo, Martin Garralaga, *LL* Armida, Lillian Molieri, Soledad Jiminez. *The Gay Cavalier* (Monogram; William Nigh) *CB* Gilbert Roland, Martin Garralaga, *LL* Ramsey Ames; *South of Monterey* (Monogram; William Nigh) *CB* Gilbert Roland, Martin Garralaga, Frank Yaconelli, *LL* Marjorie Riordan, Iris Flores; *Beauty and the Bandit* (Monogram; William Nigh) *CB* Gilbert Roland, Martin Garralaga, Frank Yaconelli, *LL* Ramsey Ames. **1947:** *Riding the California Trail* (Monogram; William Nigh) *CB* Gilbert Roland, Martin Garralaga, Frank Yaconelli, *LL* Teala Loring, Inez Cooper; *Robin Hood of Monterey* (Monogram; Christy Cabanne) *CB* Gilbert Roland, Chris Pin Martin, *LL* Evelyn Brent; *King of the Bandits* (Monogram; Christy Cabanne) *CB* Gilbert Roland, Chris Pin Martin, *LL* Angela Greene. **1949:** *The Valiant Hombre* (United Artists; Wallace Fox) *CB* Duncan Renaldo, Leo Carrillo, *LL* Barbara Billingsley; *The Gay Amigo* (United Artists; Wallace Fox) *CB* Duncan Renaldo, Leo Carrillo, *LL* Armida; *The Daring Caballero* (United Artists; Wallace Fox) *CB* Duncan Renaldo, Leo Carrillo, *LL* Kippee Valez; *Satan's Cradle* (United Artists; Ford Beebe) *CB* Duncan Renaldo, Leo Carrillo, *LL* Ann Savage. **1950:** *The Girl from San Lorenzo* (United Artists; Derwin Abrahams) *CB* Duncan Renaldo, Leo Carrillo, *LL* Jane Adams.

The Lone Rider Filmography

1941: *The Lone Rider Rides On* (PRC; Sam Newfield) *CB* George Houston, Fuzzy St. John, *LL* Hillary Brooke; *The Lone Rider Crosses the Rio* (PRC; Sam Newfield) *CB* George Houston, Fuzzy St. John, *LL* Roquel Verrin; *The Lone Rider in Ghost Town* (PRC; Sam Newfield) *CB* George Houston, Fuzzy St. John, *LL* Alaine Brandes; *Frontier Fury* (PRC; Sam Newfield) *CB* George Houston, Fuzzy St. John, *LL* Hillary Brooke; *The Lone Rider Ambushed* (PRC; Sam Newfield) *CB* George Houston, Fuzzy St. John, *LL* Maxine Leslie; *The Lone Rider Fights Back* (PRC; Sam Newfield) *CB* George Houston, Fuzzy St. John, *LL* Dorothy Short. **1942:** *Lone Rider and the Bandit* (PRC; Sam Newfield) *CB* George Houston, Fuzzy St. John, *LL* Vicki Lester; *Lone Rider in Cheyenne* (PRC; Sam Newfield) *CB* George Houston, Fuzzy St. John, *LL* Ella Neal; *Texas Justice* (PRC; Sam Newfield) *CB* George Houston, Fuzzy St. John, *LL* Wanda McKay; *Border Roundup* (PRC; Sam Newfield) *CB* George Houston, Fuzzy St. John, *LL* Patricia Knox; *Outlaws of Boulder Pass* (PRC; Sam Newfield) *CB* George Houston, Fuzzy St. John, *LL* Patricia Knox; *Overland Stagecoach* (PRC; Sam Newfield) *CB* Bob Livingston, Fuzzy St. John, *LL* Julie Duncan. **1943:** *Wild Horse Rustlers* (PRC; Sam Newfield) *CB* Bob Livingston, Fuzzy St. John, *LL* Linda Johnson; *Death Rides the Plains* (PRC; Sam Newfield) *CB* Bob Livingston, Fuzzy St. John, *LL* Nica Doret; *Wolves of the Range* (PRC; Sam Newfield) *CB* Bob Livingston, Fuzzy St. John, *LL* Frances Gladwin; *Law of the Saddle* (PRC; Melville Delay) *CB* Bob Livingston, Fuzzy St. John, *LL* Betty Miles; *Raiders of Red Gap* (PRC; Sam Newfield) *CB* Bob Livingston, Fuzzy St. John, *LL* Myrna Dell.

The Range Busters Filmography

1940: *The Range Busters* (Monogram; S. Roy Luby) *CB* Ray Corrigan, Dusty King, Max Terhune, *LL* Luana Walters; *Trailing Double Trouble* (Monogram; S. Roy Luby) *CB* Ray Corrigan, Dusty King, Max Terhune, *LL* Lita Conway; *West of Pinto Basin* (Monogram; S. Roy Luby) *CB* Ray Corrigan, Dusty King, Max Terhune, *LL* Gwen Gaze. **1941:** *Trail of the Silver Spurs* (Monogram; S. Roy Luby) *CB* Ray Corrigan, Dusty King, Max Terhune, *LL* Dorothy Short. *The Kid's Last Ride* (Monogram; S. Roy Luby) *CB* Ray Corrigan, Dusty King, Max Terhune, *LL* Luana Walters; *Tumbledown Ranch in Arizona* (Monogram; S. Roy Luby) *CB* Ray Corrigan, Dusty King, Max Terhune, *LL* Sheila Darcy, Marian Kirby; *Wrangler's Roost* (Monogram; S. Roy Luby) *CB* Ray Corrigan, Dusty King, Max Terhune, *LL* Gwen Gaze; *Fugitive Valley* (Monogram; S. Roy Luby) *CB* Ray Corrigan, Dusty King, Max Terhune, *LL* Julie Duncan; *Saddle Moun-*

tain Roundup (Monogram; S. Roy Luby) *CB* Ray Corrigan, Dusty King, Max Terhune, *LL* Lita Conway; *Tonto Basin Outlaws* (Monogram; S. Roy Luby) *CB* Ray Corrigan, Dusty King, Max Terhune, *LL* Jan Wiley; *Underground Rustlers* (Monogram; S. Roy Luby) *CB* Ray Corrigan, Dusty King, Max Terhune, *LL* Gwen Gaze. **1942:** *Thunder River Feud* (Monogram; S. Roy Luby) *CB* Ray Corrigan, Dusty King, Max Terhune, *LL* Jan Wiley; *Rock River Renegades* (Monogram; S. Roy Luby) *CB* Ray Corrigan, Dusty King, Max Terhune, *LL* Christine McIntyre, *Boot Hill Bandits* (Monogram; S. Roy Luby) *CB* Ray Corrigan, Dusty King, Max Terhune, *LL* Jean Brooks; *Texas Trouble Shooters* (Monogram; S. Roy Luby) *CB* Ray Corrigan, Dusty King, Max Terhune, *LL* Julie Duncan; *Arizona Stagecoach* (Monogram; S. Roy Luby) *CB* Ray Corrigan, Dusty King, Max Terhune, *LL* Nell O'Day; *Texas to Bataan* (Monogram; Robert Tansey) *CB* Dusty King, David Sharpe, Max Terhune, *LL* Marjorie Manners; *Trail Riders* (Monogram; Robert Tansey) *CB* Dusty King, David Sharpe, Max Terhune, *LL* Evelyn Finley. **1943:** *Two Fisted Justice* (Monogram; Robert Tansey) *CB* Dusty King, David Sharpe, Max Terhune, *LL* Gwen Gaze; *Haunted Ranch* (Monogram; Robert Tansey) *CB* Dusty King, David Sharpe, Max Terhune, *LL* Julie Duncan; *Land of Hunted Men* (Monogram; S. Roy Luby) *CB* Ray Corrigan, Dennis Moore, Max Terhune, *LL* Phyllis Adair; *Cowboy Commandos* (Monogram; S. Roy Luby) *CB* Ray Corrigan, Dennis Moore, Max Terhune, *LL* Evelyn Finley; *Black Market Rustlers* (Monogram; S. Roy Luby) *CB* Ray Corrigan, Dennis Moore, Max Terhune, *LL* Evelyn Finley; *Bullets and Saddles* (Monogram; Anthony Marshall) *CB* Ray Corrigan, Dennis Moore, Max Terhune, *LL* Julie Duncan.

Red Ryder Filmography

1944: *Tucson Raiders* (Republic; Spencer Bennett) *CB* Wild Bill Elliott, Gabby Hayes, Bobby Blake, *LL* Peggy Stewart; *Marshal of Reno* (Republic; Wallace Grissell) *CB* Wild Bill Elliott, Gabby Hayes, Bobby Blake; *The San Antonio Kid* (Republic; Howard Bretherton) *CB* Wild Bill Elliott, Bobby Blake, *LL* Linda Stirling; *Cheyenne Wildcat* (Republic; Lesley Selander) *CB* Wild Bill Elliott, Bobby Blake, *LL* Peggy Stewart; *Vigilantes of Dodge City* (Republic; Wallace Grissell) *CB* Wild Bill Elliott, Bobby Blake, *LL* Linda Stirling; *Sheriff of Las Vegas* (Republic; Lesley Selander) *CB* Wild Bill Elliott, Bobby Blake, *LL* Peggy Stewart. **1945:** *The Great Stagecoach Robbery* (Republic; Lesley Selander) *CB* Wild Bill Elliott, Bobby Blake, *LL* Sylvia Arslan; *Lone Texas Ranger* (Republic; Spencer Bennett) *CB* Wild Bill Elliott, Bobby Blake, *LL* Helen Talbot; *Phantom of the Plains* (Republic; Lesley Selander) *CB* Wild Bill Elliott, Bobby Blake, *LL* Virginia Christine; *Marshal of Laredo* (Republic; R.G. Springsteen) *CB*

Wild Bill Elliott, Bobby Blake, *LL* Peggy Stewart; *Colorado Pioneers* (Republic; R.G. Springsteen) *CB* Wild Bill Elliott, Bobby Blake; *Wagon Wheels Westward* (Republic; R.G. Springsteen) *CB* Wild Bill Elliott, Bobby Blake, *LL* Linda Stirling. **1946:** *California Gold Rush* (Republic; R.G. Springsteen) *CB* Wild Bill Elliott, Bobby Blake, *LL* Peggy Stewart; *Sun Valley Cyclone* (Republic; R.G. Springsteen) *CB* Wild Bill Elliott, Bobby Blake; *Conquest of Cheyenne* (Republic; R.G. Springsteen) *CB* Wild Bill Elliott, Bobby Blake, *LL* Peggy Stewart; *Sheriff of Redwood Valley* (Republic; R.G. Springsteen) *CB* Wild Bill Elliott, Bobby Blake, *LL* Peggy Stewart; *Santa Fe Uprising* (Republic; R.G. Springsteen) *CB* Rocky Lane, Bobby Blake; *Stagecoach to Denver* (Republic; R.G. Springsteen) *CB* Rocky Lane, Bobby Blake, *LL* Peggy Stewart. **1947:** *Vigilantes of Boomtown* (Republic; R.G. Springsteen) *CB* Rocky Lane, Bobby Blake, *LL* Peggy Stewart; *Homesteaders of Paradise Valley* (Republic; R.G. Springsteen) *CB* Rocky Lane, *LL* Ann Todd; *Oregon Trail Scouts* (Republic; R.G. Springsteen) *CB* Rocky Lane, Bobby Blake; *Rustlers of Devil's Canyon* (Republic; R.G. Springsteen) *CB* Rocky Lane, Bobby Blake, *LL* Peggy Stewart; *Marshal of Cripple Creek* (Republic; R.G. Springsteen) *CB* Rocky Lane, Bobby Blake. **1949:** *Ride, Ryder, Ride* (Eagle Lion; Lewis Collins) *CB* Jim Bannon, *LL* Peggy Stewart; *Roll, Thunder, Roll* (Eagle Lion; Lewis Collins) *CB* Jim Bannon, *LL* Nancy Gates; *The Fighting Redhead* (Eagle Lion; Lewis Collins) *CB* Jim Bannon, *LL* Peggy Stewart; *Cowboy and the Prizefighter* (Eagle Lion; Lewis Collins) *CB* Jim Bannon, *LL* Karen Randle.

Renfrew of the Royal Mounted Filmography

1937: *Renfrew of the Royal Mounted* (Grand National; Al Herman) *CB* James Newill, *LL* Carol Hughes. **1938:** *On the Great White Trail* (Grand National; Al Herman) *CB* James Newill, *LL* Terry Walker. **1939:** *Crashing Thru* (Monogram; Elmer Clifton) *CB* James Newill, *LL* Jean Carmen; *Fighting Mad* (Monogram; Sam Newfield) *CB* James Newill, Dave O'Brien, *LL* Sally Blane; *Yukon Flight* (Monogram; Ralph Staub) *CB* James Newill, Dave O'Brien, *LL* Louise Stanley. **1940:** *Danger Ahead* (Monogram; Ralph Staub) *CB* James Newill, Dave O'Brien, *LL* Dorothea Kent; *Murder on the Yukon* (Monogram; Louis Gasnier) *CB* James Newill, Dave O'Brien, *LL* Polly Ann Young; *Sky Bandits* (Monogram; Ralph Staub) *CB* James Newill, Dave O'Brien, *LL* Louise Stanley.

John Paul Revere Filmography

1943: *Beyond the Last Frontier* (Republic; Howard Bretherton) *CB* Eddie Dew, Smiley Burnette, *LL* Lorraine Miller; *Raiders of Sunset Pass* (Republic;

John English) *CB* Eddie Dew, Smiley Burnette, *LL* Jennifer Holt; *Pride of the Plains* (Republic; Wallace Fox) *CB* Robert Livingston, Smiley Burnette, *LL* Nancy Gay; *Beneath Western Skies* (Republic; Spencer Bennett) *CB* Robert Livingston, Smiley Burnette, *LL* Effie Laird.

The Rough Riders Filmography

1941: *Arizona Bound* (Monogram; Spencer Bennett) *CB* Buck Jones, Tim McCoy, Raymond Hatton, *LL* Luana Walters; *The Gunman from Bodie* (Monogram; Spencer Bennett) *CB* Buck Jones, Tim McCoy, Raymond Hatton, *LL* Christine McIntyre; *Forbidden Trails* (Monogram; R.N. Bradbury) *CB* Buck Jones, Tim McCoy, Raymond Hatton, *LL* Christine McIntyre. **1942:** *Below the Border* (Monogram; Howard Bretherton) *CB* Buck Jones, Tim McCoy, Raymond Hatton, *LL* Linda Brent; *Ghost Town Law* (Monogram; Howard Bretherton) *CB* Buck Jones, Tim McCoy, Raymond Hatton, *LL* Virginia Carpenter; *Down Texas Way* (Monogram; Howard Bretherton) *CB* Buck Jones, Tim McCoy, Raymond Hatton, *LL* Luana Walters; *Riders of the West* (Monogram; Howard Bretherton) *CB* Buck Jones, Tim McCoy, Raymond Hatton, *LL* Christine McIntyre; *West of the Law* (Monogram; Howard Bretherton) *CB* Buck Jones, Tim McCoy, Raymond Hatton, *LL* Evelyn Cook.

Texas Rangers Filmography

1942: *The Rangers Take Over* (PRC; Al Herman) *CB* James Newill, Dave O'Brien, Guy Wilkerson, *LL* Iris Meredith. **1943:** *Bad Men of Thunder Gap* (PRC; Al Herman) *CB* James Newill, Dave O'Brien, Guy Wilkerson, *LL* Janet Shaw; *West of Texas (Shootin' Irons)* (PRC; Oliver Drake) *CB* James Newill, Dave O'Brien, Guy Wilkerson, *LL* Frances Gladwin; *Border Buckaroos* (PRC; Oliver Drake) *CB* James Newill, Dave O'Brien, Guy Wilkerson, *LL* Christine McIntyre; *Fighting Valley* (PRC; Oliver Drake) *CB* James Newill, Dave O'Brien, Guy Wilkerson, *LL* Patti McCarty; *Trail of Terror* (PRC; Oliver Drake) *CB* James Newill, Dave O'Brien, Guy Wilkerson, *LL* Patricia Knox; *Return of the Rangers* (PRC; Elmer Clifton) *CB* James Newill, Dave O'Brien, Guy Wilkerson, *LL* Nell O'Day; *Boss of Rawhide* (PRC; Elmer Clifton) *CB* James Newill, Dave O'Brien, Guy Wilkerson, *LL* Nell O'Day. **1944:** *Gunsmoke Mesa* (PRC; Harry Fraser) *CB* James Newill, Dave O'Brien, Guy Wilkerson, *LL* Patti McCarty; *Outlaw Roundup* (PRC; Harry Fraser) *CB* James Newill, Dave O'Brien, Guy Wilkerson, *LL* Helen Chapman; *Guns of the Law* (PRC; Elmer Clifton) *CB* James Newill, Dave O'Brien, Guy Wilkerson; *The Pinto Bandit* (PRC;

Elmer Clifton) *CB* James Newill, Dave O'Brien, Guy Wilkerson, *LL* Mady Lawrence; *Spook Town* (PRC; Elmer Clifton) *CB* James Newill, Dave O'Brien, Guy Wilkerson, *LL* Mady Lawrence; *Brand of the Devil* (PRC; Harry Fraser) *CB* James Newill, Dave O'Brien, Guy Wilkerson, *LL* Ellen Hall; *Gangsters of the Frontier* (PRC; Elmer Clifton) *CB* Tex Ritter, Dave O'Brien, Guy Wilkerson, *LL* Patti McCarty, Betty Miles; *Dead or Alive* (PRC; Elmer Clifton) *CB* Tex Ritter, Dave O'Brien, Guy Wilkerson, *LL* Marjorie Clements; *The Whispering Skull* (PRC; Elmer Clifton) *CB* Tex Ritter, Dave O'Brien, Guy Wilkerson. **1945:** *Marked for Murder* (PRC; Elmer Clifton) *CB* Tex Ritter, Dave O'Brien, Guy Wilkerson, *LL* Marilyn McConnell; *Enemy of the Law* (PRC; Harry Fraser) *CB* Tex Ritter, Dave O'Brien, Guy Wilkerson, *LL* Kay Hughes; *Three in the Saddle* (PRC; Harry Fraser) *CB* Tex Ritter, Dave O'Brien, Guy Wilkerson, *LL* Lorraine Miller; *Frontier Fugitives* (PRC; Harry Fraser) *CB* Tex Ritter, Dave O'Brien, Guy Wilkerson, *LL* Lorraine Miller; *Flaming Bullets* (PRC; Harry Fraser) *CB* Tex Ritter, Dave O'Brien, Guy Wilkerson, *LL* Patricia Knox.

The Three Mesquiteers Filmography

1935: *Powdersmoke Range* (RKO; Wallace Fox) *CB* Harry Carey, Hoot Gibson, Big Boy Wiliams, *LL* Boots Mallory. **1936:** *The Three Mesquiteers* (Republic; Ray Taylor) *CB* Bob Livingston, Ray Corrigan, Syd Saylor, *LL* Kay Hughes; *Ghost Town Gold* (Republic; Joseph Kane) *CB* Bob Livingston, Ray Corrigan, Max Terhune, *LL* Kay Hughes; *Roarin' Lead* (Republic; Mack V. Wright, Sam Newfield) *CB* Bob Livingston, Ray Corrigan, Max Terhune, *LL* Christine Maple. **1937:** *Riders of the Whistling Skull* (Republic; Mack V. Wright) *CB* Bob Livingston, Ray Corrigan, Max Terhune, *LL* Mary Russell; *Hit the Saddle* (Republic, Mack V. Wright) *CB* Bob Livingston, Ray Corrigan, Max Terhune, *LL* Rita Cansino; *Gunsmoke Ranch* (Republic; Joseph Kane) *CB* Bob Livingston, Ray Corrigan, Max Terhune, *LL* Julia Thayer; *Come on Cowboys* (Republic; Joseph Kane) *CB* Bob Livingston, Ray Corrigan, Max Terhune, *LL* Maxine Doyle; *Range Defenders* (Republic; Mack V. Wright) *CB* Bob Livingston, Ray Corrigan, Max Terhune, *LL* Eleanor Stewart; *Heart of the Rockies* (Republic; Joseph Kane) *CB* Bob Livingston, Ray Corrigan, Max Terhune, *LL* Lynne Roberts; *The Trigger Trio* (Republic; William Witney) *CB* Ray Corrigan, Max Terhune, Ralph Byrd, *LL* Sandra Corday; *Wild Horse Rodeo* (Republic; George Sherman) *CB* Bob Livingston, Ray Corrigan, Max Terhune, *LL* June Martel. **1938:** *The Purple Vigilantes* (Republic; George Sherman) *CB* Bob Livingston, Ray Corrigan, Max Terhune, *LL* Joan Barclay; *Call the Mesquiteers* (Republic; John English) *CB* Bob Livingston, Ray Corrigan, Max Terhune, *LL* Lynne Roberts; *Outlaws of Sonora* (Republic; George

Sherman) *CB* Bob Livingston, Ray Corrigan, Max Terhune, *LL* Jean Joyce; *Riders of the Black Hills* (Republic; George Sherman) *CB* Bob Livingston, Ray Corrigan, Max Terhune, *LL* Ann Evers; *Heroes of the Hills* (Republic; George Sherman) *CB* Bob Livingston, Ray Corrigan, Max Terhune, *LL* Priscilla Lawson; *Pals of the Saddle* (Republic; George Sherman) *CB* John Wayne, Ray Corrigan, Max Terhune, *LL* Doreen McKay; *Overland Stage Raiders* (Republic; George Sherman) *CB* John Wayne, Ray Corrigan, Max Terhune, *LL* Louise Brooks; *Santa Fe Stampede* (Republic; George Sherman) *CB* John Wayne, Ray Corrigan, Max Terhune, *LL* June Martel; *Red River Range* (Republic; George Sherman) *CB* John Wayne, Ray Corrigan, Max Terhune, *LL* Polly Moran, Lorna Gray; *The Night Riders* (Republic; George Sherman) *CB* John Wayne, Ray Corrigan, Max Terhune, *LL* Doreen McKay, Ruth Rogers. **1939:** *Three Texas Steers* (Republic; George Sherman) *CB* John Wayne, Ray Corrigan, Max Terhune, *LL* Carole Landis; *Wyoming Outlaw* (Republic; George Sherman) *CB* John Wayne, Ray Corrigan, Raymond Hatton, *LL* Adele Pearce; *New Frontier* (Republic; George Sherman) *CB* John Wayne, Ray Corrigan, Raymond Hatton, *LL* Phyllis Isley; *The Kansas Terror* (Republic; George Sherman) *CB* Robert Livingston, Raymond Hatton, Duncan Renaldo, *LL* Jacqueline Wells; *Cowboys from Texas* (Republic; George Sherman) *CB* Robert Livingston, Raymond Hatton, Duncan Renaldo, *LL* Carole Landis. **1940:** *Heroes of the Saddle* (Republic; William Witney) *CB* Robert Livingston, Raymond Hatton, Duncan Renaldo, *LL* Loretta Weaver, Patsy Lee Parsons; *Pioneers of the West* (Republic; Lester Orlebeck) *CB* Robert Livingston, Raymond Hatton, Duncan Renaldo, *LL* Beatrice Roberts; *Covered Wagon Days* (Republic; George Sherman) *CB* Robert Livingston, Raymond Hatton, Duncan Renaldo, *LL* Kay Griffith, Ruth Robinson; *Rocky Mountain Rangers* (Republic; George Sherman) *CB* Robert Livingston, Raymond Hatton, Duncan Renaldo, *LL* Rosella Towne; *Oklahoma Renegades* (Republic; Nate Watt) *CB* Robert Livingston, Raymond Hatton, Duncan Renaldo, *LL* Florine McKinney; *Under Texas Skies* (Republic; George Sherman) *CB* Robert Livingston, Bob Steele, Rufe Davis, *LL* Lois Ransom; *The Trail Blazers* (Republic; George Sherman) *CB* Robert Livingston, Bob Steele, Rufe Davis, *LL* Pauline Moore; *Lone Star Raiders* (Republic; George Sherman) *CB* Robert Livingston, Bob Steele, Rufe Davis), *LL* June Johnson, Sarah Padden. **1941:** *Prairie Pioneers* (Republic; Lester Orlebeck) *CB* Robert Livingston, Bob Steele, Rufe Davis, *LL* Esther Estrella; *Pals of the Pecos* (Republic; Lester Orlebeck) *CB* Robert Livingston, Bob Steele, Rufe Davis, *LL* June Johnson; *Saddlemates* (Republic; Lester Orlebeck) *CB* Robert Livingston, Bob Steele, Rufe Davis, *LL* Gale Storm; *Gangs of Sonora* (Republic; John English) *CB* Robert Livingston, Bob Steele, Rufe Davis, *LL* Helen McKellar; *Outlaws of the Cherokee Trail* (Republic; Lester Orlebeck) *CB* Bob Steele, Tom Tyler, Rufe Davis, *LL* Lois Collier; *Gauchos* *of El Dorado* (Republic; Lester Orlebeck) *CB* Bob Steele, Tom Tyler, Rufe Davis, *LL* Lois Collier, Rosina Galli; *West of Cimarron* (Republic; Lester Orlebeck) *CB* Bob Steele, Tom Tyler, Rufe Davis, *LL* Lois Collier. **1942:** *Code of the Outlaw* (Republic; John English) *CB* Bob Steele, Tom Tyler, Rufe Davis, *LL* Melinda Leighton; *Raiders of the Range* (Republic; John English) *CB* Bob Steele, Tom Tyler, Rufe Davis, *LL* Lois Collier; *Westward Ho* (Republic; John English) *CB* Bob Steele, Tom Tyler, Rufe Davis, *LL* Evelyn Brent; *The Phantom Plainsmen* (Republic; John English) *CB* Bob Steele, Tom Tyler, Rufe Davis, *LL* Lois Collier; *Shadows on the Sage* (Republic; John English) *CB* Bob Steele, Tom Tyler, Jimmie Dodd, *LL* Cheryl Walker; *Valley of Hunted Men* (Republic; John English) *CB* Bob Steele, Tom Tyler, Jimmie Dodd, *LL* Anna Marie Stewart. **1943:** *Thundering Trails* (Republic; John English) *CB* Bob Steele, Tom Tyler, Jimmie Dodd, *LL* Nell O'Day; *The Blocked Trail* (Republic; Elmer Clifton) *CB* Bob Steele, Tom Tyler, Jimmie Dodd, *LL* Helen Deverell; *Santa Fe Scouts* (Republic; Howard Bretherton) *CB* Bob Steele, Tom Tyler, Jimmie Dodd, *LL* Lois Collier; *Riders of the Rio Grande* (Republic; Howard Bretherton) *CB* Bob Steele, Tom Tyler, Jimmie Dodd, *LL* Lorraine Miller.

The Trail Blazers Filmography

1943: *Wild Horse Stampede* (Monogram; Alan James) *CB* Ken Maynard, Hoot Gibson, *LL* Betty Miles; *The Law Rides Again* (Monogram; Alan James) *CB* Ken Maynard, Hoot Gibson, *LL* Betty Miles; *Blazing Guns* (Monogram; Robert Tansey) *CB* Ken Maynard, Hoot Gibson, *LL* Kay Forrester; *Death Valley Rangers* (Monogram; Robert Tansey) *CB* Ken Maynard, Hoot Gibson, Bob Steele, *LL* Betty Miles. **1944:** *Westward Bound* (Monogram; Robert Tansey) *CB* Ken Maynard, Hoot Gibson, Bob Steele, *LL* Betty Miles; *Arizona Whirlwind* (Monogram; Robert Tansey) *CB* Ken Maynard, Hoot Gibson, Bob Steele, *LL* Myrna Dell; *Outlaw Trail* (Monogram; Robert Tansey) *CB* Bob Steele, Hoot Gibson, Chief Thundercloud, *LL* Jennifer Holt; *Sonora Stagecoach* (Monogram; Robert Tansey) *CB* Bob Steele, Hoot Gibson, Chief Thundercloud, *LL* Betty Miles; *Marked Trails* (Monogram; J.P. McCarthy) *CB* Hoot Gibson, Bob Steele, *LL* Veda Ann Borg.

Bibliography

Books

Adams, Les, and Buck Rainey. *Shoot 'em Ups.* New Rochelle, N.Y.: Arlington House, 1978.

Barbour, Alan G. *The Thrill of It All.* New York: Macmillan, 1971.

Brooks, Tim, and Earl Marsh. *The Complete Dictionary to Prime Time Network TV Shows.* New York: Ballantine Books, 1979.

Corneau, Ernest. *The Hall of Fame of Western Film Stars.* N. Quincy, Mass.: Christopher, 1969.

De Marco, Mario. *Tom Mix.* Privately published.

Everson, William K. *The Bad Guys.* New York: Citadel Press, 1964.

_____. *A Pictorial History of the Western Film.* Secaucus, New Jersey: Citadel Press, 1969.

Fitzgerald, Michael. *Universal Pictures.* New Rochelle, New York: Arlington House, 1977.

Halliwell, Leslie. *The Filmgoers Companion*, 4th ed. New York: Hill and Wang, 1974.

Lackey, Wayne. *Western Star Roundup.* Privately published.

Maltin, Leonard. *The Great Movie Shorts.* New York: Bonanza Books, 1972.

Marschall, Rick. *The Encyclopedia of Country & Western Music.* New York: 1985.

The New York Times Directory of Film. New York: Arno Pres, 1971.

Nye, Douglas. *Six Gun Heroes: A Viewers Guide Vols. I and II.* Columbia, S.C.: The Producers Inc., 1983 and 1984.

Oermann, Robert K., and Douglas B. Green. *The Listener's Guide to Country Music.* New York: Facts on File, 1983.

Parish, James Robert. *Great Western Stars.* New York: Ace Books, 1976.

Rogers, Roy, and Dale Evans, and Carlton Stowers. *Happy Trails.* Waco, Tex.: Word Books, 1979.

Rothel, David. *The Singing Cowboys.* New York: A.S. Barnes, 1978.

————. *Those Great Cowboy Sidekicks.* Metuchen, N.J.: Scarecrow Press, 1984.

Terrace, Vincent. *The Complete Encyclopedia of Television Programs, 1947–1976.* Vols. I and II. Cranbury, N.J.: A.S. Barnes, 1976.

Truitt, Evelyn Mack. *Who Was Who on Screen.* New York: R.R. Bowker, 1984.

Weiss, Ken, and Ed Goodgold. *To Be Continued.* New York: Crown, 1972.

Zinman, David. *Saturday Afternoon at the Bijou.* New Rochelle, N.Y.: Arlington House, 1973.

Specialty Publications

Favorite Westerns. Issues #1–18. Mankato, Minn.: Keitzer.

Under Western Skies. Issues #1–28. Waynesville, N.C.: World of Yesterday.

Name Index

Numbers appearing in **boldface** indicate photographs.

B

Baer, Max 327
Bailey, Carmen 152
Baker, Betty 38
Baker, Bob 14–15, **15**, 256, 257, 308,
    330, 338, 362, 454, 462
Balenda, Carla 7
Ballew, Smith 16–17, **17**
Bannon, Jim 16–17, **18**, 19, 259, 270,
    271, 279, 378
Barclay, Joan 15, 24, 54, 57, 75, 80,
    89, 90, 118, 122, 183, 309–310, **309**
Barcroft, Roy 46, 387, 393–397, **394**,
    412
Bardette, Trevor 398
Bare, Richard 316
Barnett, Vince 144, 209
Barrett, Claudia 84, 111
Barrie, Mona 99
Barry, Don "Red" 19–20, **20**, 207,
    238, 259, 261, 280, 288, 350, 383,
    399, 412, 432
Barry, Judith 133
Barsha, Leon 176
Barton, Buzz 24, 147, 193, 194,
    210
Basquette, Lina 24, 79, 102
Baugh, Slingin' Sammy 105
Baxter, Warner 75, 165
Beatty, Clyde 46, 280, 355
Bedford, Barbara 99
Beebe, Ford 33, 42, 77, 154, 191, 192
Beery, Noah, Jr. 21–22, **22**
Beery, Noah, Sr. 399, **400**
Beery, Wallace 21, 356
Bell, Marjorie 15
Bell, Rex 22–24, **23**, 24, 127, 210, 265,
    277, 346, 353, 356, 371, 372, 383
Belmont, Virginia 19, 35
Benet, Joile 38
Bennett, Spencer G. 4, 21, 46, 69,
    70, 118, 125, 152, 157
Bergen, Connie 24, 201
Berke, William 87, 94, 108, 147, 178
Berkley, Lynne 8
Bernds, Edward 144
Ben Bernie Orchestra 105
Bickford, Charles 75
Blackjack 108
Black King 49

Blaine, Sally 79
Blair, George 7, 135
Blair, Reno 35, 192, 310–311
Blake, Bobby 70, 108, 110, 210–212,
    211, 472, 473
Blake, Pamela 112
Blakewell, William 334
Blangstead, Folmer 176
Blondell, Joan 383
Blue, Monte 75
Boardman, Eleanor 33
Bogart, Humphrey 75, 112, 130, 135
Bond, Johnny 190
Bond, Ward 388
Booth, Adrian 69, 83, 84, 176,
    311–312, **313**
Booth, Edwina 40, 42
Borg, Veda Ann 69, 70, 80, 184
Boutel, Genee 38
Bow, Clara 22, 23
The Bowery Boys 102
Boyd, Bill "Cowboy Rambler" 24–25,
    25, 149, 390
Boyd, William 25–31, **26**, **27**, **29**,
    376, **425**
Boyer, Charles 383
Bradbury, Robert N. 33, 50, 63, 103,
    150, 151, 157, 182, 183, 197, 198
Bradford, Lane 400–401
Brady, Pat 212–214, **213**, 164
Brannon, Fred C. 19, 61, 103, 110
Brave Heart 144
Brennan, Walter 227
Brent, Evelyn 30, 35, 128, 165, 184,
    388
Brent, Linda 99, 118, 122, 127, 184
Bretherton, Howard 16, 21, 28, 29,
    34, 35, 39, 66, 69, 87, 104, 110,
    178, 191, 203
Bridge, Alan 401–402
Britton, Barbara 13, 30
Bronson, Betty 12
Brooke, Hillary 91
Brooks, Rand 25, 30, 31, 214, 215
Brower, Otto 42, 79, 166
Brown, Clarence 42
Brown, Harry Joe 125
Brown, Johnny Mack 31–36, **32**, 49,
    71, 73, 77, 155, 208, 229, 237, 256,
    257, 261, 264, 265, 280, 311, 317,
    334, 335, 337, 338, 344, 349, 355,